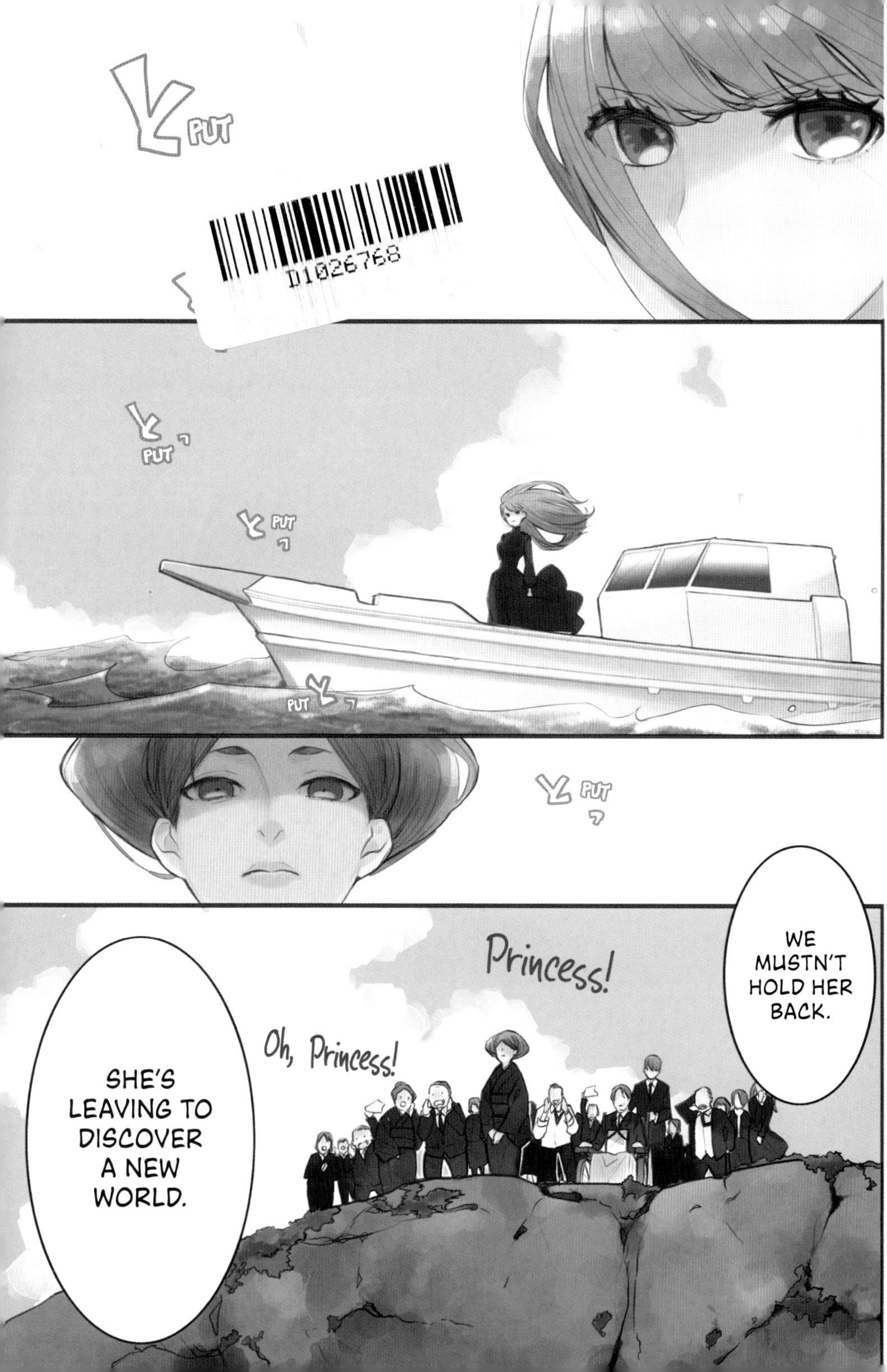
PUT
PUT
PUT
PUT
PUT
WE MUSTN'T HOLD HER BACK.
Princess!
Oh, Princess!
SHE'S LEAVING TO DISCOVER A NEW WORLD.

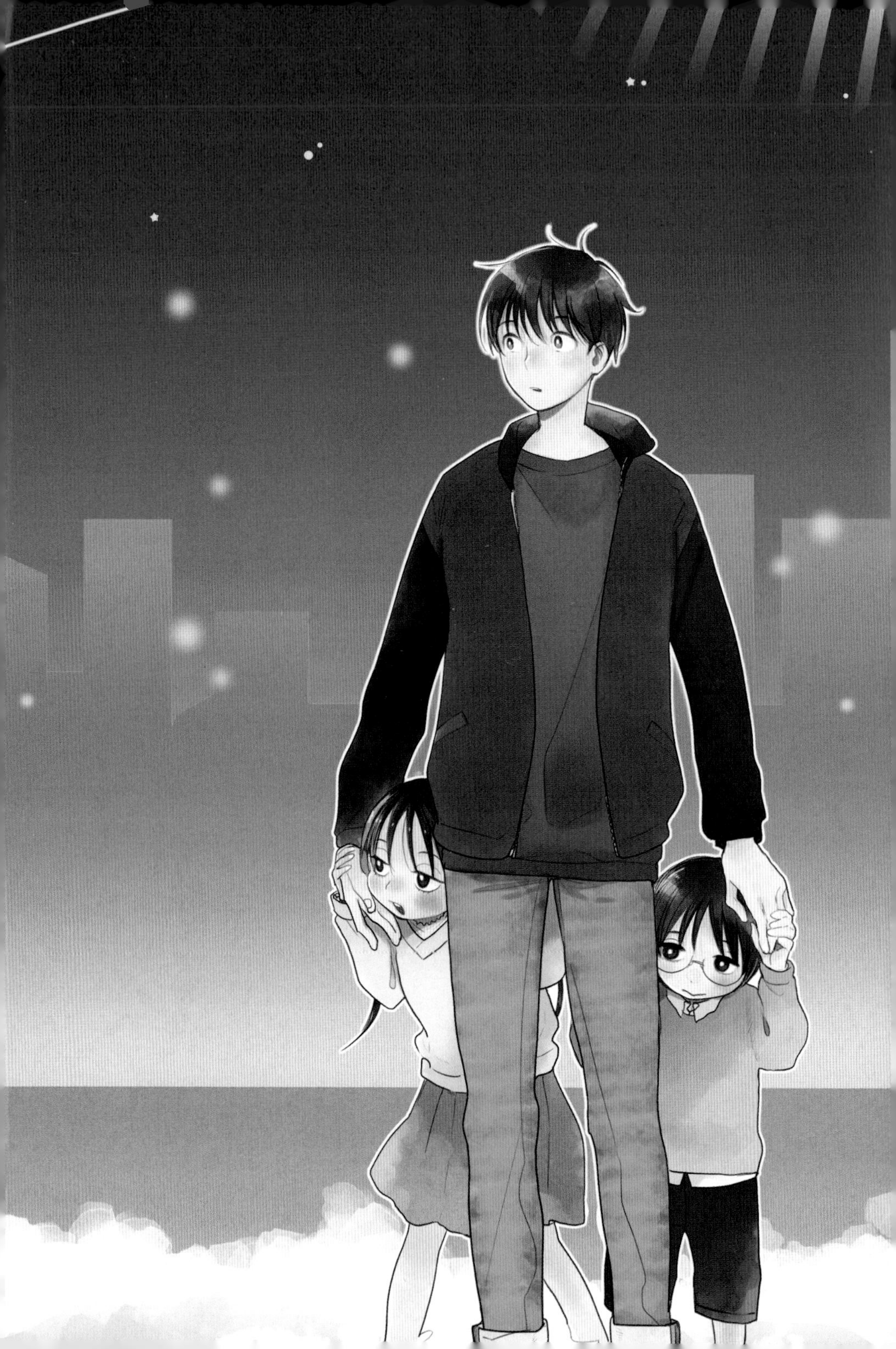

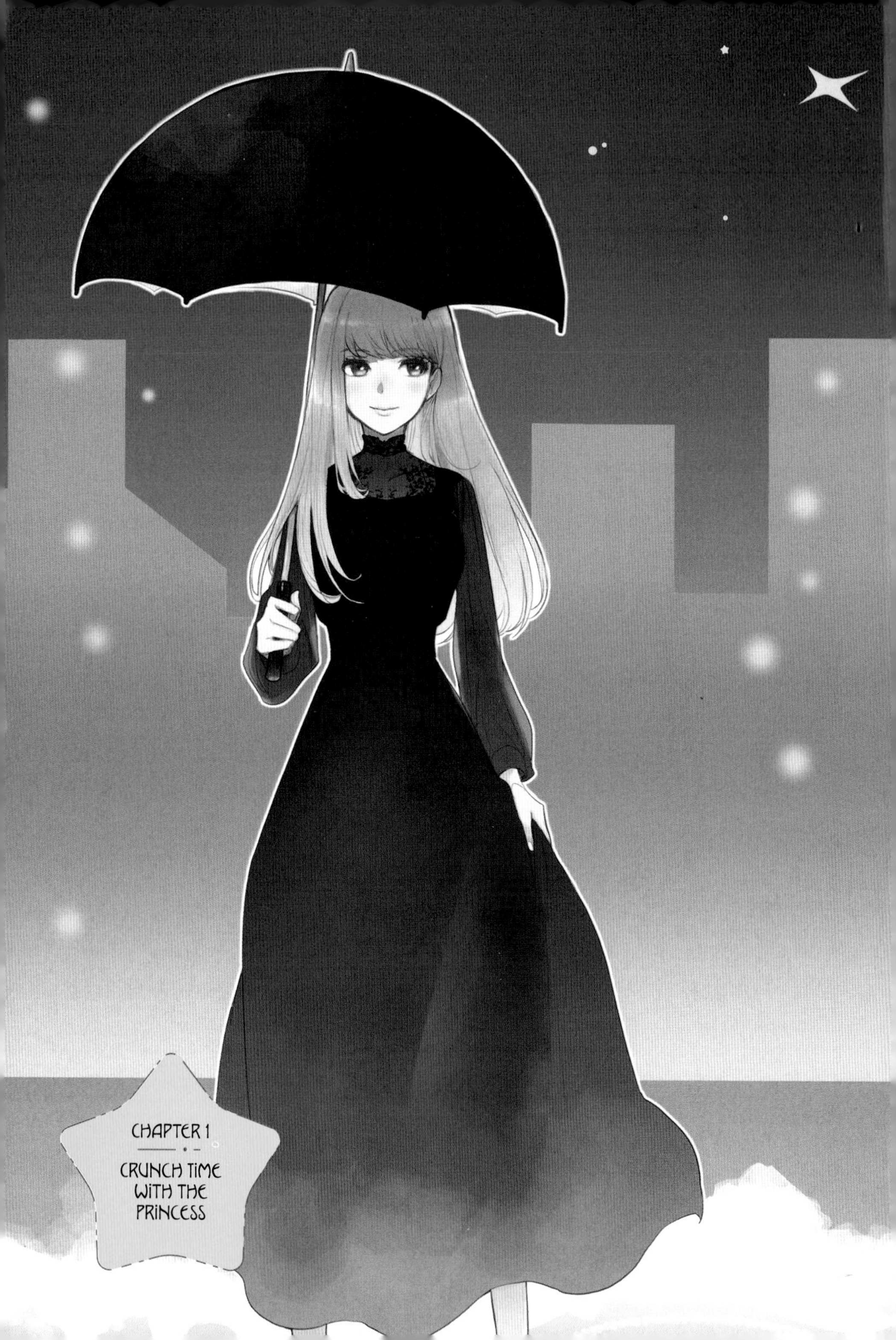
CHAPTER 1
CRUNCH TIME WITH THE PRINCESS

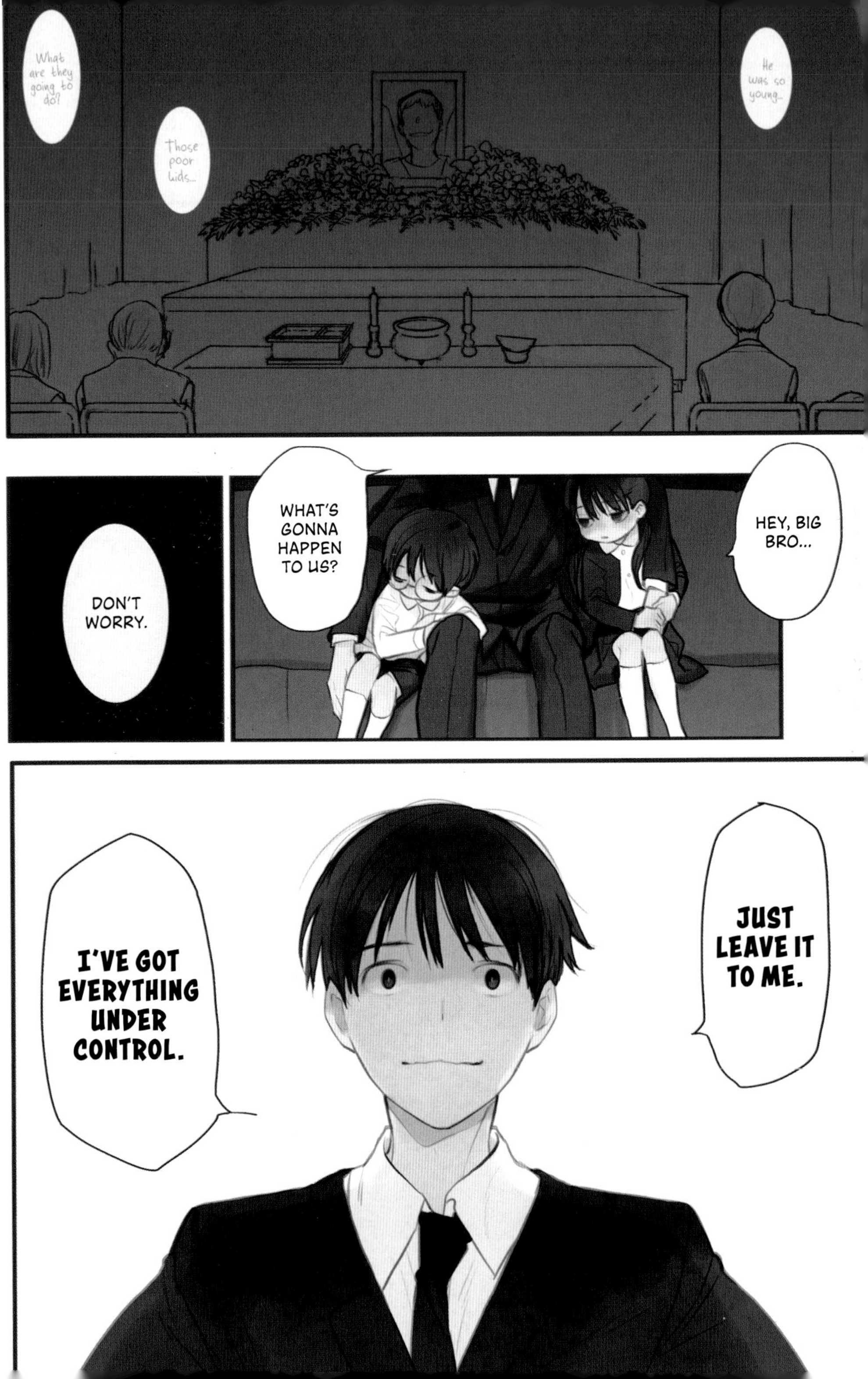
He was so young...
What are they going to do?
Those poor kids...
HEY, BIG BRO...
WHAT'S GONNA HAPPEN TO US?
DON'T WORRY.
JUST LEAVE IT TO ME.
I'VE GOT EVERYTHING UNDER CONTROL.

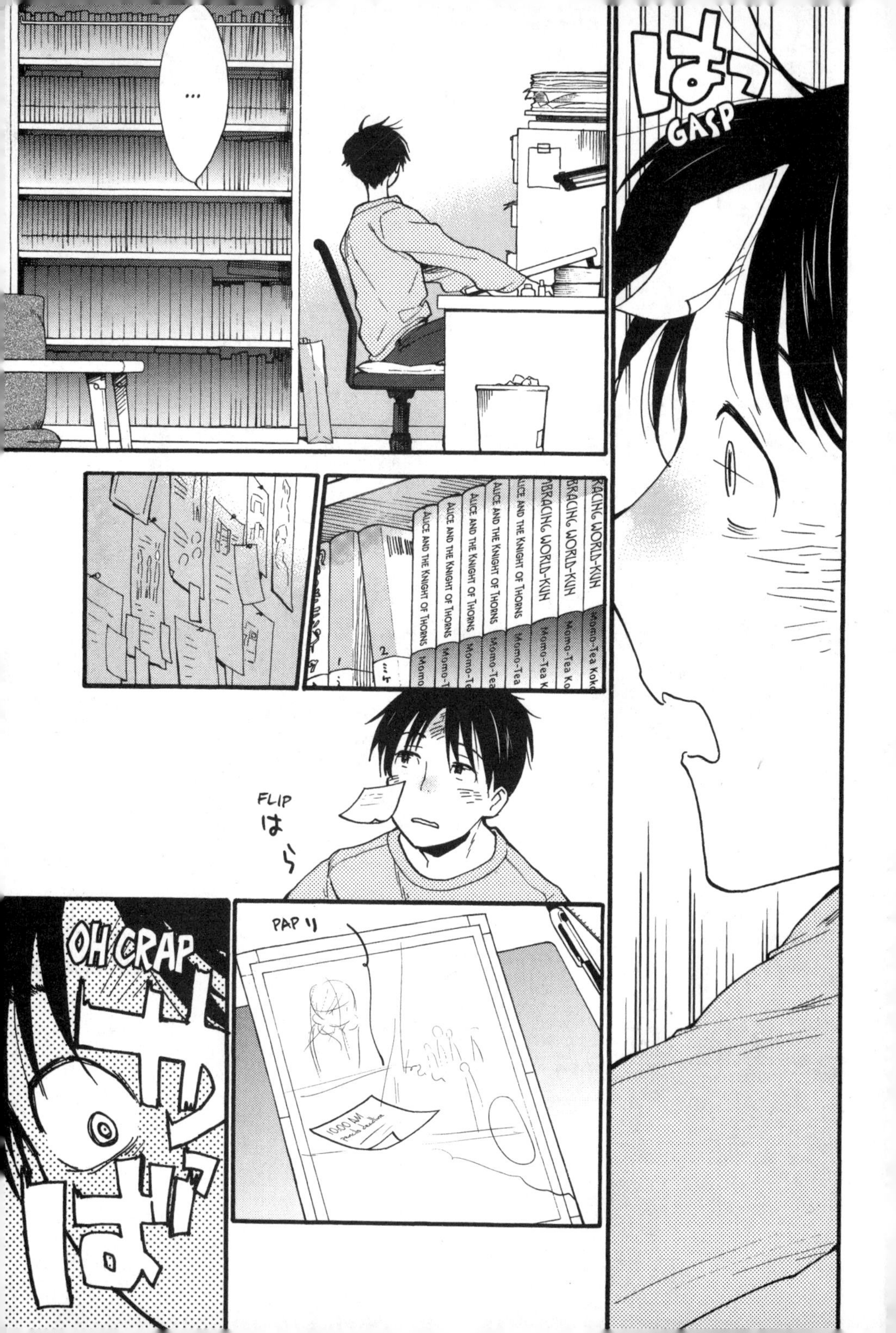
はっ
GASP
...
RACING WORLD-KUN
BRACING WORLD-KUN
BRACING WORLD-KUN
ALICE AND THE KNIGHT OF THORNS
ALICE AND THE KNIGHT OF THORNS
ALICE AND THE KNIGHT OF THORNS
ALICE AND THE KNIGHT OF THORNS
ALICE AND THE KNIGHT OF THORNS
FLIP
はら
PAP り
10:00 AM
pencils deadline
OH CRAP
やばっ

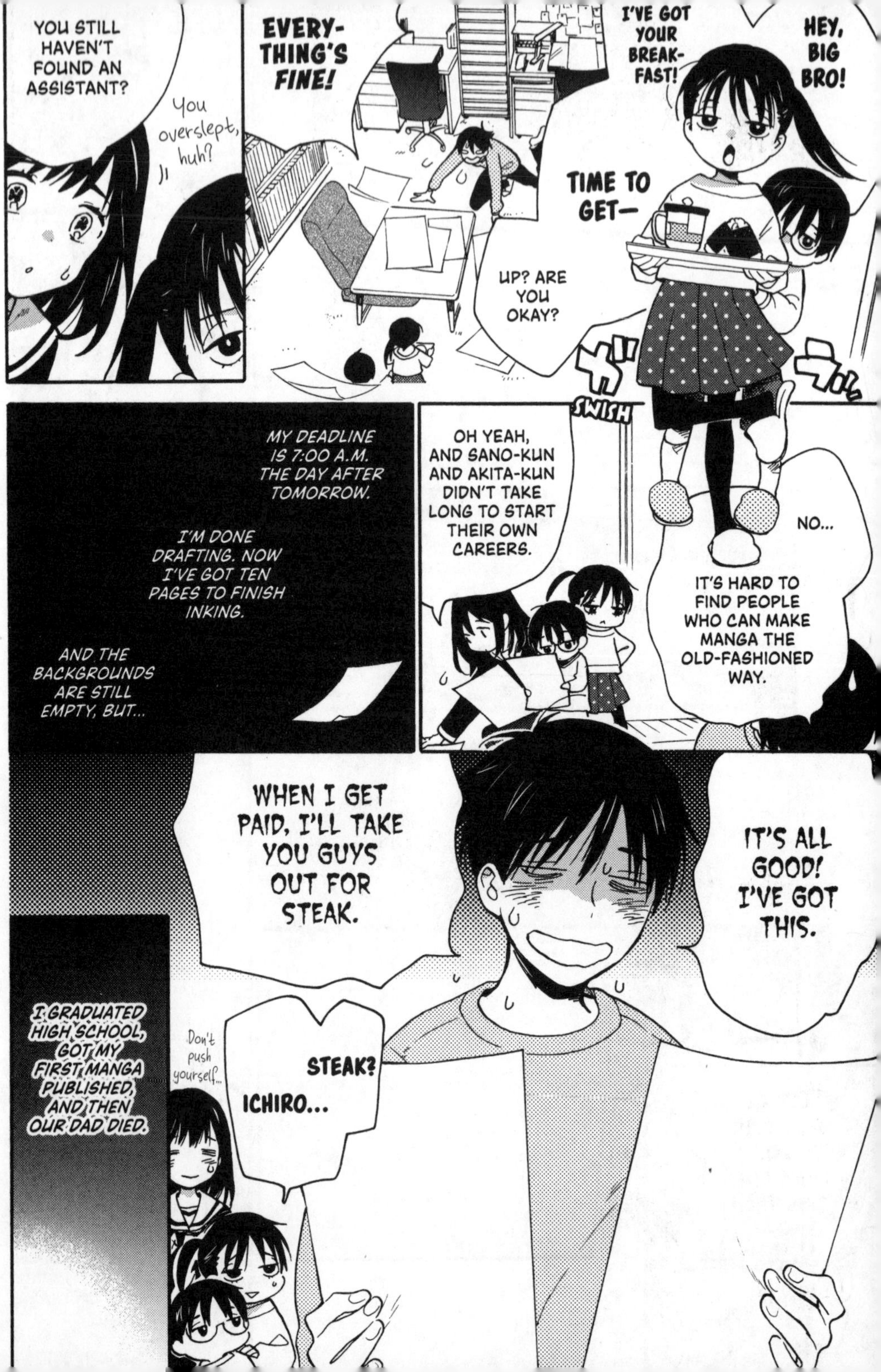
HEY, BIG BRO!
I'VE GOT YOUR BREAK-FAST!
TIME TO GET—
UP? ARE YOU OKAY?
SWISH
EVERY-THING'S FINE!
YOU STILL HAVEN'T FOUND AN ASSISTANT?
You overslept, huh?
OH YEAH, AND SANO-KUN AND AKITA-KUN DIDN'T TAKE LONG TO START THEIR OWN CAREERS.
NO...
IT'S HARD TO FIND PEOPLE WHO CAN MAKE MANGA THE OLD-FASHIONED WAY.
MY DEADLINE IS 7:00 A.M. THE DAY AFTER TOMORROW.
I'M DONE DRAFTING. NOW I'VE GOT TEN PAGES TO FINISH INKING.
AND THE BACKGROUNDS ARE STILL EMPTY, BUT...
IT'S ALL GOOD! I'VE GOT THIS.
WHEN I GET PAID, I'LL TAKE YOU GUYS OUT FOR STEAK.
STEAK?
ICHIRO...
Don't push yourself...
I GRADUATED HIGH SCHOOL, GOT MY FIRST MANGA PUBLISHED, AND THEN OUR DAD DIED.

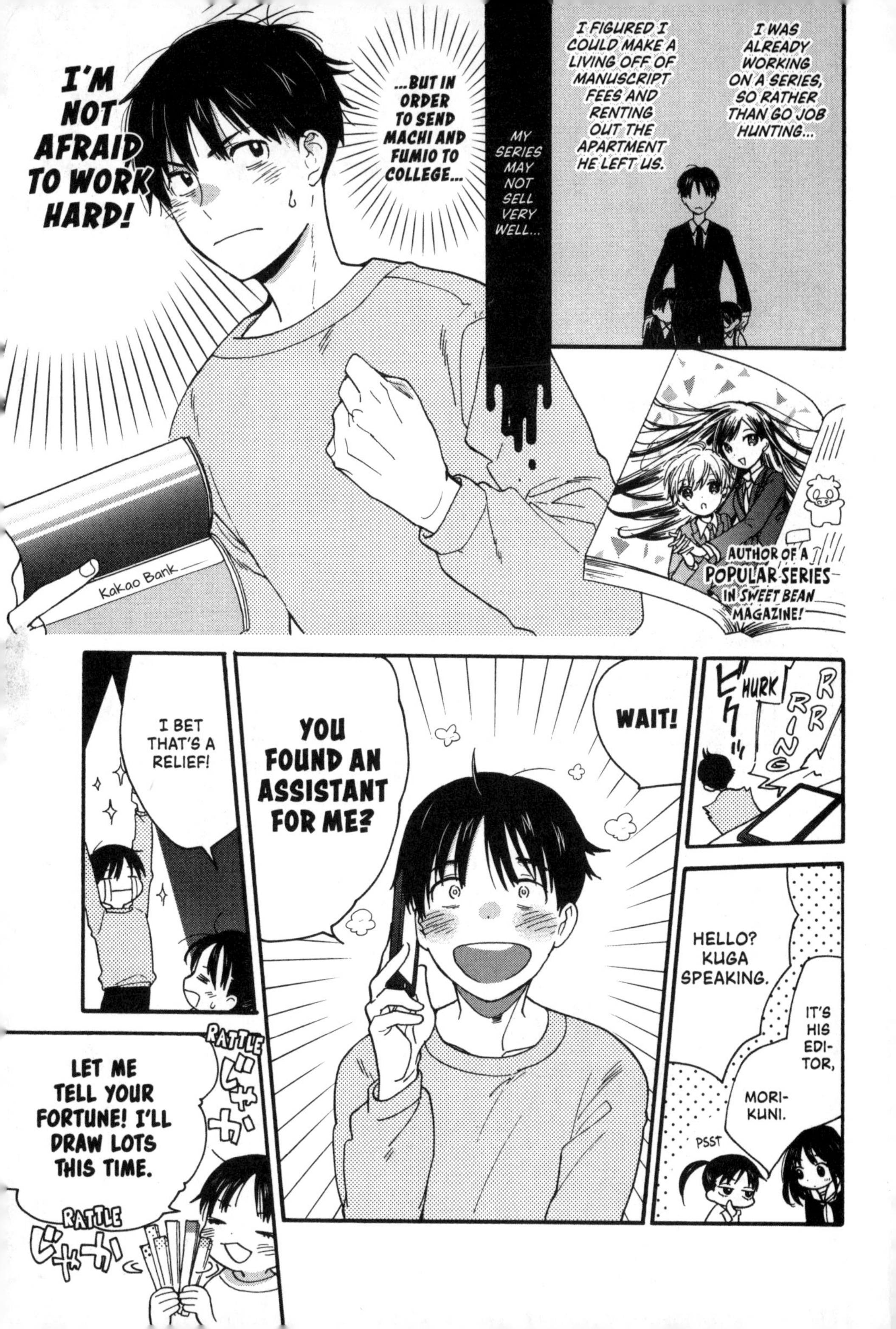
I WAS ALREADY WORKING ON A SERIES, SO RATHER THAN GO JOB HUNTING...
I FIGURED I COULD MAKE A LIVING OFF OF MANUSCRIPT FEES AND RENTING OUT THE APARTMENT HE LEFT US.
AUTHOR OF A POPULAR SERIES IN SWEET BEAN MAGAZINE!
MY SERIES MAY NOT SELL VERY WELL...
...BUT IN ORDER TO SEND MACHI AND FUMIO TO COLLEGE...
I'M NOT AFRAID TO WORK HARD!
Kakao Bank
RRRING
HURK
HELLO? KUGA SPEAKING.
IT'S HIS EDITOR,
MORI-KUNI.
PSST
WAIT!
YOU FOUND AN ASSISTANT FOR ME?
I BET THAT'S A RELIEF!
RATTLE
LET ME TELL YOUR FORTUNE! I'LL DRAW LOTS THIS TIME.
RATTLE

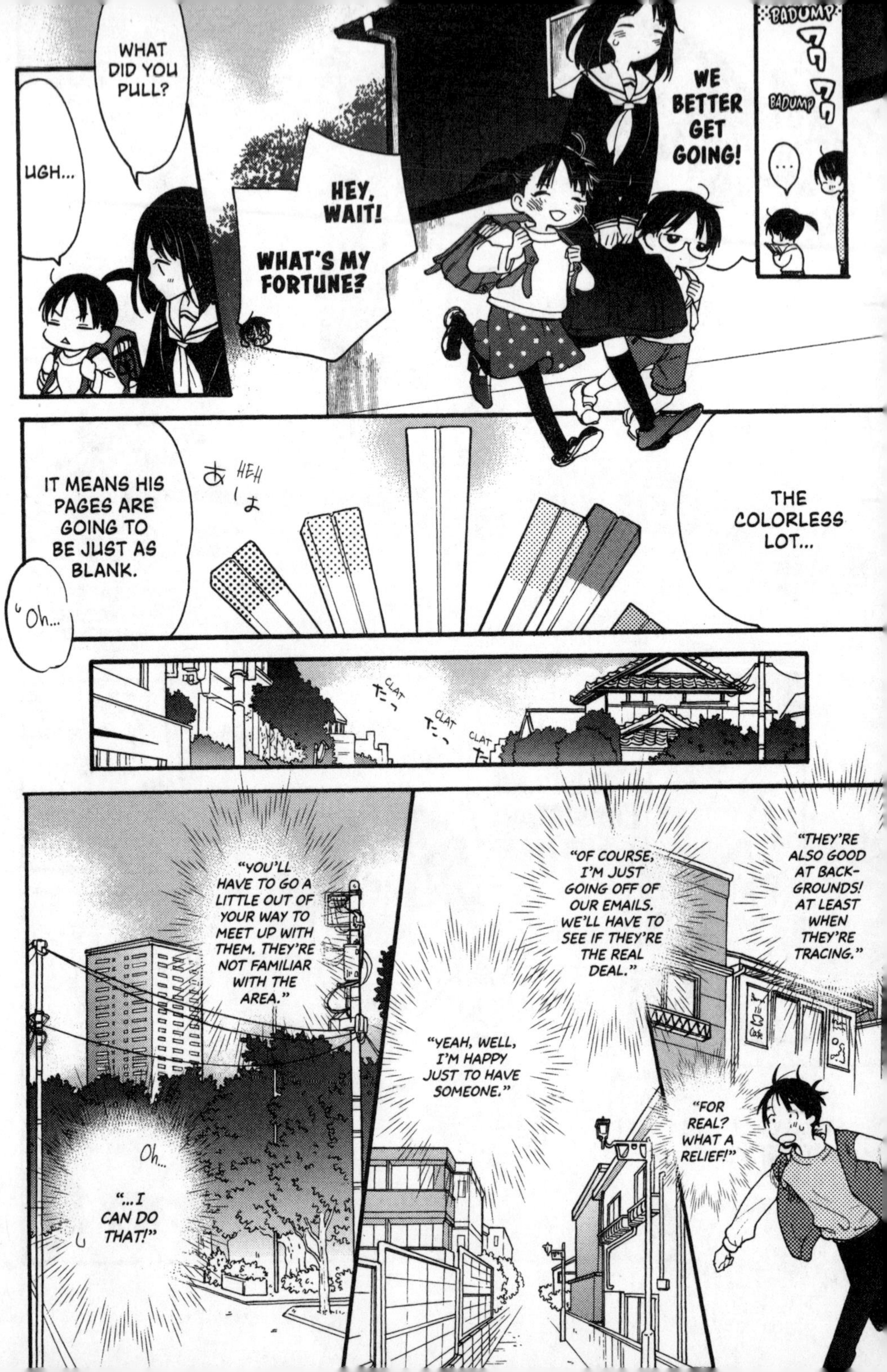
BADUMP
BADUMP
...
WE BETTER GET GOING!
HEY, WAIT!
WHAT'S MY FORTUNE?
WHAT DID YOU PULL?
UGH...
THE COLORLESS LOT...
HEH
IT MEANS HIS PAGES ARE GOING TO BE JUST AS BLANK.
Oh...
CLAT
CLAT
CLAT
"THEY'RE ALSO GOOD AT BACK-GROUNDS! AT LEAST WHEN THEY'RE TRACING."
"OF COURSE, I'M JUST GOING OFF OF OUR EMAILS. WE'LL HAVE TO SEE IF THEY'RE THE REAL DEAL."
"FOR REAL? WHAT A RELIEF!"
"YEAH, WELL, I'M HAPPY JUST TO HAVE SOMEONE."
"YOU'LL HAVE TO GO A LITTLE OUT OF YOUR WAY TO MEET UP WITH THEM. THEY'RE NOT FAMILIAR WITH THE AREA."
Oh...
"...I CAN DO THAT!"

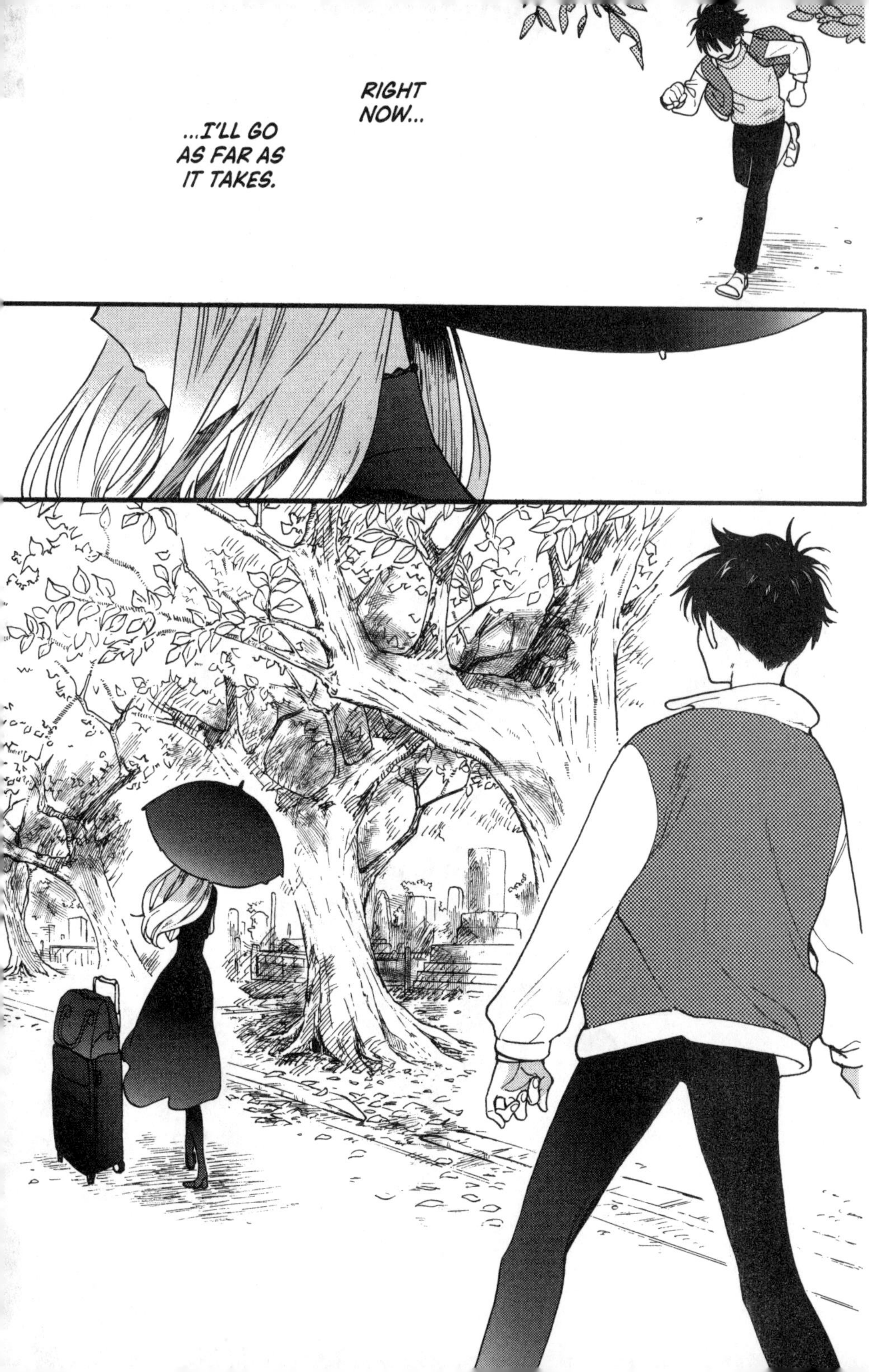
RIGHT NOW...
...I'LL GO AS FAR AS IT TAKES.

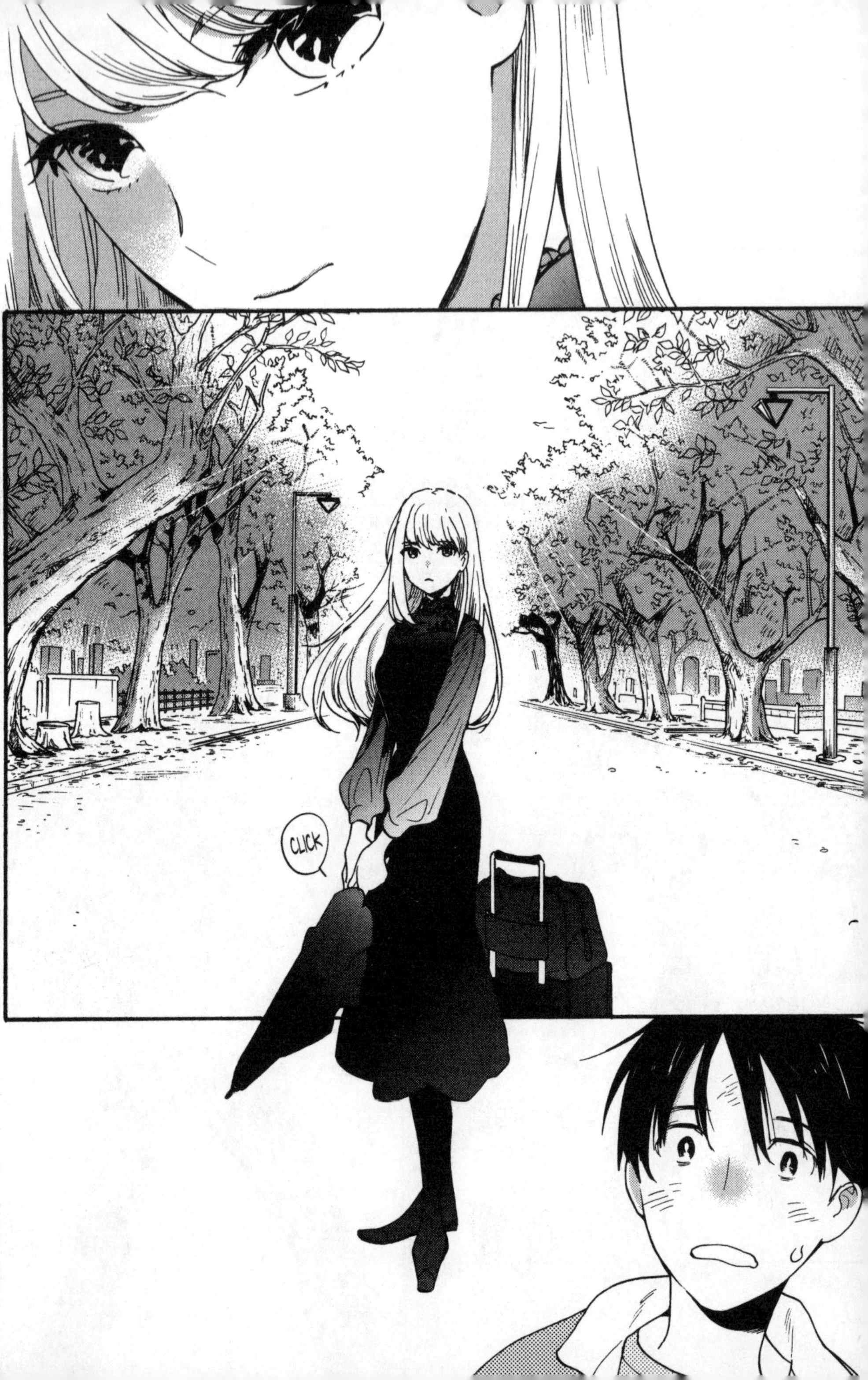
CLICK

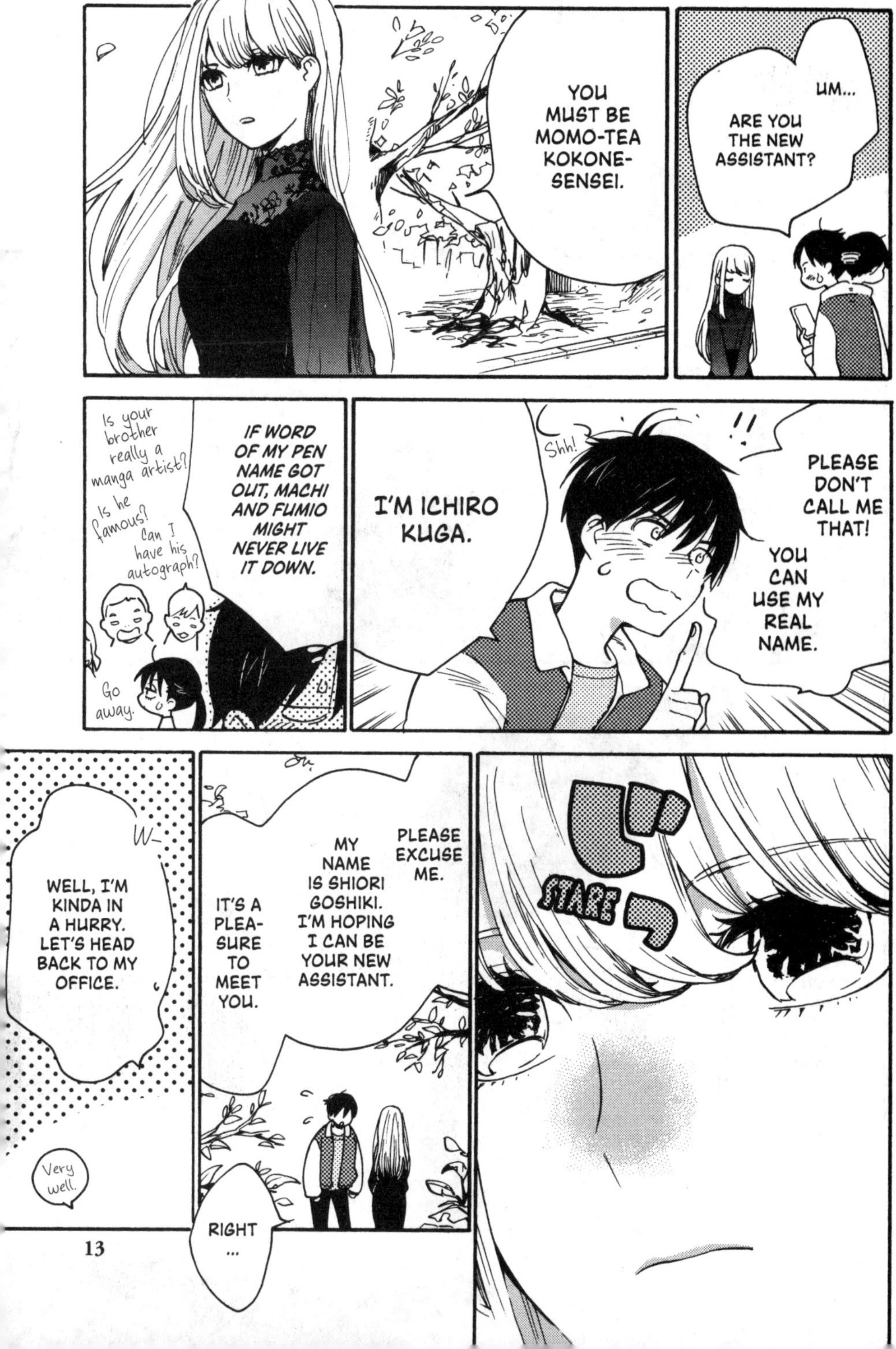
UM...
ARE YOU THE NEW ASSISTANT?
YOU MUST BE MOMO-TEA KOKONE-SENSEI.
!!
Shh!
PLEASE DON'T CALL ME THAT!
YOU CAN USE MY REAL NAME.
I'M ICHIRO KUGA.
IF WORD OF MY PEN NAME GOT OUT, MACHI AND FUMIO MIGHT NEVER LIVE IT DOWN.
Is your brother really a manga artist?
Is he famous?
Can I have his autograph?
Go away.
STARE
PLEASE EXCUSE ME.
MY NAME IS SHIORI GOSHIKI. I'M HOPING I CAN BE YOUR NEW ASSISTANT.
IT'S A PLEASURE TO MEET YOU.
RIGHT ...
W–
WELL, I'M KINDA IN A HURRY. LET'S HEAD BACK TO MY OFFICE.
Very well.

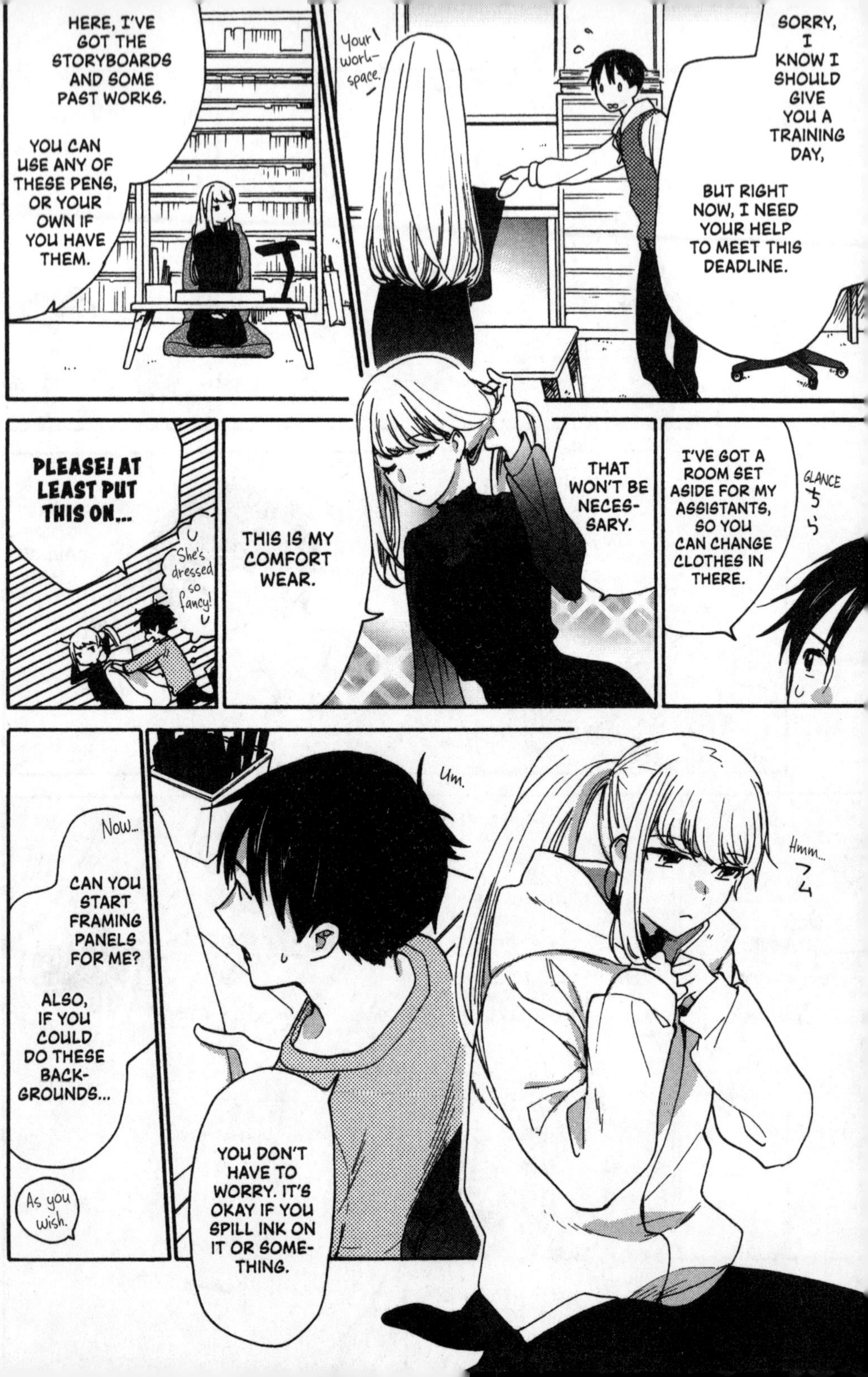

SORRY, I KNOW I SHOULD GIVE YOU A TRAINING DAY,
BUT RIGHT NOW, I NEED YOUR HELP TO MEET THIS DEADLINE.
Your workspace.
HERE, I'VE GOT THE STORYBOARDS AND SOME PAST WORKS.
YOU CAN USE ANY OF THESE PENS, OR YOUR OWN IF YOU HAVE THEM.
GLANCE
ちら
I'VE GOT A ROOM SET ASIDE FOR MY ASSISTANTS, SO YOU CAN CHANGE CLOTHES IN THERE.
THAT WON'T BE NECES-SARY.
THIS IS MY COMFORT WEAR.
PLEASE! AT LEAST PUT THIS ON...
She's dressed so fancy!
Hmm...
フム
Um.
Now...
CAN YOU START FRAMING PANELS FOR ME?
ALSO, IF YOU COULD DO THESE BACK-GROUNDS...
YOU DON'T HAVE TO WORRY. IT'S OKAY IF YOU SPILL INK ON IT OR SOME-THING.
As you wish.

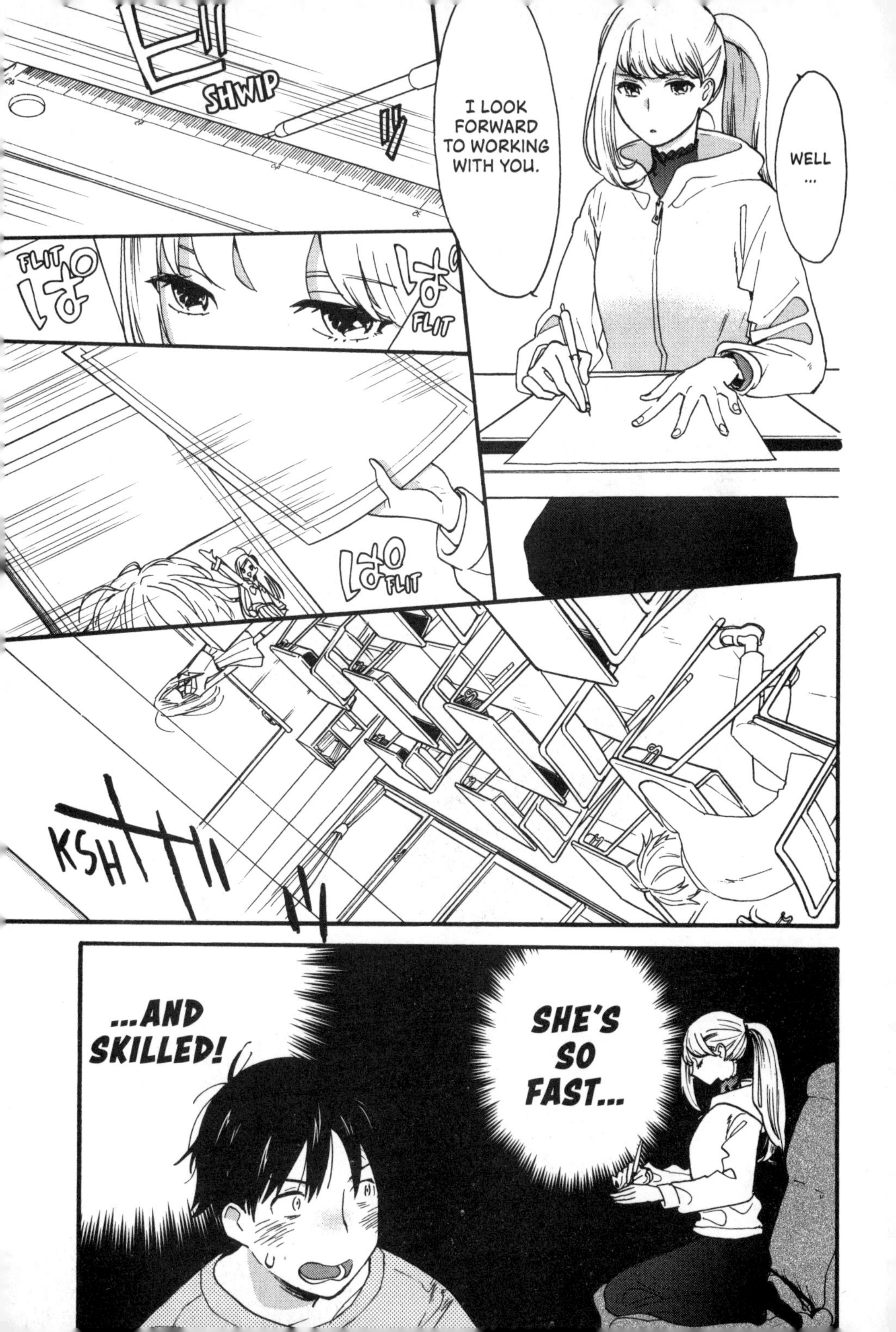

WELL ...
I LOOK FORWARD TO WORKING WITH YOU.
SHWIP
FLIT
FLIT
FLIT
KSH
SHE'S SO FAST...
...AND SKILLED!

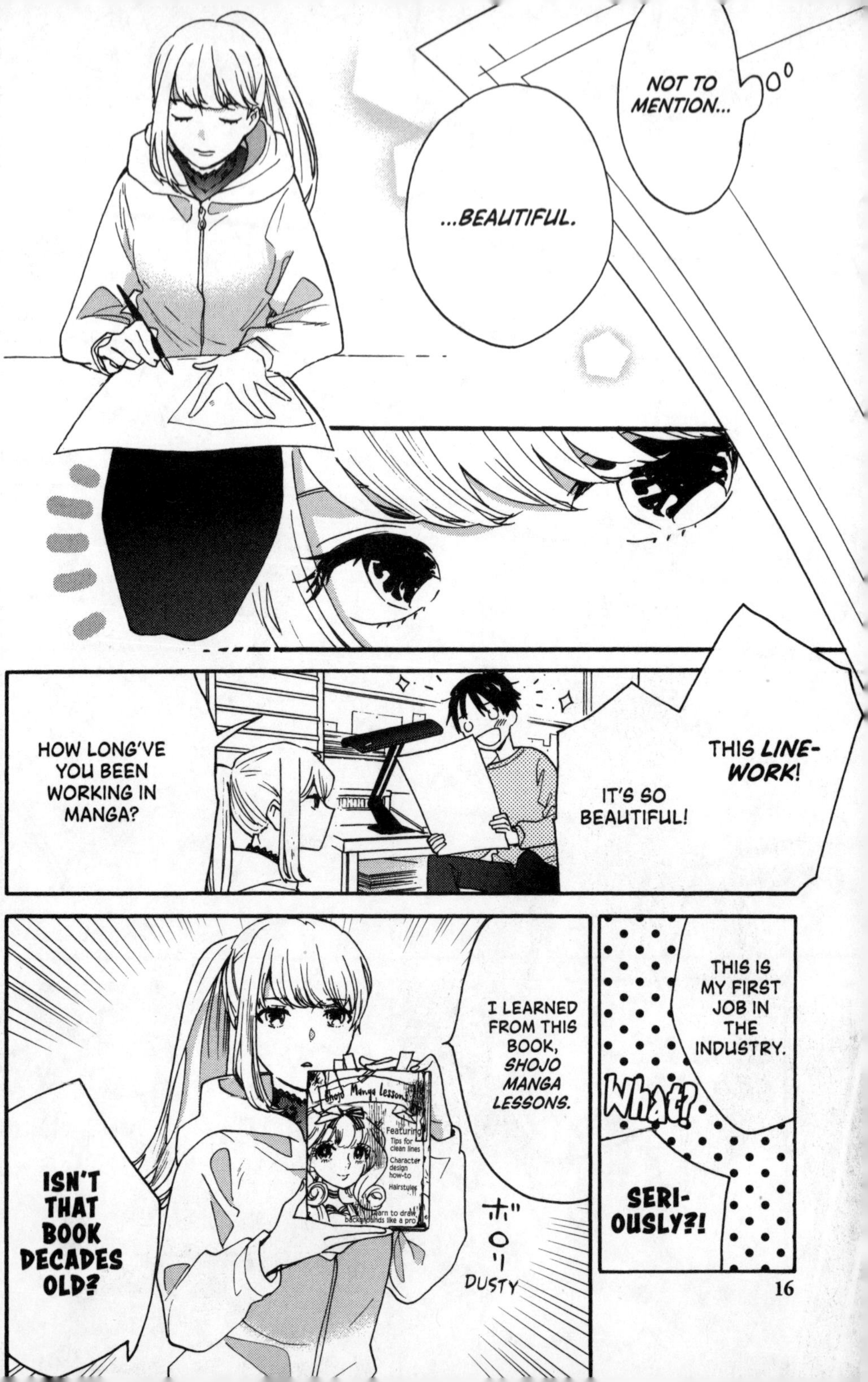

NOT TO MENTION...
...BEAUTIFUL.
THIS *LINE-WORK*!
IT'S SO BEAUTIFUL!
HOW LONG'VE YOU BEEN WORKING IN MANGA?
THIS IS MY FIRST JOB IN THE INDUSTRY.
What?
SERI-OUSLY?!
I LEARNED FROM THIS BOOK, *SHOJO MANGA LESSONS*.
Shojo Manga Lessons
Featuring
Tips for clean lines
Character design how-to
Hairstyles
DUSTY
ISN'T THAT BOOK DECADES OLD?

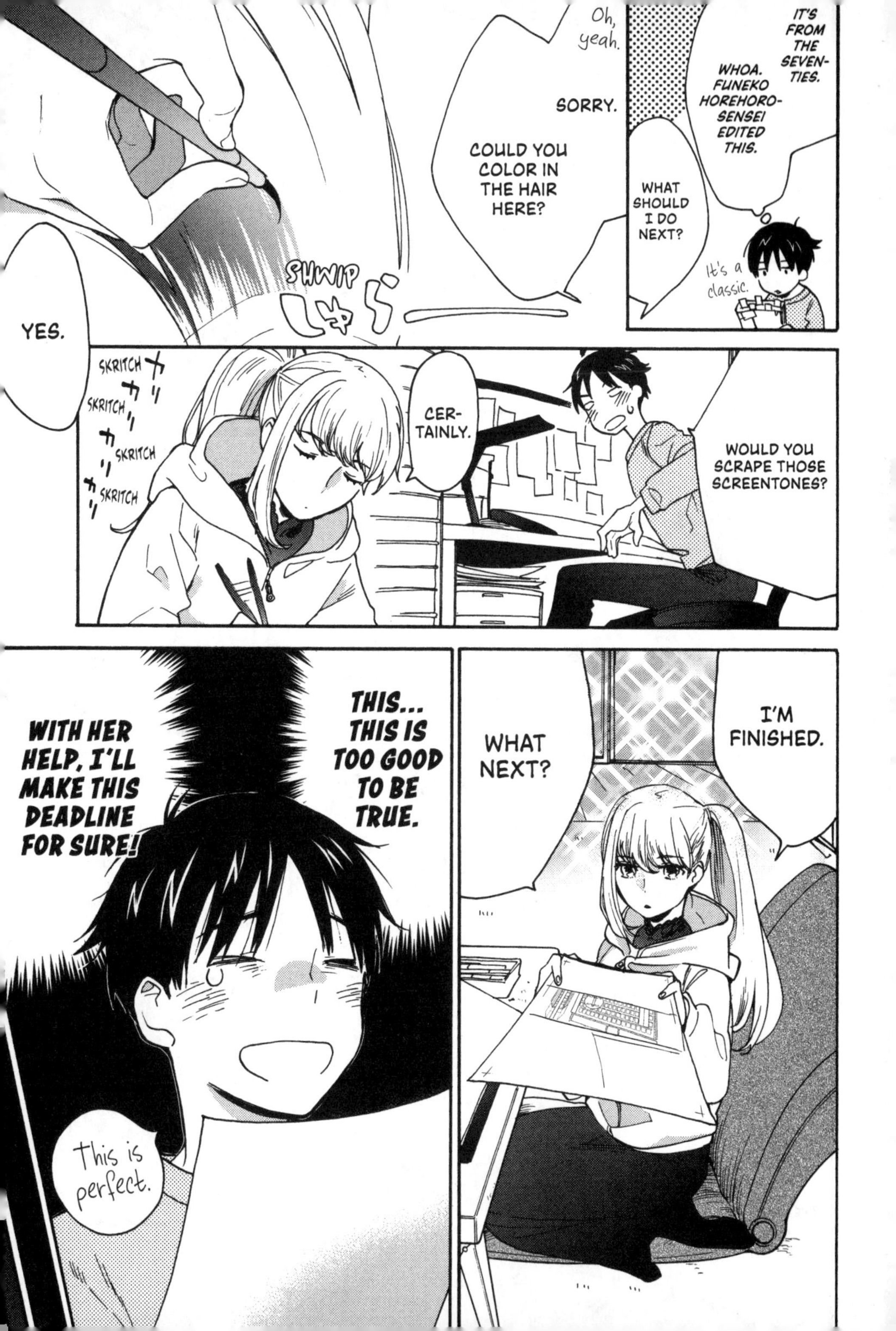
IT'S FROM THE SEVENTIES.
WHOA. FUNEKO HOREHORO-SENSEI EDITED THIS.
WHAT SHOULD I DO NEXT?
It's a classic.
Oh, yeah.
SORRY.
COULD YOU COLOR IN THE HAIR HERE?
SHWIP
YES.
WOULD YOU SCRAPE THOSE SCREENTONES?
CER-TAINLY.
SKRITCH
SKRITCH
SKRITCH
SKRITCH
I'M FINISHED.
WHAT NEXT?
THIS... THIS IS TOO GOOD TO BE TRUE.
WITH HER HELP, I'LL MAKE THIS DEADLINE FOR SURE!
This is perfect.

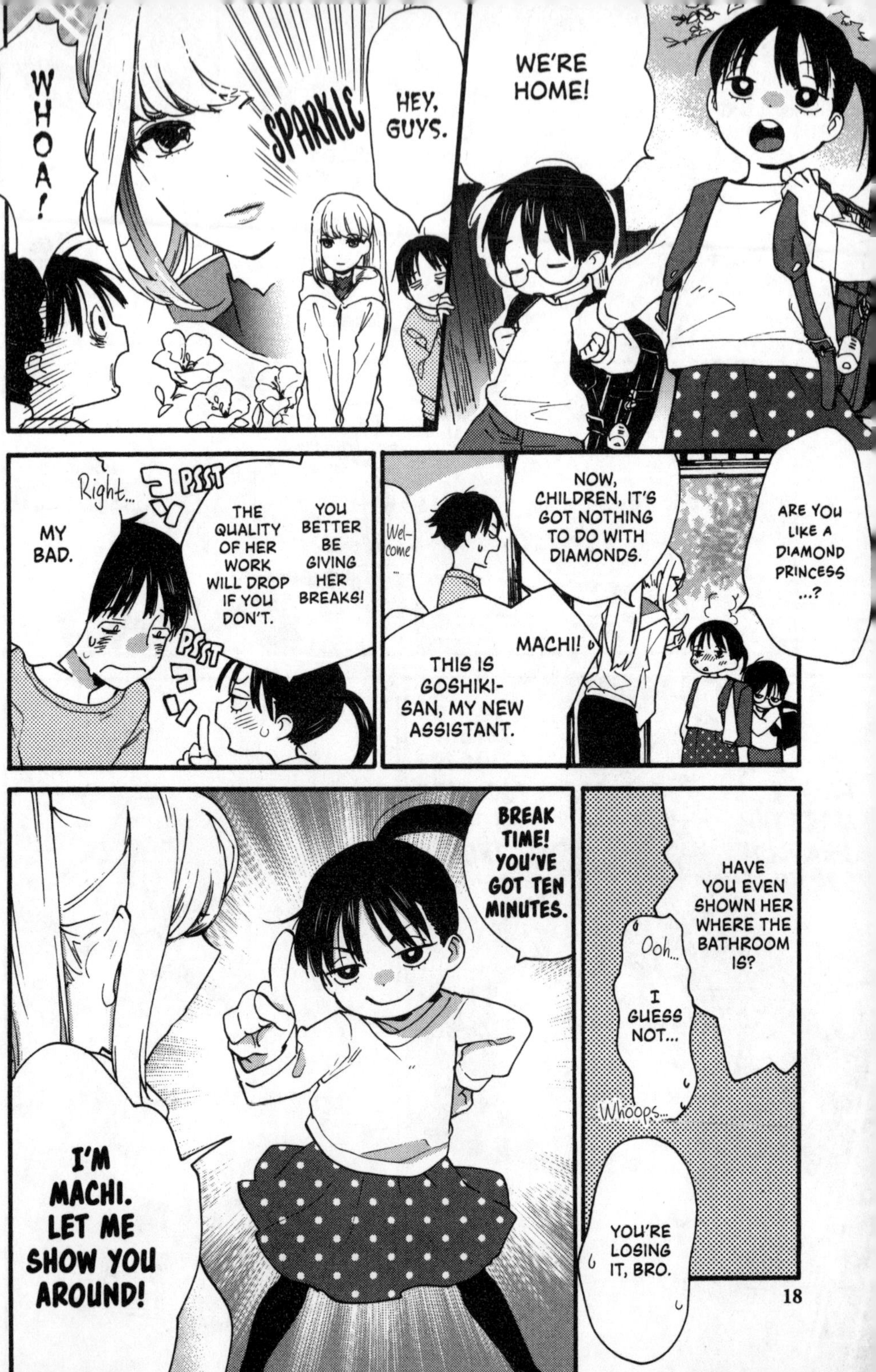
WE'RE HOME!
HEY, GUYS.
SPARKLE
WHOA!
ARE YOU LIKE A DIAMOND PRINCESS ...?
NOW, CHILDREN, IT'S GOT NOTHING TO DO WITH DIAMONDS.
Wel-come...
MACHI!
THIS IS GOSHIKI-SAN, MY NEW ASSISTANT.
YOU BETTER BE GIVING HER BREAKS!
THE QUALITY OF HER WORK WILL DROP IF YOU DON'T.
PSST
Right...
MY BAD.
PSST
HAVE YOU EVEN SHOWN HER WHERE THE BATHROOM IS?
Ooh...
I GUESS NOT...
Whoops...
YOU'RE LOSING IT, BRO.
BREAK TIME! YOU'VE GOT TEN MINUTES.
I'M MACHI. LET ME SHOW YOU AROUND!

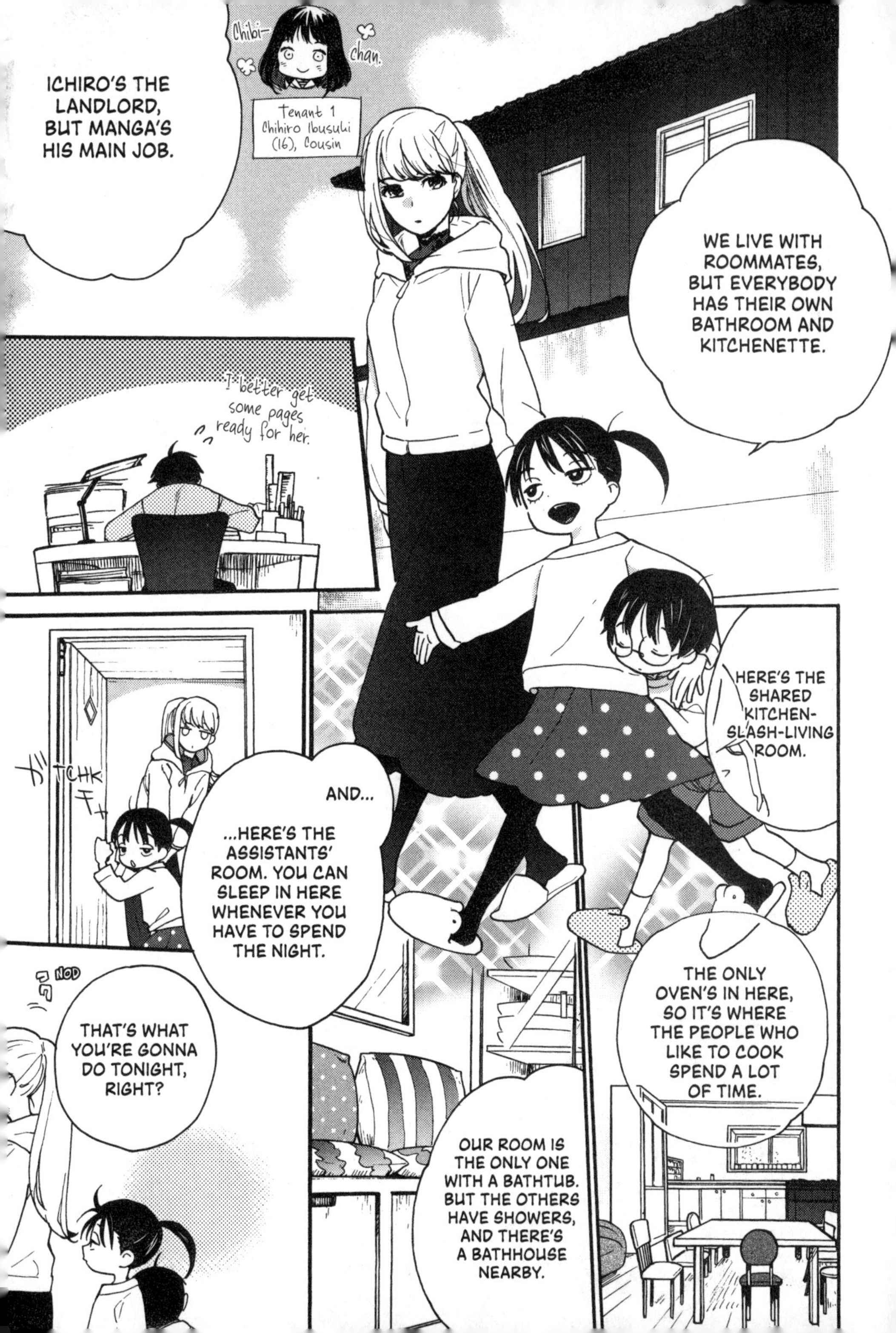

Chibi-chan.
Tenant 1 Chihiro Ibusuki (16), Cousin
ICHIRO'S THE LANDLORD, BUT MANGA'S HIS MAIN JOB.
I better get some pages ready for her.
WE LIVE WITH ROOMMATES, BUT EVERYBODY HAS THEIR OWN BATHROOM AND KITCHENETTE.
HERE'S THE SHARED KITCHEN-SLASH-LIVING ROOM.
THE ONLY OVEN'S IN HERE, SO IT'S WHERE THE PEOPLE WHO LIKE TO COOK SPEND A LOT OF TIME.
OUR ROOM IS THE ONLY ONE WITH A BATHTUB. BUT THE OTHERS HAVE SHOWERS, AND THERE'S A BATHHOUSE NEARBY.
TCHK
AND...
...HERE'S THE ASSISTANTS' ROOM. YOU CAN SLEEP IN HERE WHENEVER YOU HAVE TO SPEND THE NIGHT.
NOD
THAT'S WHAT YOU'RE GONNA DO TONIGHT, RIGHT?

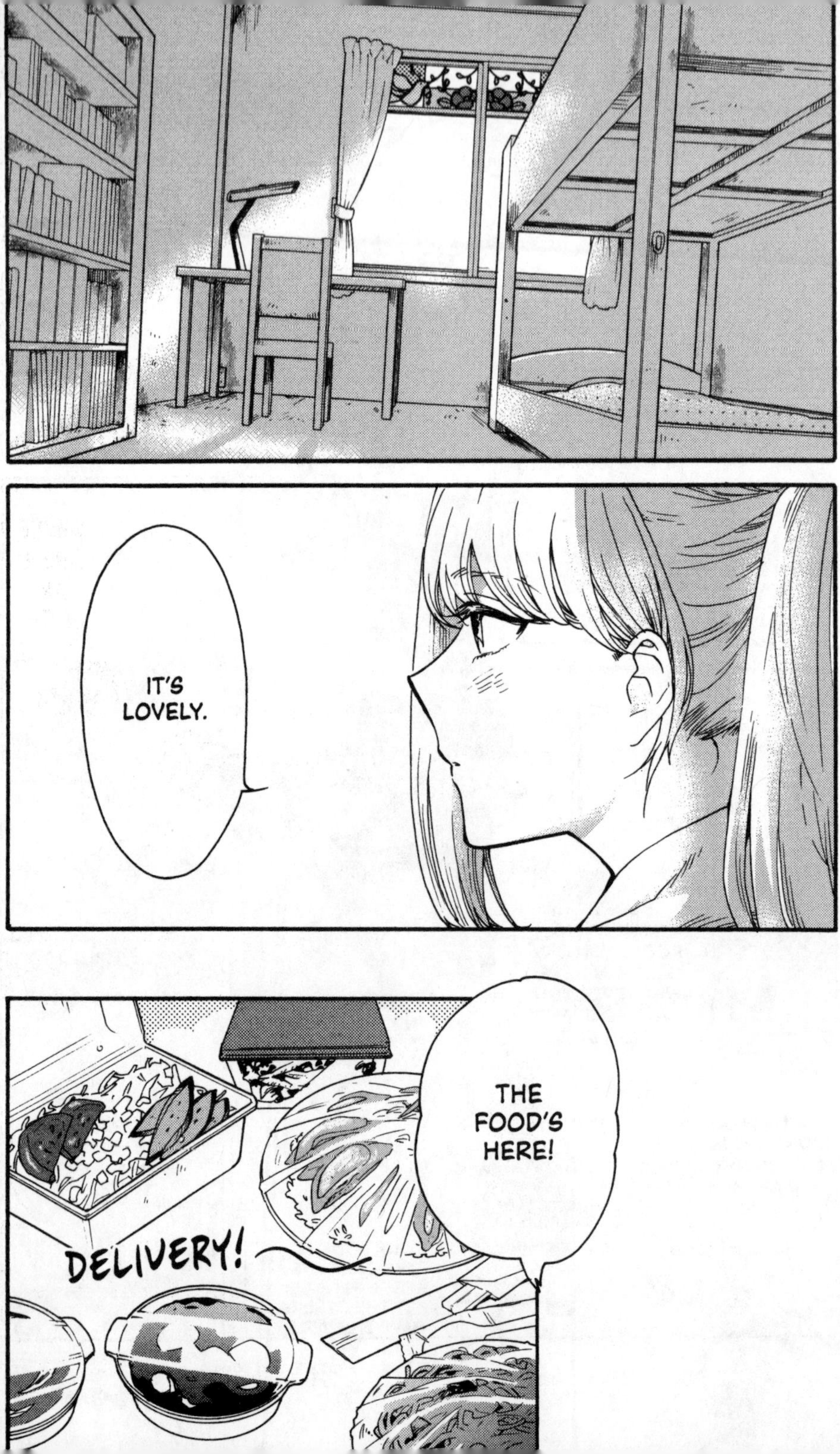
IT'S LOVELY.
THE FOOD'S HERE!
DELIVERY!

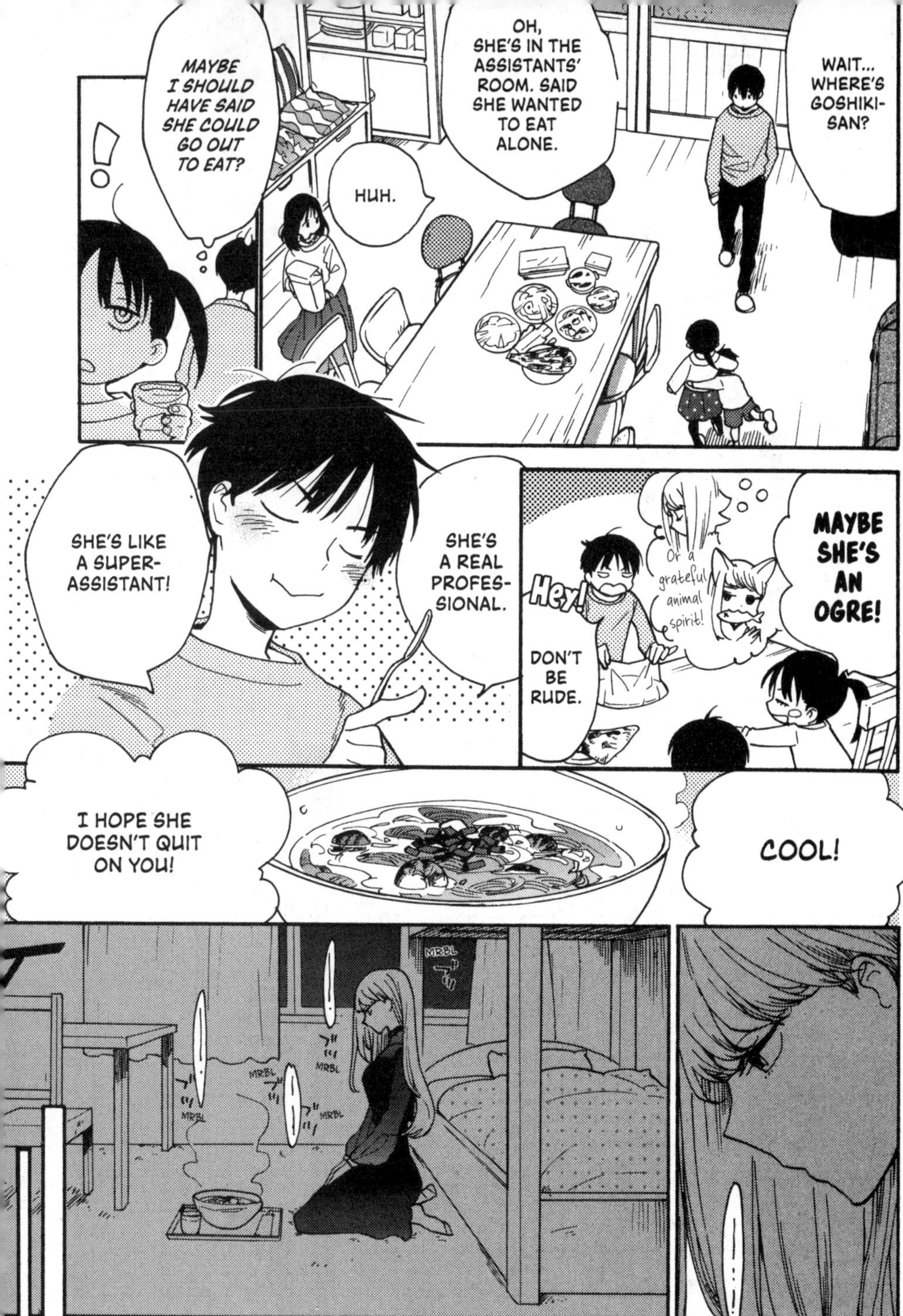
WAIT... WHERE'S GOSHIKI-SAN?
OH, SHE'S IN THE ASSISTANTS' ROOM. SAID SHE WANTED TO EAT ALONE.
HUH.
MAYBE I SHOULD HAVE SAID SHE COULD GO OUT TO EAT?
MAYBE SHE'S AN OGRE!
Or a grateful animal spirit!
Hey!
DON'T BE RUDE.
SHE'S A REAL PROFESSIONAL.
SHE'S LIKE A SUPER-ASSISTANT!
COOL!
I HOPE SHE DOESN'T QUIT ON YOU!
MRBL
MRBL
MRBL
MRBL
MRBL

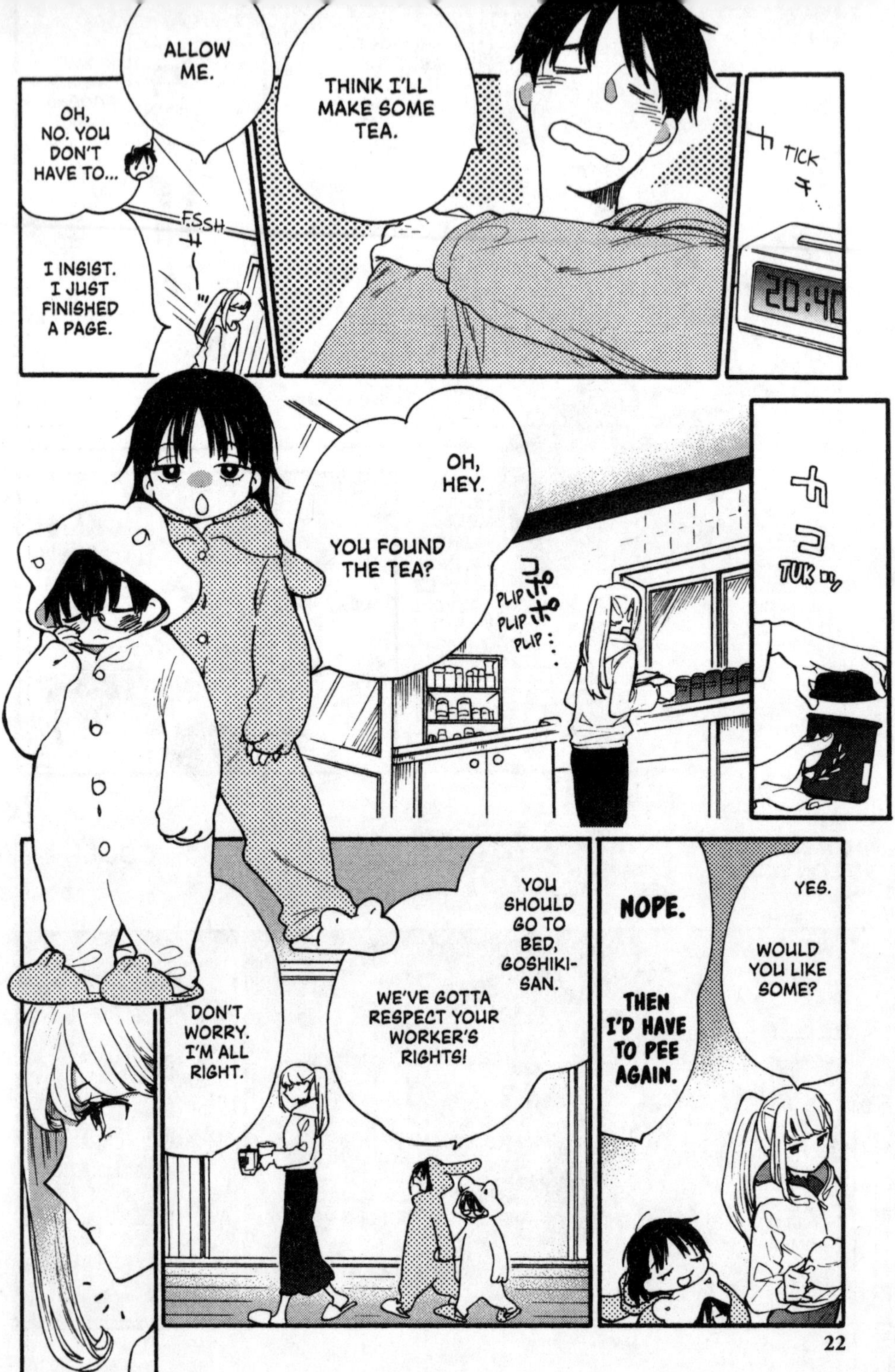
TICK
THINK I'LL MAKE SOME TEA.
ALLOW ME.
OH, NO. YOU DON'T HAVE TO...
FSSH
I INSIST. I JUST FINISHED A PAGE.
TUK
PLIP PLIP PLIP...
OH, HEY.
YOU FOUND THE TEA?
YES.
WOULD YOU LIKE SOME?
NOPE.
THEN I'D HAVE TO PEE AGAIN.
YOU SHOULD GO TO BED, GOSHIKI-SAN.
WE'VE GOTTA RESPECT YOUR WORKER'S RIGHTS!
DON'T WORRY. I'M ALL RIGHT.

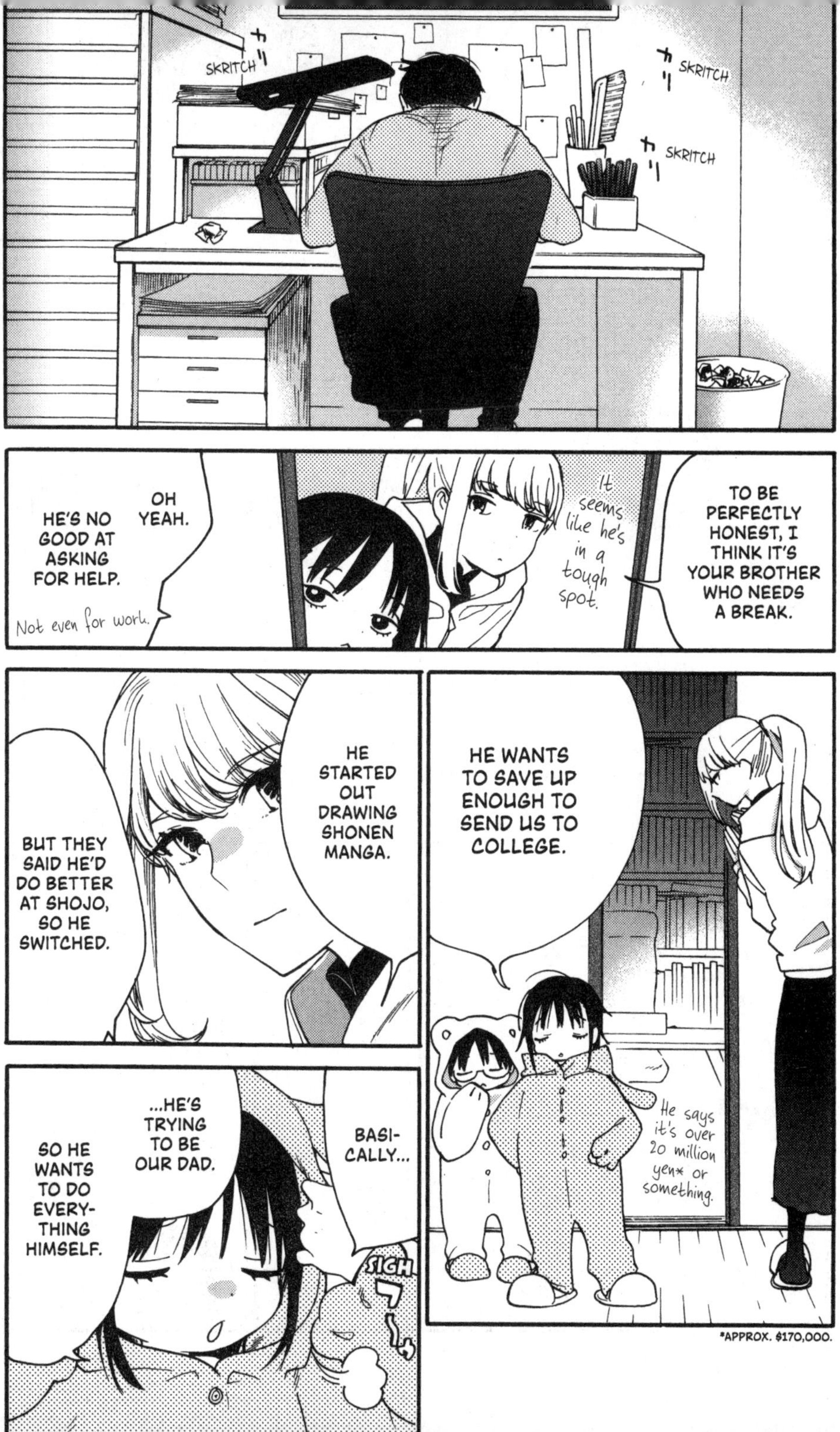
SKRITCH
SKRITCH
SKRITCH
TO BE PERFECTLY HONEST, I THINK IT'S YOUR BROTHER WHO NEEDS A BREAK.
It seems like he's in a tough spot.
OH YEAH.
HE'S NO GOOD AT ASKING FOR HELP.
Not even for work.
HE WANTS TO SAVE UP ENOUGH TO SEND US TO COLLEGE.
He says it's over 20 million yen* or something.
HE STARTED OUT DRAWING SHONEN MANGA.
BUT THEY SAID HE'D DO BETTER AT SHOJO, SO HE SWITCHED.
BASI-CALLY...
...HE'S TRYING TO BE OUR DAD.
SO HE WANTS TO DO EVERY-THING HIMSELF.
SIGH

*APPROX. $170,000.

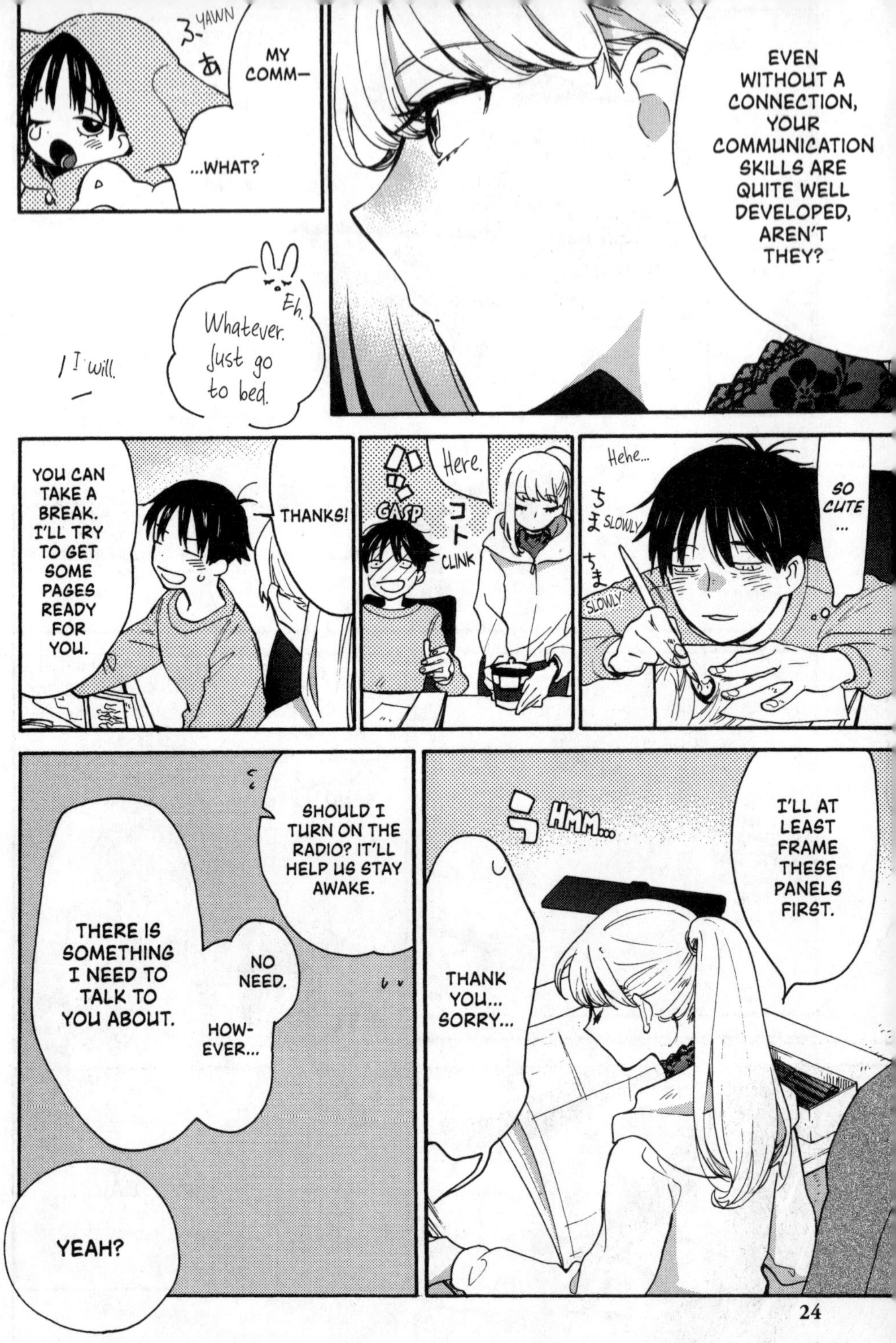
EVEN WITHOUT A CONNECTION, YOUR COMMUNICATION SKILLS ARE QUITE WELL DEVELOPED, AREN'T THEY?
ふあ YAWN
MY COMM—
...WHAT?
Eh. Whatever. Just go to bed.
I will.
Hehe...
SO CUTE...
ちま SLOWLY
ちま SLOWLY
Here.
GASP
コト CLINK
THANKS!
YOU CAN TAKE A BREAK. I'LL TRY TO GET SOME PAGES READY FOR YOU.
I'LL AT LEAST FRAME THESE PANELS FIRST.
HMM...
THANK YOU... SORRY...
SHOULD I TURN ON THE RADIO? IT'LL HELP US STAY AWAKE.
NO NEED.
HOW-EVER...
THERE IS SOMETHING I NEED TO TALK TO YOU ABOUT.
YEAH?

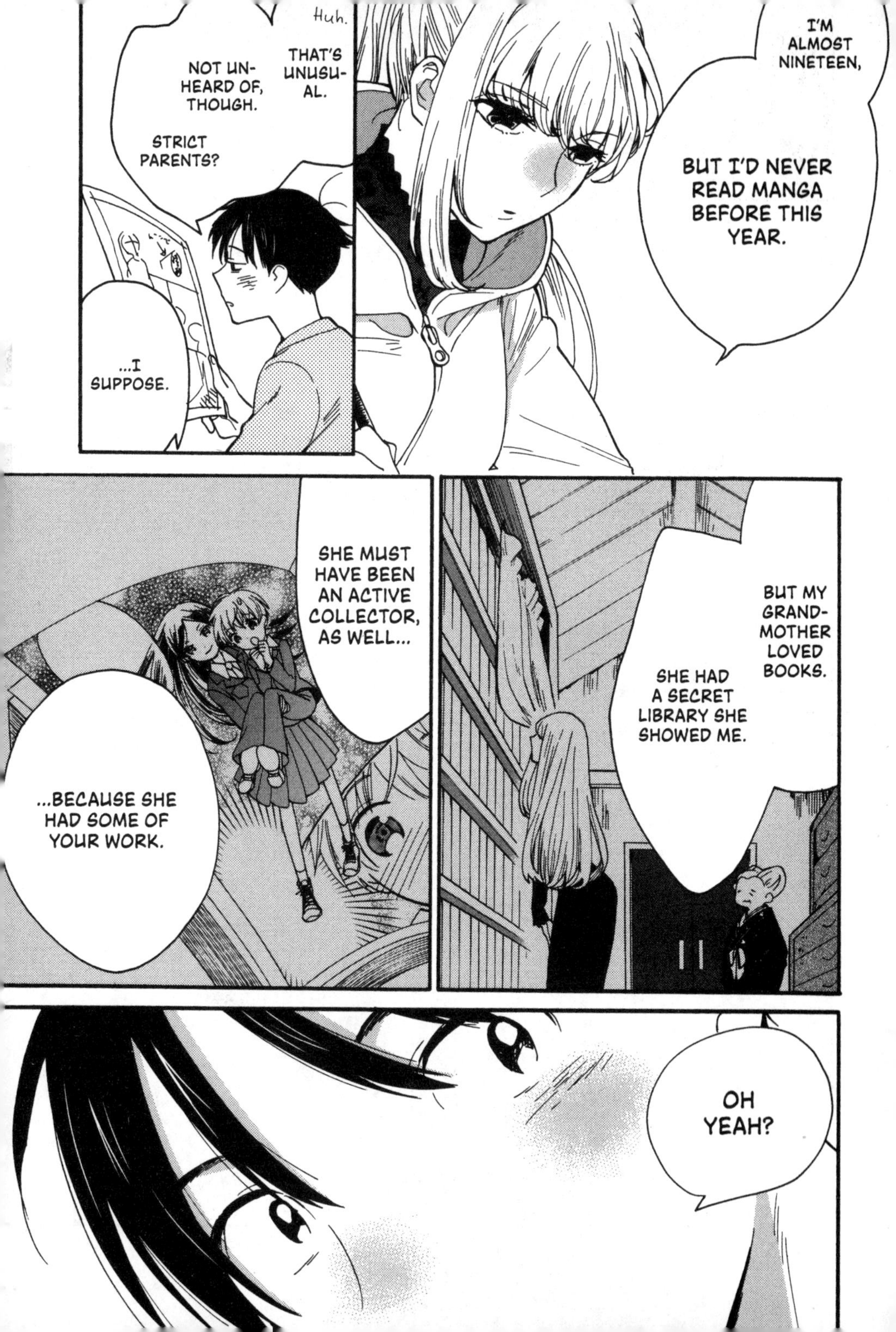
I'M ALMOST NINETEEN,
BUT I'D NEVER READ MANGA BEFORE THIS YEAR.
Huh.
THAT'S UNUSU-AL.
NOT UN-HEARD OF, THOUGH.
STRICT PARENTS?
...I SUPPOSE.
BUT MY GRAND-MOTHER LOVED BOOKS.
SHE HAD A SECRET LIBRARY SHE SHOWED ME.
SHE MUST HAVE BEEN AN ACTIVE COLLECTOR, AS WELL...
...BECAUSE SHE HAD SOME OF YOUR WORK.
OH YEAH?

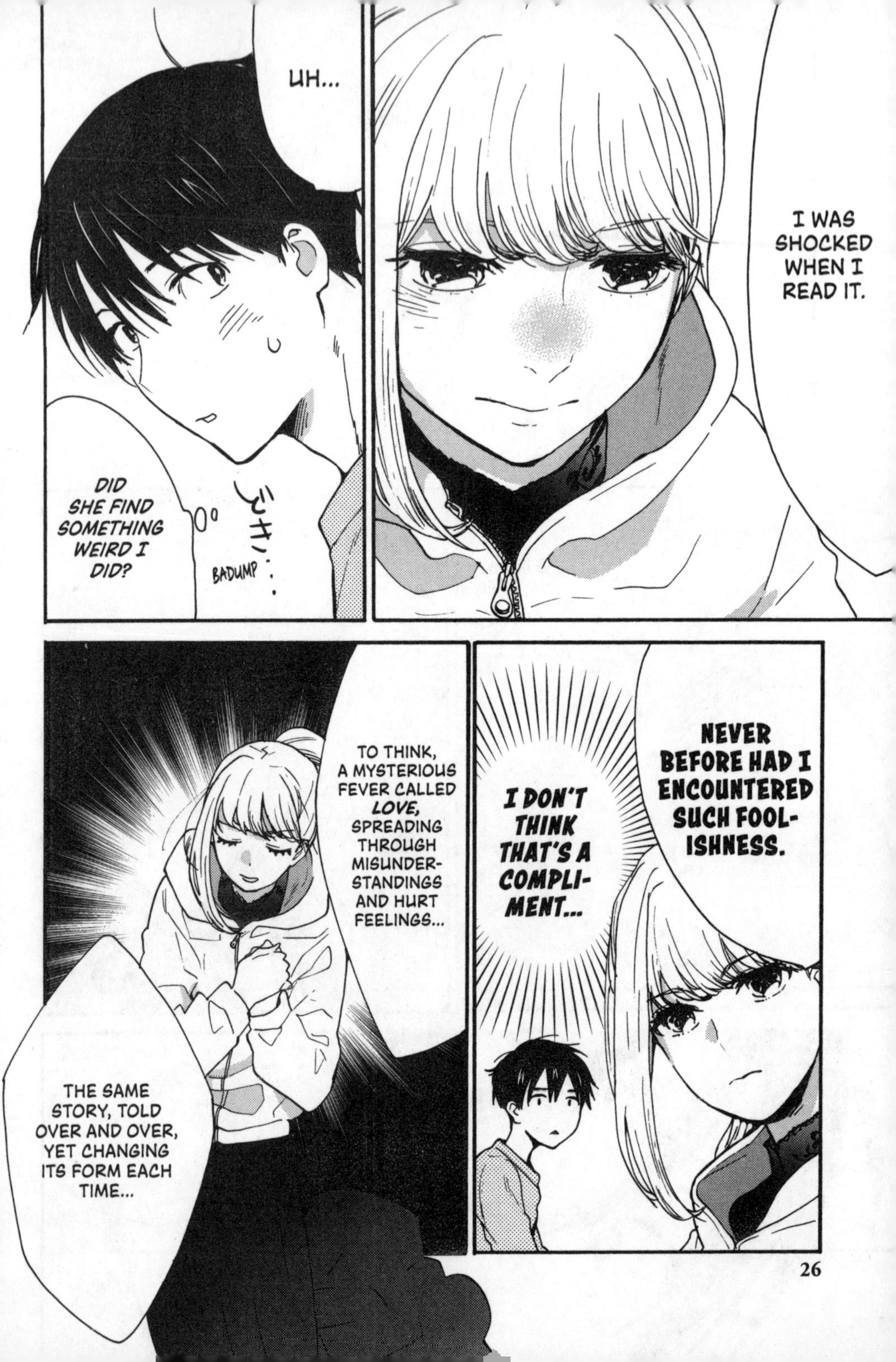
I WAS SHOCKED WHEN I READ IT.
UH...
DID SHE FIND SOMETHING WEIRD I DID?
BADUMP
NEVER BEFORE HAD I ENCOUNTERED SUCH FOOL-ISHNESS.
I DON'T THINK THAT'S A COMPLI-MENT...
TO THINK, A MYSTERIOUS FEVER CALLED *LOVE*, SPREADING THROUGH MISUNDER-STANDINGS AND HURT FEELINGS...
THE SAME STORY, TOLD OVER AND OVER, YET CHANGING ITS FORM EACH TIME...

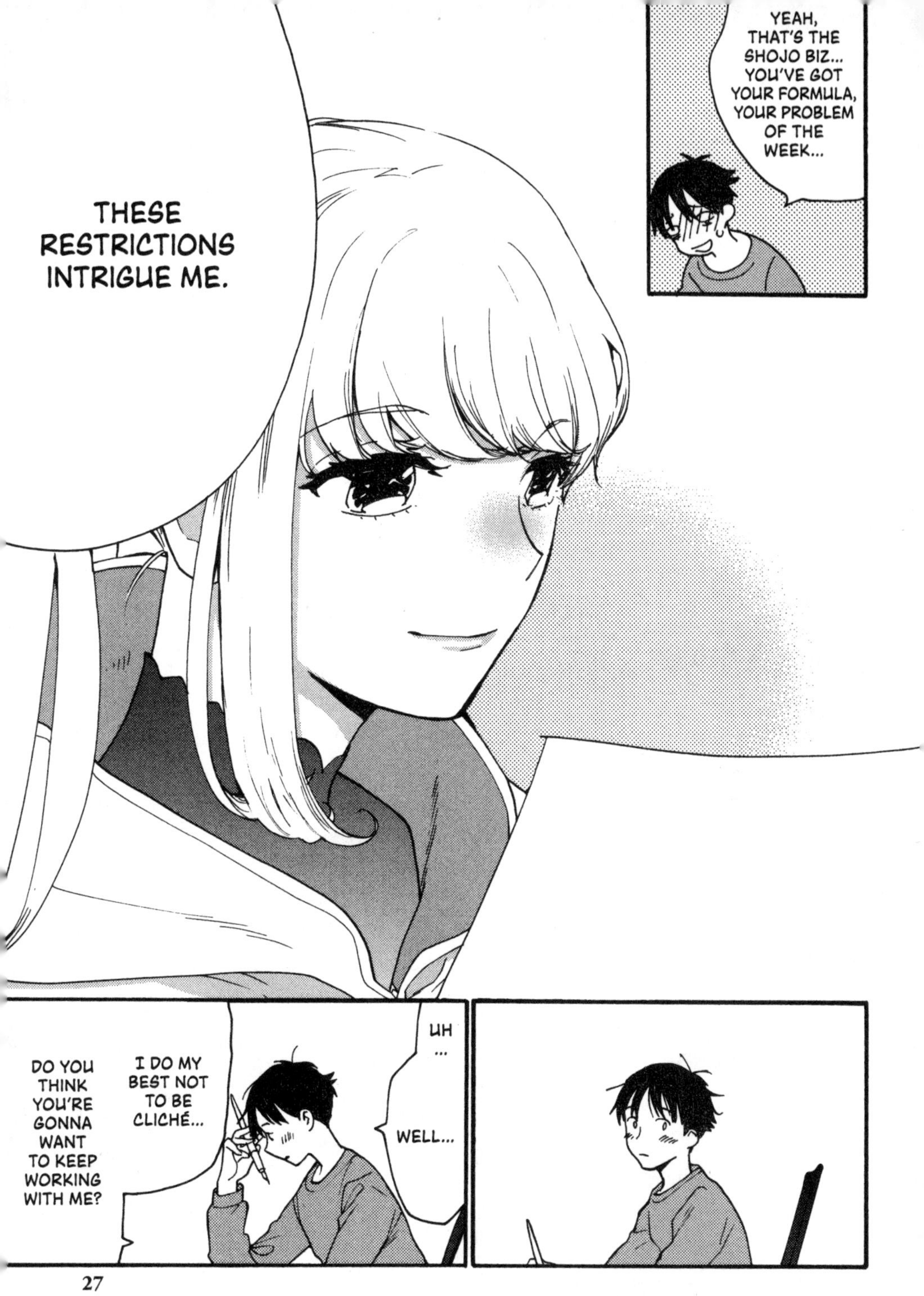
YEAH, THAT'S THE SHOJO BIZ... YOU'VE GOT YOUR FORMULA, YOUR PROBLEM OF THE WEEK...
THESE RESTRICTIONS INTRIGUE ME.
UH... WELL...
I DO MY BEST NOT TO BE CLICHÉ...
DO YOU THINK YOU'RE GONNA WANT TO KEEP WORKING WITH ME?

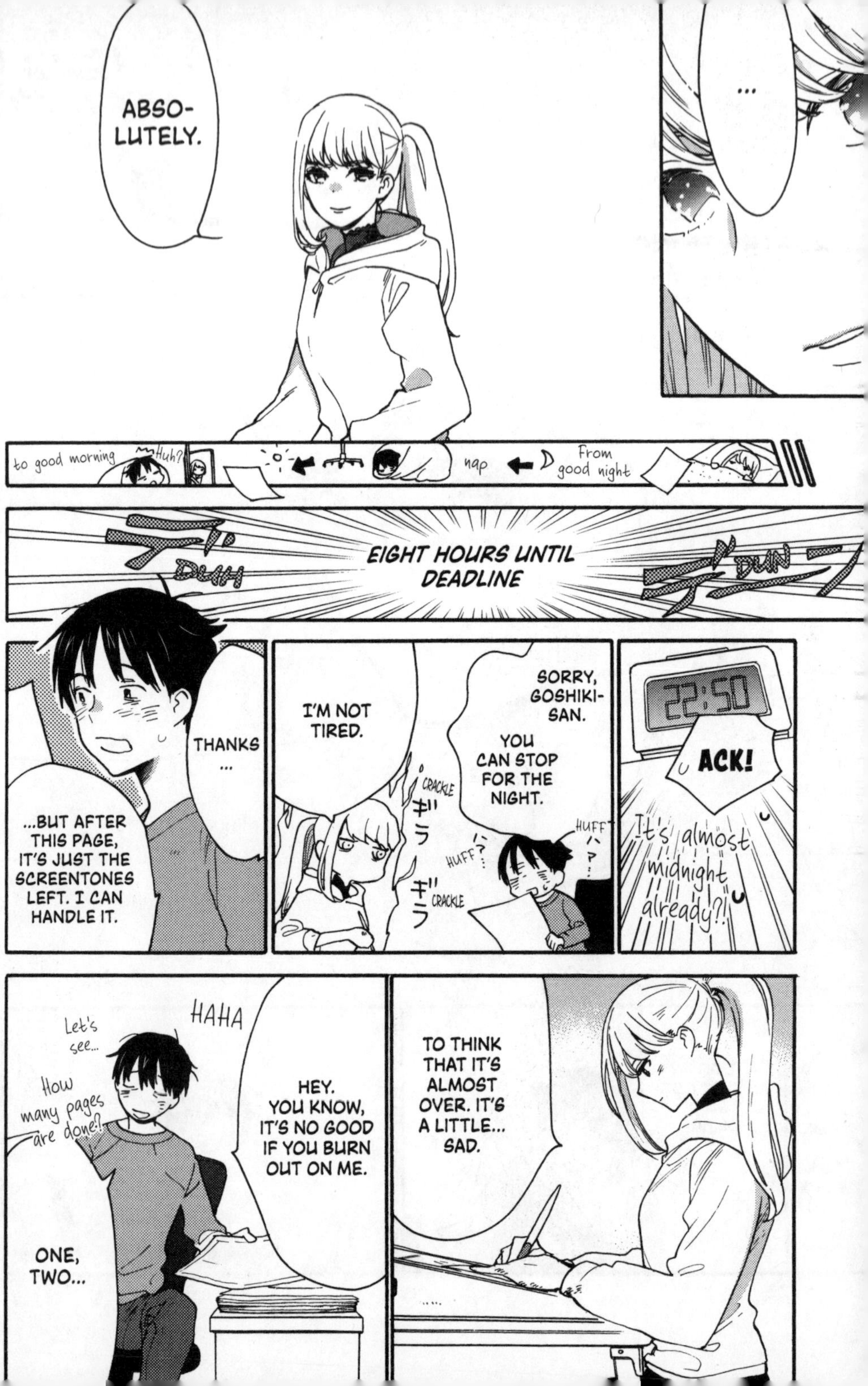
...
ABSO-LUTELY.
From good night
nap
Huh?
to good morning
DUN
EIGHT HOURS UNTIL DEADLINE
DUH
22:50
ACK!
It's almost midnight already?!
SORRY, GOSHIKI-SAN.
YOU CAN STOP FOR THE NIGHT.
HUFF
HUFF
I'M NOT TIRED.
CRACKLE
CRACKLE
THANKS...
...BUT AFTER THIS PAGE, IT'S JUST THE SCREENTONES LEFT. I CAN HANDLE IT.
TO THINK THAT IT'S ALMOST OVER. IT'S A LITTLE... SAD.
.....
HEY. YOU KNOW, IT'S NO GOOD IF YOU BURN OUT ON ME.
HAHA
Let's see...
How many pages are done?
ONE, TWO...

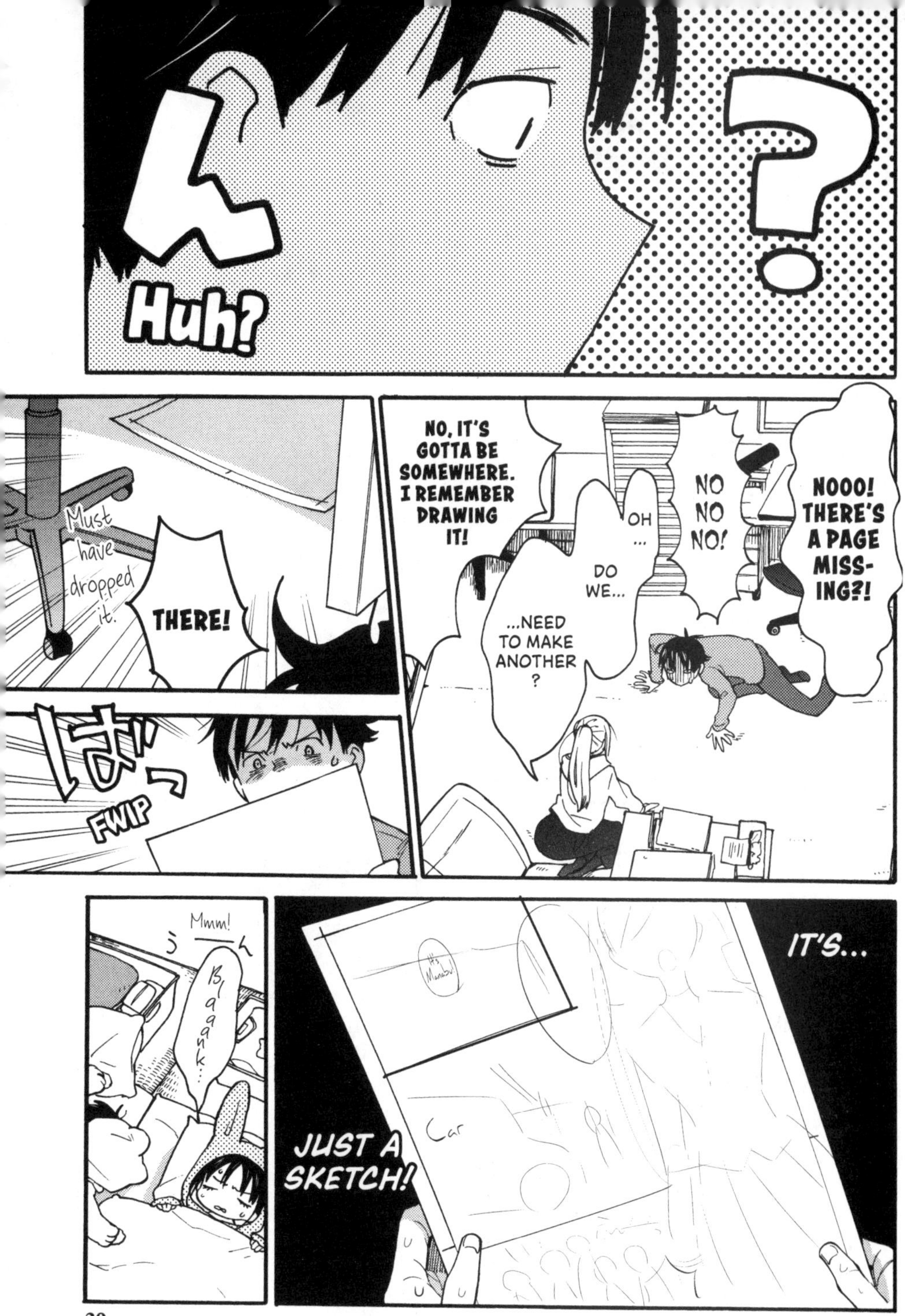
ん?
Huh?
NOOO! THERE'S A PAGE MISS-ING?!
NO NO NO!
OH ...
DO WE...
...NEED TO MAKE ANOTHER ?
NO, IT'S GOTTA BE SOMEWHERE. I REMEMBER DRAWING IT!
THERE!
Must have dropped it.
はっ
FWIP
IT'S...
It's Manabu!
Car
JUST A SKETCH!
Mmm!
うーん
Blaaank...

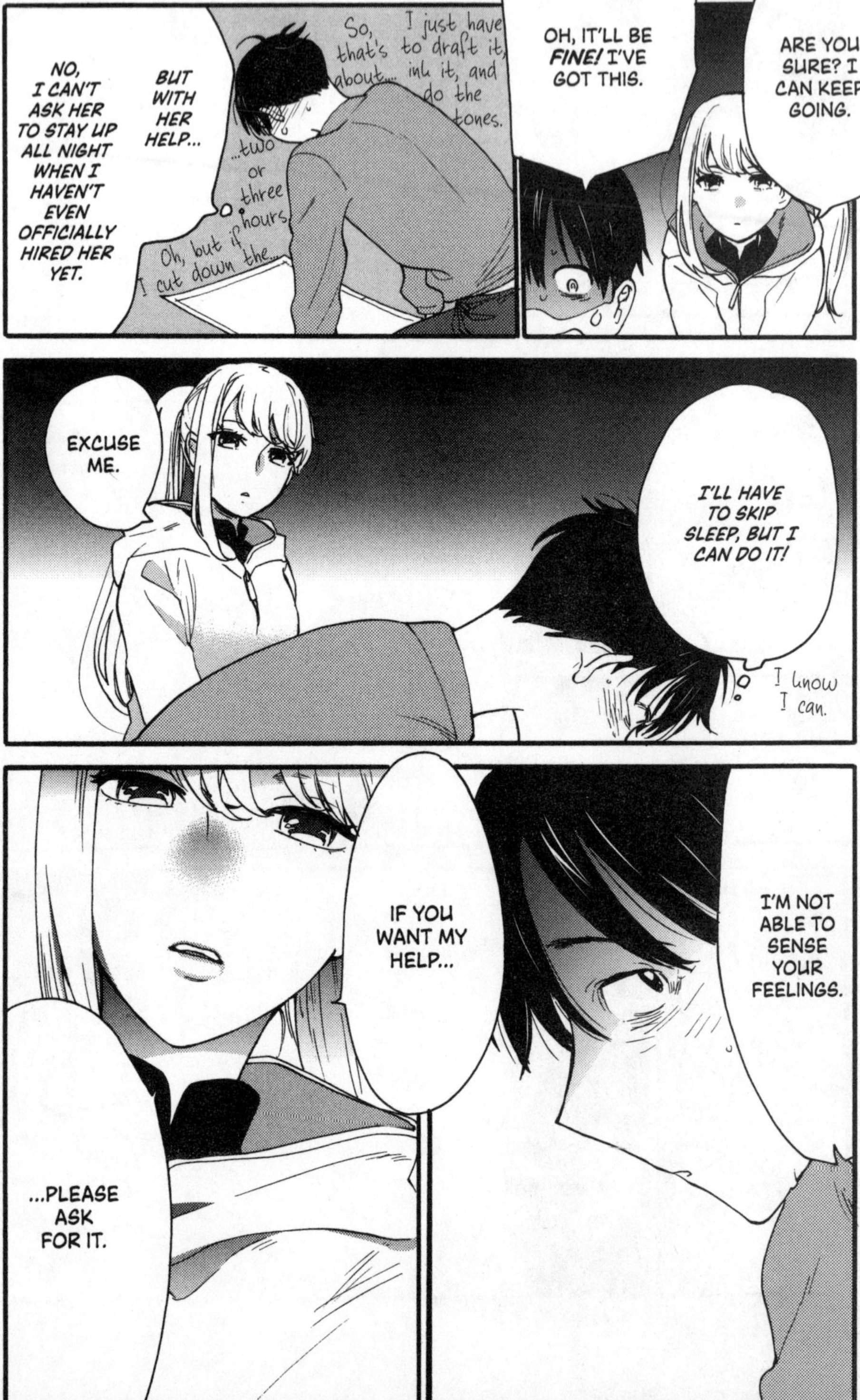
ARE YOU SURE? I CAN KEEP GOING.
OH, IT'LL BE *FINE!* I'VE GOT THIS.
I just have to draft it, ink it, and do the tones.
So, that's about...
...two or three hours.
Oh, but if I cut down the...
BUT WITH HER HELP...
NO, I CAN'T ASK HER TO STAY UP ALL NIGHT WHEN I HAVEN'T EVEN OFFICIALLY HIRED HER YET.
I'LL HAVE TO SKIP SLEEP, BUT I CAN DO IT!
I know I can.
EXCUSE ME.
I'M NOT ABLE TO SENSE YOUR FEELINGS.
IF YOU WANT MY HELP...
...PLEASE ASK FOR IT.

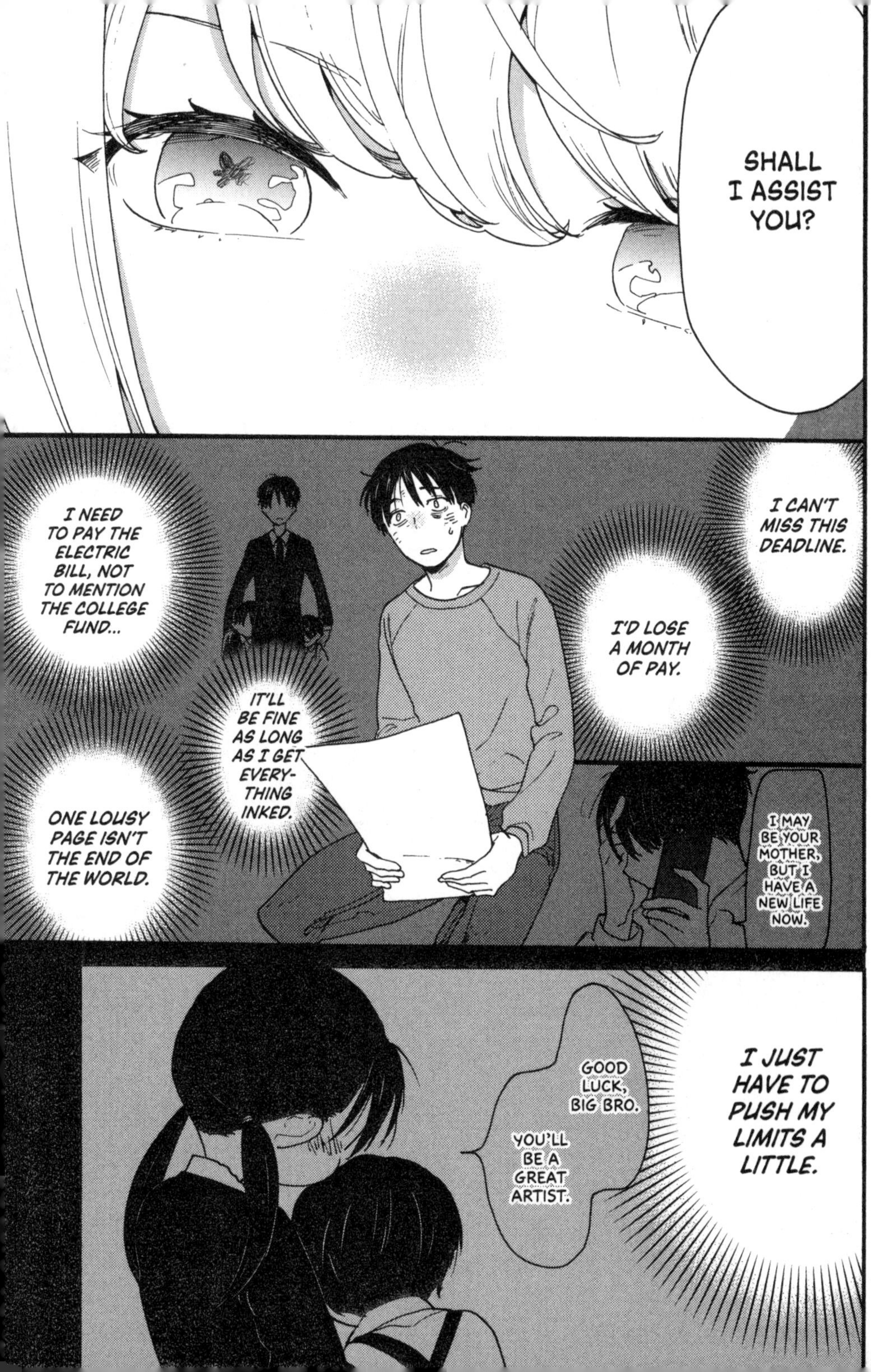
SHALL I ASSIST YOU?
I CAN'T MISS THIS DEADLINE.
I'D LOSE A MONTH OF PAY.
I NEED TO PAY THE ELECTRIC BILL, NOT TO MENTION THE COLLEGE FUND...
IT'LL BE FINE AS LONG AS I GET EVERY-THING INKED.
ONE LOUSY PAGE ISN'T THE END OF THE WORLD.
I MAY BE YOUR MOTHER, BUT I HAVE A NEW LIFE NOW.
I JUST HAVE TO PUSH MY LIMITS A LITTLE.
GOOD LUCK, BIG BRO.
YOU'LL BE A GREAT ARTIST.

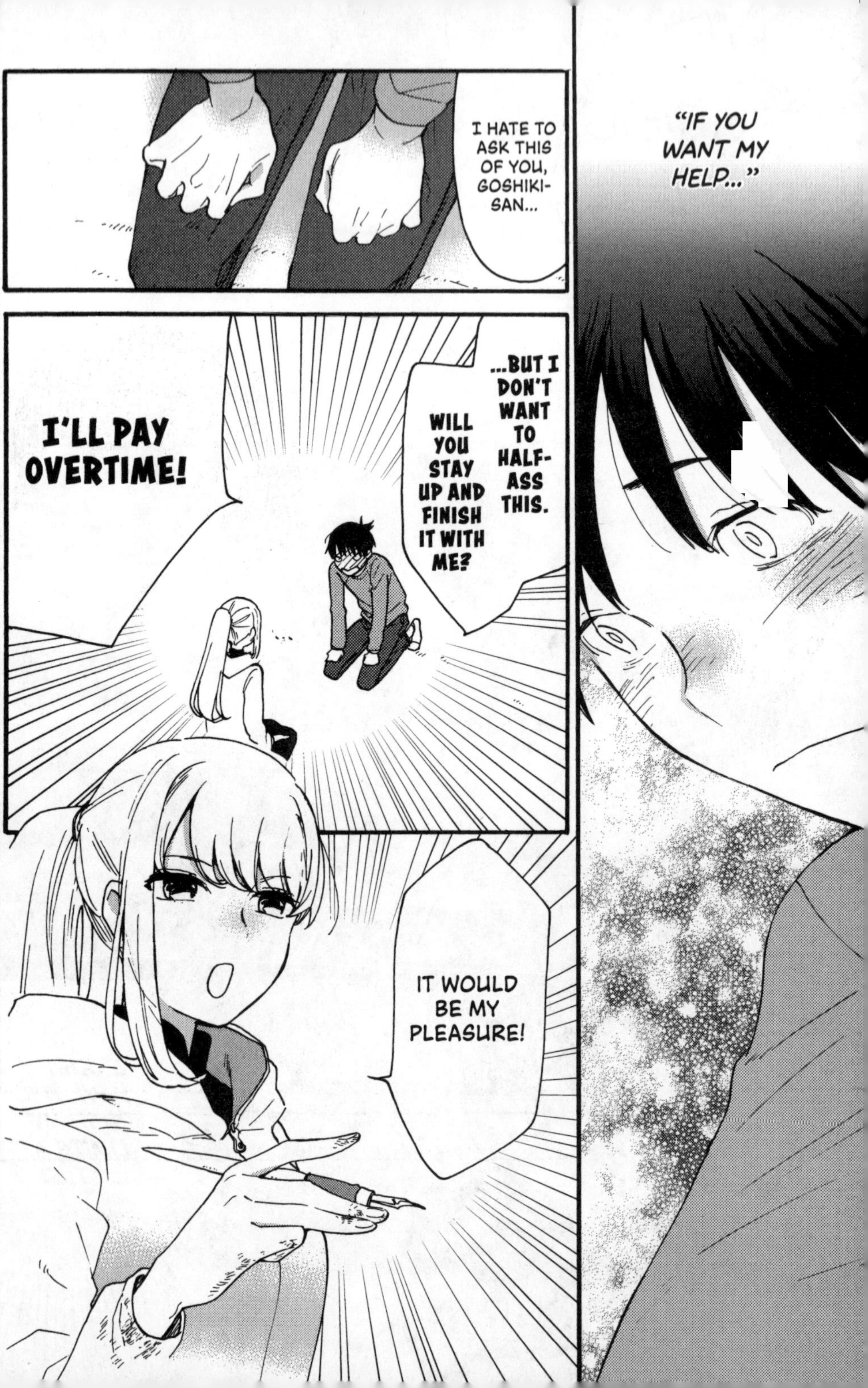
"IF YOU WANT MY HELP..."
I HATE TO ASK THIS OF YOU, GOSHIKI-SAN...
...BUT I DON'T WANT TO HALF-ASS THIS.
WILL YOU STAY UP AND FINISH IT WITH ME?
I'LL PAY OVERTIME!
IT WOULD BE MY PLEASURE!

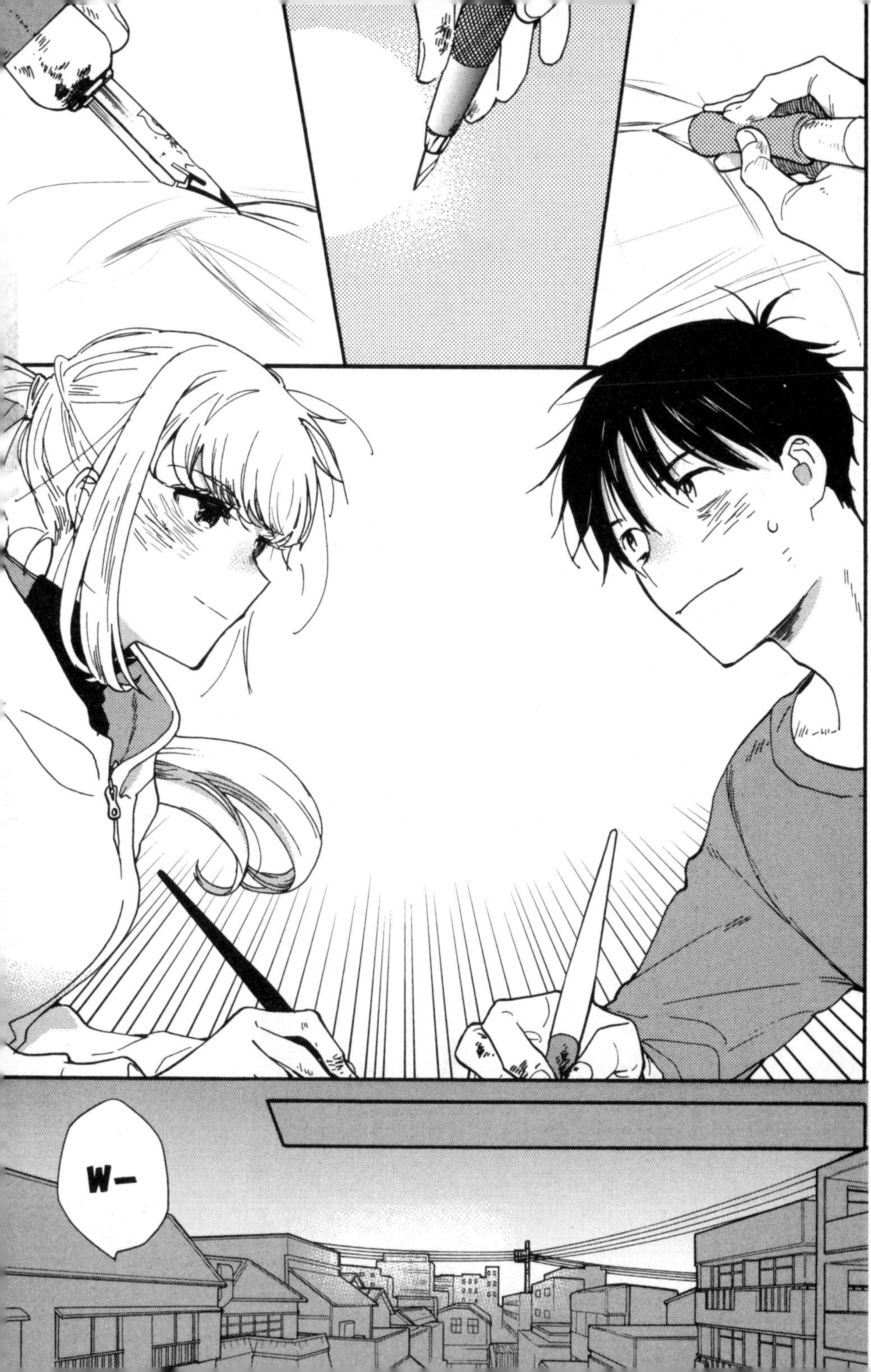
W–

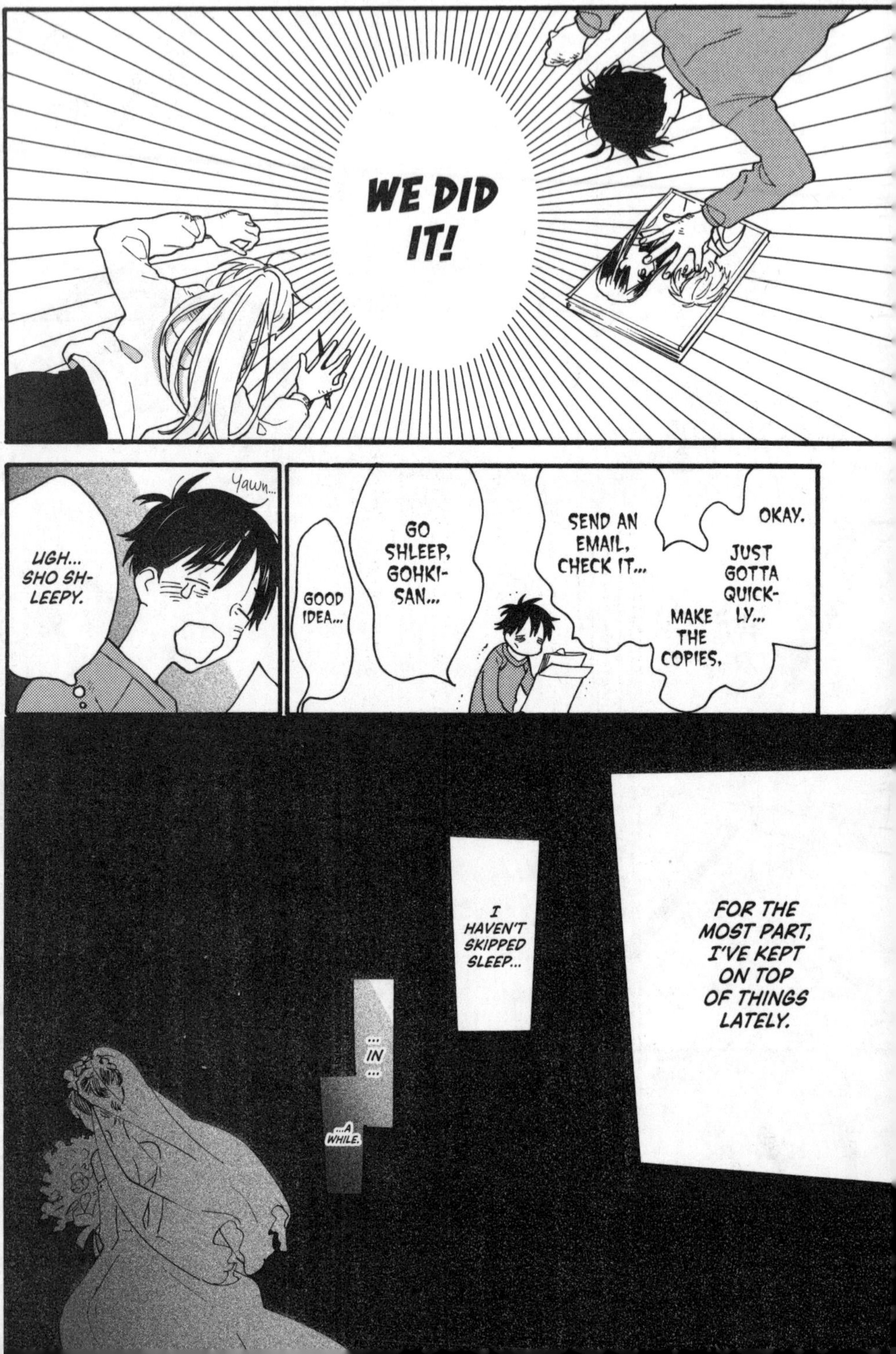
WE DID IT!
OKAY.
JUST GOTTA QUICK-LY...
MAKE THE COPIES,
SEND AN EMAIL, CHECK IT...
GO SHLEEP, GOHKI-SAN...
GOOD IDEA...
Yawn...
UGH... SHO SH-LEEPY.
FOR THE MOST PART, I'VE KEPT ON TOP OF THINGS LATELY.
I HAVEN'T SKIPPED SLEEP...
...IN...
...A WHILE.

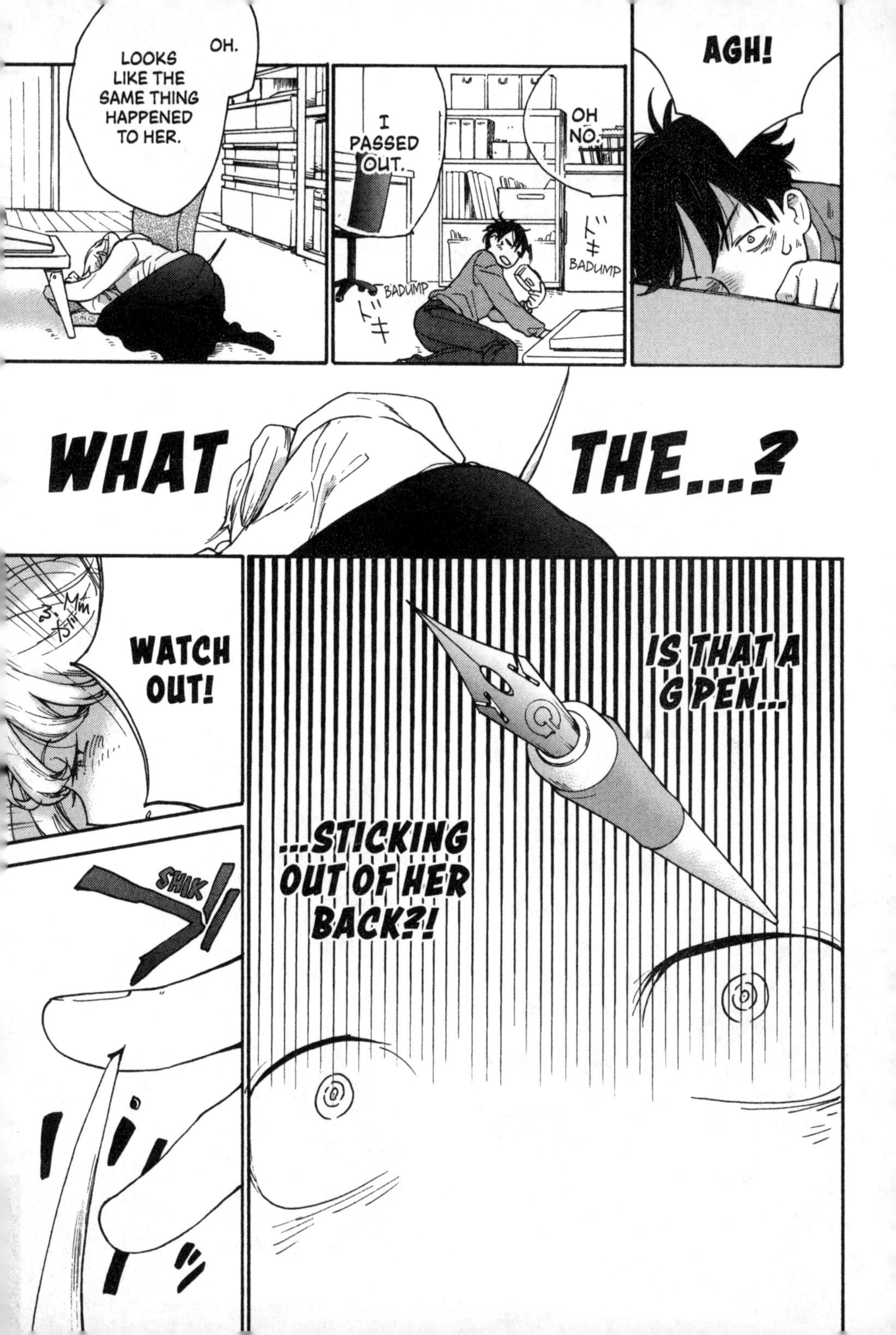
AGH!
OH NO.
I PASSED OUT.
ドキ BADUMP
ドキ BADUMP
OH.
LOOKS LIKE THE SAME THING HAPPENED TO HER.
WHAT THE...?
IS THAT A G PEN...
...STICKING OUT OF HER BACK?!
Mm
WATCH OUT!
SHIK

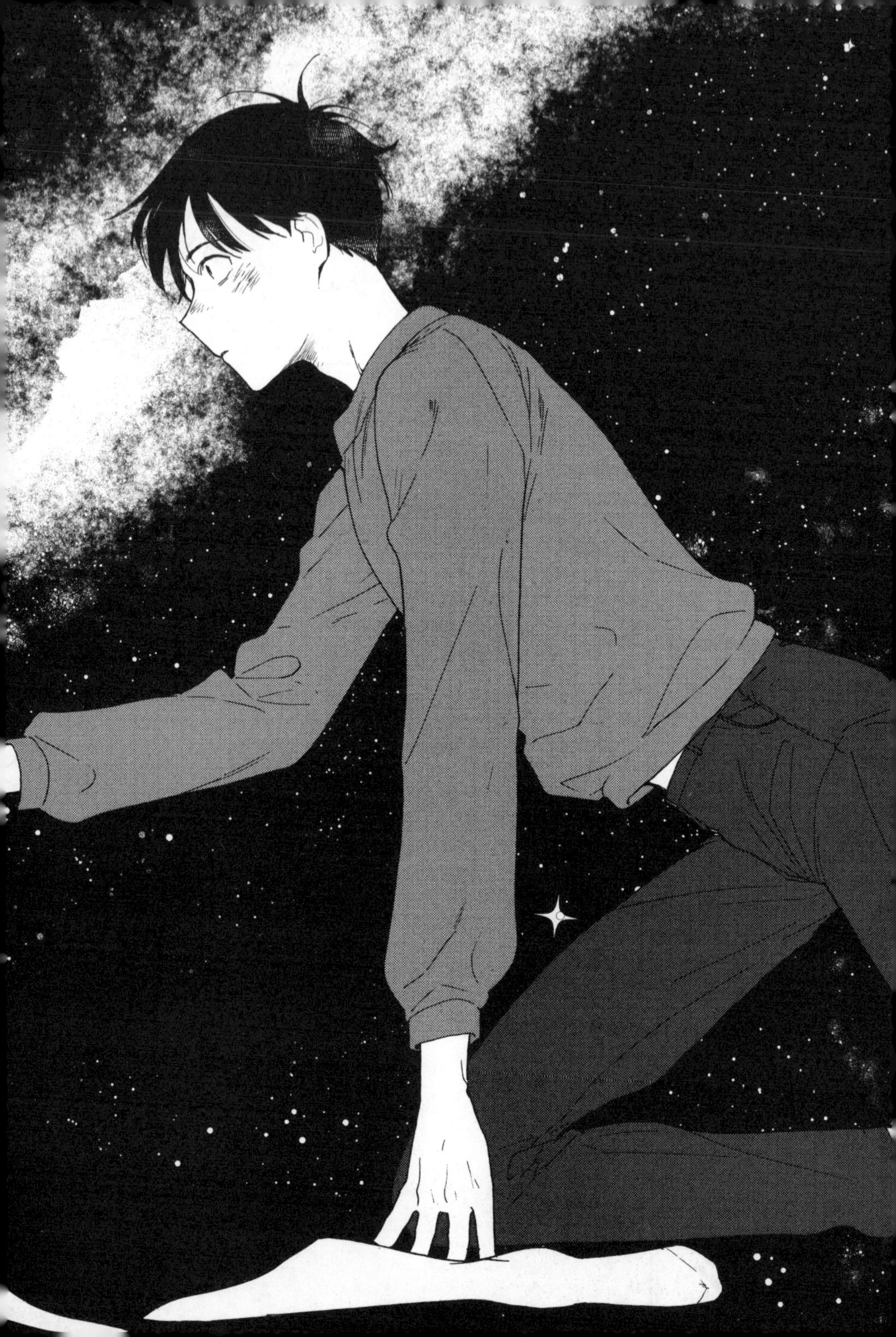

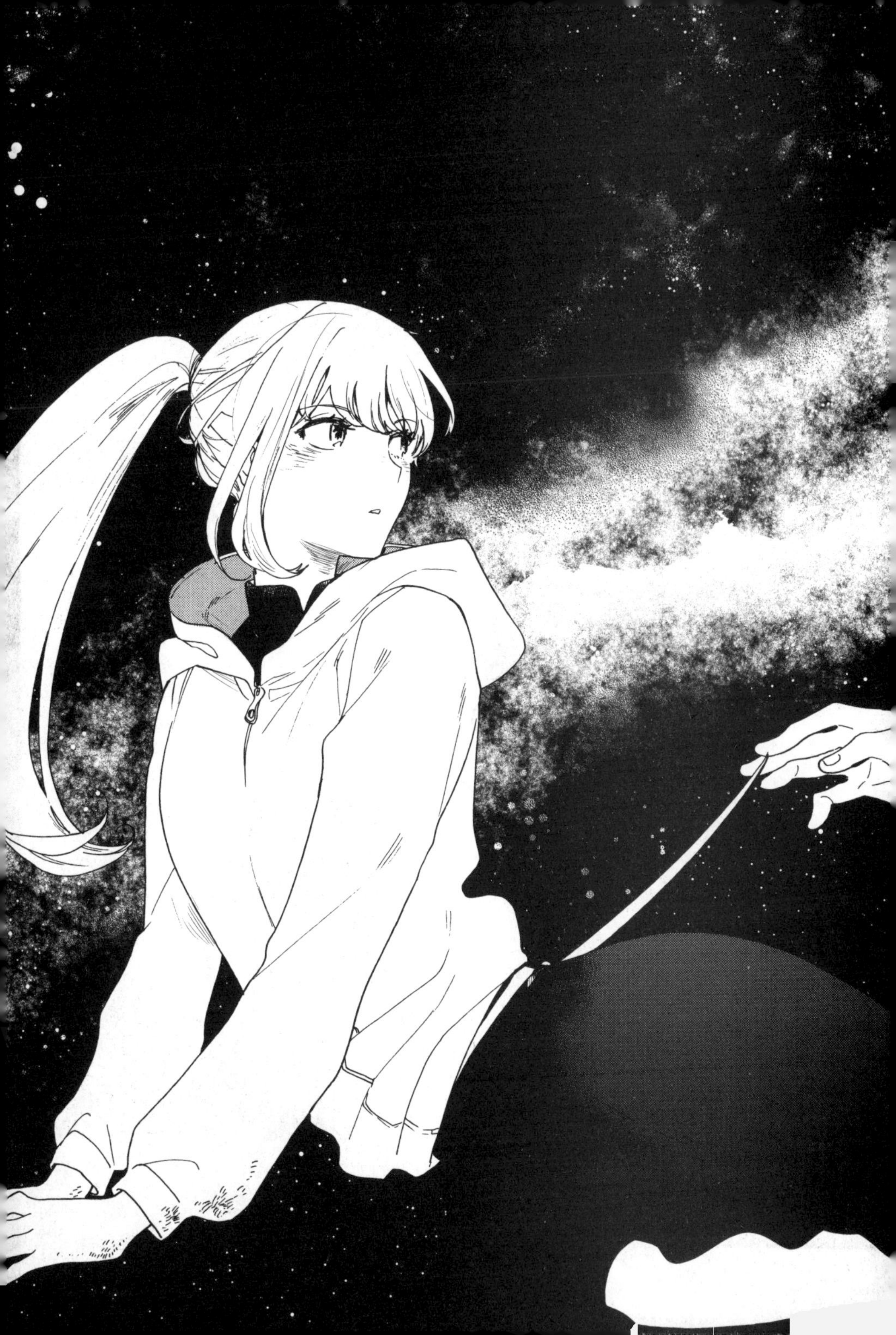

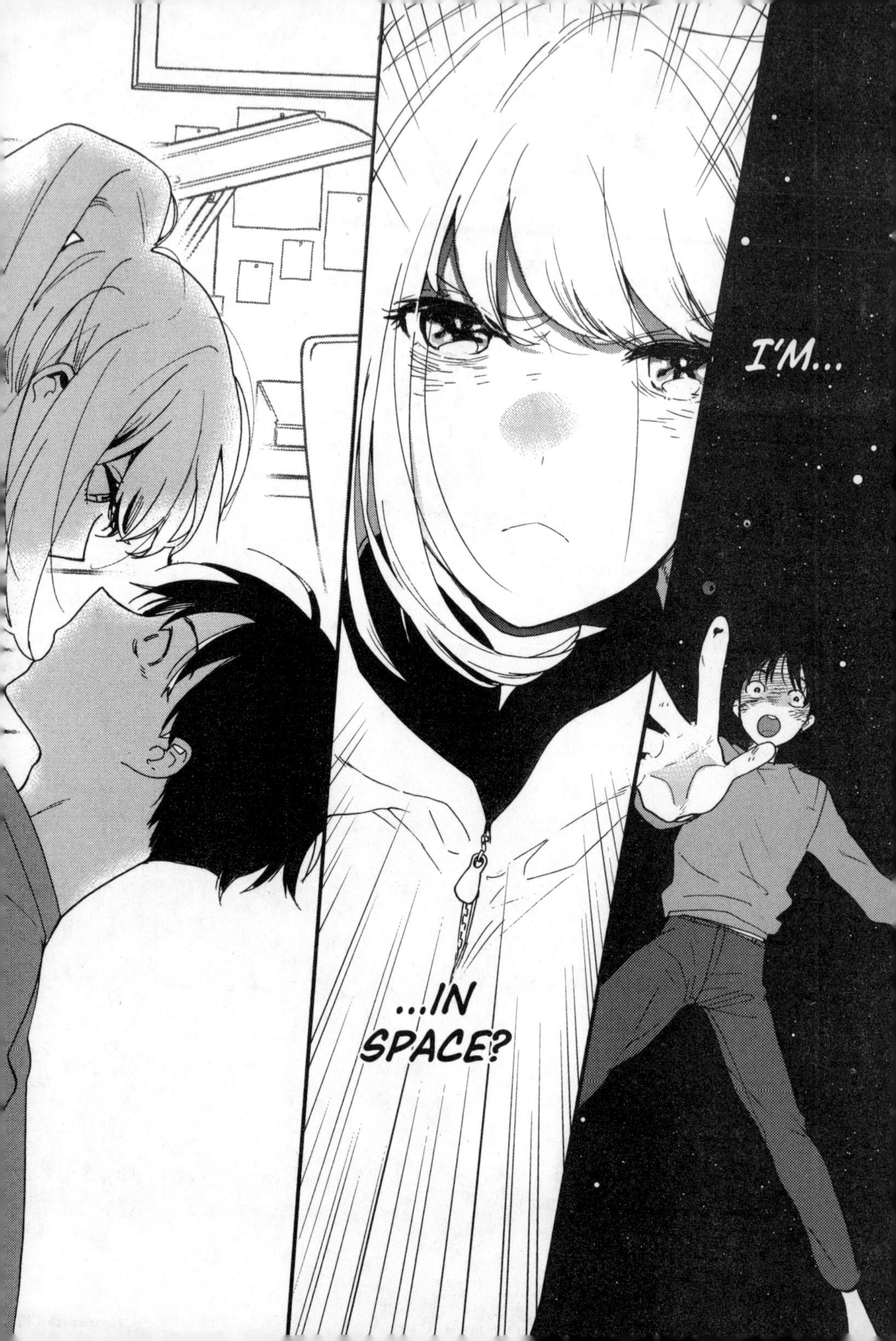
I'M...
...IN SPACE?

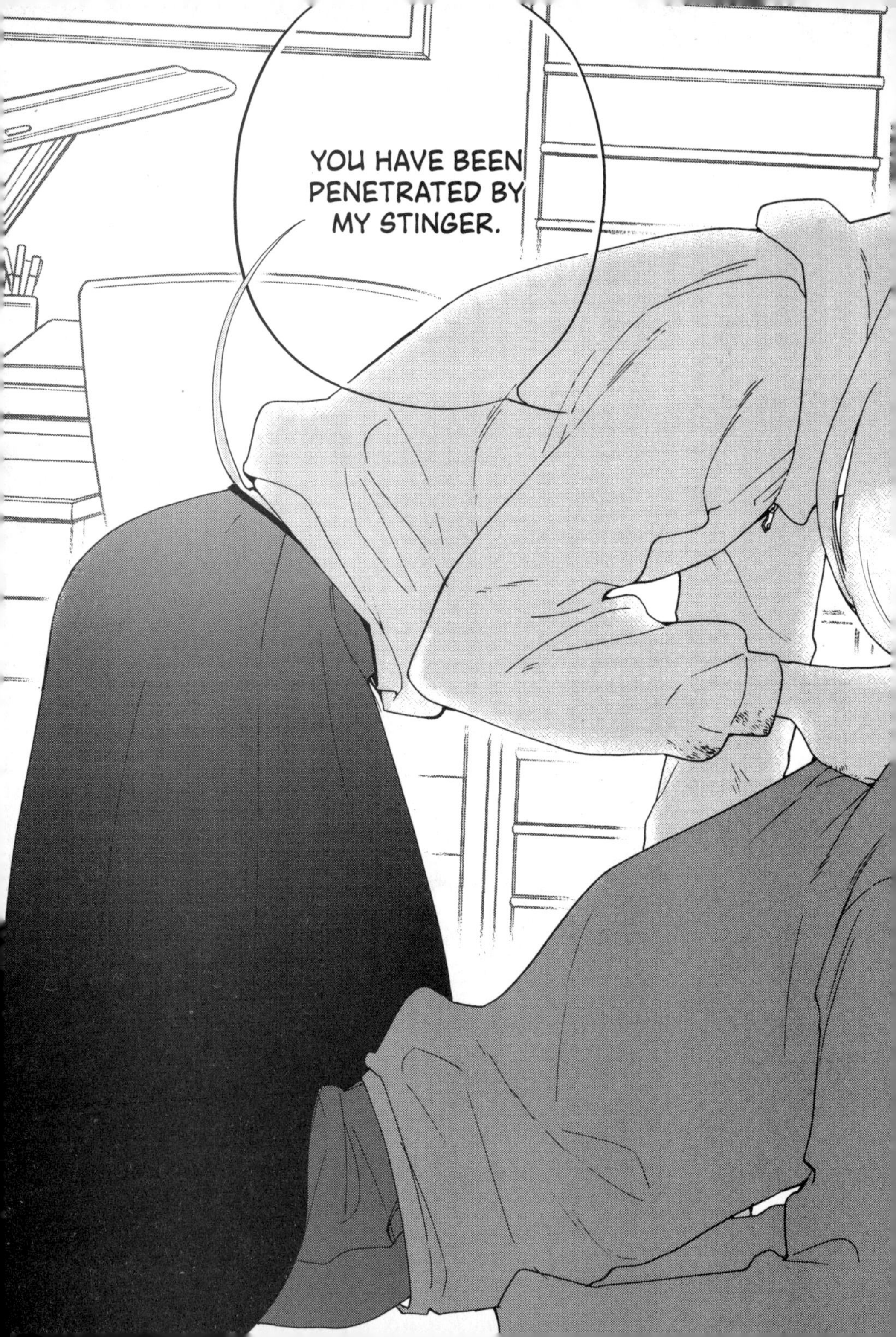
YOU HAVE BEEN PENETRATED BY MY STINGER.

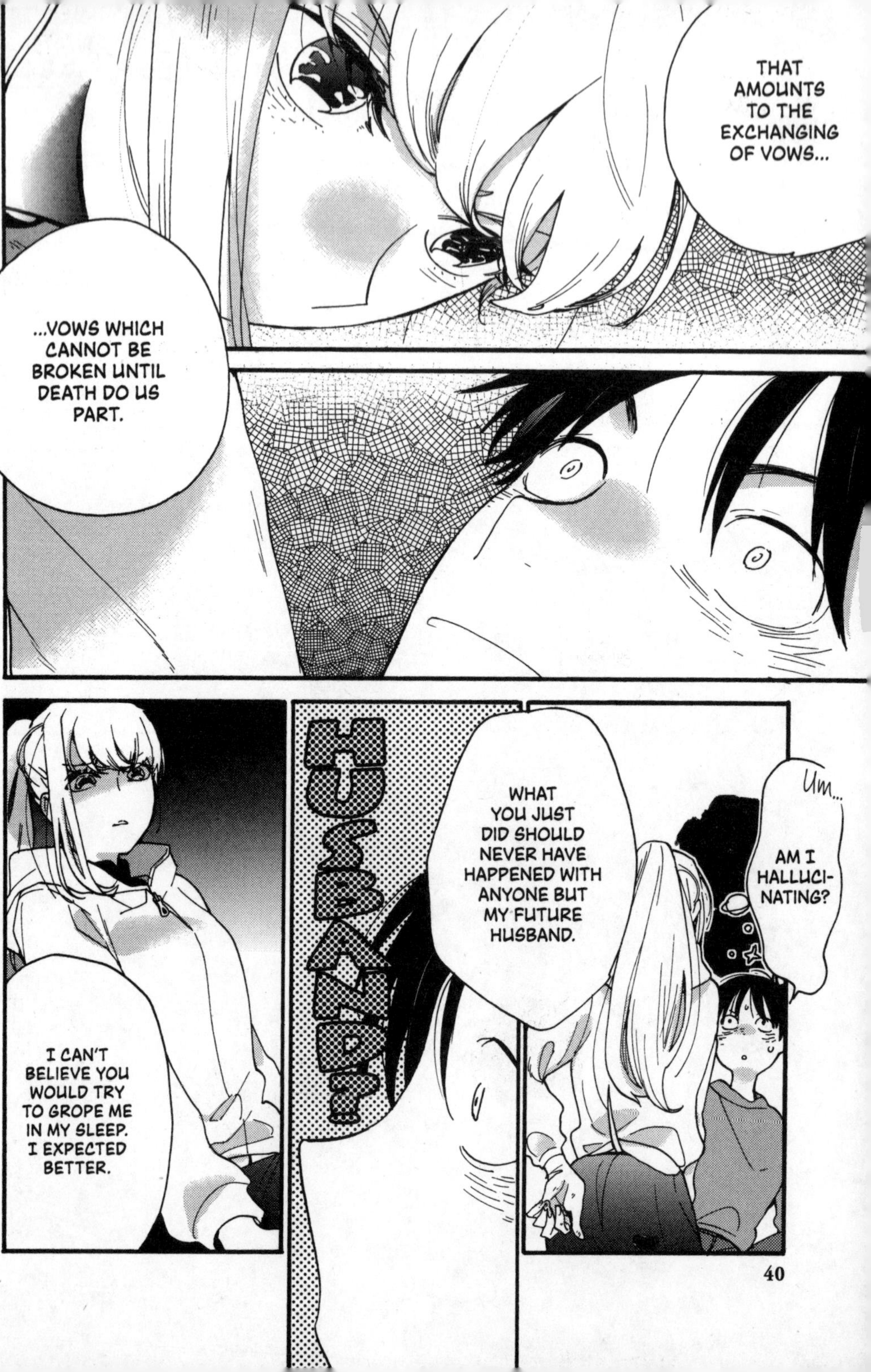
THAT AMOUNTS TO THE EXCHANGING OF VOWS...
...VOWS WHICH CANNOT BE BROKEN UNTIL DEATH DO US PART.
WHAT YOU JUST DID SHOULD NEVER HAVE HAPPENED WITH ANYONE BUT MY FUTURE HUSBAND.
Um...
AM I HALLUCINATING?
I CAN'T BELIEVE YOU WOULD TRY TO GROPE ME IN MY SLEEP. I EXPECTED BETTER.

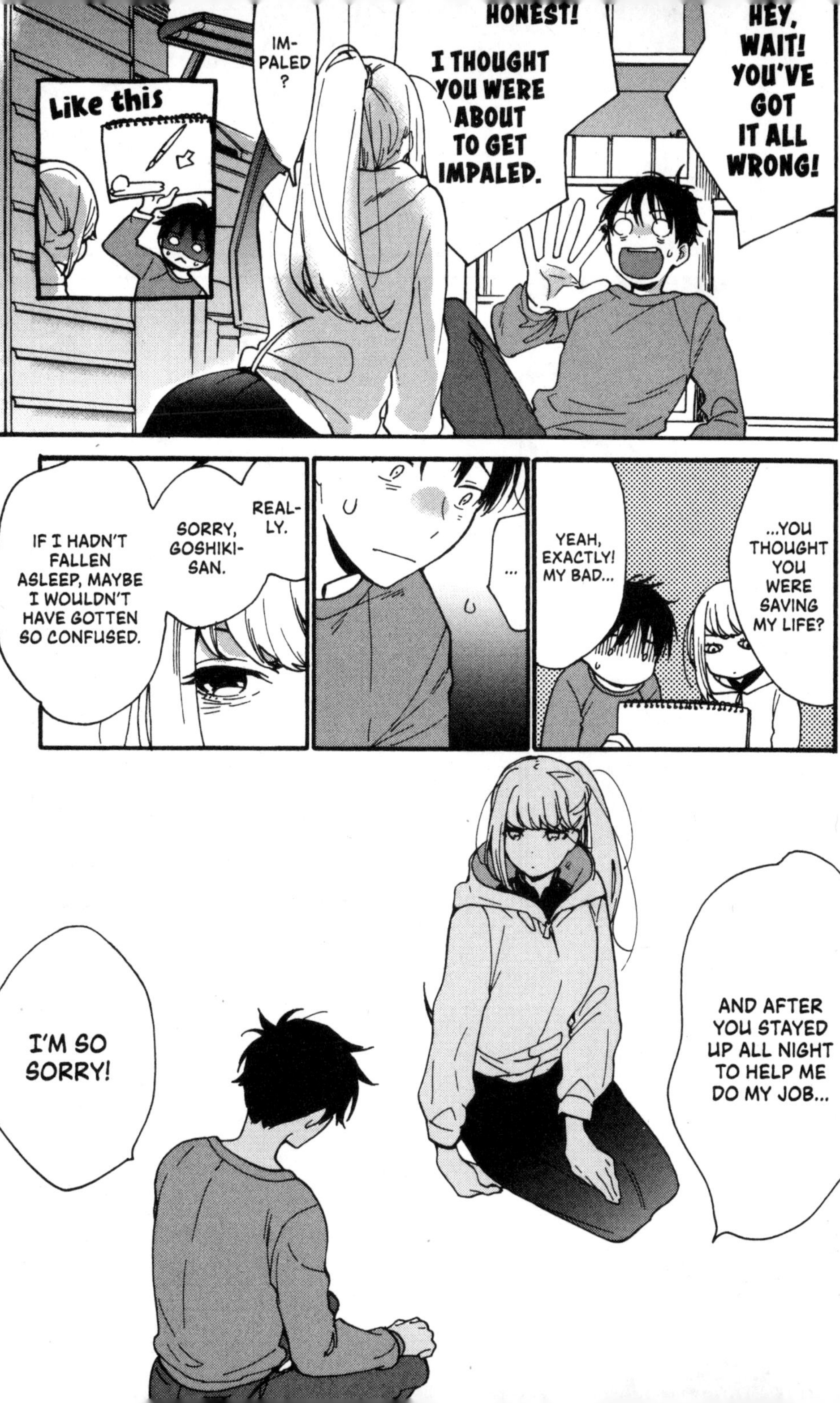
HEY, WAIT! YOU'VE GOT IT ALL WRONG!
HONEST!
I THOUGHT YOU WERE ABOUT TO GET IMPALED.
IM-PALED?
Like this
...YOU THOUGHT YOU WERE SAVING MY LIFE?
YEAH, EXACTLY! MY BAD...
...
REAL-LY.
SORRY, GOSHIKI-SAN.
IF I HADN'T FALLEN ASLEEP, MAYBE I WOULDN'T HAVE GOTTEN SO CONFUSED.
AND AFTER YOU STAYED UP ALL NIGHT TO HELP ME DO MY JOB...
I'M SO SORRY!

...

YOU THOUGHT I WAS IN DANGER.

WELL...

I'M PARTIALLY TO BLAME.

I APPRECIATE THAT YOU WERE TRYING TO HELP.

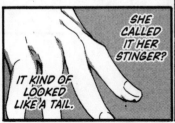

SHE CALLED IT HER STINGER?

IT KIND OF LOOKED LIKE A TAIL.

THERE ARE PEOPLE WHO HAVE TAILS, RIGHT?

I MEAN, IT WOULD PROBABLY BE RUDE TO ASK...

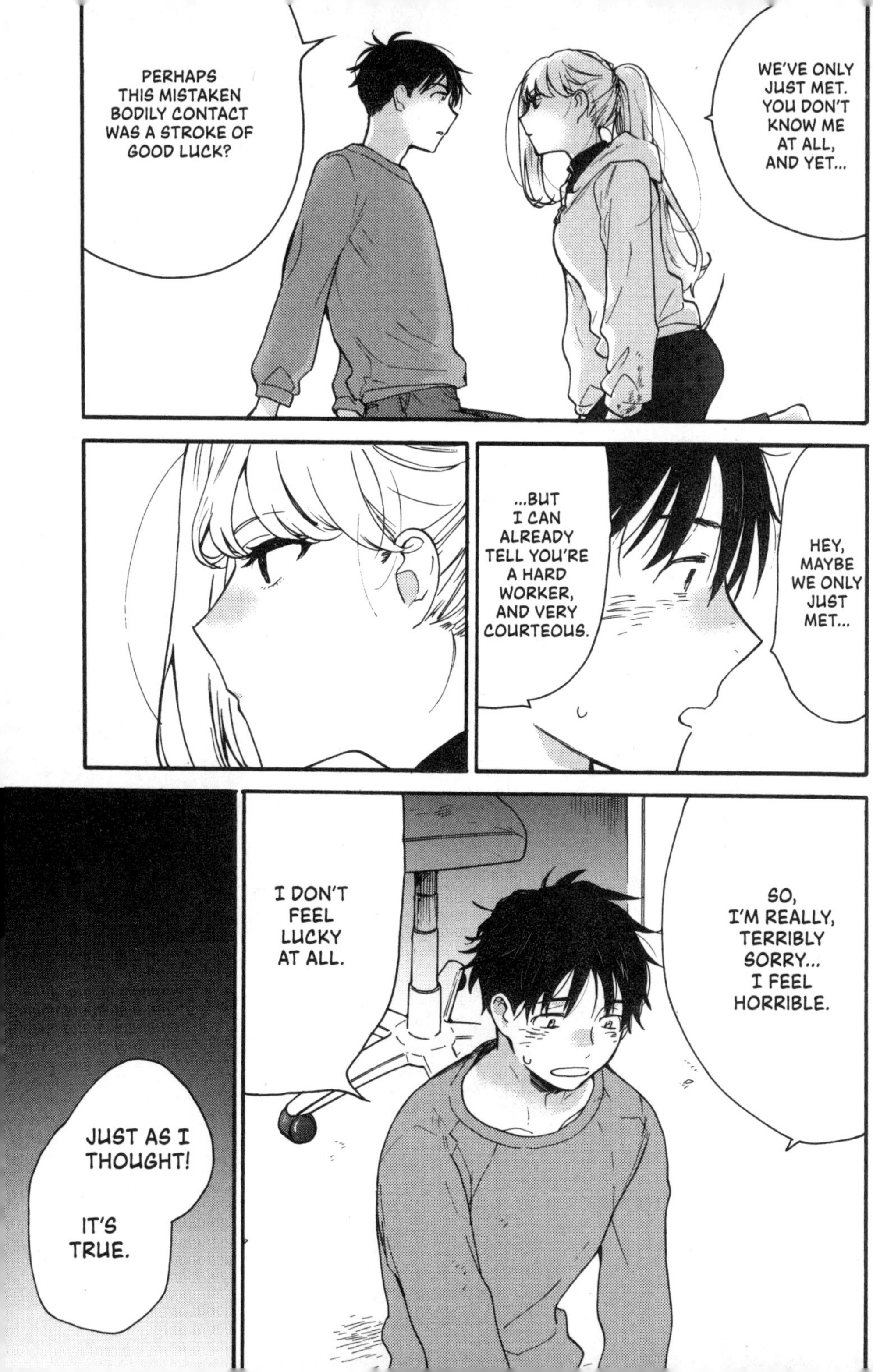
WE'VE ONLY JUST MET. YOU DON'T KNOW ME AT ALL, AND YET...
PERHAPS THIS MISTAKEN BODILY CONTACT WAS A STROKE OF GOOD LUCK?
HEY, MAYBE WE ONLY JUST MET...
...BUT I CAN ALREADY TELL YOU'RE A HARD WORKER, AND VERY COURTEOUS.
SO, I'M REALLY, TERRIBLY SORRY... I FEEL HORRIBLE.
I DON'T FEEL LUCKY AT ALL.
JUST AS I THOUGHT!
IT'S TRUE.

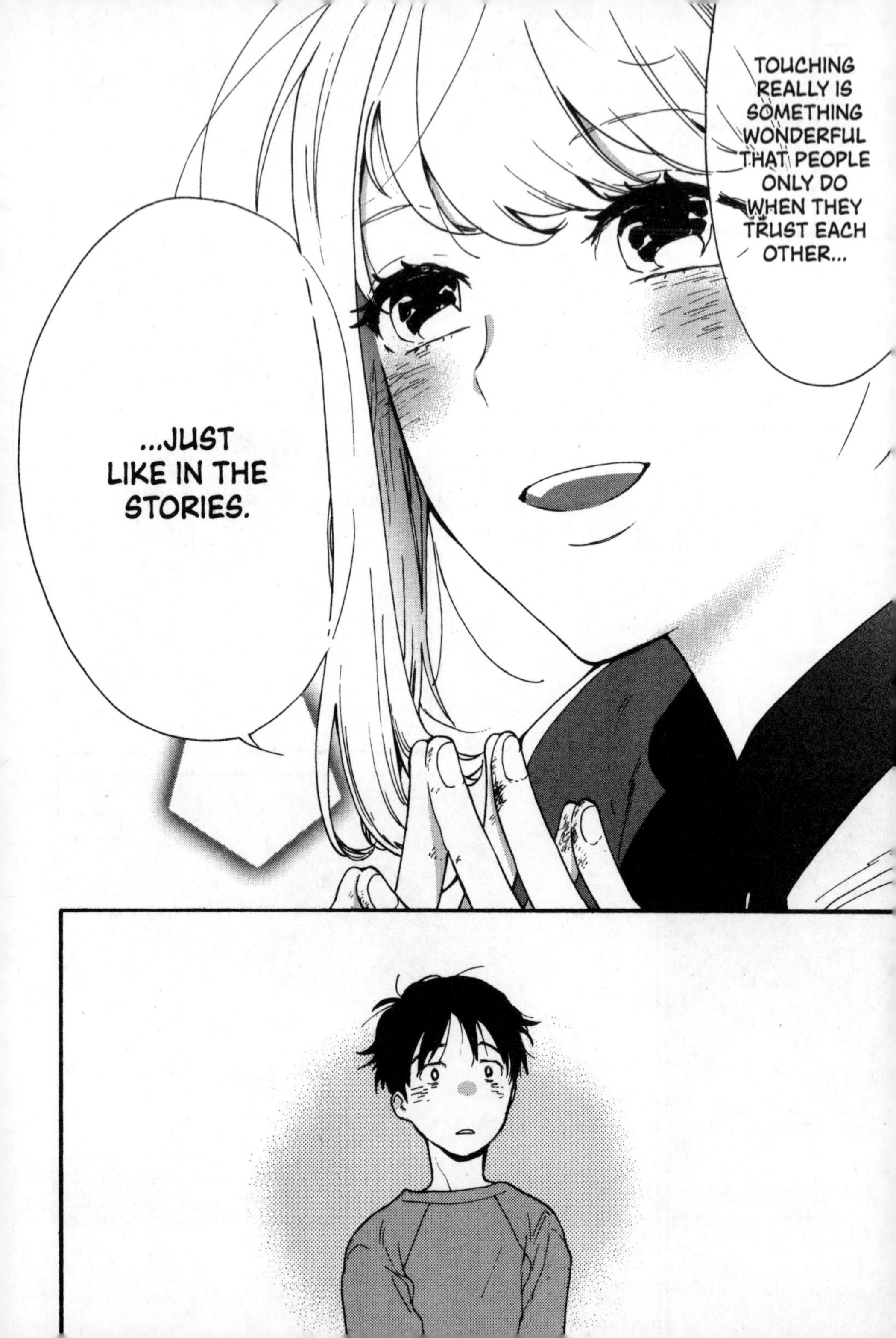
TOUCHING REALLY IS SOMETHING WONDERFUL THAT PEOPLE ONLY DO WHEN THEY TRUST EACH OTHER...
...JUST LIKE IN THE STORIES.

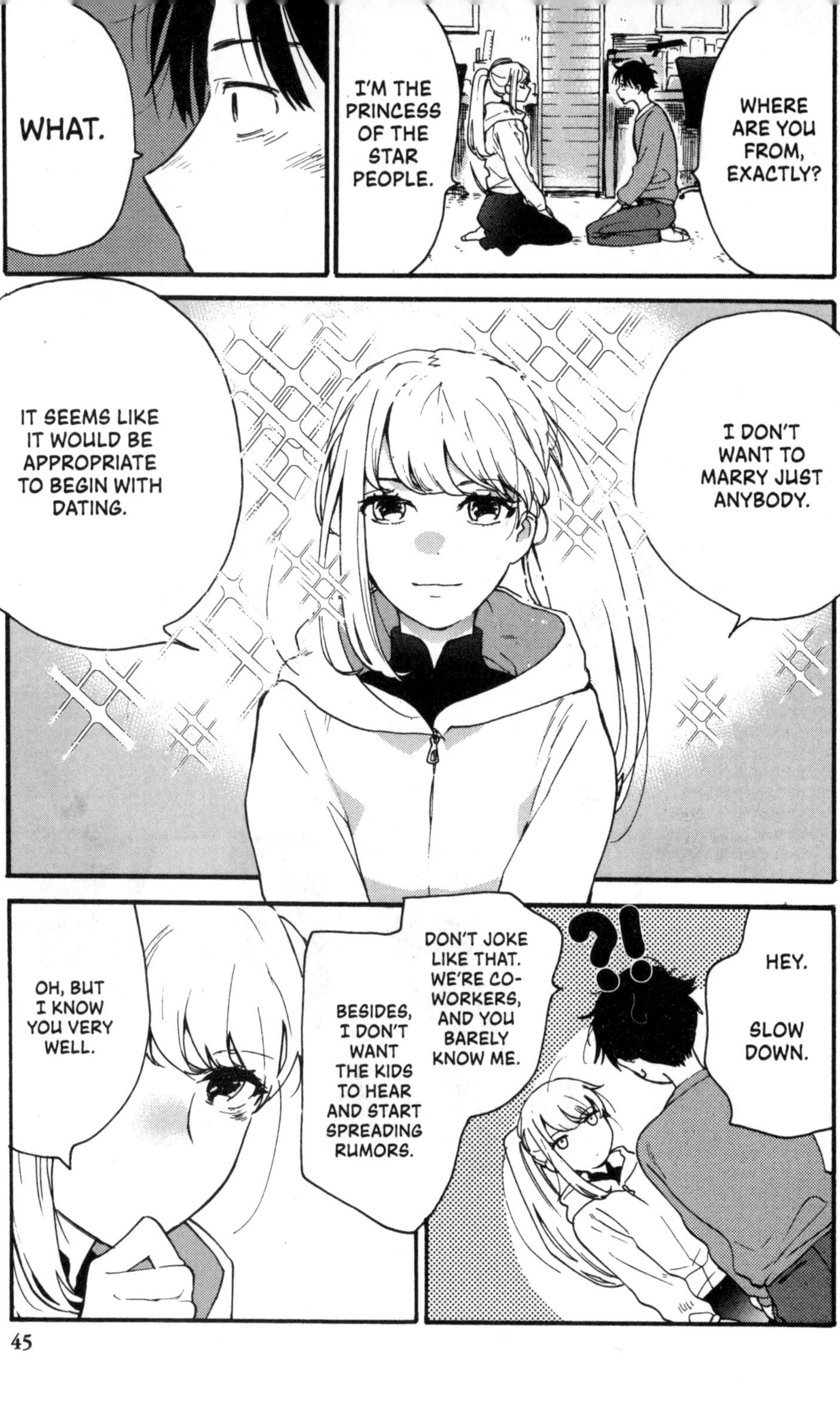
WHERE ARE YOU FROM, EXACTLY?
I'M THE PRINCESS OF THE STAR PEOPLE.
WHAT.
I DON'T WANT TO MARRY JUST ANYBODY.
IT SEEMS LIKE IT WOULD BE APPROPRIATE TO BEGIN WITH DATING.
HEY.
SLOW DOWN.
?!
DON'T JOKE LIKE THAT. WE'RE CO-WORKERS, AND YOU BARELY KNOW ME.
BESIDES, I DON'T WANT THE KIDS TO HEAR AND START SPREADING RUMORS.
OH, BUT I KNOW YOU VERY WELL.

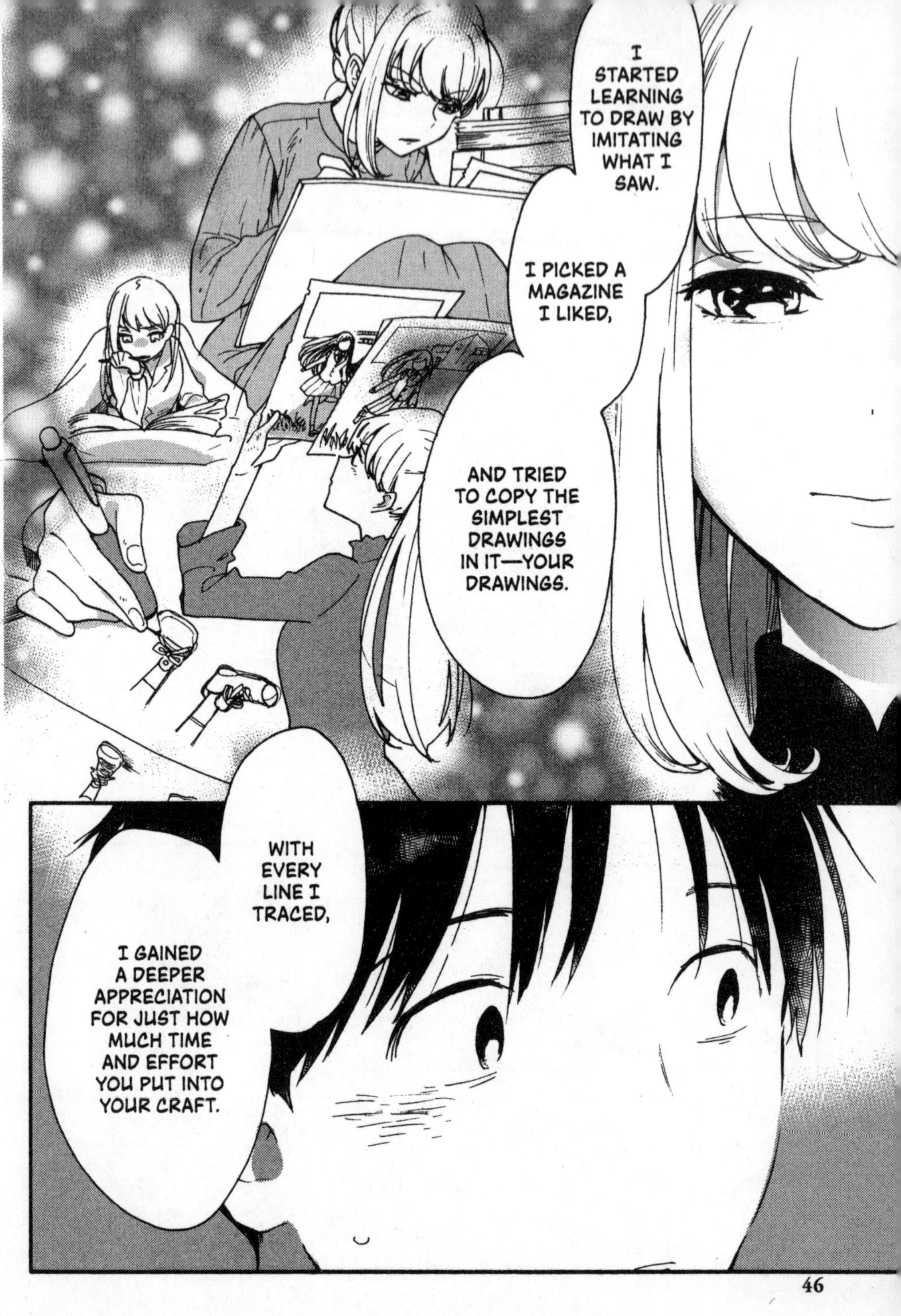
I STARTED LEARNING TO DRAW BY IMITATING WHAT I SAW.
I PICKED A MAGAZINE I LIKED,
AND TRIED TO COPY THE SIMPLEST DRAWINGS IN IT—YOUR DRAWINGS.
WITH EVERY LINE I TRACED,
I GAINED A DEEPER APPRECIATION FOR JUST HOW MUCH TIME AND EFFORT YOU PUT INTO YOUR CRAFT.

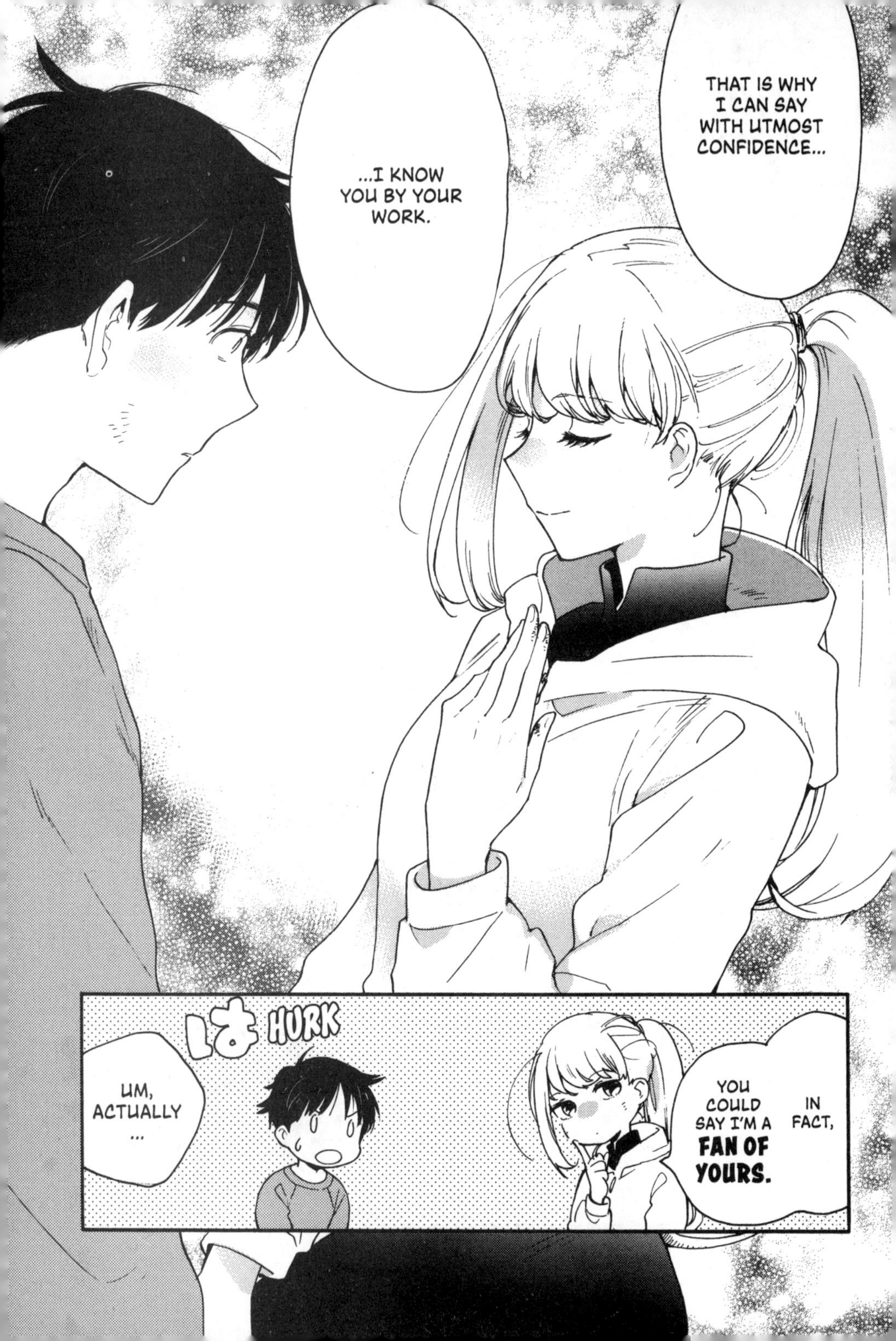
THAT IS WHY I CAN SAY WITH UTMOST CONFIDENCE...
...I KNOW YOU BY YOUR WORK.
IN FACT,
YOU COULD SAY I'M A FAN OF YOURS.
HURK
UM, ACTUALLY...

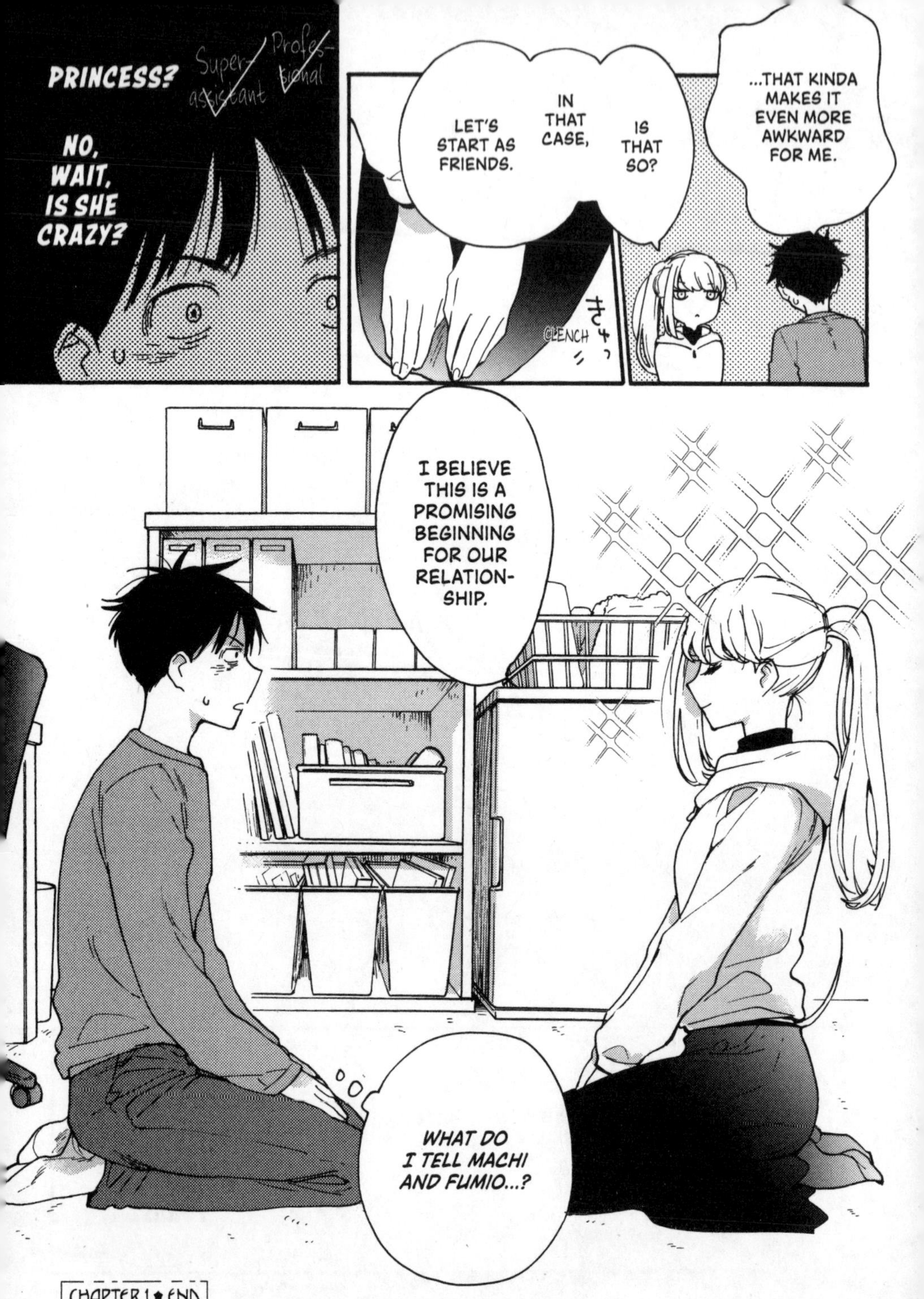
...THAT KINDA MAKES IT EVEN MORE AWKWARD FOR ME.
IS THAT SO?
IN THAT CASE,
LET'S START AS FRIENDS.
CLENCH
PRINCESS?
Super-assistant
Profes-sional
NO, WAIT, IS SHE CRAZY?
I BELIEVE THIS IS A PROMISING BEGINNING FOR OUR RELATION-SHIP.
WHAT DO I TELL MACHI AND FUMIO...?
CHAPTER 1 END

So this is manga in its raw form...

Hee hee...

A Galaxy
Next Door

Gido
Amagakure

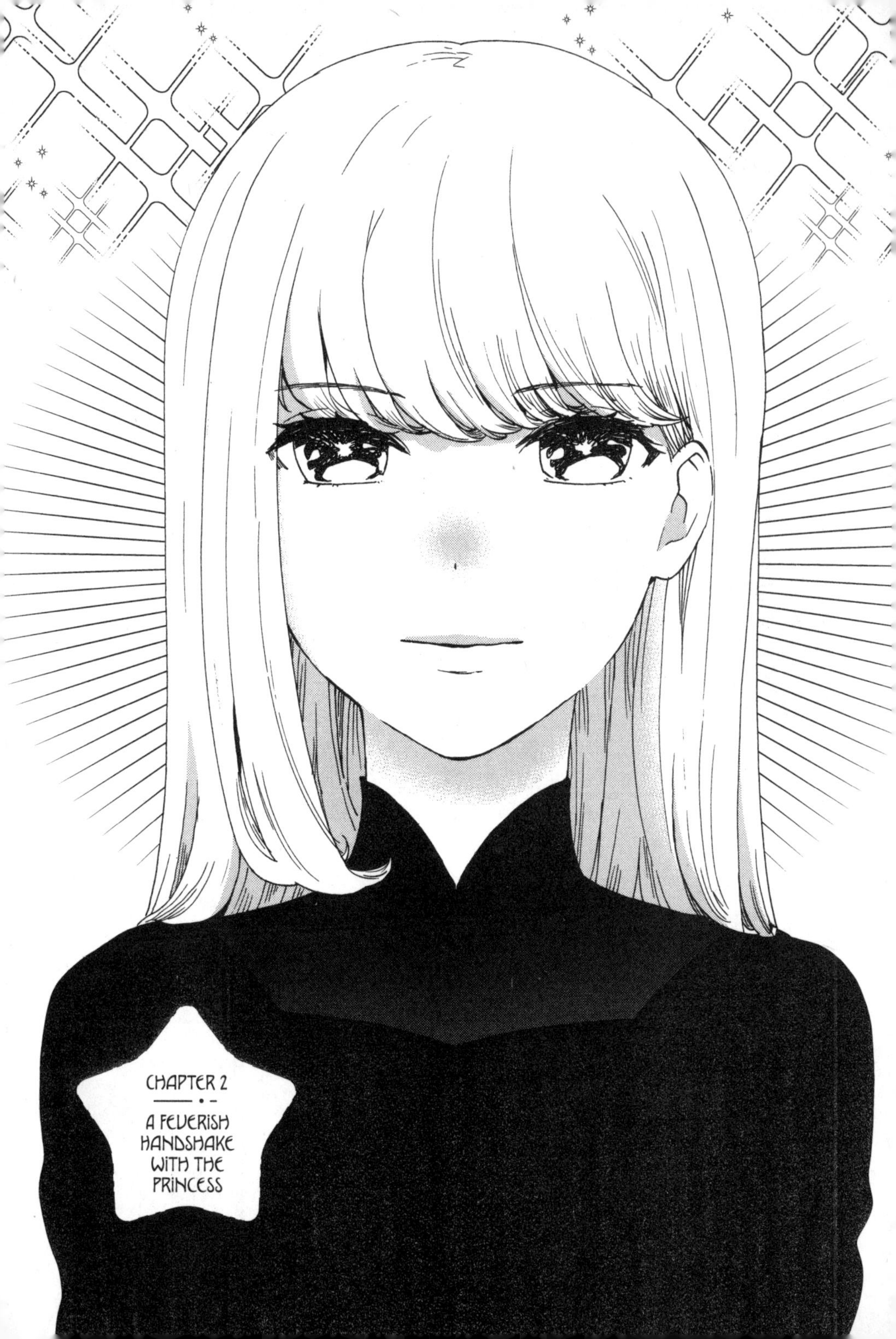
CHAPTER 2
A FEVERISH HANDSHAKE WITH THE PRINCESS

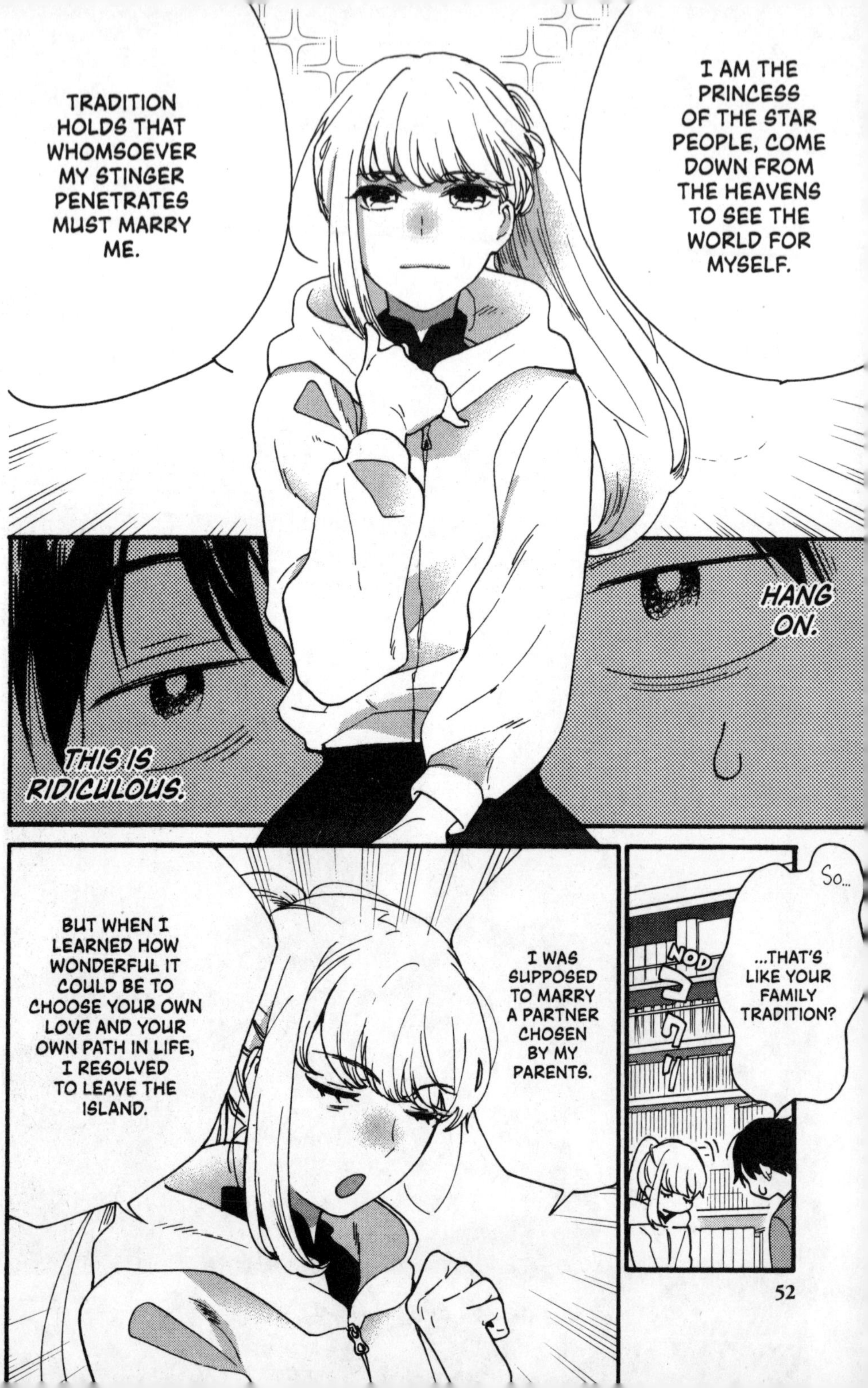
I AM THE PRINCESS OF THE STAR PEOPLE, COME DOWN FROM THE HEAVENS TO SEE THE WORLD FOR MYSELF.
TRADITION HOLDS THAT WHOMSOEVER MY STINGER PENETRATES MUST MARRY ME.
HANG ON.
THIS IS RIDICULOUS.
So...
...THAT'S LIKE YOUR FAMILY TRADITION?
NOD
I WAS SUPPOSED TO MARRY A PARTNER CHOSEN BY MY PARENTS.
BUT WHEN I LEARNED HOW WONDERFUL IT COULD BE TO CHOOSE YOUR OWN LOVE AND YOUR OWN PATH IN LIFE, I RESOLVED TO LEAVE THE ISLAND.

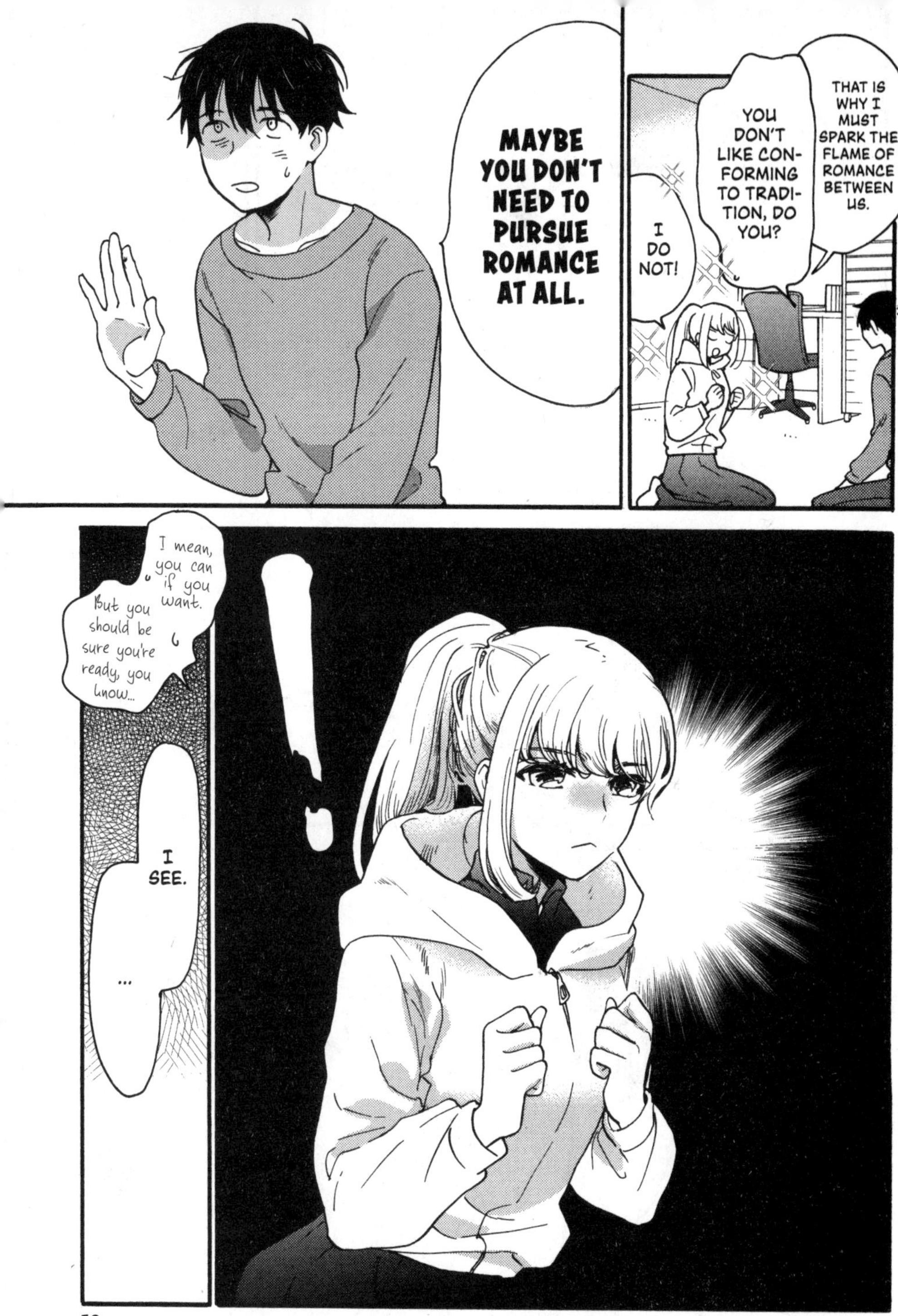
THAT IS WHY I MUST SPARK THE FLAME OF ROMANCE BETWEEN US.
YOU DON'T LIKE CON-FORMING TO TRADI-TION, DO YOU?
I DO NOT!
MAYBE YOU DON'T NEED TO PURSUE ROMANCE AT ALL.
I mean, you can if you want.
But you should be sure you're ready, you know...
I SEE.
...

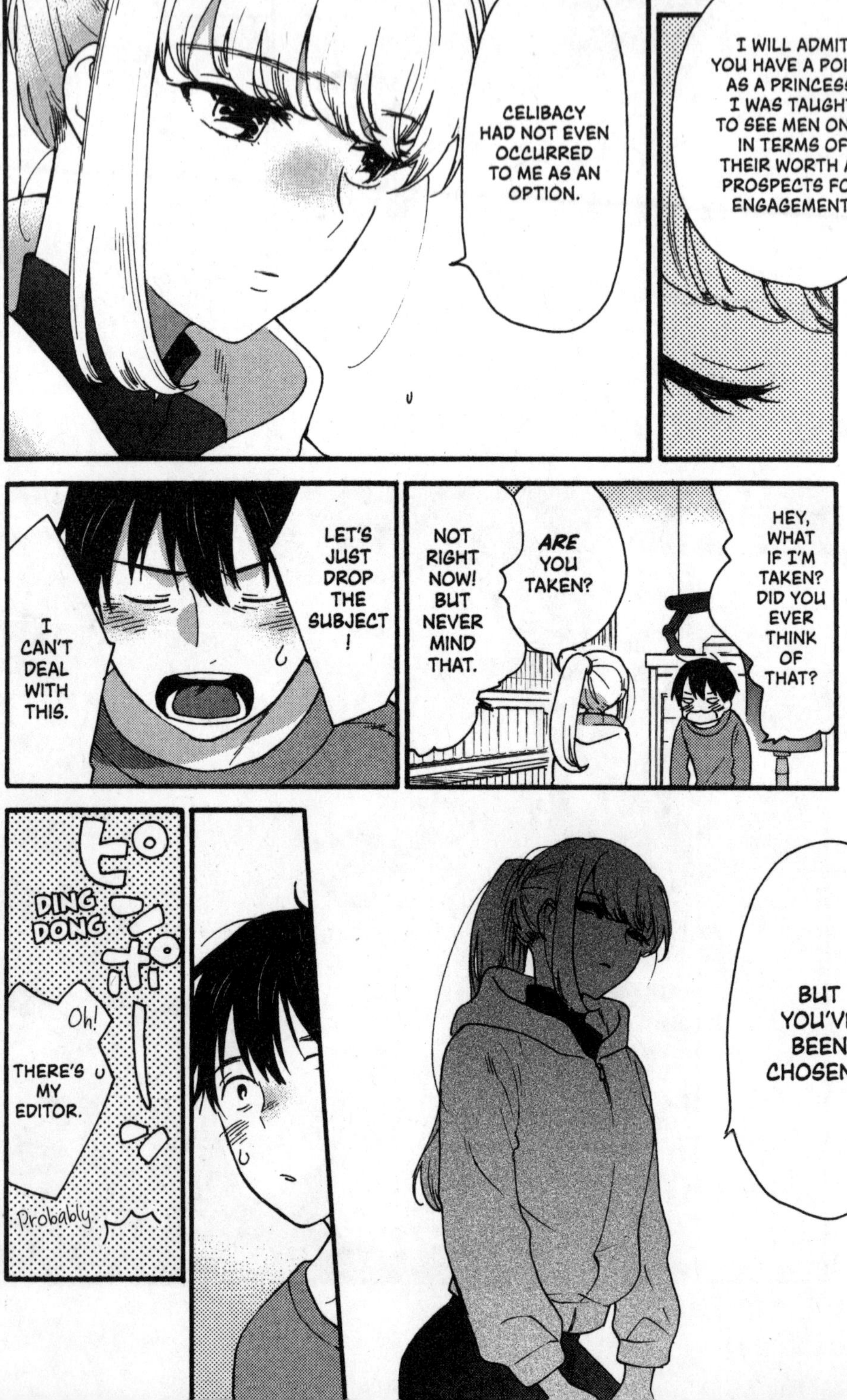
I WILL ADMIT YOU HAVE A POINT. AS A PRINCESS, I WAS TAUGHT TO SEE MEN ONLY IN TERMS OF THEIR WORTH AS PROSPECTS FOR ENGAGEMENT.
CELIBACY HAD NOT EVEN OCCURRED TO ME AS AN OPTION.
HEY, WHAT IF I'M TAKEN? DID YOU EVER THINK OF THAT?
ARE YOU TAKEN?
NOT RIGHT NOW! BUT NEVER MIND THAT.
LET'S JUST DROP THE SUBJECT!
I CAN'T DEAL WITH THIS.
BUT YOU'VE BEEN CHOSEN...
DING DONG
Oh!
THERE'S MY EDITOR.
Probably.

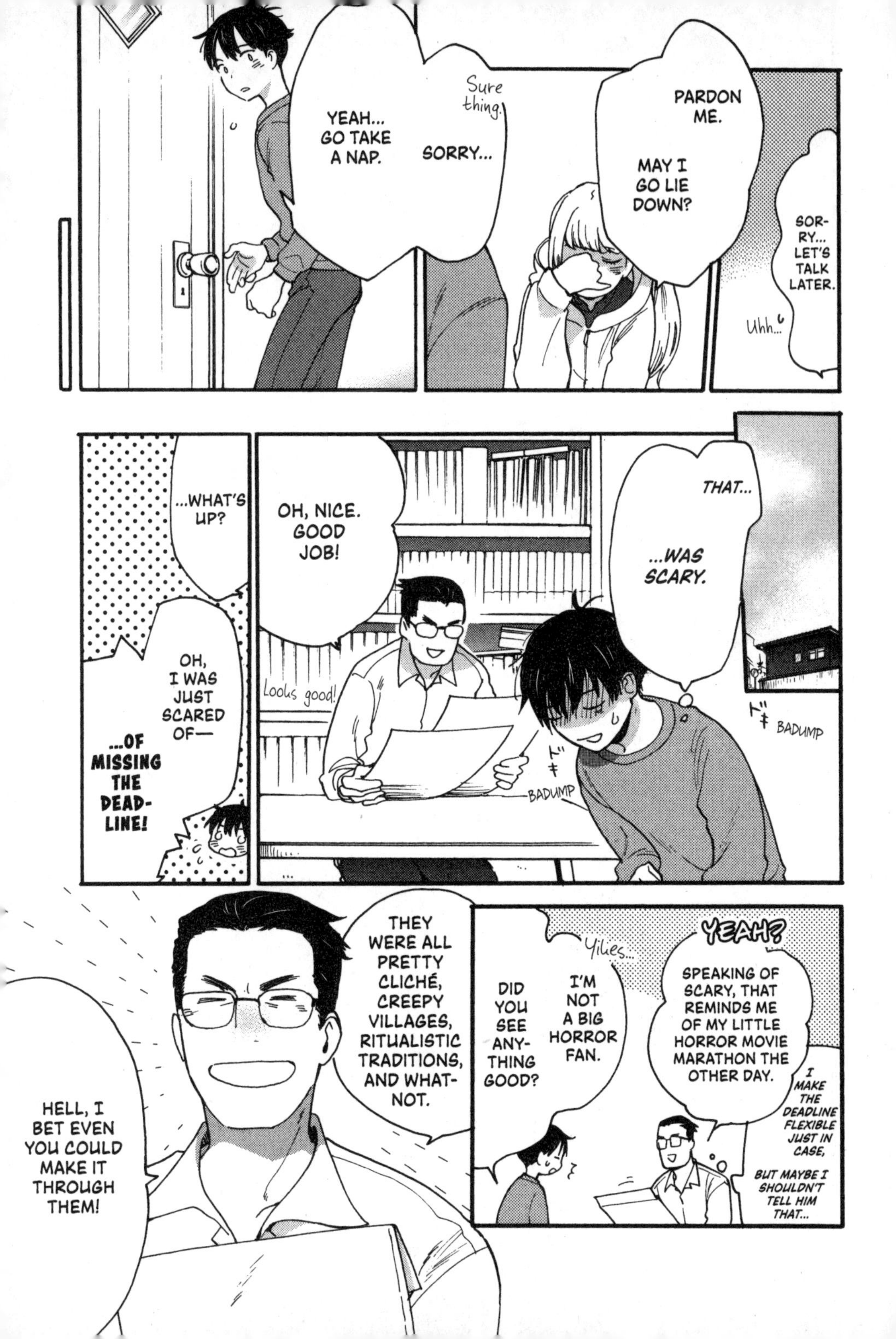
PARDON ME.
MAY I GO LIE DOWN?
SORRY... LET'S TALK LATER.
Uhh...
SORRY...
Sure thing.
YEAH... GO TAKE A NAP.
THAT...
...WAS SCARY.
ドキ BADUMP
ドキ BADUMP
OH, NICE. GOOD JOB!
Looks good!
...WHAT'S UP?
OH, I WAS JUST SCARED OF—
...OF MISSING THE DEADLINE!
...
YEAH?
SPEAKING OF SCARY, THAT REMINDS ME OF MY LITTLE HORROR MOVIE MARATHON THE OTHER DAY.
I MAKE THE DEADLINE FLEXIBLE JUST IN CASE,
BUT MAYBE I SHOULDN'T TELL HIM THAT...
Yikes...
I'M NOT A BIG HORROR FAN.
DID YOU SEE ANYTHING GOOD?
THEY WERE ALL PRETTY CLICHÉ, CREEPY VILLAGES, RITUALISTIC TRADITIONS, AND WHAT-NOT.
HELL, I BET EVEN YOU COULD MAKE IT THROUGH THEM!

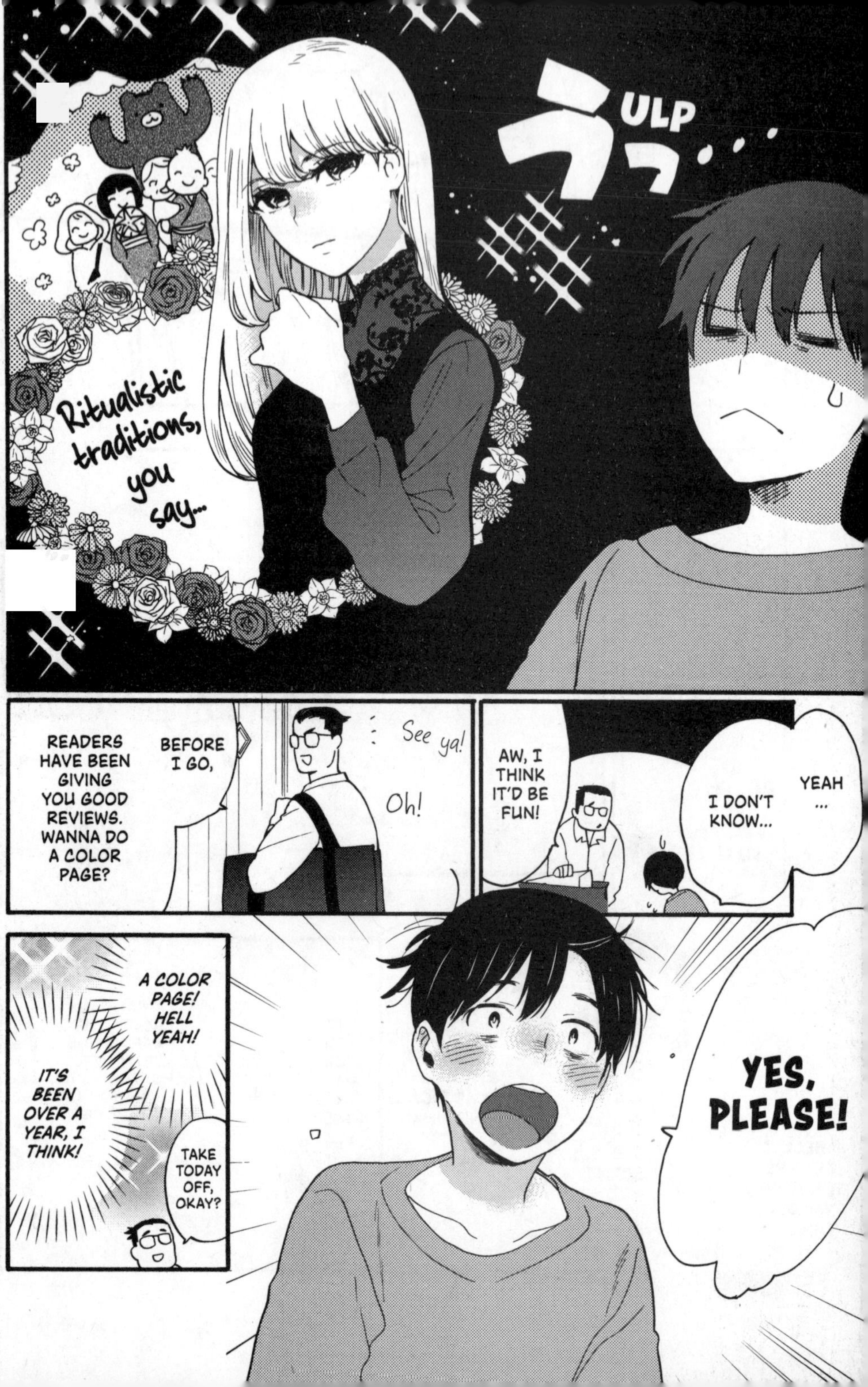
ULP
Ritualistic traditions, you say...
YEAH ...
I DON'T KNOW...
AW, I THINK IT'D BE FUN!
See ya!
Oh!
BEFORE I GO,
READERS HAVE BEEN GIVING YOU GOOD REVIEWS. WANNA DO A COLOR PAGE?
YES, PLEASE!
A COLOR PAGE! HELL YEAH!
IT'S BEEN OVER A YEAR, I THINK!
TAKE TODAY OFF, OKAY?

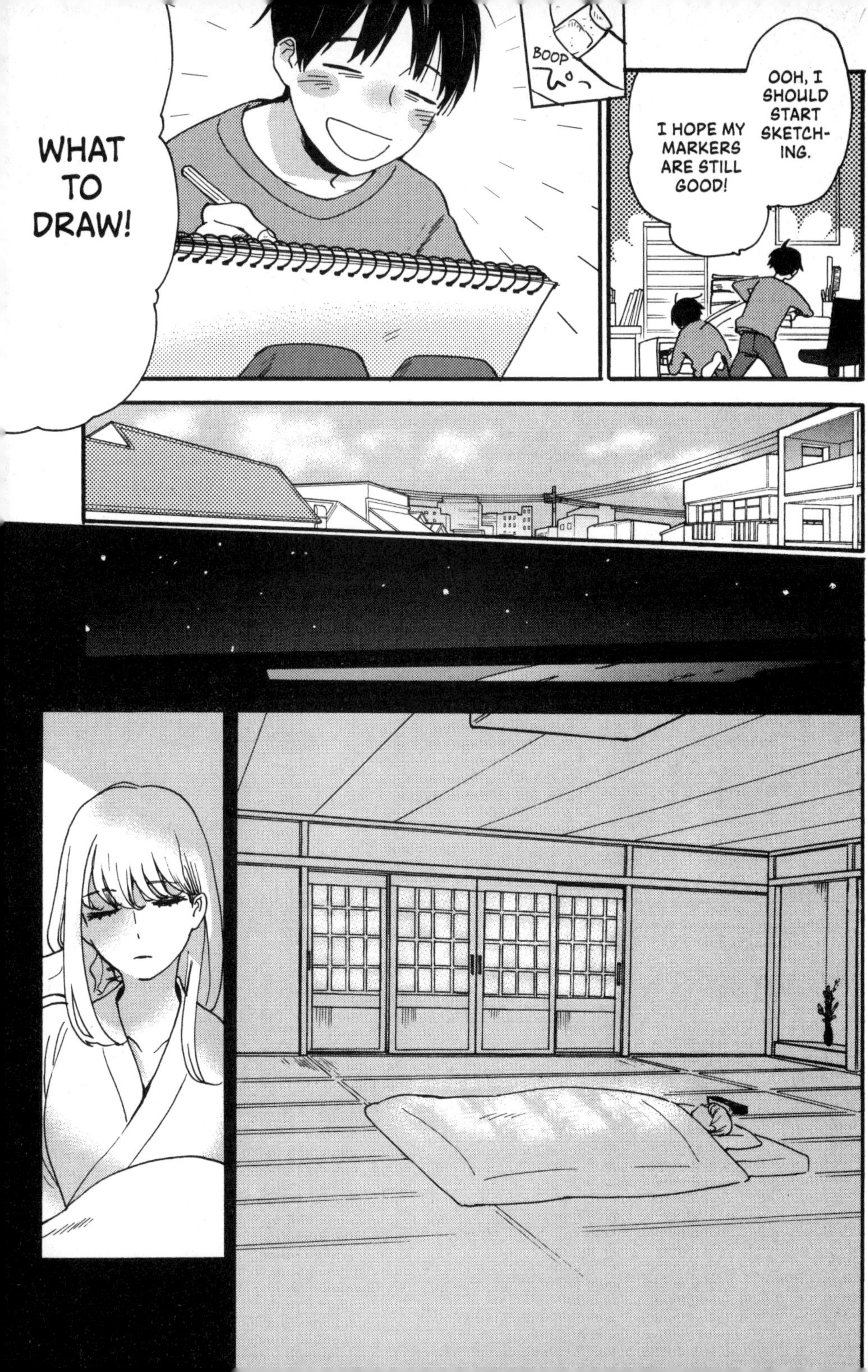
BOOP
ぴっ
OOH, I SHOULD START SKETCH-ING.
I HOPE MY MARKERS ARE STILL GOOD!
WHAT TO DRAW!

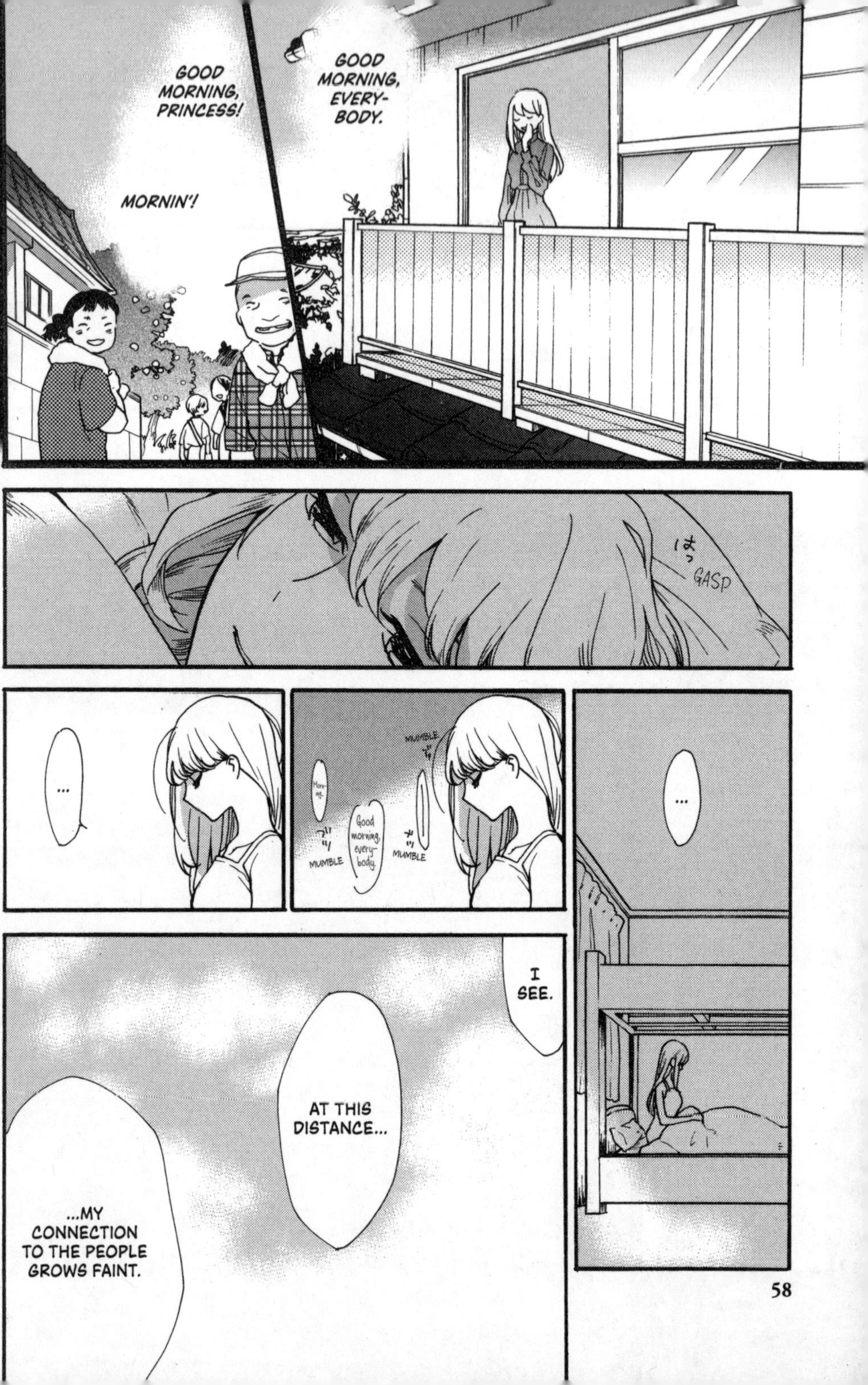
GOOD MORNING, EVERY-BODY.
GOOD MORNING, PRINCESS!
MORNIN'!
はっ
GASP
...
MUMBLE
Good morning, every-body.
Morn-ing...
MUMBLE
...
I SEE.
AT THIS DISTANCE...
...MY CONNECTION TO THE PEOPLE GROWS FAINT.

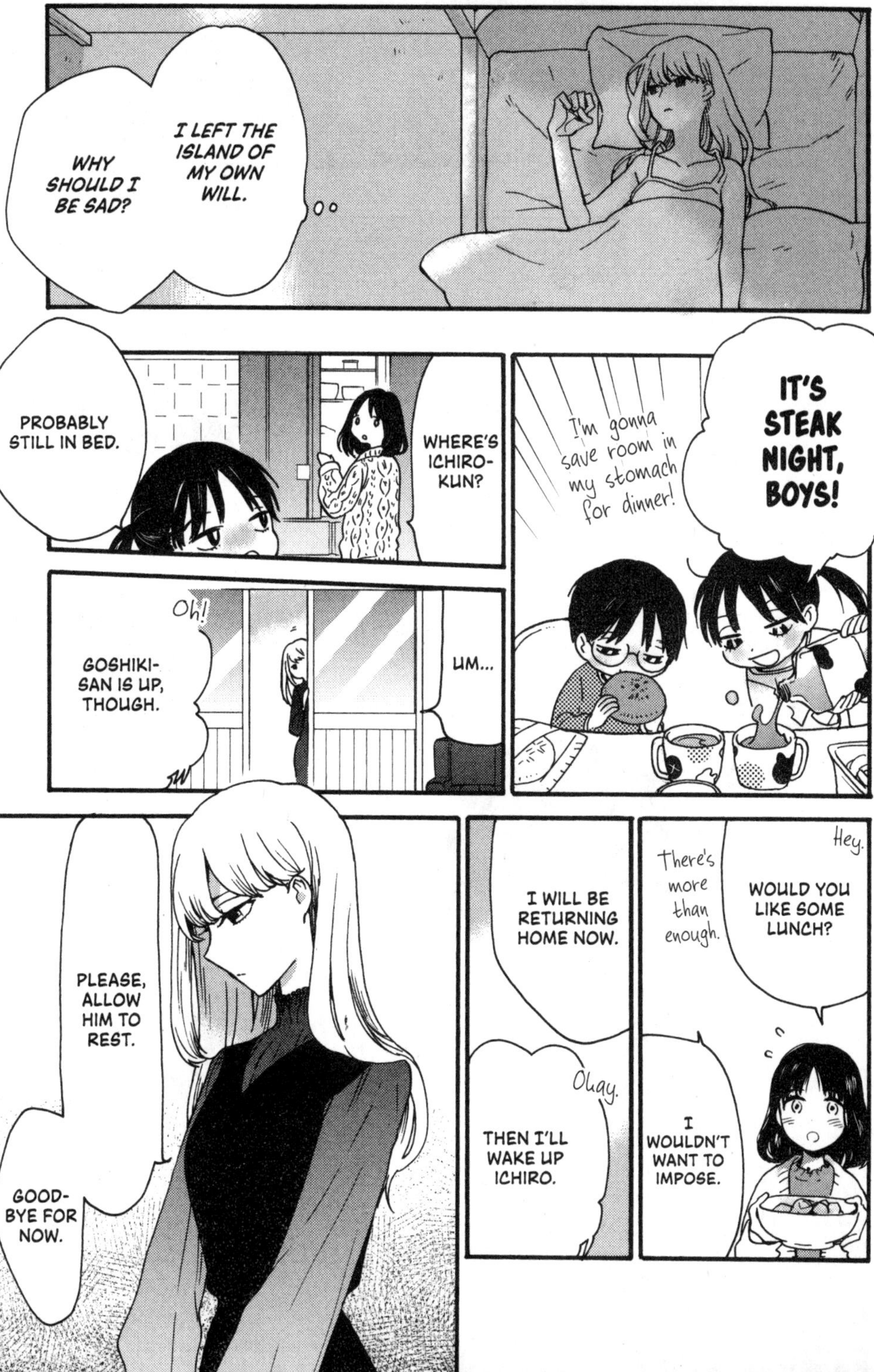
I LEFT THE ISLAND OF MY OWN WILL.
WHY SHOULD I BE SAD?
IT'S STEAK NIGHT, BOYS!
I'm gonna save room in my stomach for dinner!
WHERE'S ICHIRO-KUN?
PROBABLY STILL IN BED.
UM...
Oh!
GOSHIKI-SAN IS UP, THOUGH.
Hey.
WOULD YOU LIKE SOME LUNCH?
There's more than enough.
I WOULDN'T WANT TO IMPOSE.
I WILL BE RETURNING HOME NOW.
Okay.
THEN I'LL WAKE UP ICHIRO.
PLEASE, ALLOW HIM TO REST.
GOOD-BYE FOR NOW.

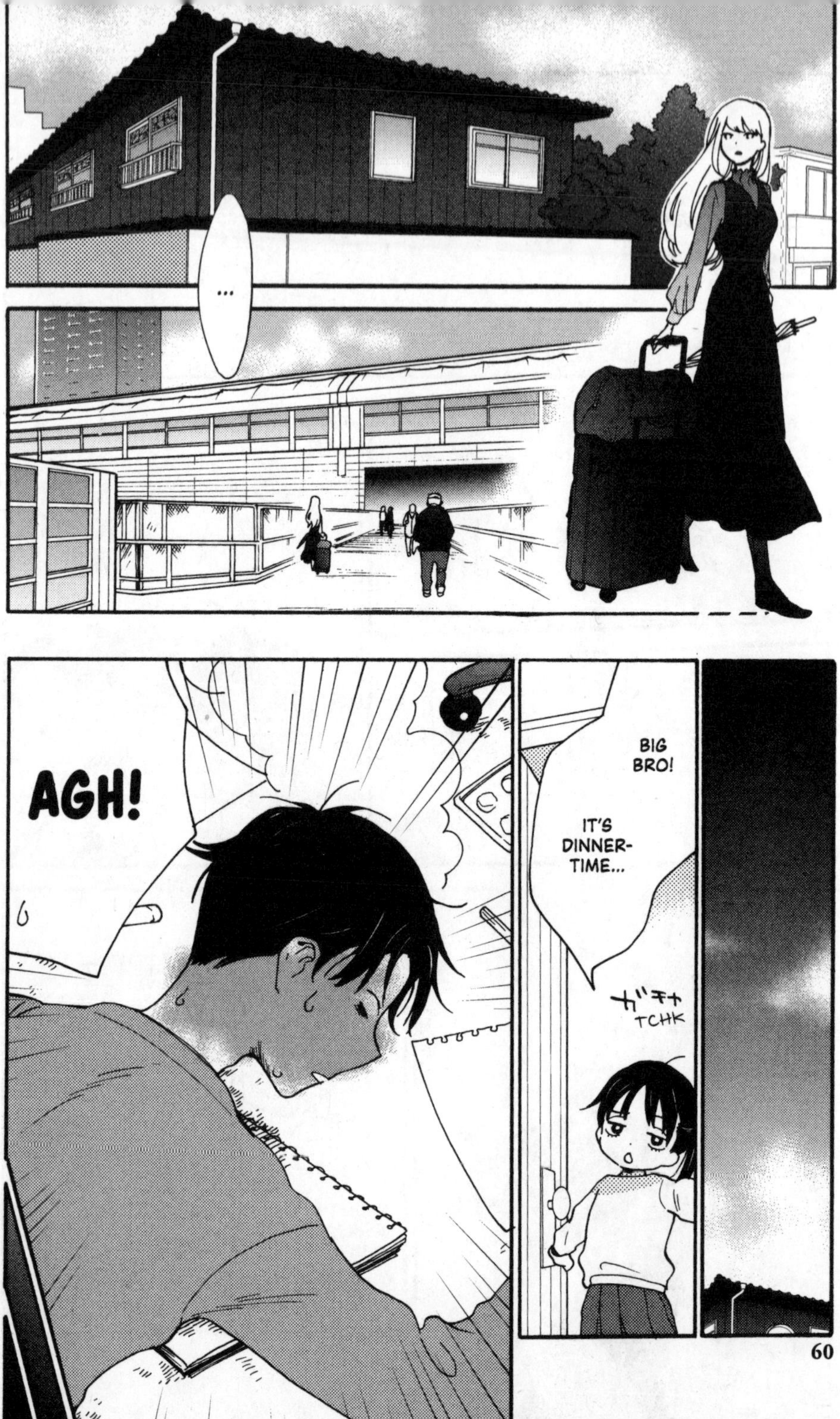
…
BIG BRO!
IT'S DINNER-TIME…
ガチャ
TCHK
AGH!

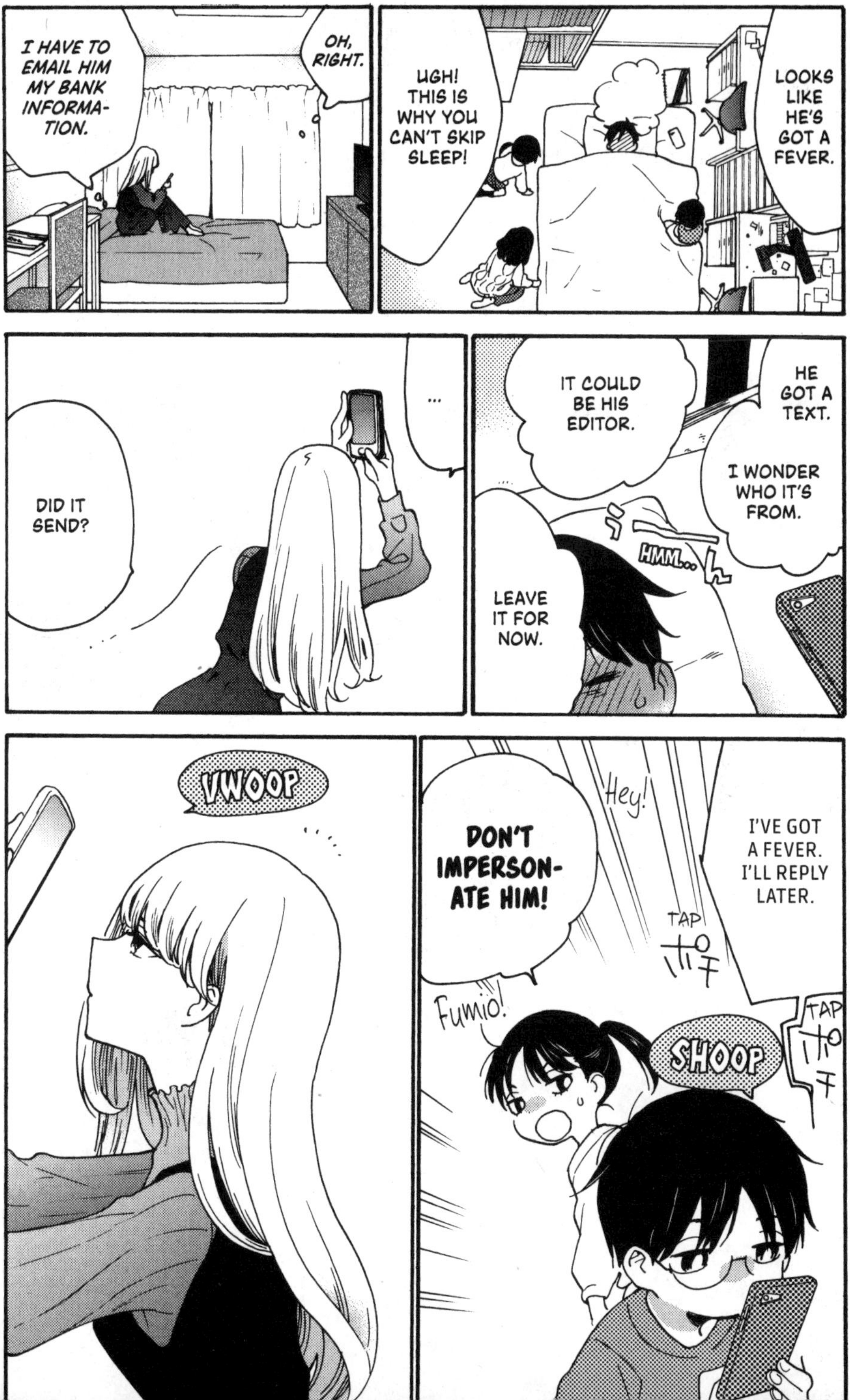
LOOKS LIKE HE'S GOT A FEVER.
UGH! THIS IS WHY YOU CAN'T SKIP SLEEP!
OH, RIGHT.
I HAVE TO EMAIL HIM MY BANK INFORMATION.
HE GOT A TEXT.
I WONDER WHO IT'S FROM.
IT COULD BE HIS EDITOR.
HMM...
LEAVE IT FOR NOW.
...
DID IT SEND?
I'VE GOT A FEVER. I'LL REPLY LATER.
Hey!
DON'T IMPERSONATE HIM!
TAP
Fumio!
SHOOP
TAP
VWOOP

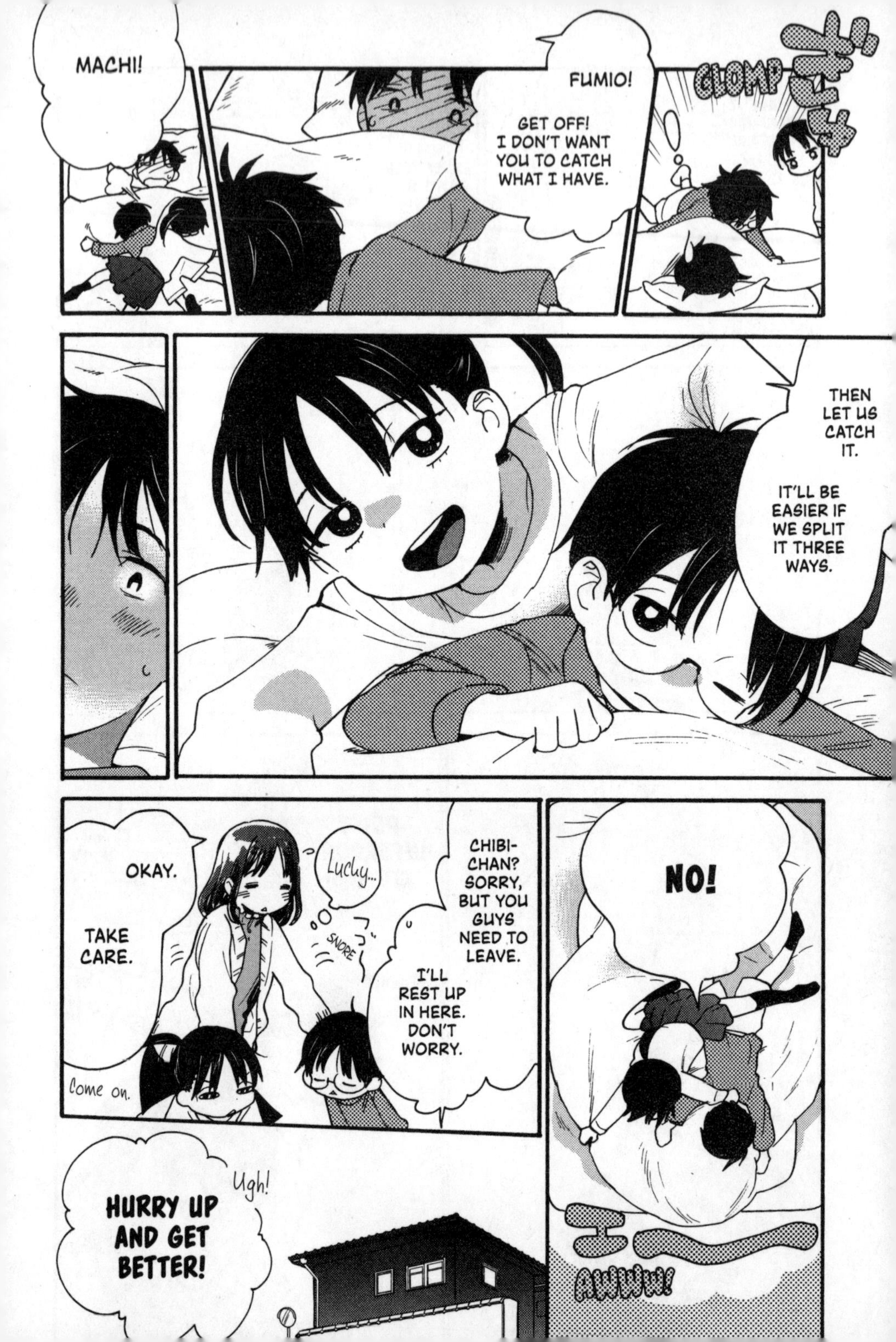
CLOMP
FUMIO!
GET OFF! I DON'T WANT YOU TO CATCH WHAT I HAVE.
MACHI!
THEN LET US CATCH IT.
IT'LL BE EASIER IF WE SPLIT IT THREE WAYS.
NO!
AWWW!
CHIBI-CHAN? SORRY, BUT YOU GUYS NEED TO LEAVE.
I'LL REST UP IN HERE. DON'T WORRY.
Lucky...
SNORE
OKAY.
TAKE CARE.
Come on.
HURRY UP AND GET BETTER!
Ugh!

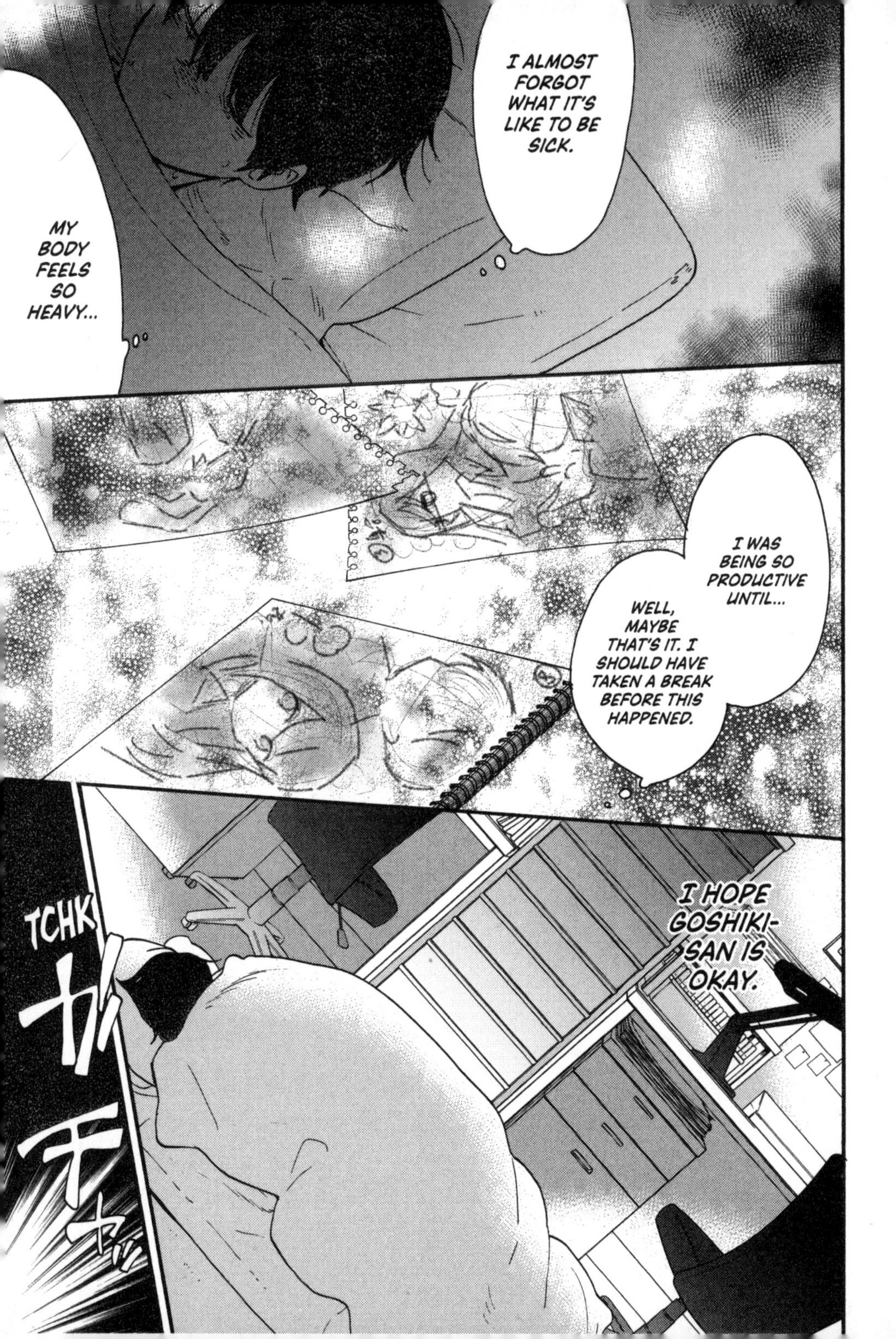
I ALMOST FORGOT WHAT IT'S LIKE TO BE SICK.
MY BODY FEELS SO HEAVY...
I WAS BEING SO PRODUCTIVE UNTIL...
WELL, MAYBE THAT'S IT. I SHOULD HAVE TAKEN A BREAK BEFORE THIS HAPPENED.
I HOPE GOSHIKI-SAN IS OKAY.
TCHK
カチャッ

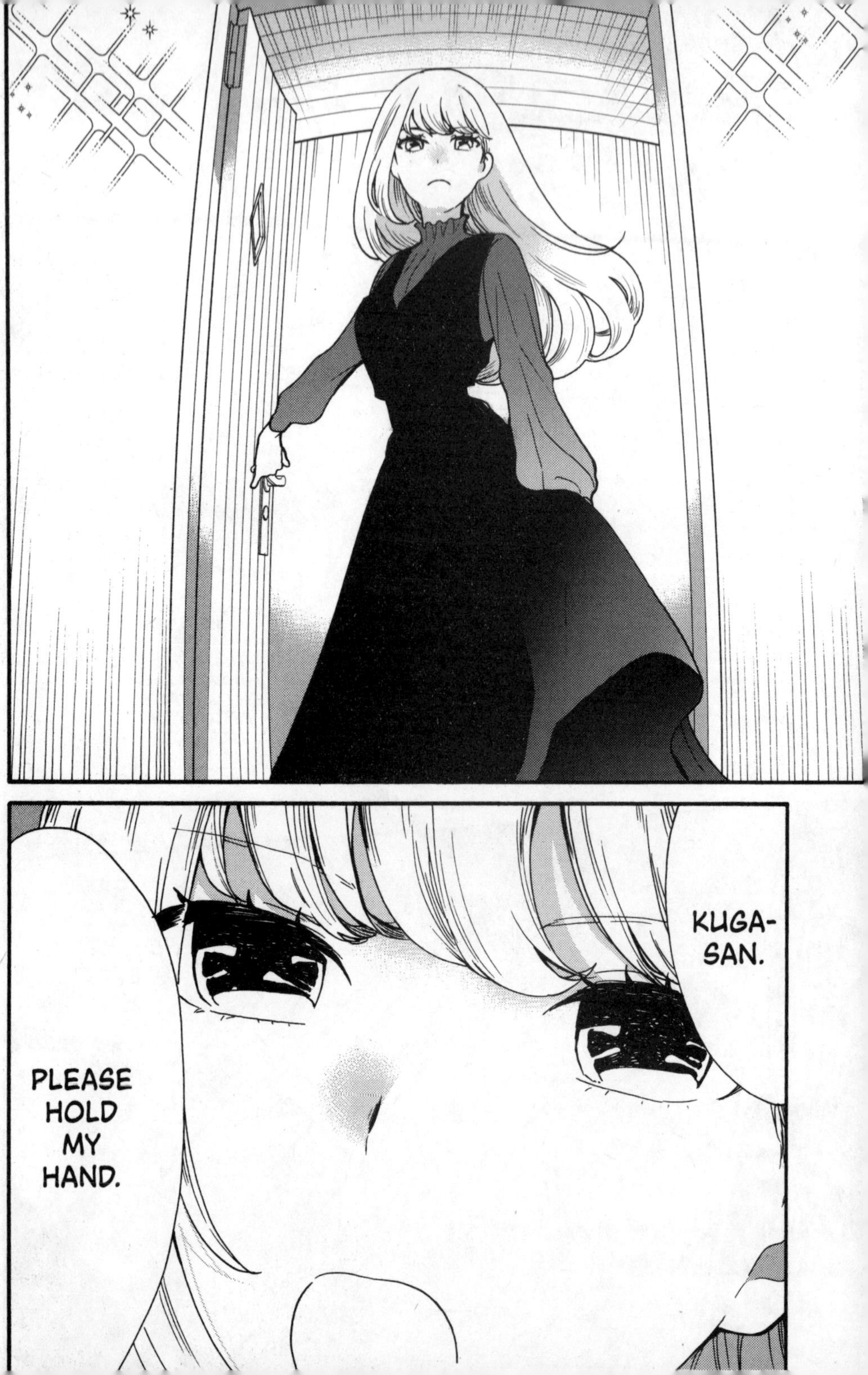
KUGA-SAN.
PLEASE HOLD MY HAND.

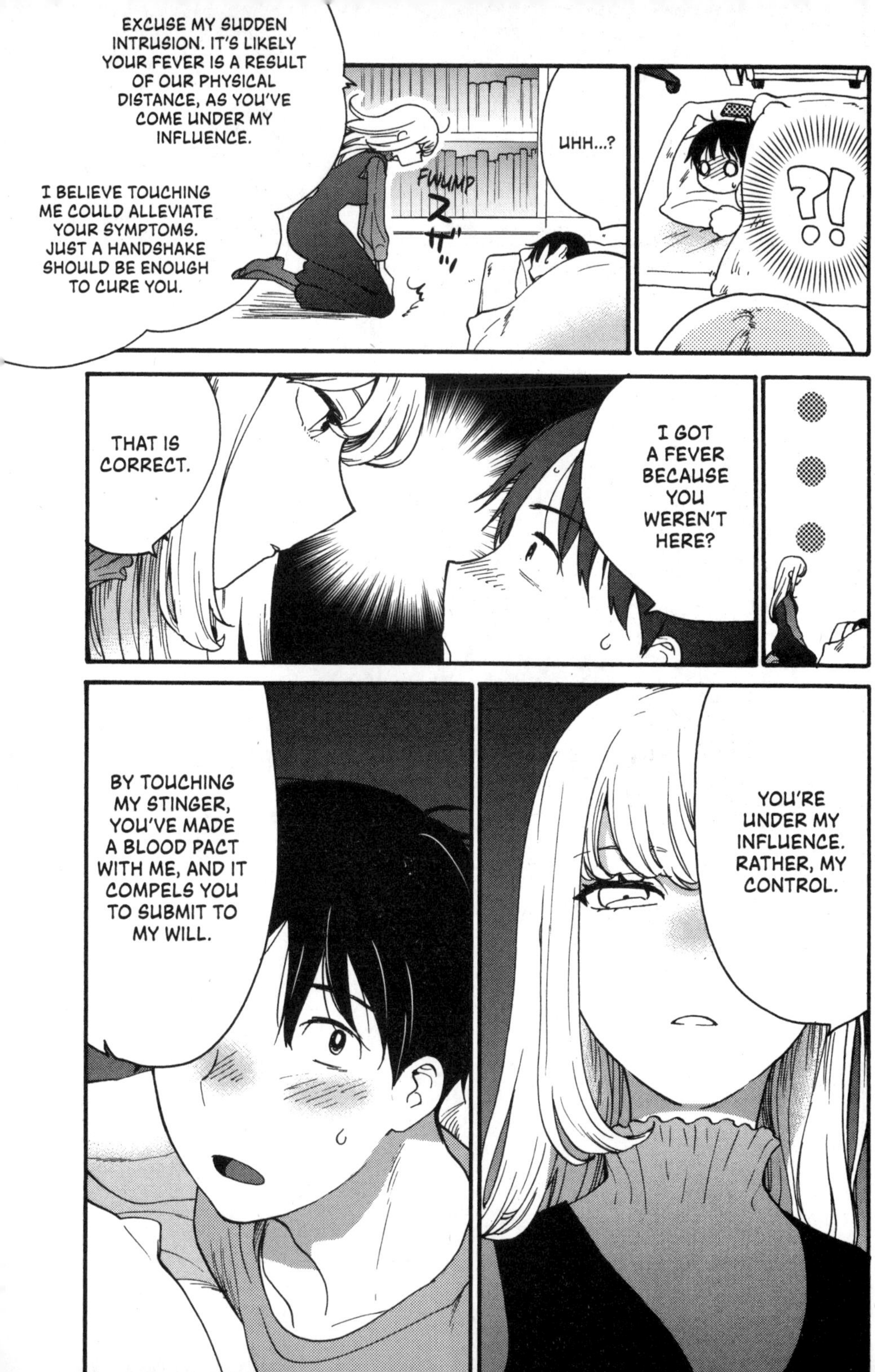
?!
UHH...?
EXCUSE MY SUDDEN INTRUSION. IT'S LIKELY YOUR FEVER IS A RESULT OF OUR PHYSICAL DISTANCE, AS YOU'VE COME UNDER MY INFLUENCE.
FWUMP
I BELIEVE TOUCHING ME COULD ALLEVIATE YOUR SYMPTOMS. JUST A HANDSHAKE SHOULD BE ENOUGH TO CURE YOU.
I GOT A FEVER BECAUSE YOU WEREN'T HERE?
THAT IS CORRECT.
YOU'RE UNDER MY INFLUENCE. RATHER, MY CONTROL.
BY TOUCHING MY STINGER, YOU'VE MADE A BLOOD PACT WITH ME, AND IT COMPELS YOU TO SUBMIT TO MY WILL.

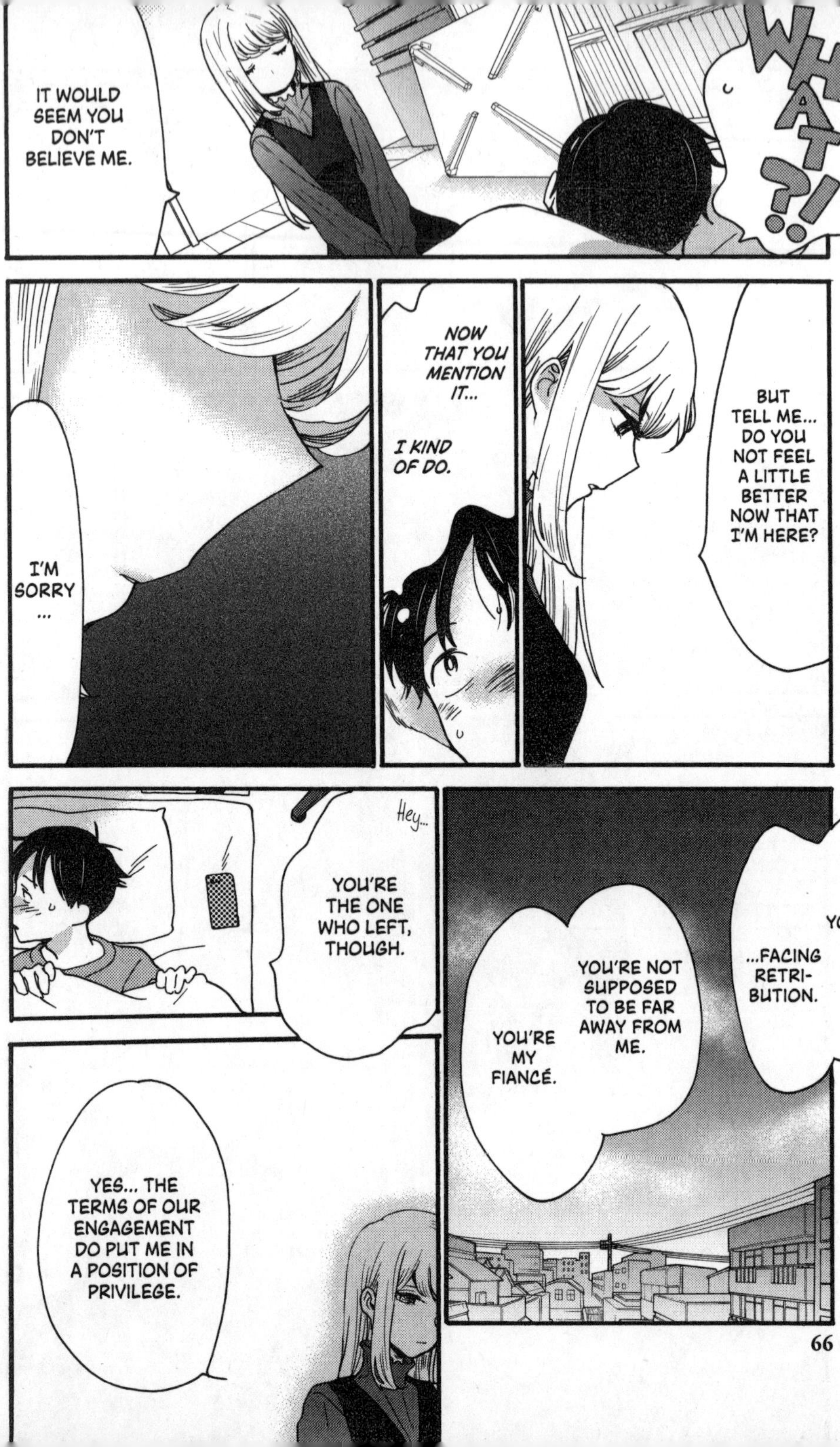
WHAT?!
IT WOULD SEEM YOU DON'T BELIEVE ME.
BUT TELL ME... DO YOU NOT FEEL A LITTLE BETTER NOW THAT I'M HERE?
NOW THAT YOU MENTION IT...
I KIND OF DO.
I'M SORRY ...
YOU'RE ...
...FACING RETRIBUTION.
YOU'RE NOT SUPPOSED TO BE FAR AWAY FROM ME.
YOU'RE MY FIANCÉ.
Hey...
YOU'RE THE ONE WHO LEFT, THOUGH.
YES... THE TERMS OF OUR ENGAGEMENT DO PUT ME IN A POSITION OF PRIVILEGE.

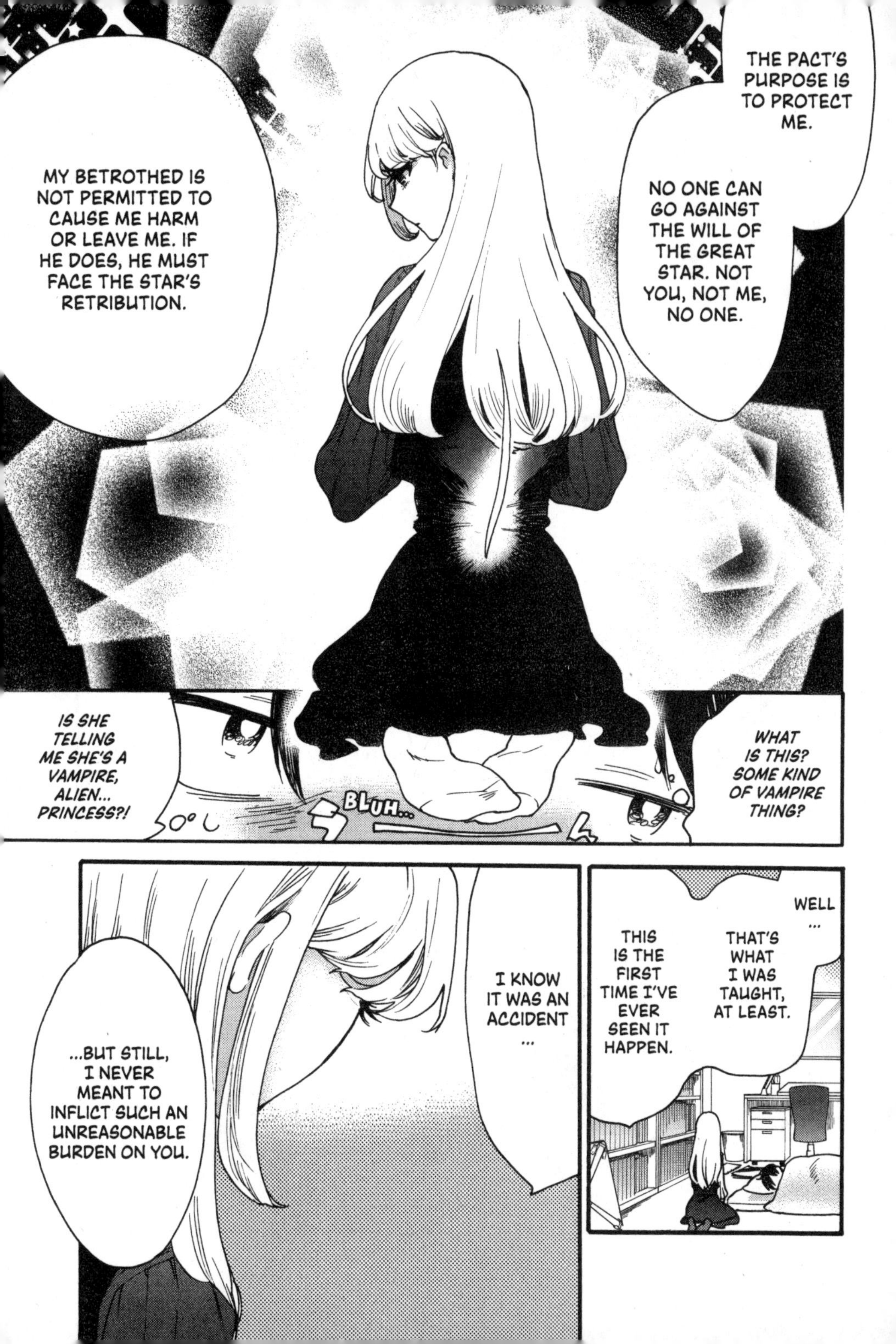
THE PACT'S PURPOSE IS TO PROTECT ME.
NO ONE CAN GO AGAINST THE WILL OF THE GREAT STAR. NOT YOU, NOT ME, NO ONE.
MY BETROTHED IS NOT PERMITTED TO CAUSE ME HARM OR LEAVE ME. IF HE DOES, HE MUST FACE THE STAR'S RETRIBUTION.
WHAT IS THIS? SOME KIND OF VAMPIRE THING?
BLUH...
IS SHE TELLING ME SHE'S A VAMPIRE, ALIEN... PRINCESS?!
WELL ...
THAT'S WHAT I WAS TAUGHT, AT LEAST.
THIS IS THE FIRST TIME I'VE EVER SEEN IT HAPPEN.
I KNOW IT WAS AN ACCIDENT ...
...BUT STILL, I NEVER MEANT TO INFLICT SUCH AN UNREASONABLE BURDEN ON YOU.

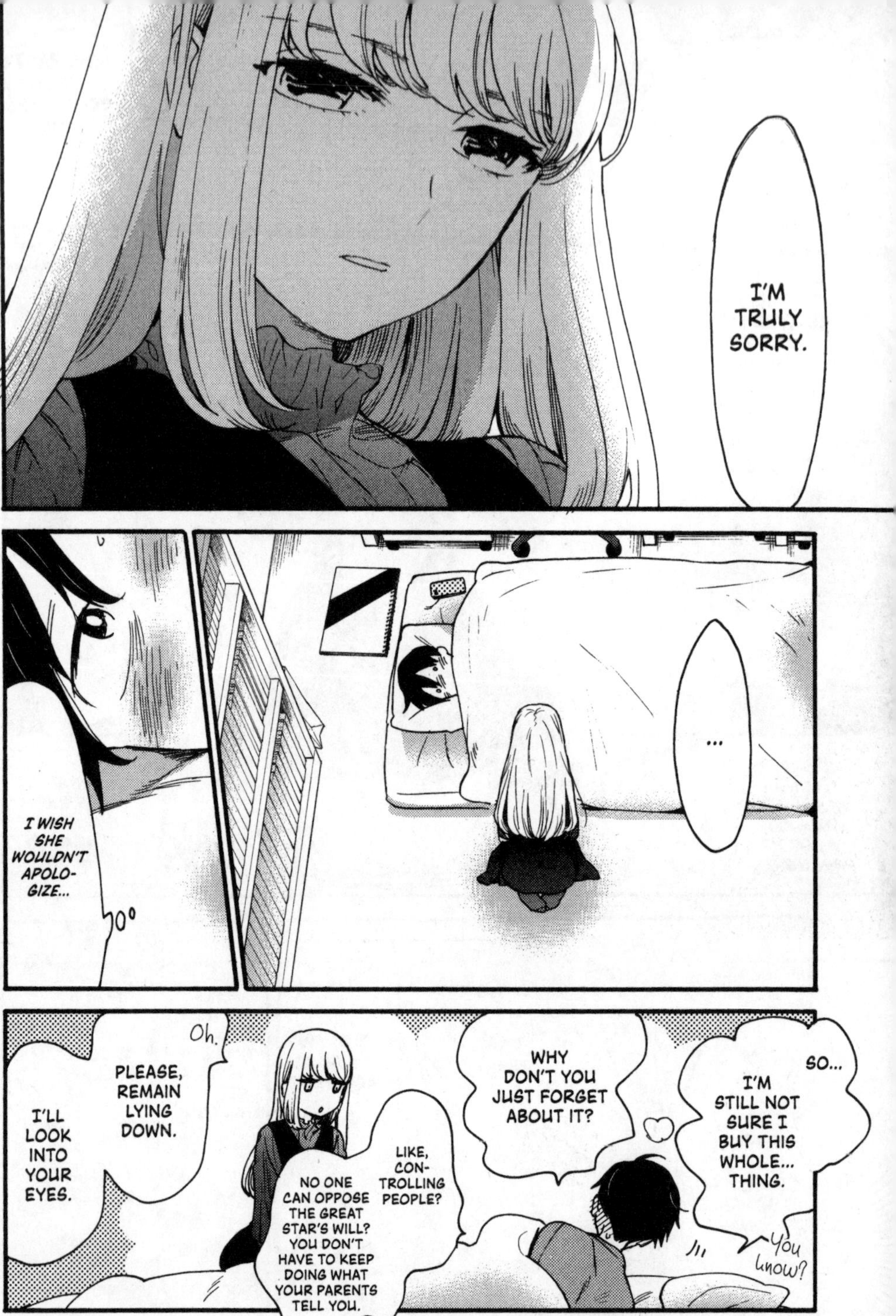
I'M TRULY SORRY.
...
I WISH SHE WOULDN'T APOLO-GIZE...
SO... I'M STILL NOT SURE I BUY THIS WHOLE... THING.
You know?
WHY DON'T YOU JUST FORGET ABOUT IT?
LIKE, CON-TROLLING PEOPLE?
NO ONE CAN OPPOSE THE GREAT STAR'S WILL? YOU DON'T HAVE TO KEEP DOING WHAT YOUR PARENTS TELL YOU.
Oh.
PLEASE, REMAIN LYING DOWN.
I'LL LOOK INTO YOUR EYES.

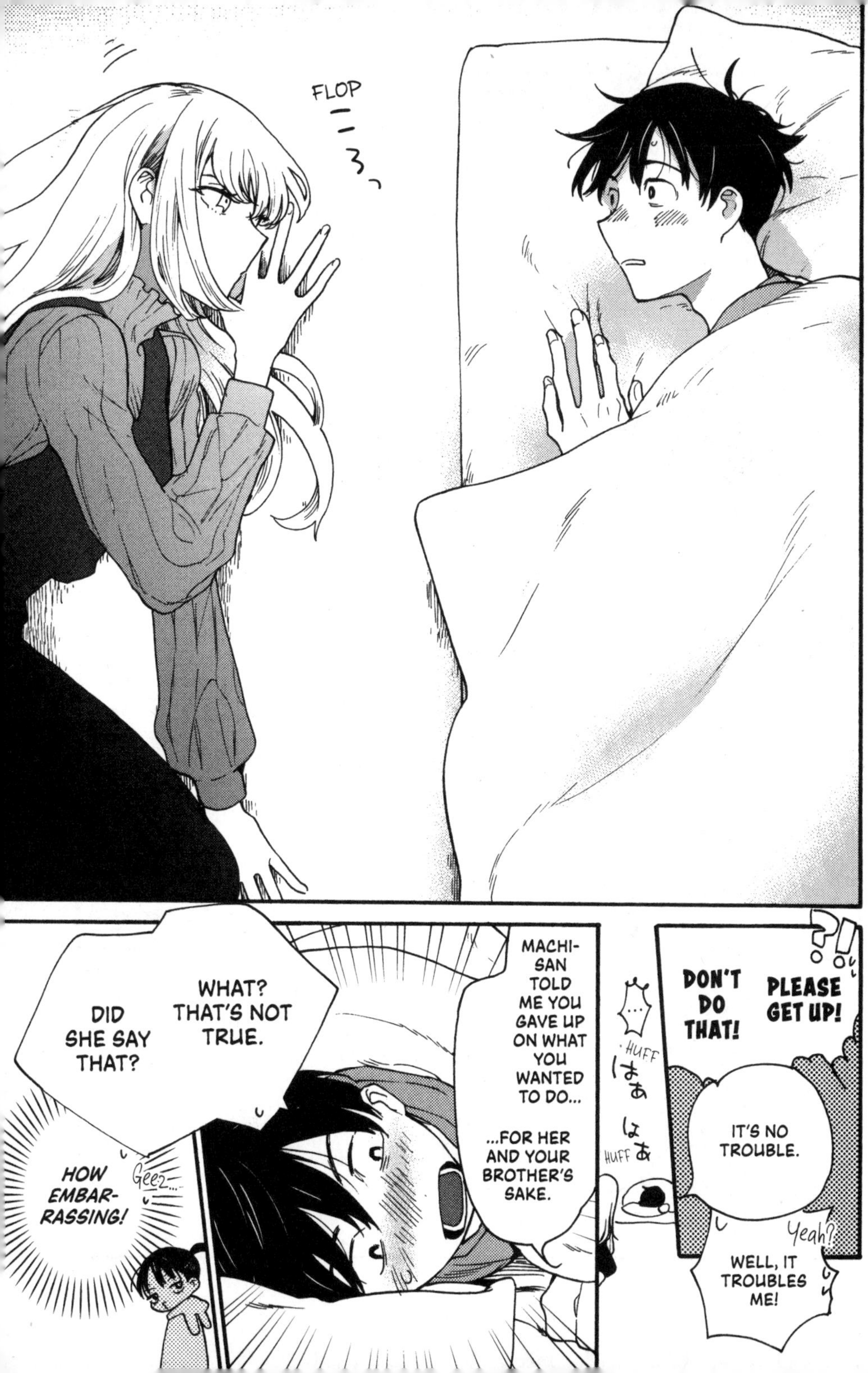
FLOP
PLEASE GET UP!
DON'T DO THAT!
IT'S NO TROUBLE.
Yeah?
WELL, IT TROUBLES ME!
HUFF
HUFF
...
MACHI-SAN TOLD ME YOU GAVE UP ON WHAT YOU WANTED TO DO...
...FOR HER AND YOUR BROTHER'S SAKE.
WHAT? THAT'S NOT TRUE.
DID SHE SAY THAT?
HOW EMBARRASSING!
Geez...

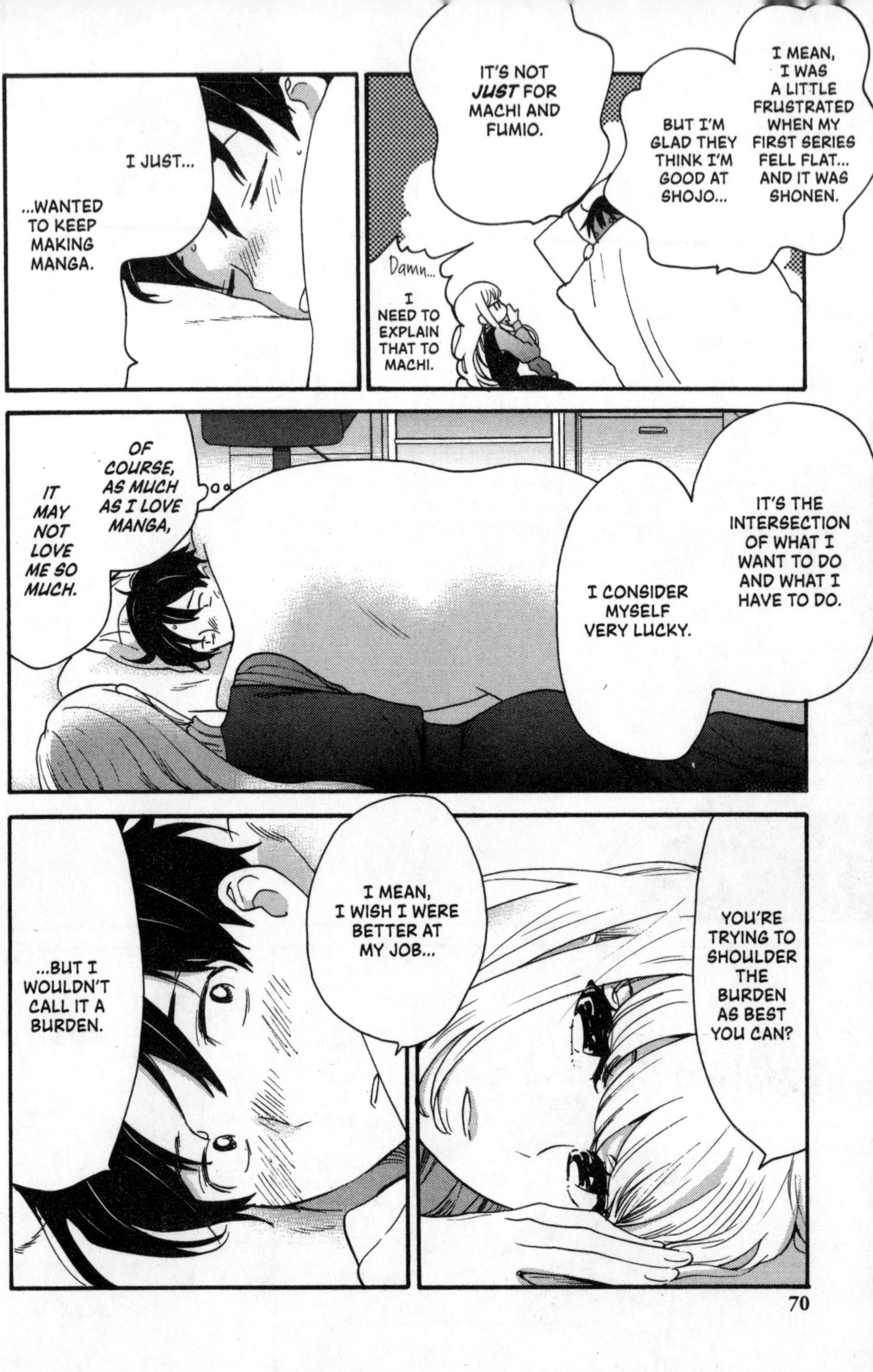
I MEAN, I WAS A LITTLE FRUSTRATED WHEN MY FIRST SERIES FELL FLAT... AND IT WAS SHONEN.
BUT I'M GLAD THEY THINK I'M GOOD AT SHOJO...
IT'S NOT *JUST* FOR MACHI AND FUMIO.
Damn...
I NEED TO EXPLAIN THAT TO MACHI.
I JUST...
...WANTED TO KEEP MAKING MANGA.
IT'S THE INTERSECTION OF WHAT I WANT TO DO AND WHAT I HAVE TO DO.
I CONSIDER MYSELF VERY LUCKY.
OF COURSE, AS MUCH AS I LOVE MANGA,
IT MAY NOT LOVE ME SO MUCH.
YOU'RE TRYING TO SHOULDER THE BURDEN AS BEST YOU CAN?
I MEAN, I WISH I WERE BETTER AT MY JOB...
...BUT I WOULDN'T CALL IT A BURDEN.

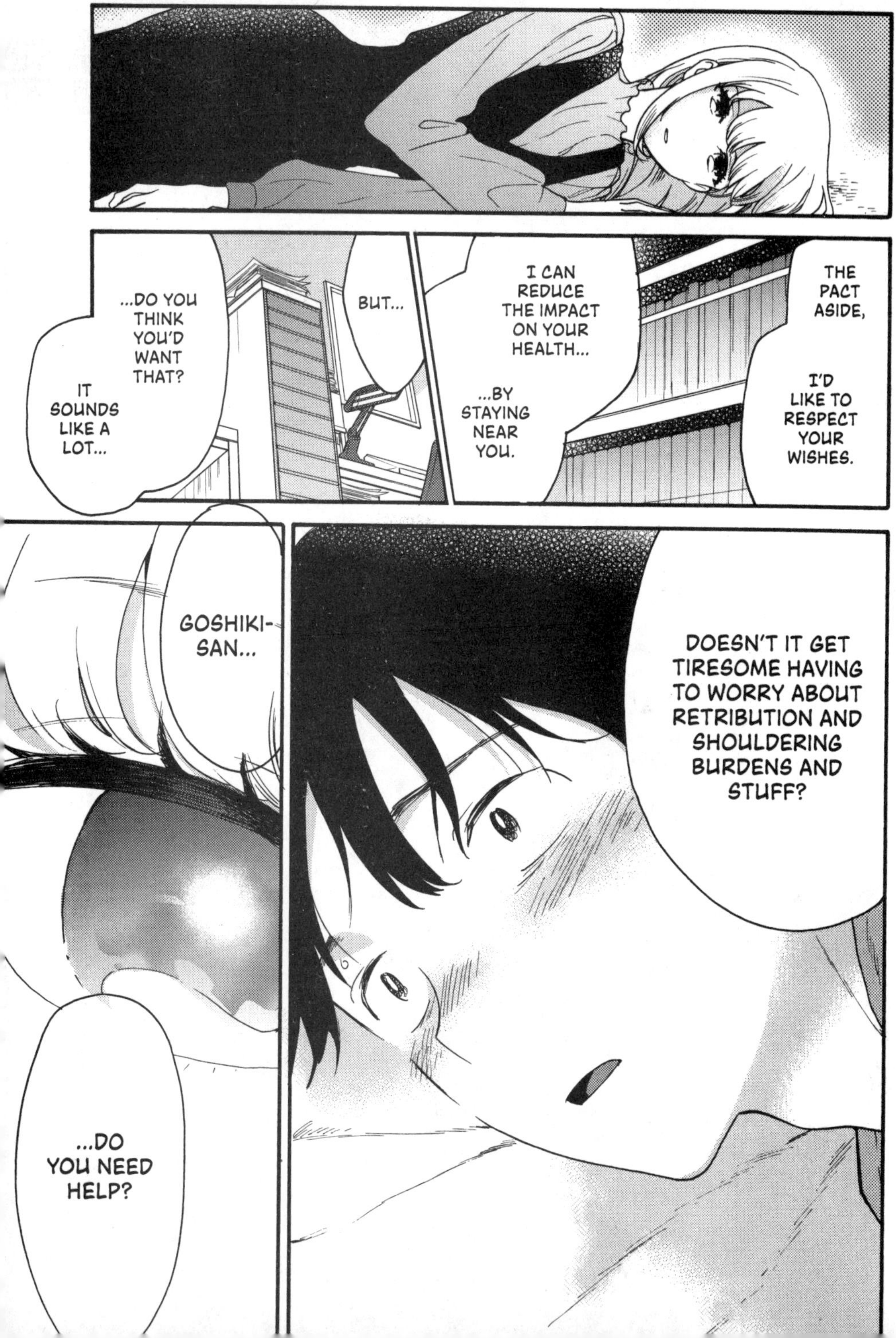
THE PACT ASIDE,
I'D LIKE TO RESPECT YOUR WISHES.
I CAN REDUCE THE IMPACT ON YOUR HEALTH...
...BY STAYING NEAR YOU.
BUT...
...DO YOU THINK YOU'D WANT THAT?
IT SOUNDS LIKE A LOT...
DOESN'T IT GET TIRESOME HAVING TO WORRY ABOUT RETRIBUTION AND SHOULDERING BURDENS AND STUFF?
GOSHIKI-SAN...
...DO YOU NEED HELP?

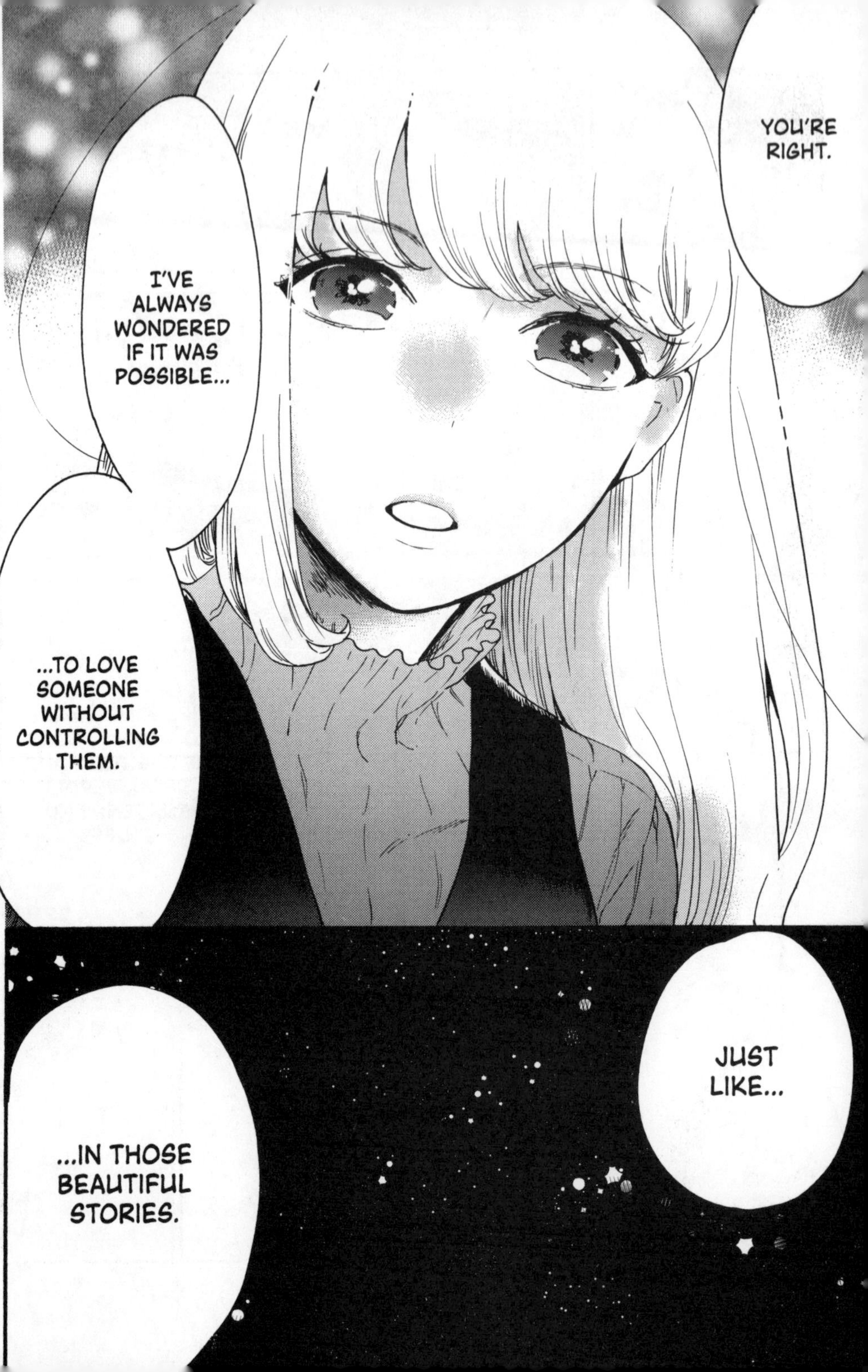
YOU'RE RIGHT.
I'VE ALWAYS WONDERED IF IT WAS POSSIBLE...
...TO LOVE SOMEONE WITHOUT CONTROLLING THEM.
JUST LIKE...
...IN THOSE BEAUTIFUL STORIES.

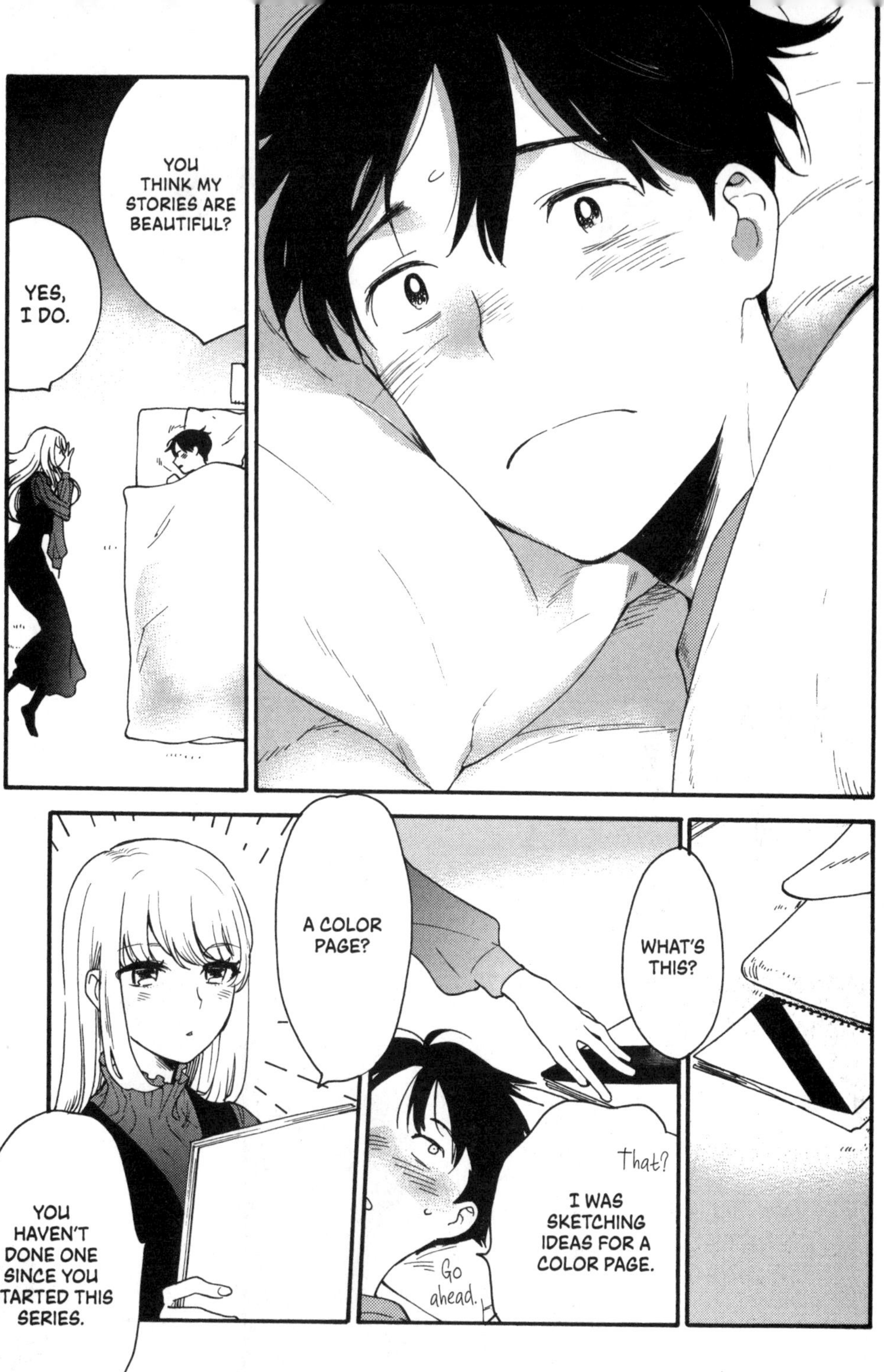

YOU THINK MY STORIES ARE BEAUTIFUL?
YES, I DO.
WHAT'S THIS?
That?
I WAS SKETCHING IDEAS FOR A COLOR PAGE.
Go ahead.
A COLOR PAGE?
YOU HAVEN'T DONE ONE SINCE YOU STARTED THIS SERIES.

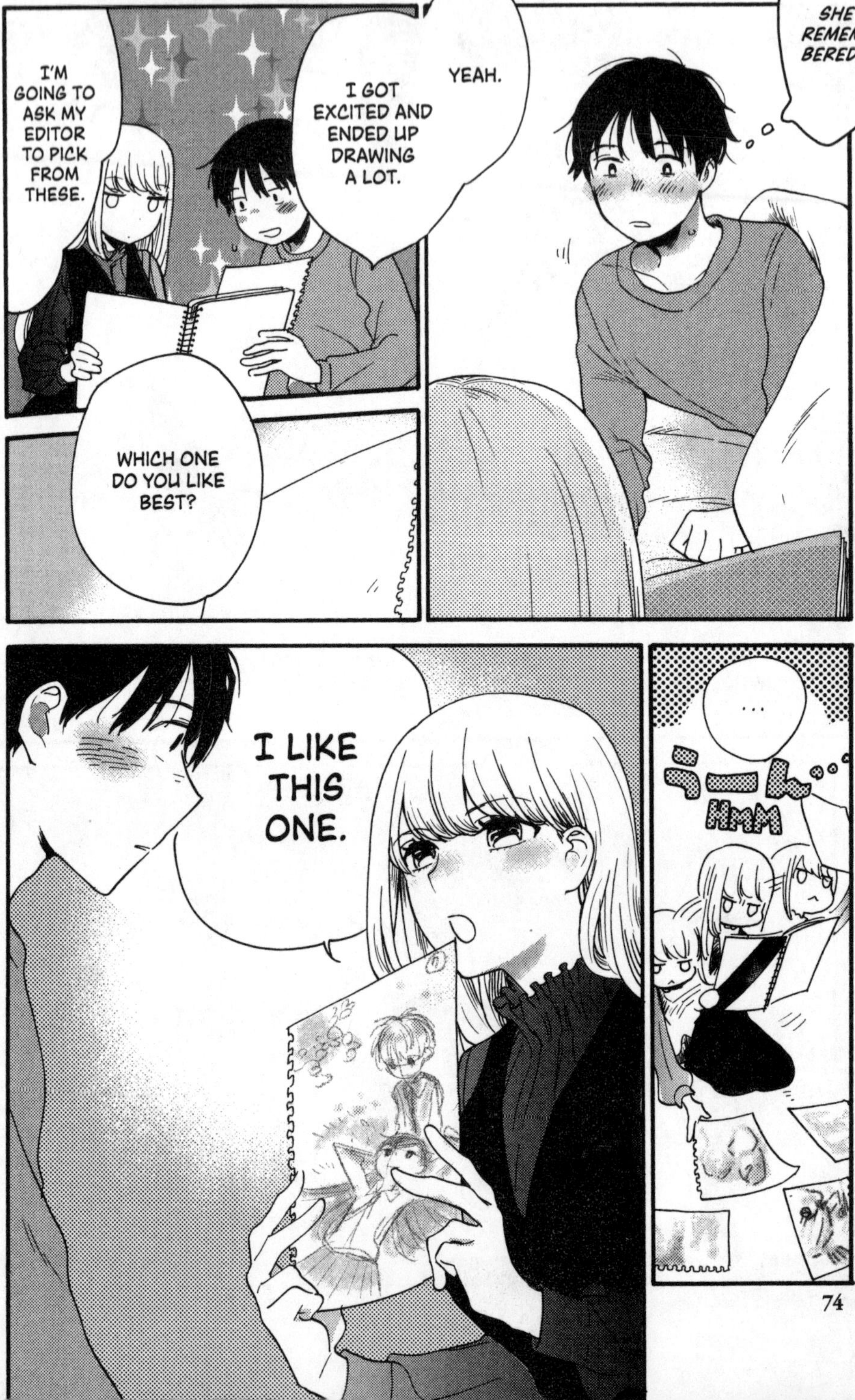
SHE REMEMBERED...
YEAH.
I GOT EXCITED AND ENDED UP DRAWING A LOT.
I'M GOING TO ASK MY EDITOR TO PICK FROM THESE.
WHICH ONE DO YOU LIKE BEST?
...
うーん…
HMM
I LIKE THIS ONE.

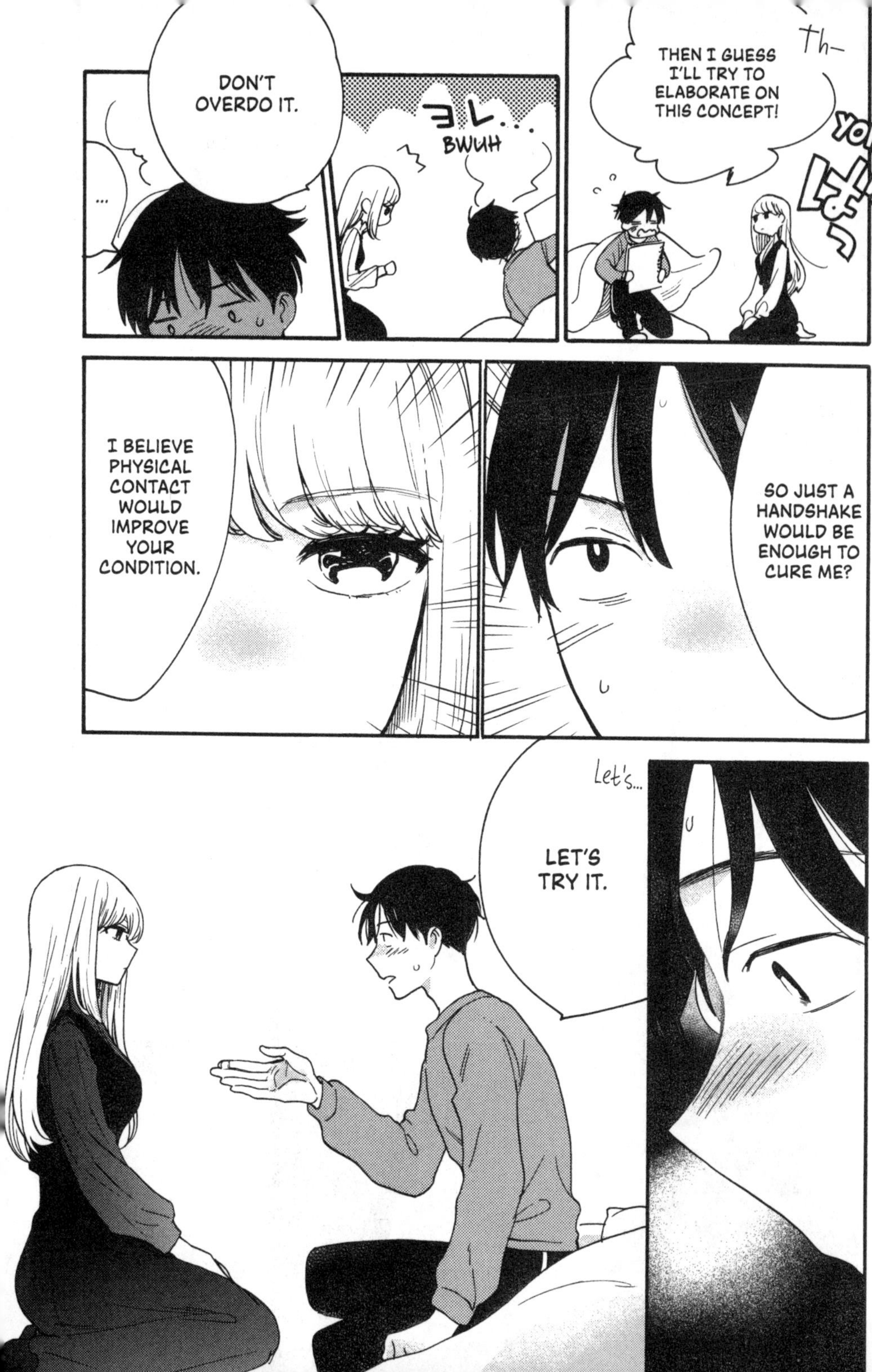
Th–
THEN I GUESS I'LL TRY TO ELABORATE ON THIS CONCEPT!
YOINK
ばっ
ヨレ...
BWUH
DON'T OVERDO IT.
...
SO JUST A HANDSHAKE WOULD BE ENOUGH TO CURE ME?
I BELIEVE PHYSICAL CONTACT WOULD IMPROVE YOUR CONDITION.
Let's...
LET'S TRY IT.

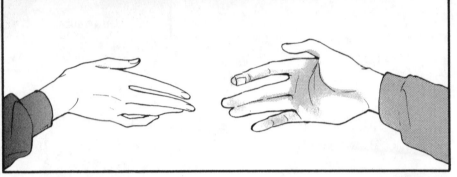

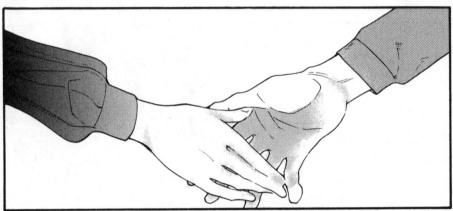

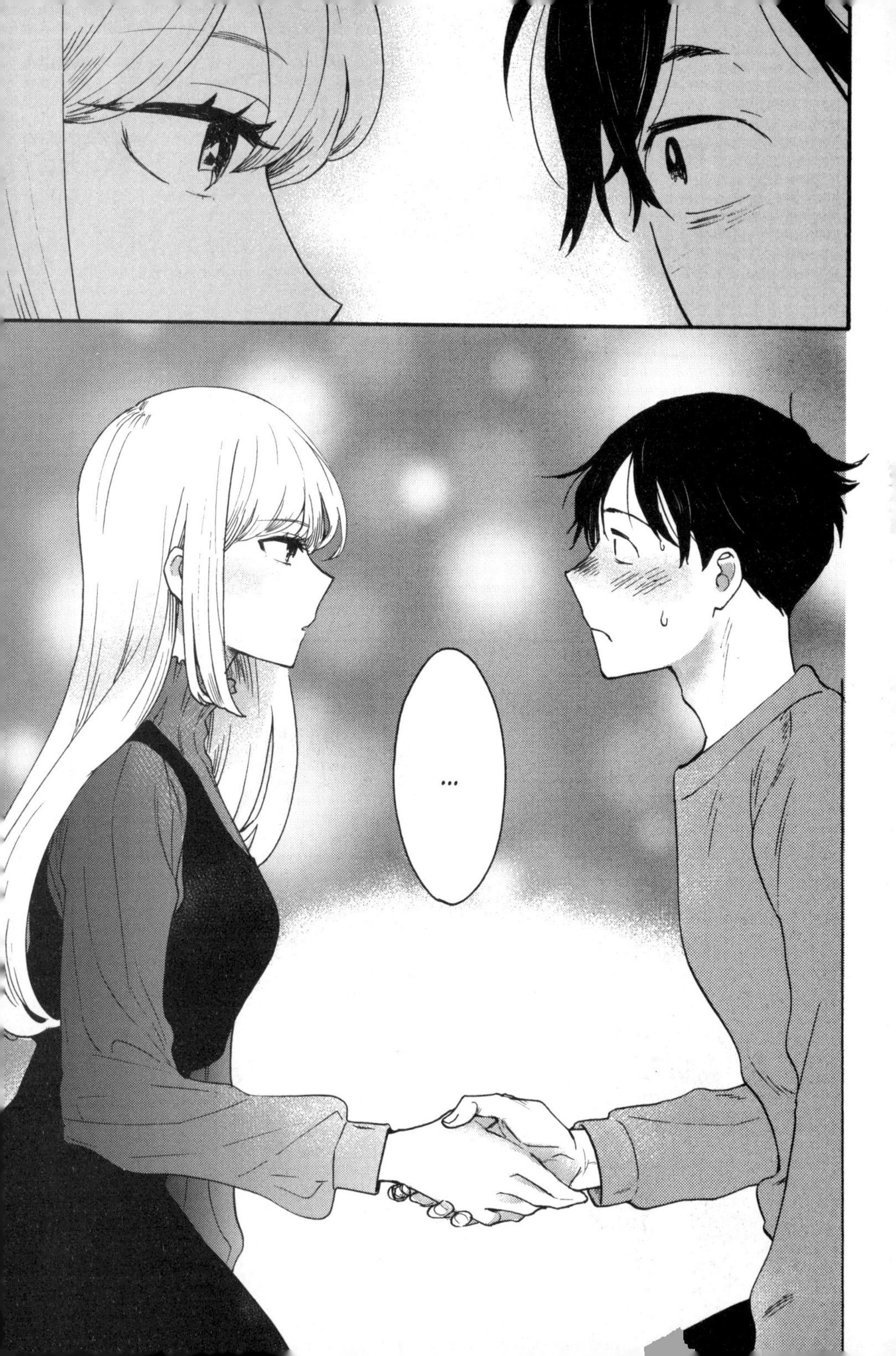
...

WHOA.

I DO FEEL BETTER.

FSH

HUH.

I GUESS SHE'S BEEN TELLING THE TRUTH THIS WHOLE TIME.

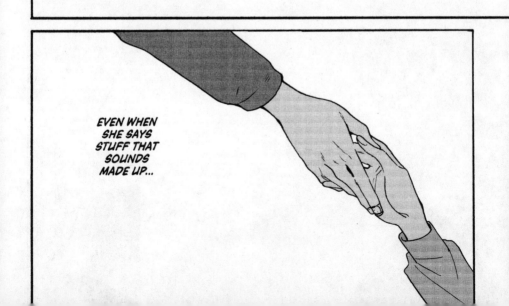

EVEN WHEN SHE SAYS STUFF THAT SOUNDS MADE UP...

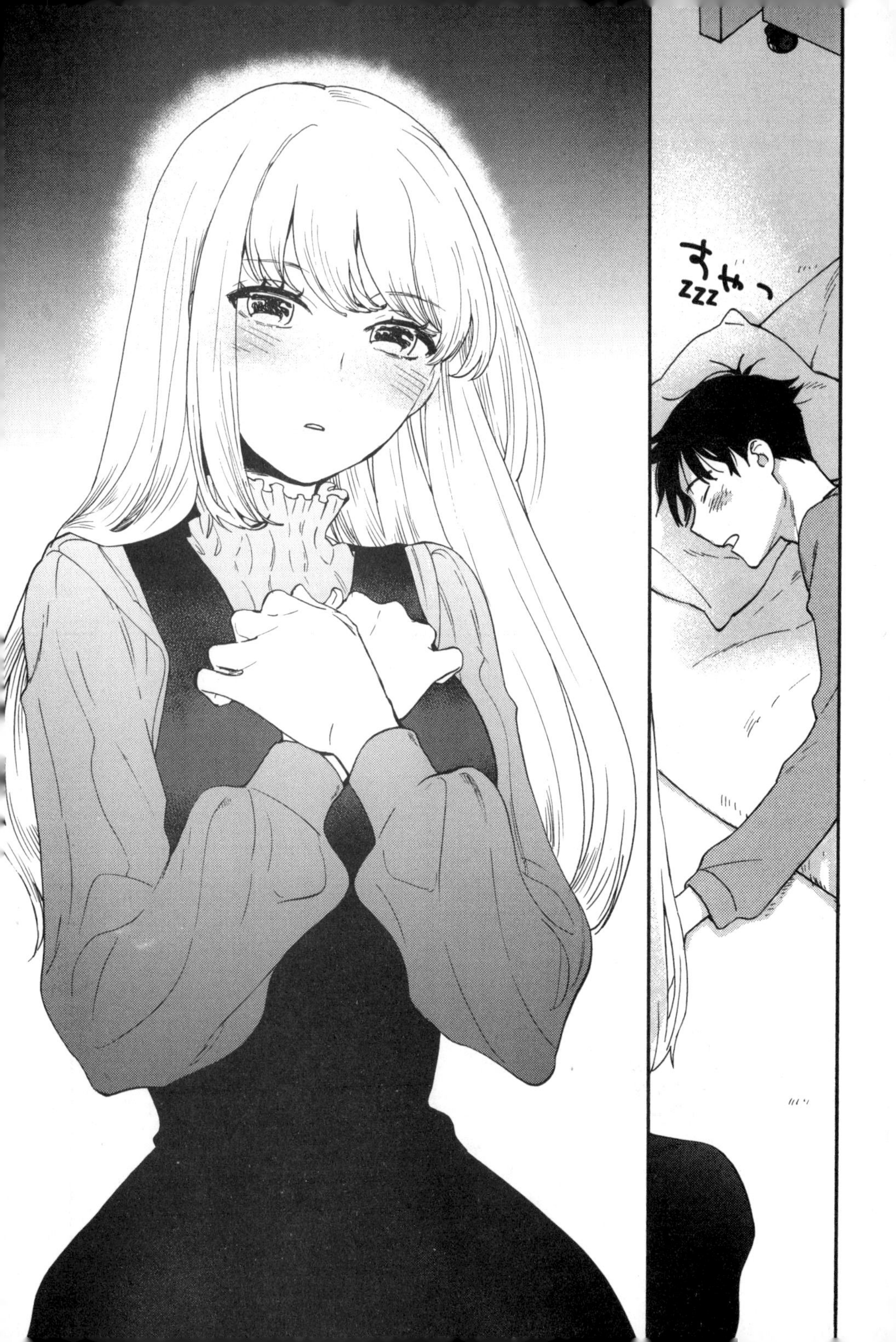
すやっ
zzz

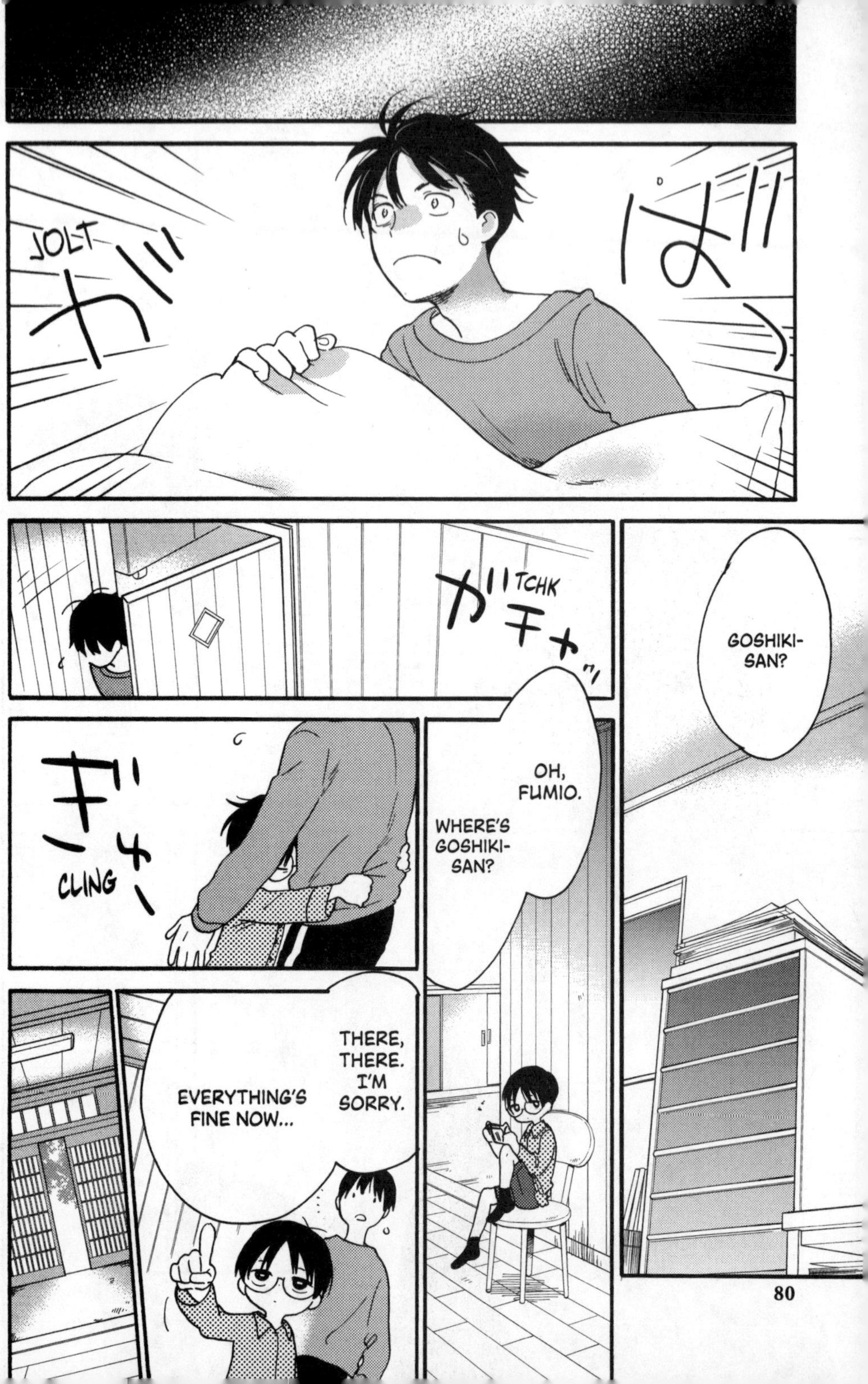
ばっ
JOLT
がば
GOSHIKI-SAN?
TCHK
ガチャ
OH, FUMIO.
WHERE'S GOSHIKI-SAN?
CLING
ぎゅ
THERE, THERE. I'M SORRY.
EVERYTHING'S FINE NOW...

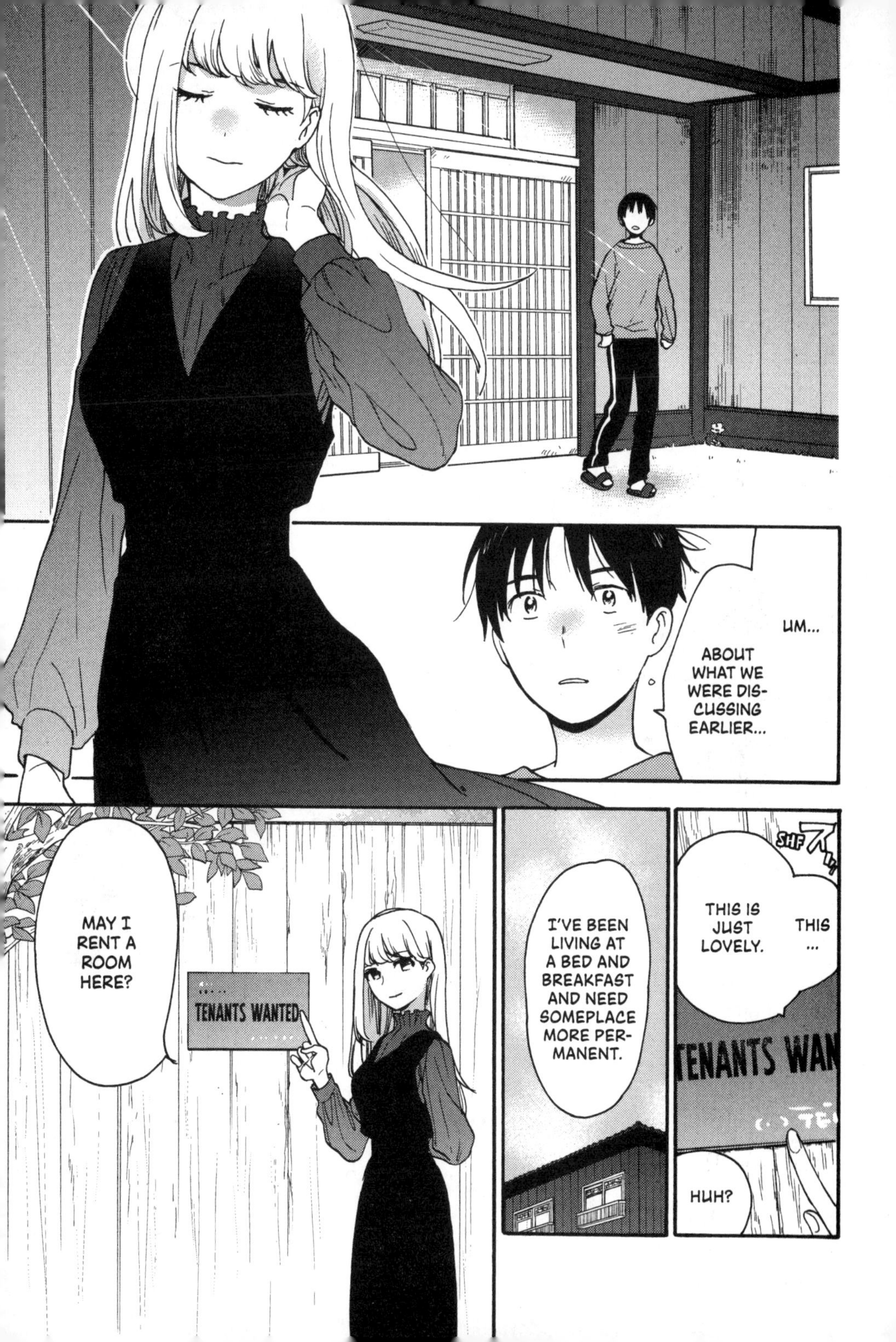
UM...
ABOUT WHAT WE WERE DIS-CUSSING EARLIER...
SHF
THIS ...
THIS IS JUST LOVELY.
HUH?
I'VE BEEN LIVING AT A BED AND BREAKFAST AND NEED SOMEPLACE MORE PER-MANENT.
MAY I RENT A ROOM HERE?
TENANTS WANTED

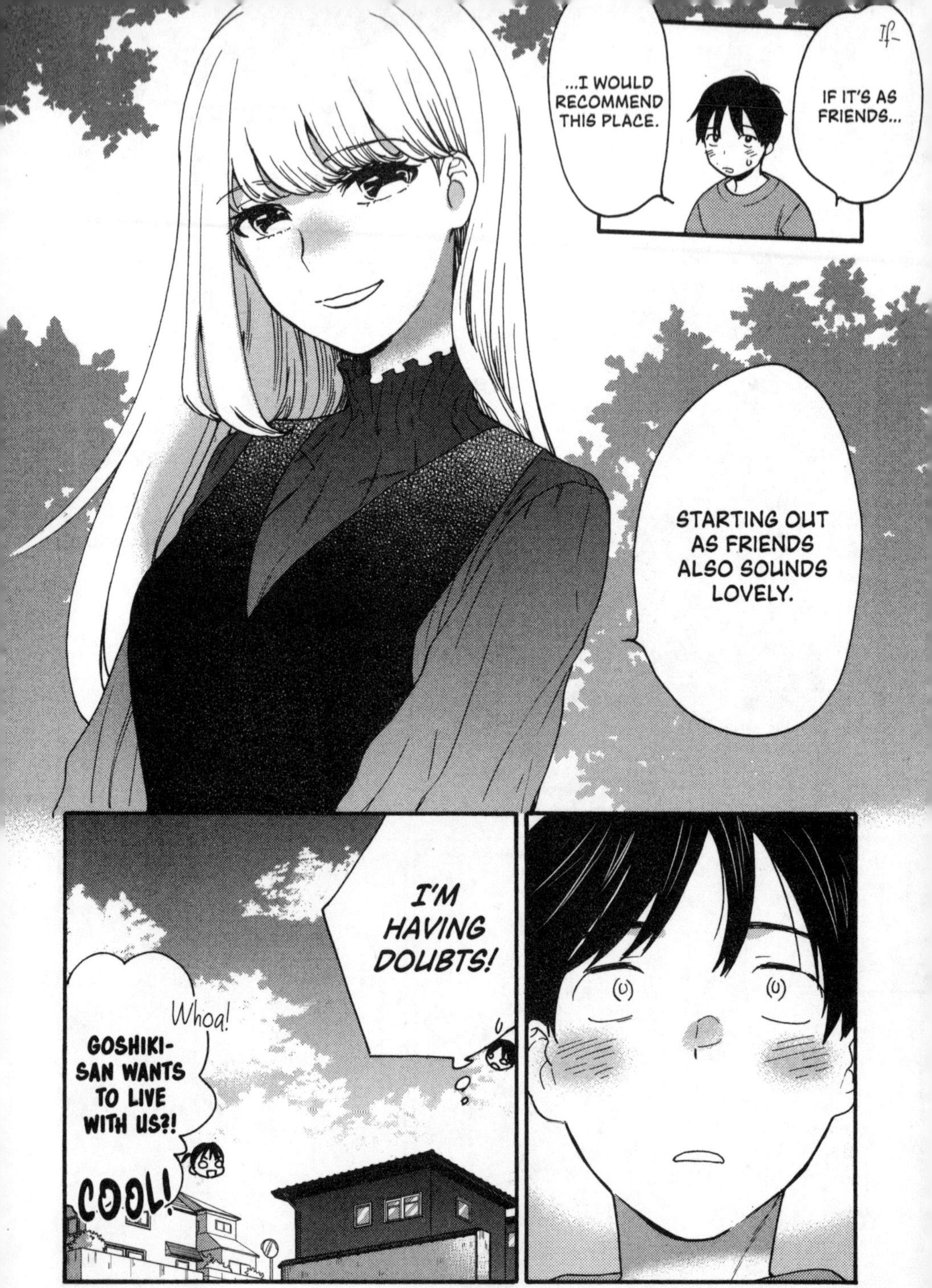
IF IT'S AS FRIENDS...
...I WOULD RECOMMEND THIS PLACE.
STARTING OUT AS FRIENDS ALSO SOUNDS LOVELY.
I'M HAVING DOUBTS!
Whoa!
GOSHIKI-SAN WANTS TO LIVE WITH US?!
COOL!

CHAPTER 2 ★ END

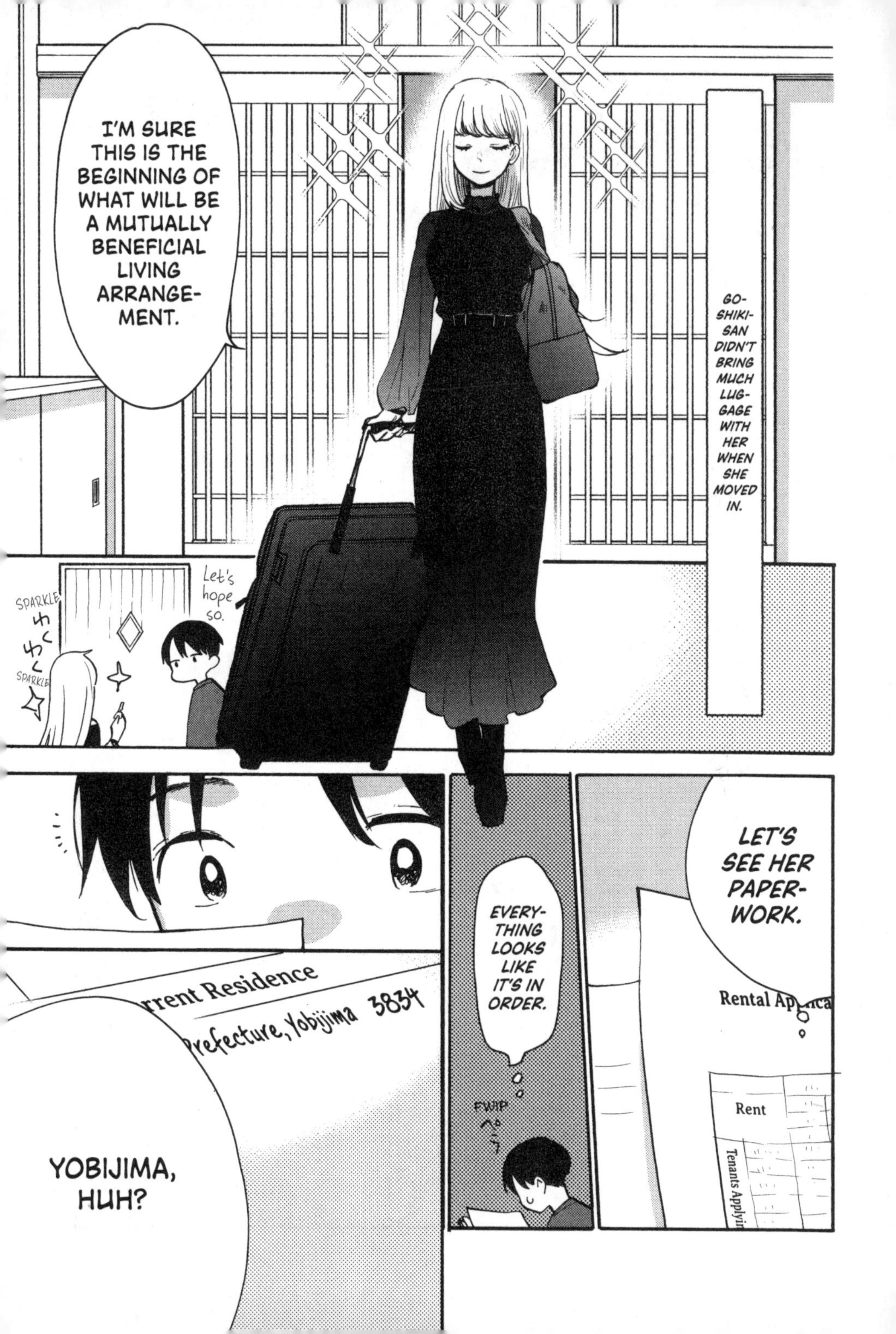
GO-SHIKI-SAN DIDN'T BRING MUCH LUGGAGE WITH HER WHEN SHE MOVED IN.
I'M SURE THIS IS THE BEGINNING OF WHAT WILL BE A MUTUALLY BENEFICIAL LIVING ARRANGE-MENT.
Let's hope so.
SPARKLE わく わく SPARKLE
LET'S SEE HER PAPER-WORK.
Rent
EVERY-THING LOOKS LIKE IT'S IN ORDER.
FWIP
Prefecture, Yobijima 3834
YOBIJIMA, HUH?

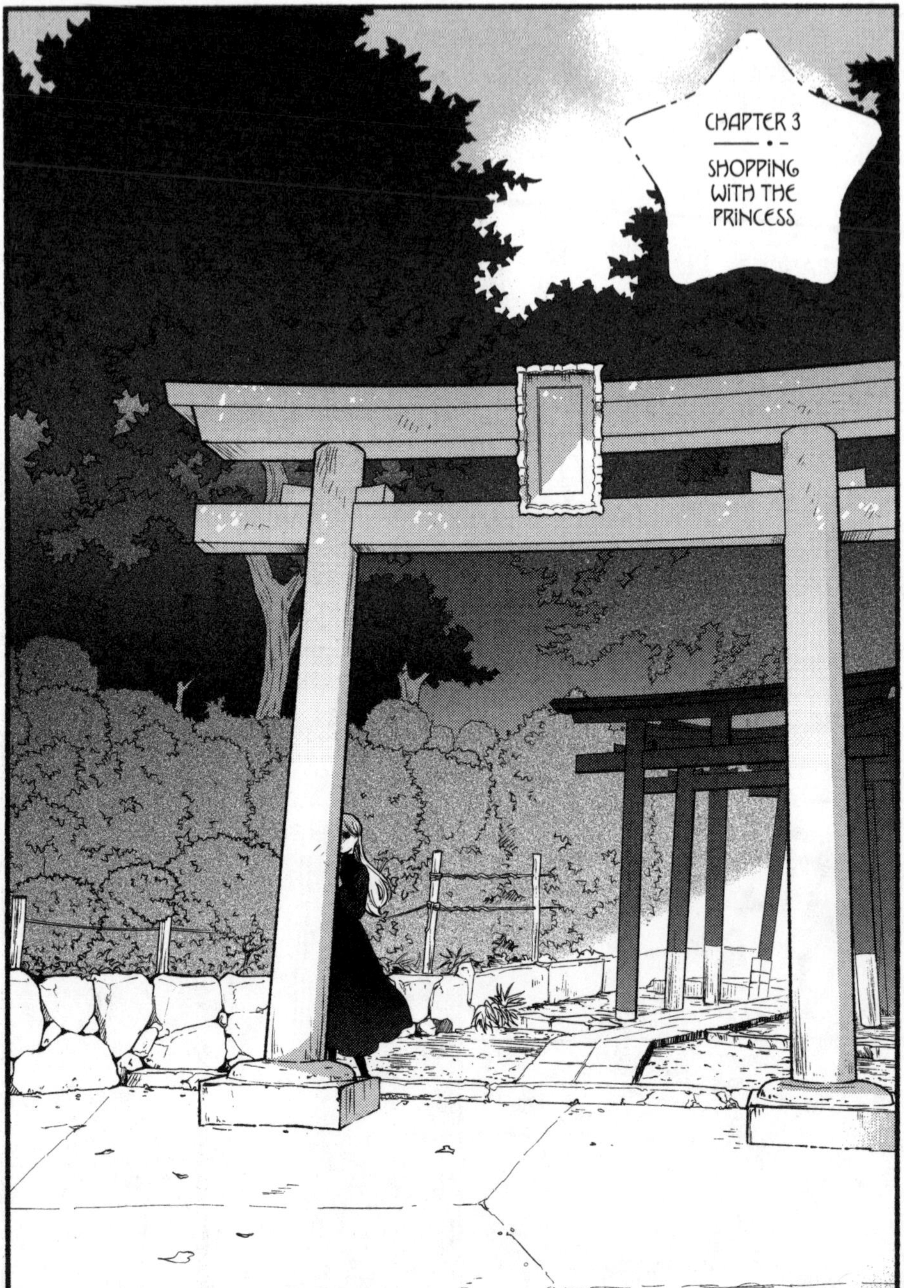
CHAPTER 3
SHOPPING WITH THE PRINCESS

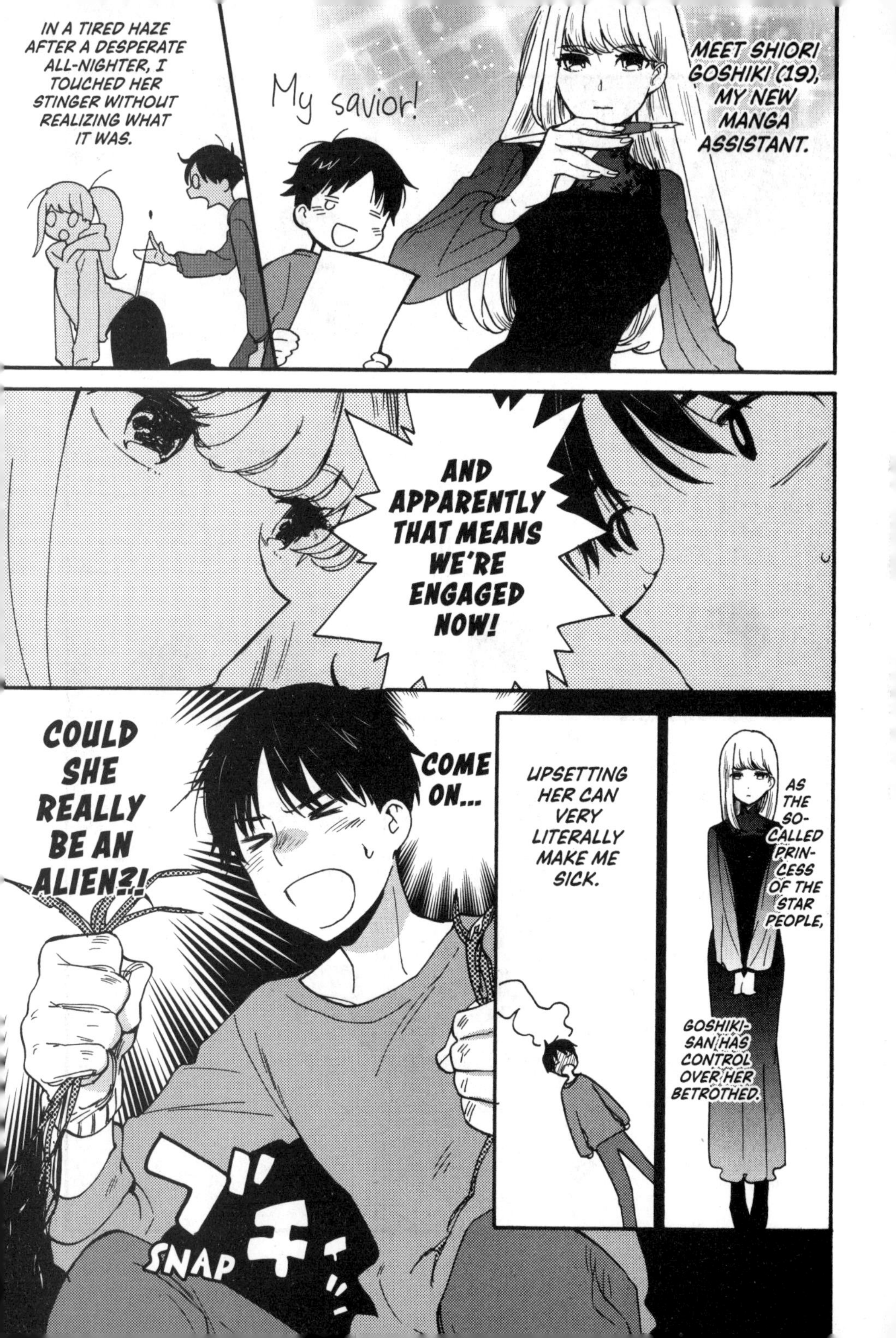
MEET SHIORI GOSHIKI (19), MY NEW MANGA ASSISTANT.
My savior!
IN A TIRED HAZE AFTER A DESPERATE ALL-NIGHTER, I TOUCHED HER STINGER WITHOUT REALIZING WHAT IT WAS.
AND APPARENTLY THAT MEANS WE'RE ENGAGED NOW!
AS THE SO-CALLED PRINCESS OF THE STAR PEOPLE,
GOSHIKI-SAN HAS CONTROL OVER HER BETROTHED.
UPSETTING HER CAN VERY LITERALLY MAKE ME SICK.
COME ON...
COULD SHE REALLY BE AN ALIEN?!
ブチ
SNAP

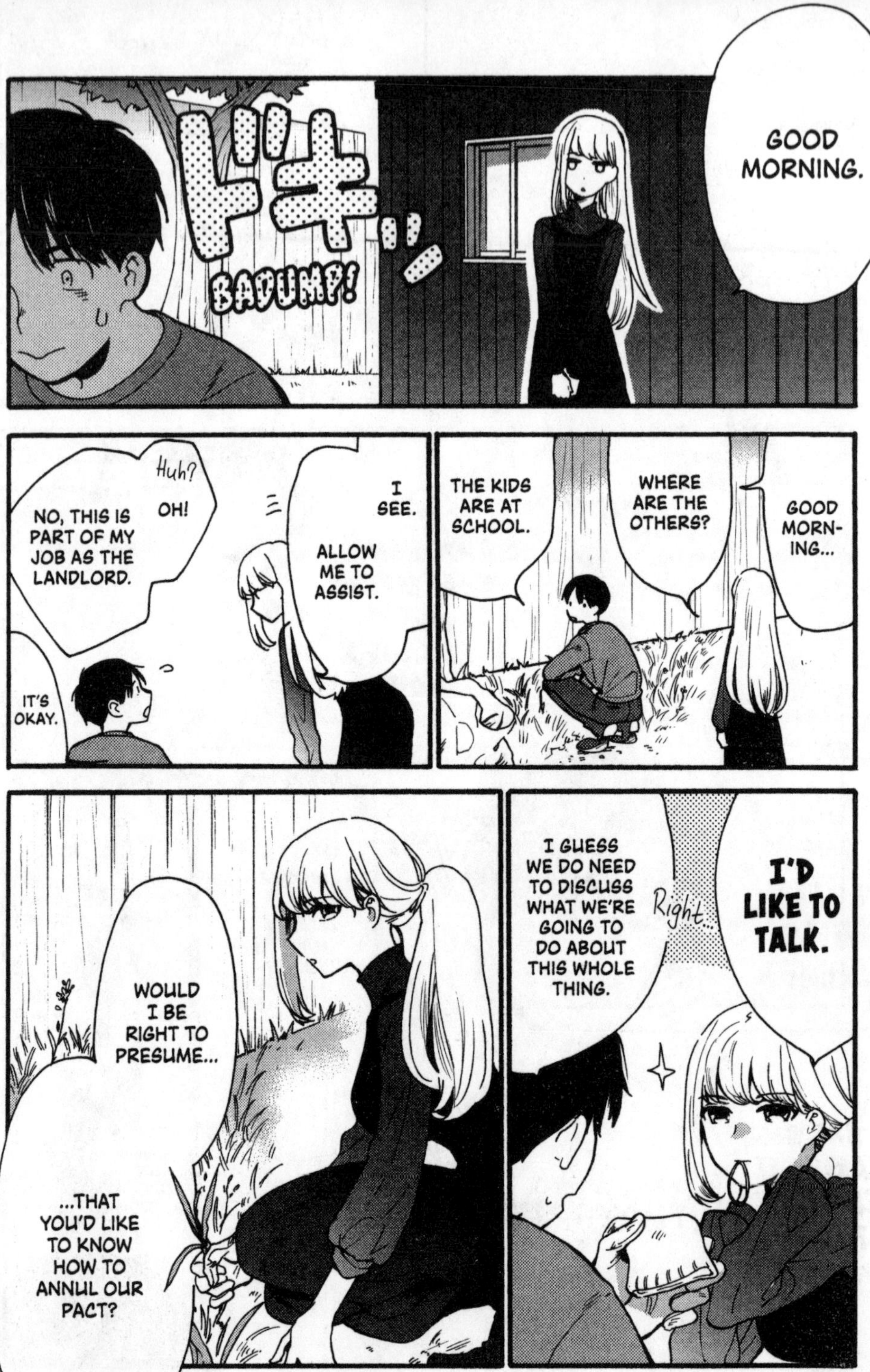
GOOD MORNING.
ドキッ
BADUMP!
GOOD MORNING...
WHERE ARE THE OTHERS?
THE KIDS ARE AT SCHOOL.
I SEE.
ALLOW ME TO ASSIST.
Huh?
OH!
NO, THIS IS PART OF MY JOB AS THE LANDLORD.
IT'S OKAY.
I'D LIKE TO TALK.
Right...
I GUESS WE DO NEED TO DISCUSS WHAT WE'RE GOING TO DO ABOUT THIS WHOLE THING.
WOULD I BE RIGHT TO PRESUME...
...THAT YOU'D LIKE TO KNOW HOW TO ANNUL OUR PACT?

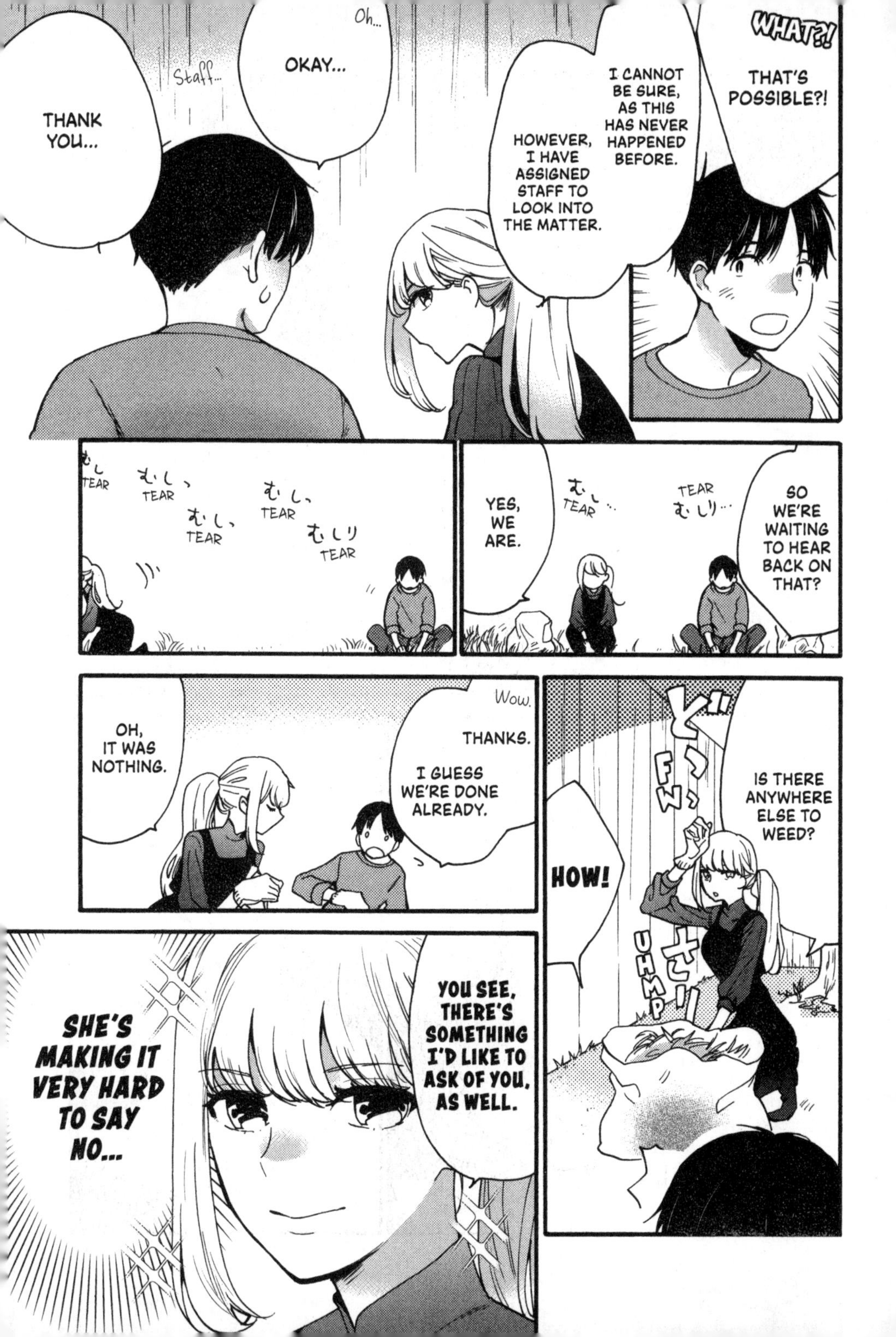
WHAT?!
THAT'S POSSIBLE?!
I CANNOT BE SURE, AS THIS HAS NEVER HAPPENED BEFORE.
HOWEVER, I HAVE ASSIGNED STAFF TO LOOK INTO THE MATTER.
Oh...
OKAY...
Staff...
THANK YOU...
SO WE'RE WAITING TO HEAR BACK ON THAT?
TEAR
むしり…
むし TEAR
YES, WE ARE.
むしり TEAR
むしっ TEAR
むしっ TEAR
むしっ TEAR
むし TEAR
どさっ
FW
UHMP
IS THERE ANYWHERE ELSE TO WEED?
HOW!
Wow.
THANKS.
I GUESS WE'RE DONE ALREADY.
OH, IT WAS NOTHING.
YOU SEE, THERE'S SOMETHING I'D LIKE TO ASK OF YOU, AS WELL.
SHE'S MAKING IT VERY HARD TO SAY NO...

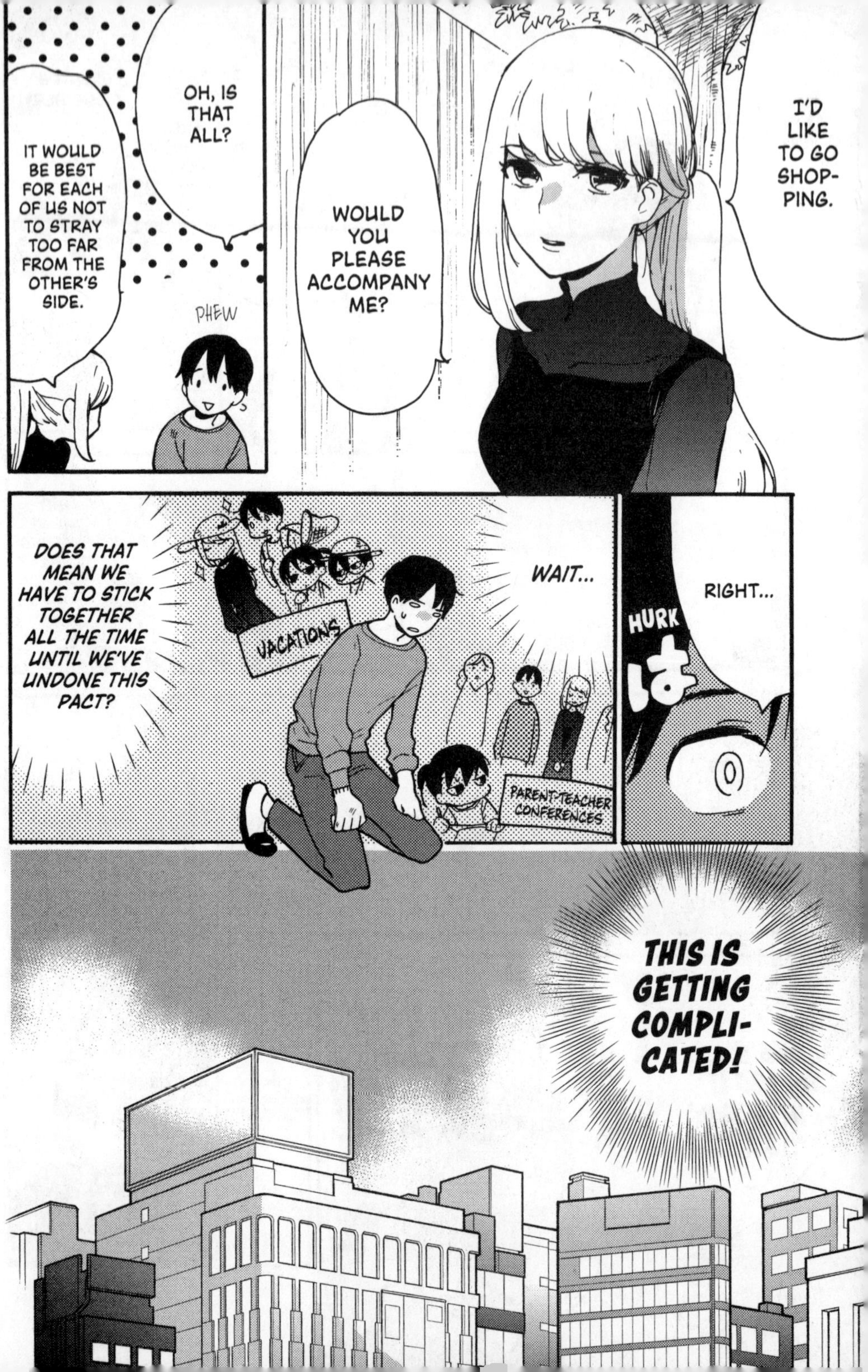
I'D LIKE TO GO SHOPPING.
WOULD YOU PLEASE ACCOMPANY ME?
OH, IS THAT ALL?
IT WOULD BE BEST FOR EACH OF US NOT TO STRAY TOO FAR FROM THE OTHER'S SIDE.
PHEW
RIGHT...
HURK
は
WAIT...
DOES THAT MEAN WE HAVE TO STICK TOGETHER ALL THE TIME UNTIL WE'VE UNDONE THIS PACT?
VACATIONS
PARENT-TEACHER CONFERENCES
THIS IS GETTING COMPLICATED!

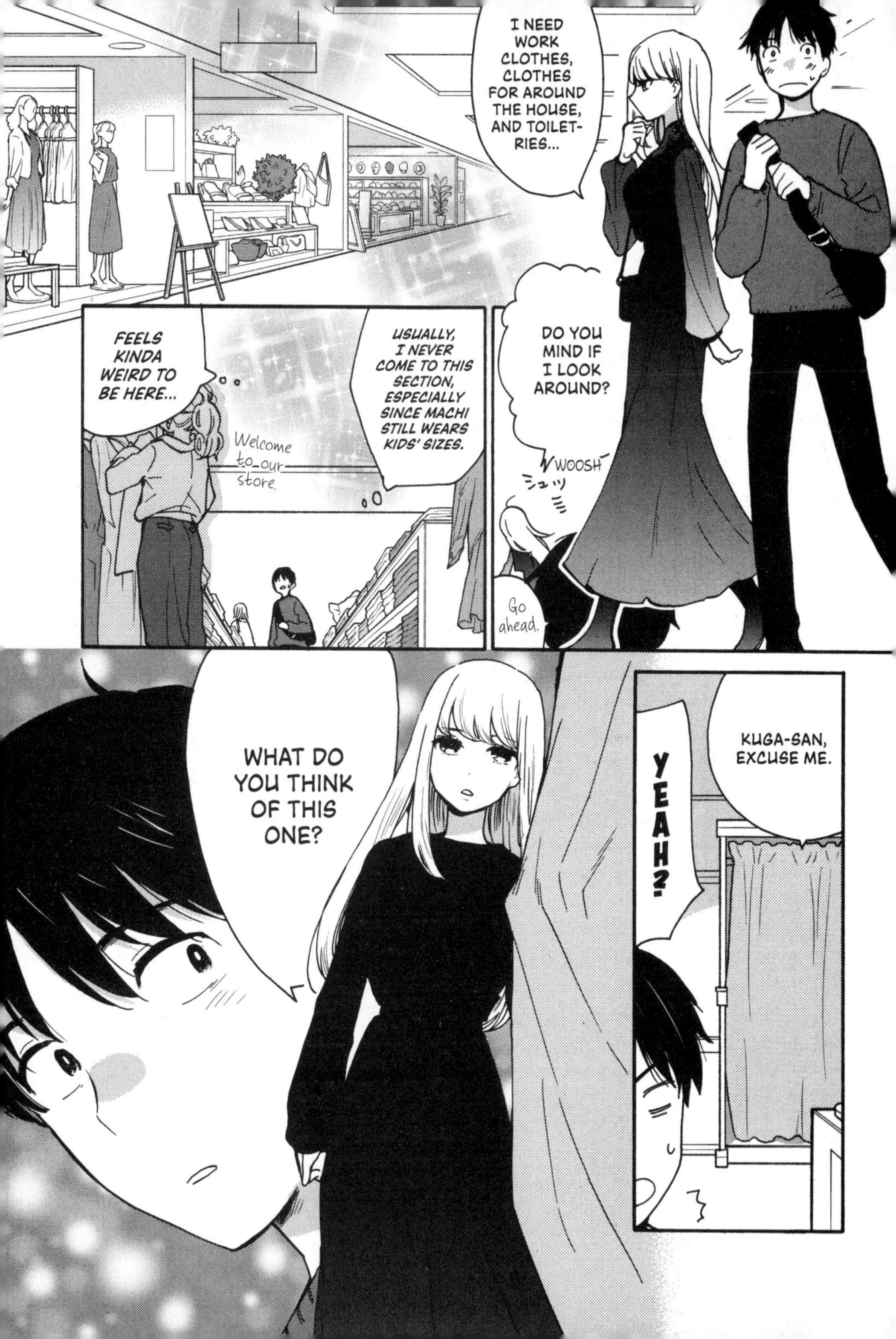
I NEED WORK CLOTHES, CLOTHES FOR AROUND THE HOUSE, AND TOILETRIES...
DO YOU MIND IF I LOOK AROUND?
WOOSH
シュッ
Go ahead.
USUALLY, I NEVER COME TO THIS SECTION, ESPECIALLY SINCE MACHI STILL WEARS KIDS' SIZES.
Welcome to our store.
FEELS KINDA WEIRD TO BE HERE...
KUGA-SAN, EXCUSE ME.
YEAH?
WHAT DO YOU THINK OF THIS ONE?

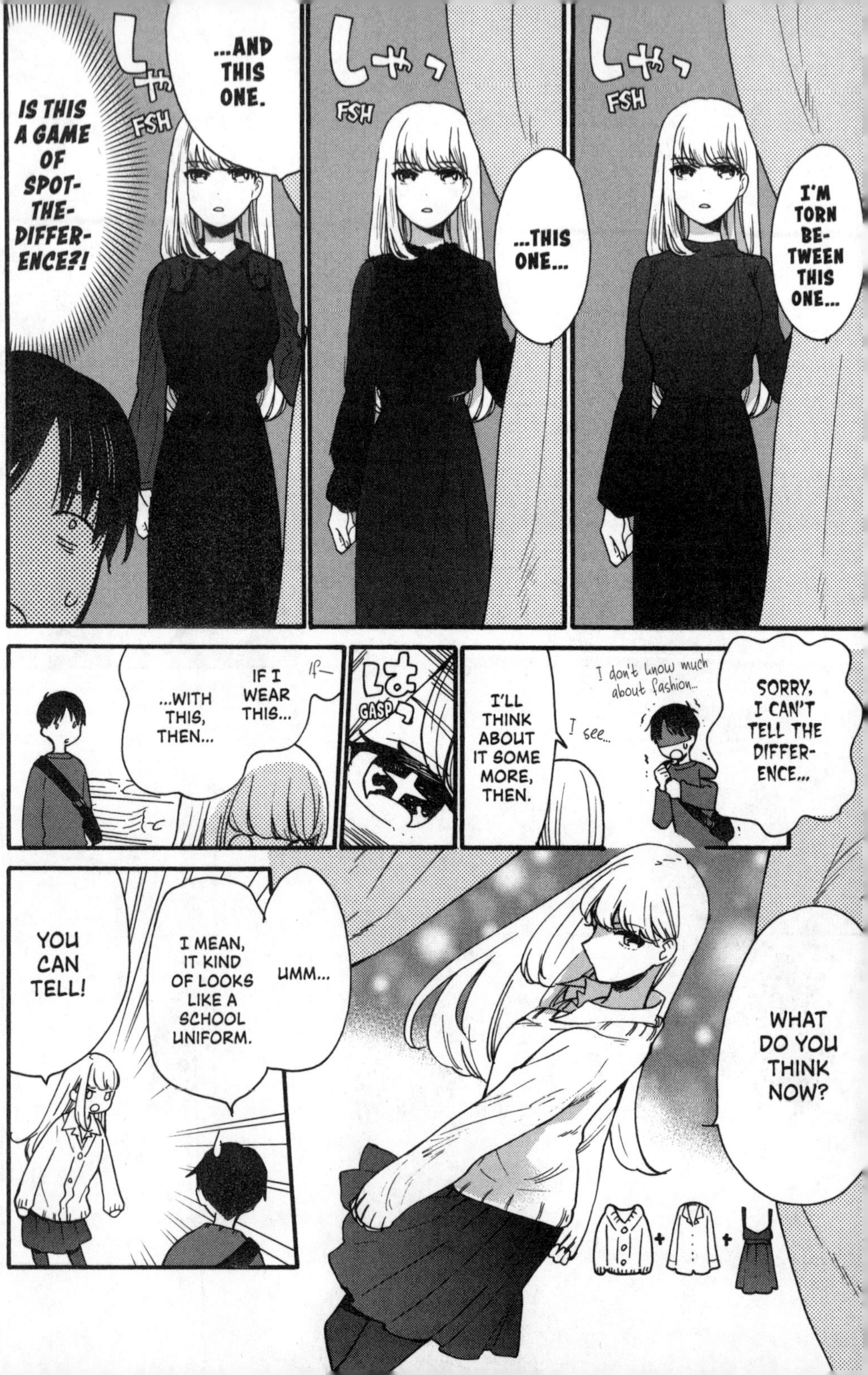
しゃっ
FSH
I'M TORN BETWEEN THIS ONE...
しゃっ
FSH
...THIS ONE...
FSH
...AND THIS ONE.
IS THIS A GAME OF SPOT-THE-DIFFERENCE?!
SORRY, I CAN'T TELL THE DIFFERENCE...
I don't know much about fashion...
I see...
I'LL THINK ABOUT IT SOME MORE, THEN.
GASP
IF I WEAR THIS...
If—
...WITH THIS, THEN...
WHAT DO YOU THINK NOW?
UMM...
I MEAN, IT KIND OF LOOKS LIKE A SCHOOL UNIFORM.
YOU CAN TELL!

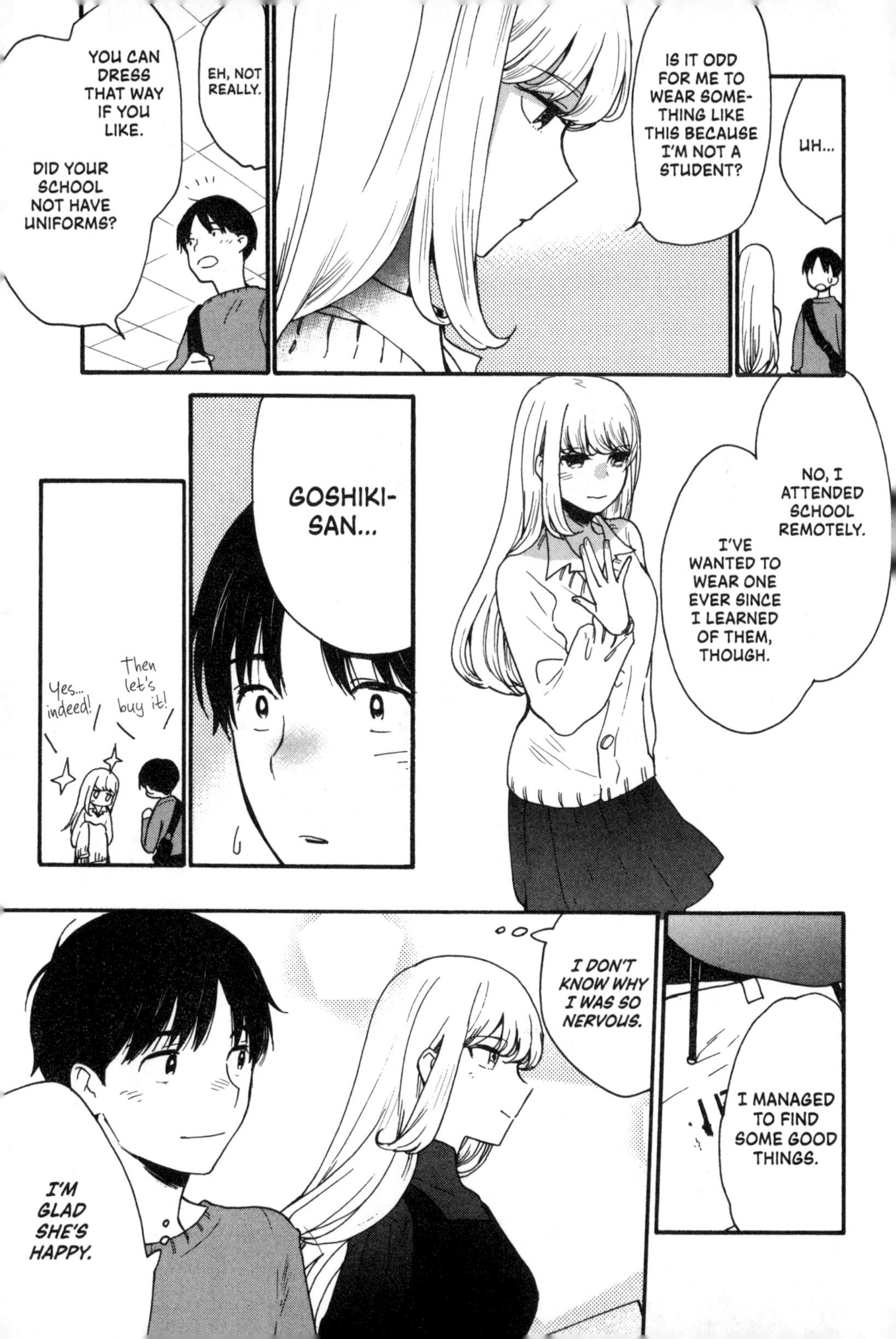
UH...
IS IT ODD FOR ME TO WEAR SOME-THING LIKE THIS BECAUSE I'M NOT A STUDENT?
EH, NOT REALLY.
YOU CAN DRESS THAT WAY IF YOU LIKE.
DID YOUR SCHOOL NOT HAVE UNIFORMS?
NO, I ATTENDED SCHOOL REMOTELY.
I'VE WANTED TO WEAR ONE EVER SINCE I LEARNED OF THEM, THOUGH.
GOSHIKI-SAN...
Then let's buy it!
Yes... indeed!
I MANAGED TO FIND SOME GOOD THINGS.
I DON'T KNOW WHY I WAS SO NERVOUS.
I'M GLAD SHE'S HAPPY.

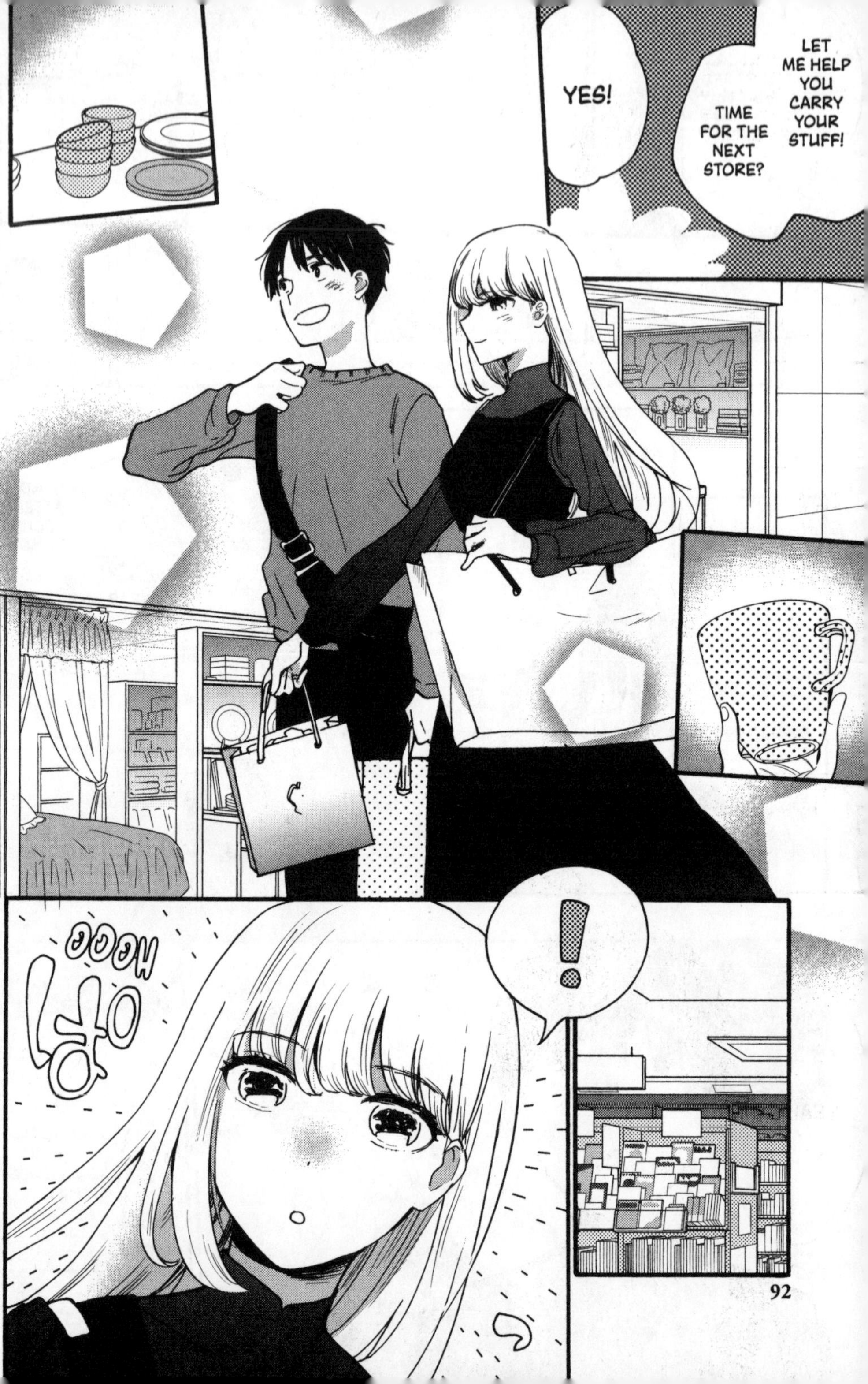
LET ME HELP YOU CARRY YOUR STUFF!
TIME FOR THE NEXT STORE?
YES!
!
HOOO

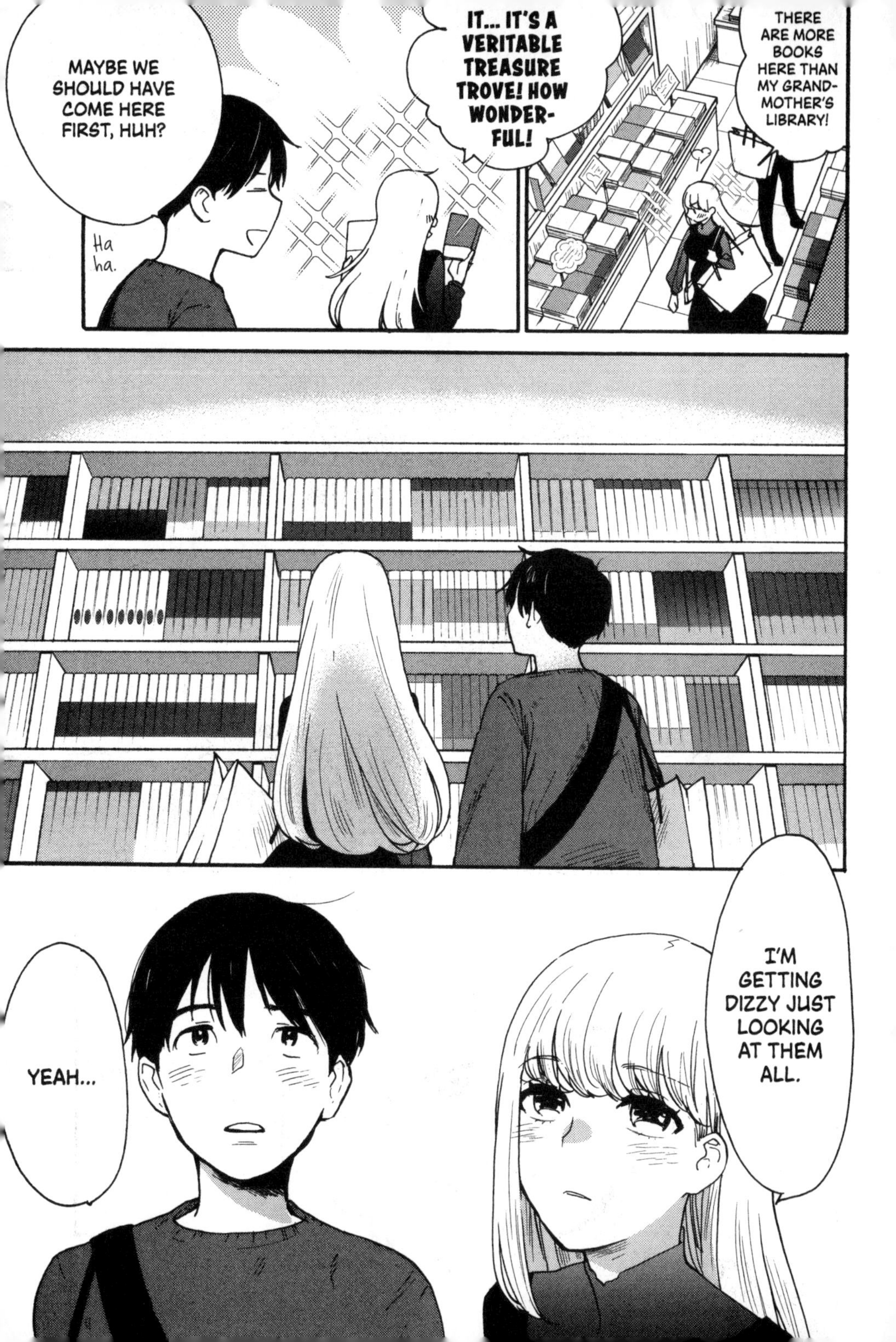
THERE ARE MORE BOOKS HERE THAN MY GRAND-MOTHER'S LIBRARY!
IT... IT'S A VERITABLE TREASURE TROVE! HOW WONDER-FUL!
MAYBE WE SHOULD HAVE COME HERE FIRST, HUH?
Ha ha.
I'M GETTING DIZZY JUST LOOKING AT THEM ALL.
YEAH...

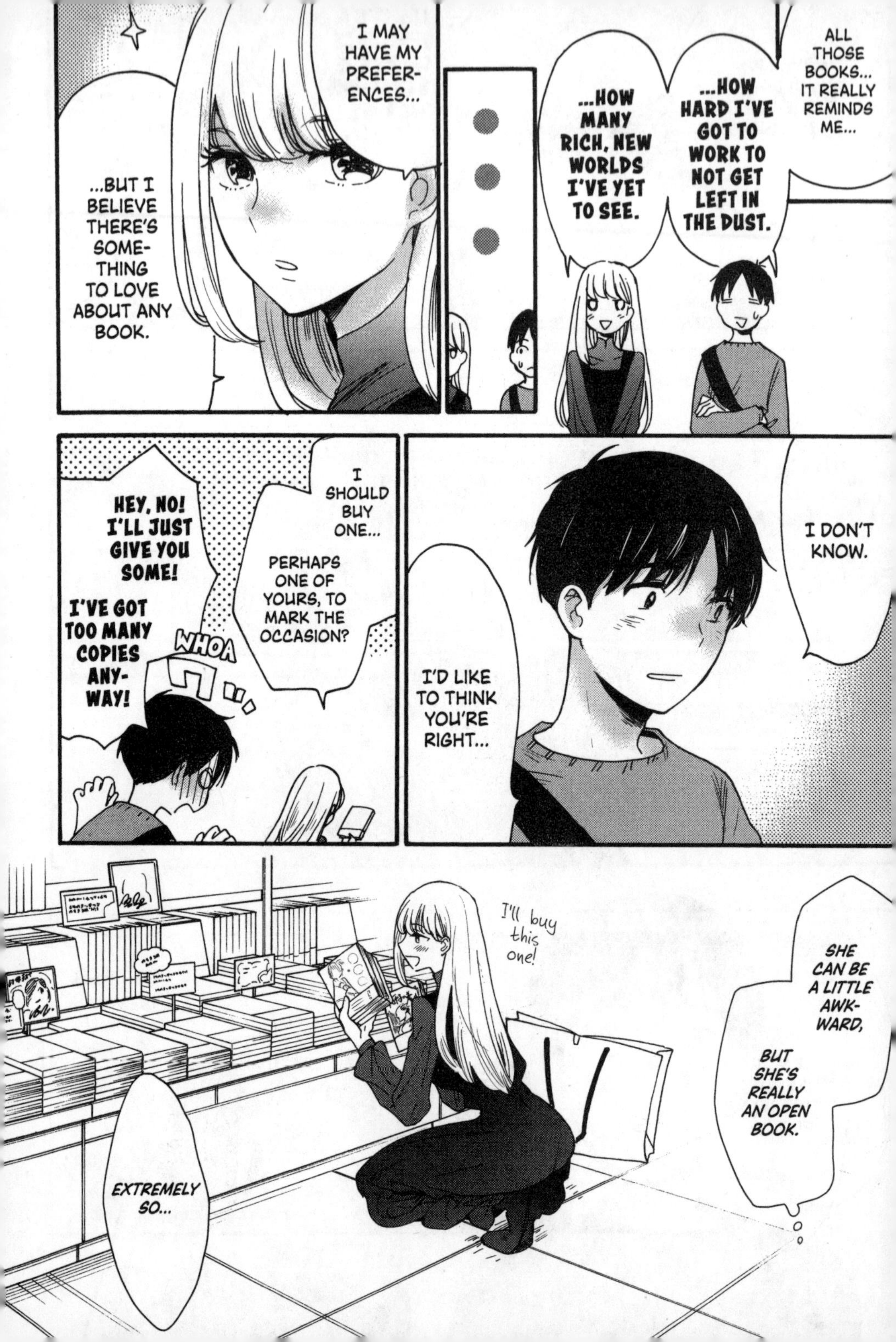
ALL THOSE BOOKS... IT REALLY REMINDS ME...
...HOW HARD I'VE GOT TO WORK TO NOT GET LEFT IN THE DUST.
...HOW MANY RICH, NEW WORLDS I'VE YET TO SEE.
I MAY HAVE MY PREFER-ENCES...
...BUT I BELIEVE THERE'S SOME-THING TO LOVE ABOUT ANY BOOK.
I DON'T KNOW.
I'D LIKE TO THINK YOU'RE RIGHT...
I SHOULD BUY ONE...
PERHAPS ONE OF YOURS, TO MARK THE OCCASION?
WHOA
HEY, NO! I'LL JUST GIVE YOU SOME!
I'VE GOT TOO MANY COPIES ANY-WAY!
SHE CAN BE A LITTLE AWK-WARD,
BUT SHE'S REALLY AN OPEN BOOK.
I'll buy this one!
EXTREMELY SO...

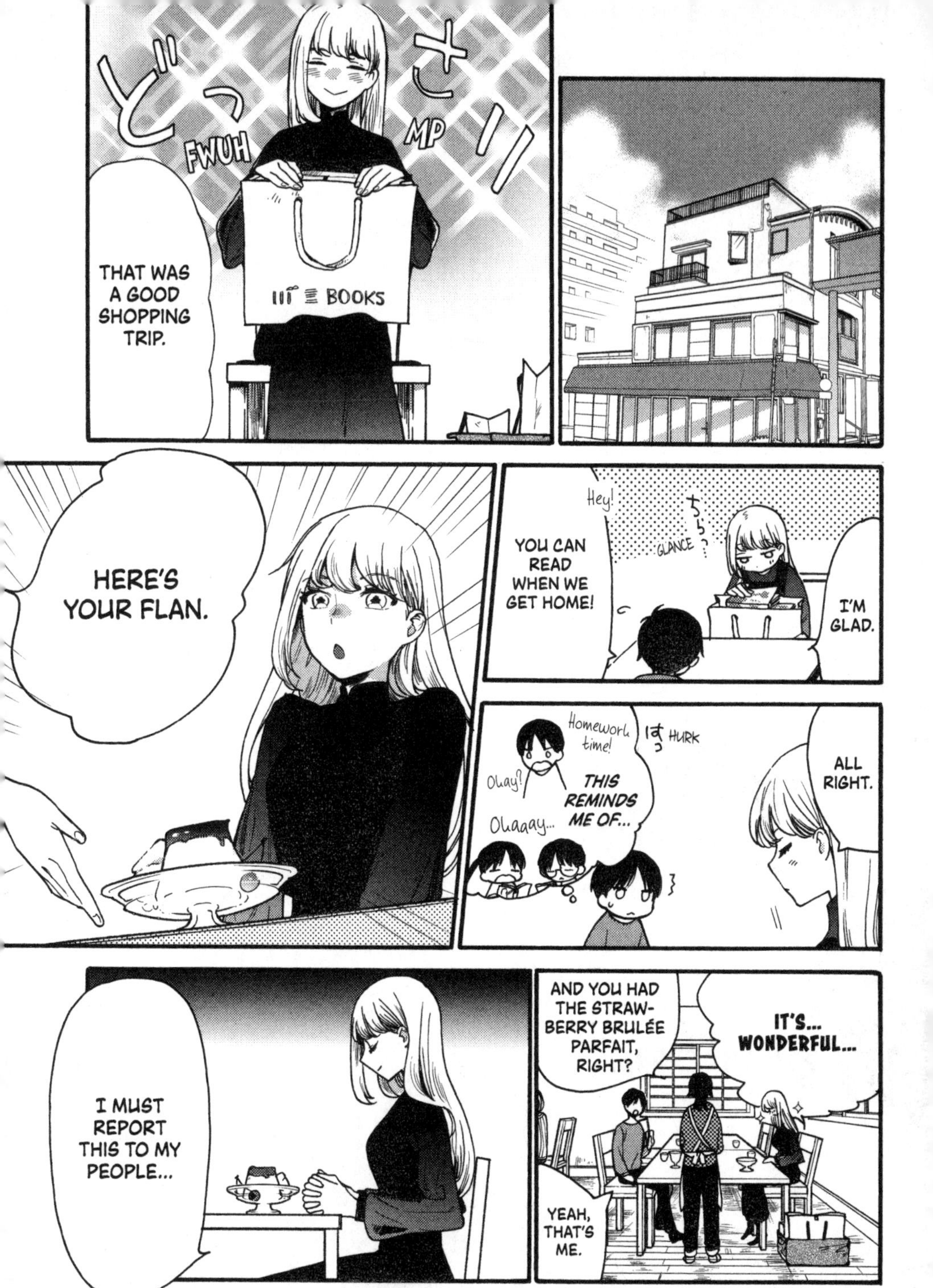
どっさ
FWUH
MP
THAT WAS A GOOD SHOPPING TRIP.
BOOKS
I'M GLAD.
Hey!
YOU CAN READ WHEN WE GET HOME!
ちら
GLANCE
ALL RIGHT.
はっ HURK
THIS REMINDS ME OF...
Homework time!
Okay?
Okaaay...
HERE'S YOUR FLAN.
IT'S... WONDERFUL...
AND YOU HAD THE STRAW-BERRY BRULÉE PARFAIT, RIGHT?
YEAH, THAT'S ME.
I MUST REPORT THIS TO MY PEOPLE...

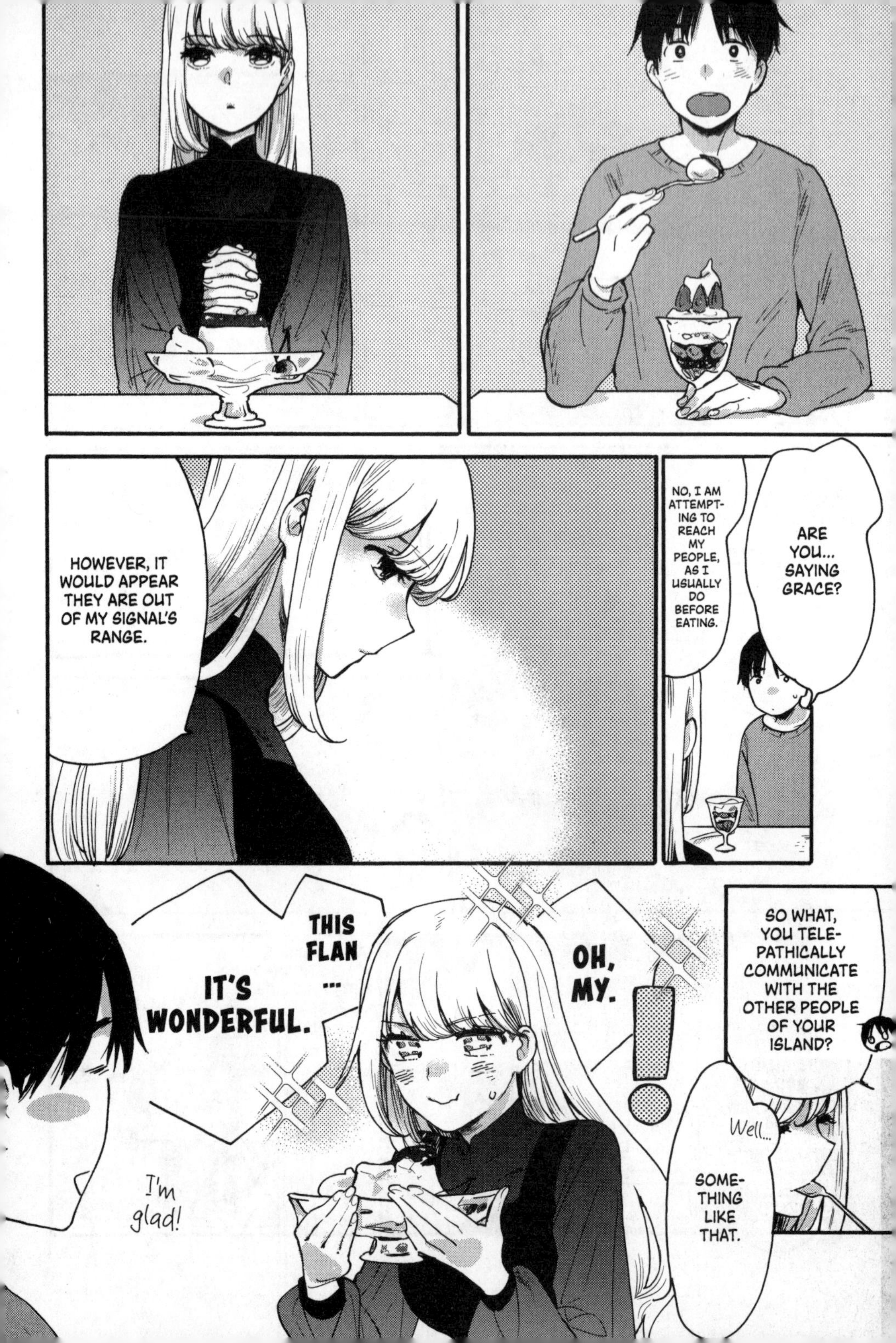
ARE YOU... SAYING GRACE?
NO, I AM ATTEMPTING TO REACH MY PEOPLE, AS I USUALLY DO BEFORE EATING.
HOWEVER, IT WOULD APPEAR THEY ARE OUT OF MY SIGNAL'S RANGE.
SO WHAT, YOU TELEPATHICALLY COMMUNICATE WITH THE OTHER PEOPLE OF YOUR ISLAND?
Well...
SOMETHING LIKE THAT.
OH, MY.
!
THIS FLAN ...
IT'S WONDERFUL.
I'm glad!

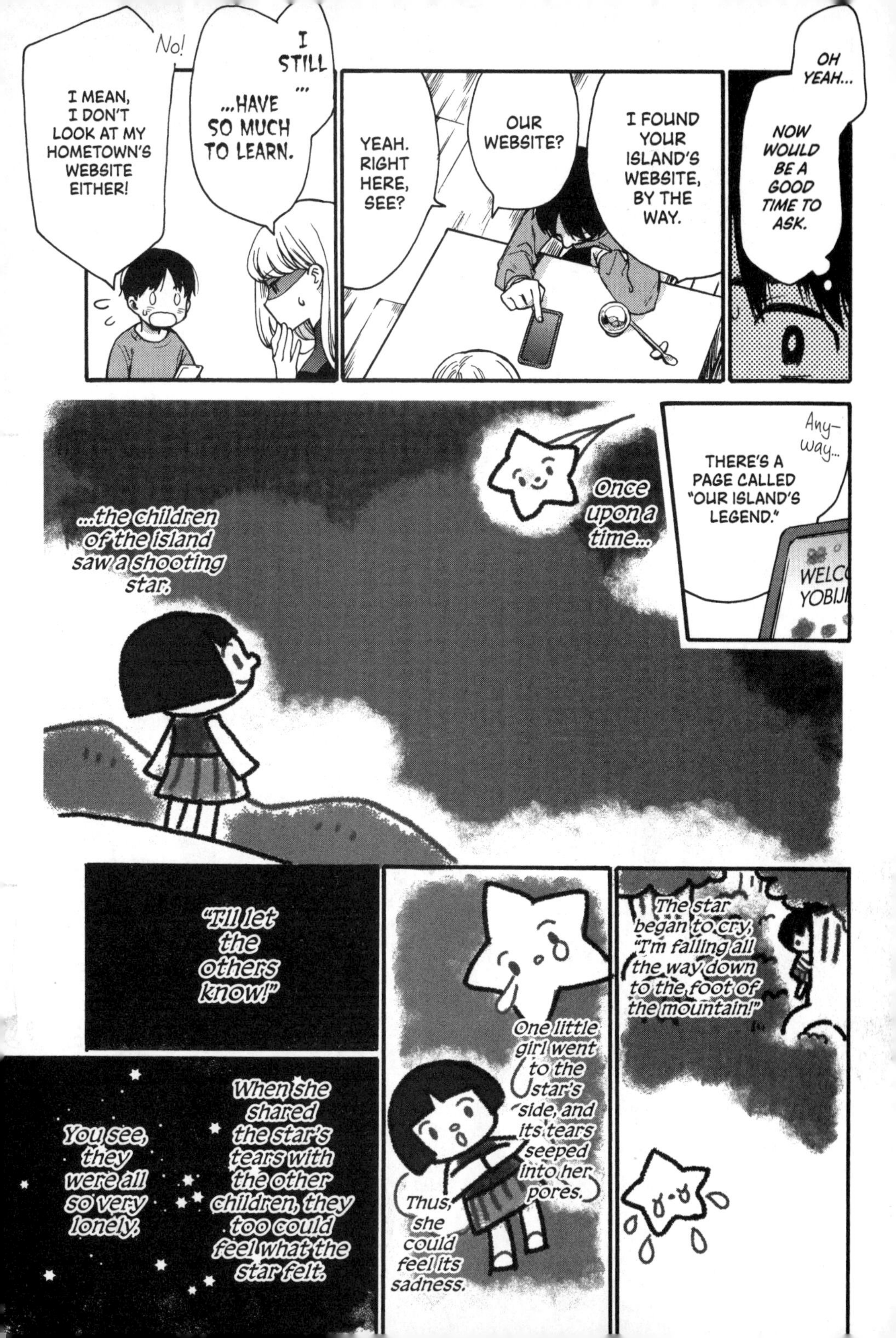
OH YEAH...
NOW WOULD BE A GOOD TIME TO ASK.
I FOUND YOUR ISLAND'S WEBSITE, BY THE WAY.
OUR WEBSITE?
YEAH. RIGHT HERE, SEE?
I STILL...
...HAVE SO MUCH TO LEARN.
No!
I MEAN, I DON'T LOOK AT MY HOMETOWN'S WEBSITE EITHER!
Any-way...
THERE'S A PAGE CALLED "OUR ISLAND'S LEGEND."
Once upon a time...
...the children of the island saw a shooting star.
The star began to cry, "I'm falling all the way down to the foot of the mountain!"
One little girl went to the star's side, and its tears seeped into her pores.
Thus, she could feel its sadness.
"I'll let the others know!"
When she shared the star's tears with the other children, they too could feel what the star felt.
You see, they were all so very lonely.

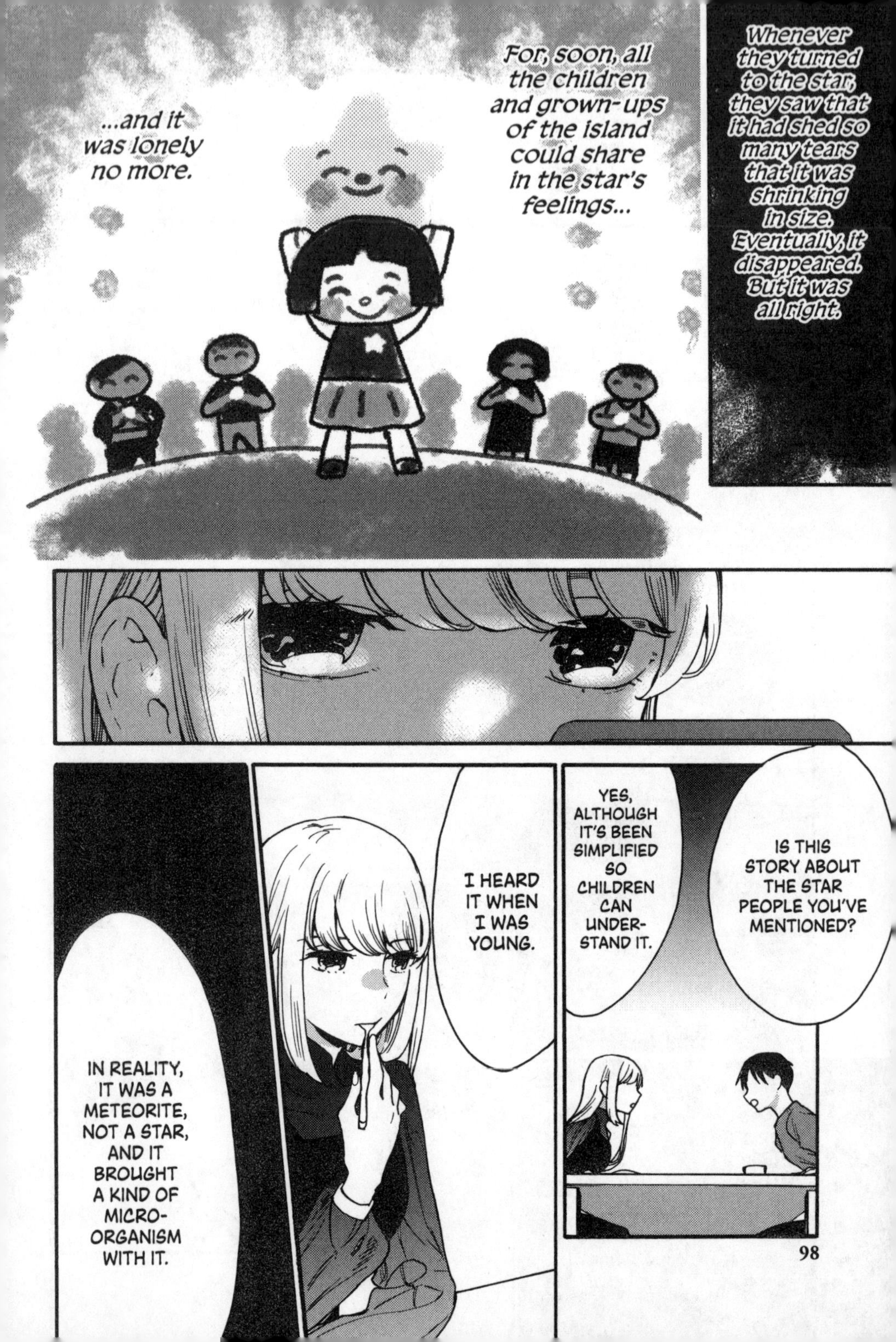

Whenever they turned to the star, they saw that it had shed so many tears that it was shrinking in size. Eventually, it disappeared. But it was all right.
For, soon, all the children and grown-ups of the island could share in the star's feelings...
...and it was lonely no more.
IS THIS STORY ABOUT THE STAR PEOPLE YOU'VE MENTIONED?
YES, ALTHOUGH IT'S BEEN SIMPLIFIED SO CHILDREN CAN UNDER-STAND IT.
I HEARD IT WHEN I WAS YOUNG.
IN REALITY, IT WAS A METEORITE, NOT A STAR, AND IT BROUGHT A KIND OF MICRO-ORGANISM WITH IT.

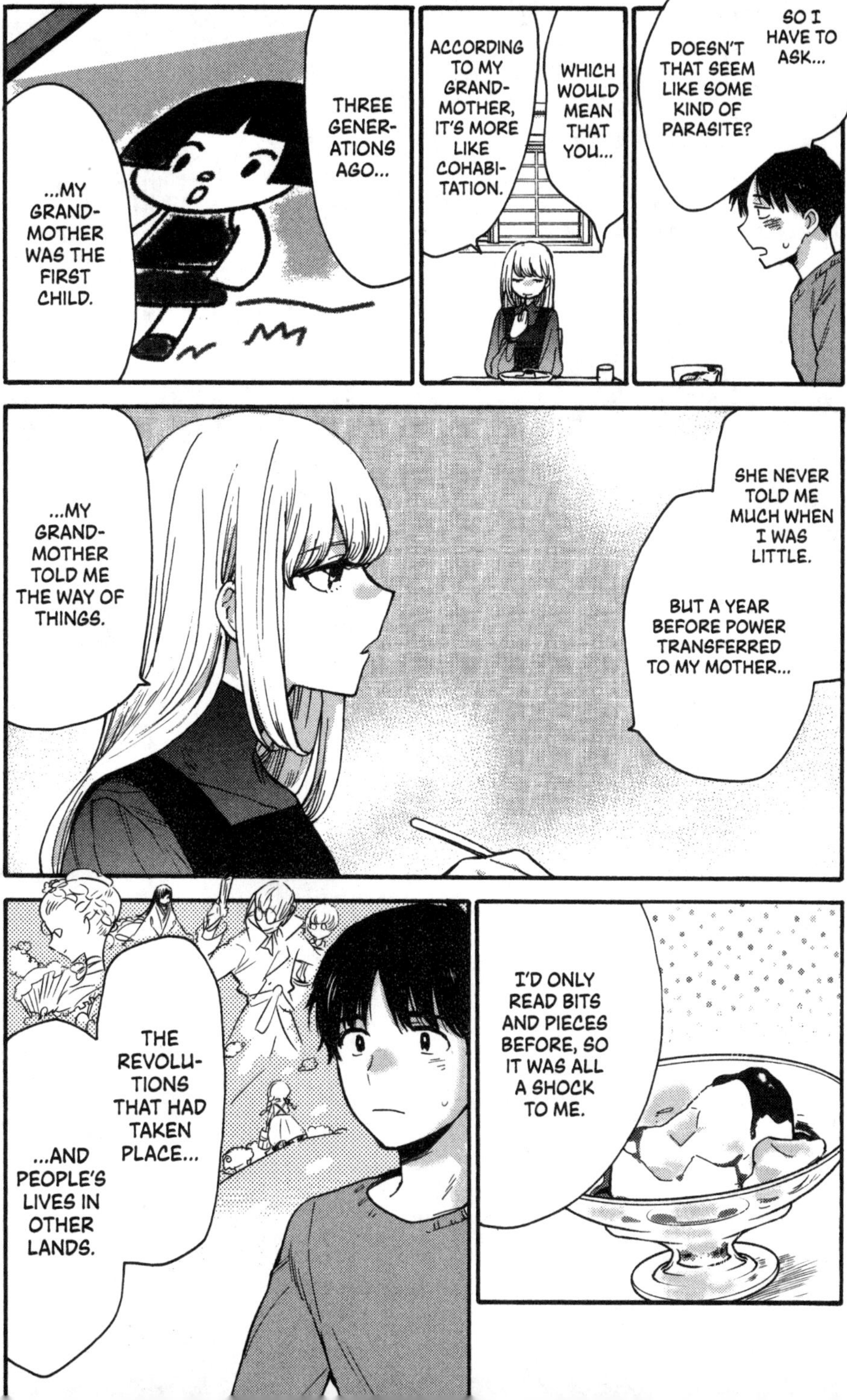
SO I HAVE TO ASK...
DOESN'T THAT SEEM LIKE SOME KIND OF PARASITE?
WHICH WOULD MEAN THAT YOU...
ACCORDING TO MY GRAND-MOTHER, IT'S MORE LIKE COHABI-TATION.
THREE GENER-ATIONS AGO...
...MY GRAND-MOTHER WAS THE FIRST CHILD.
SHE NEVER TOLD ME MUCH WHEN I WAS LITTLE.
BUT A YEAR BEFORE POWER TRANSFERRED TO MY MOTHER...
...MY GRAND-MOTHER TOLD ME THE WAY OF THINGS.
I'D ONLY READ BITS AND PIECES BEFORE, SO IT WAS ALL A SHOCK TO ME.
THE REVOLU-TIONS THAT HAD TAKEN PLACE...
...AND PEOPLE'S LIVES IN OTHER LANDS.

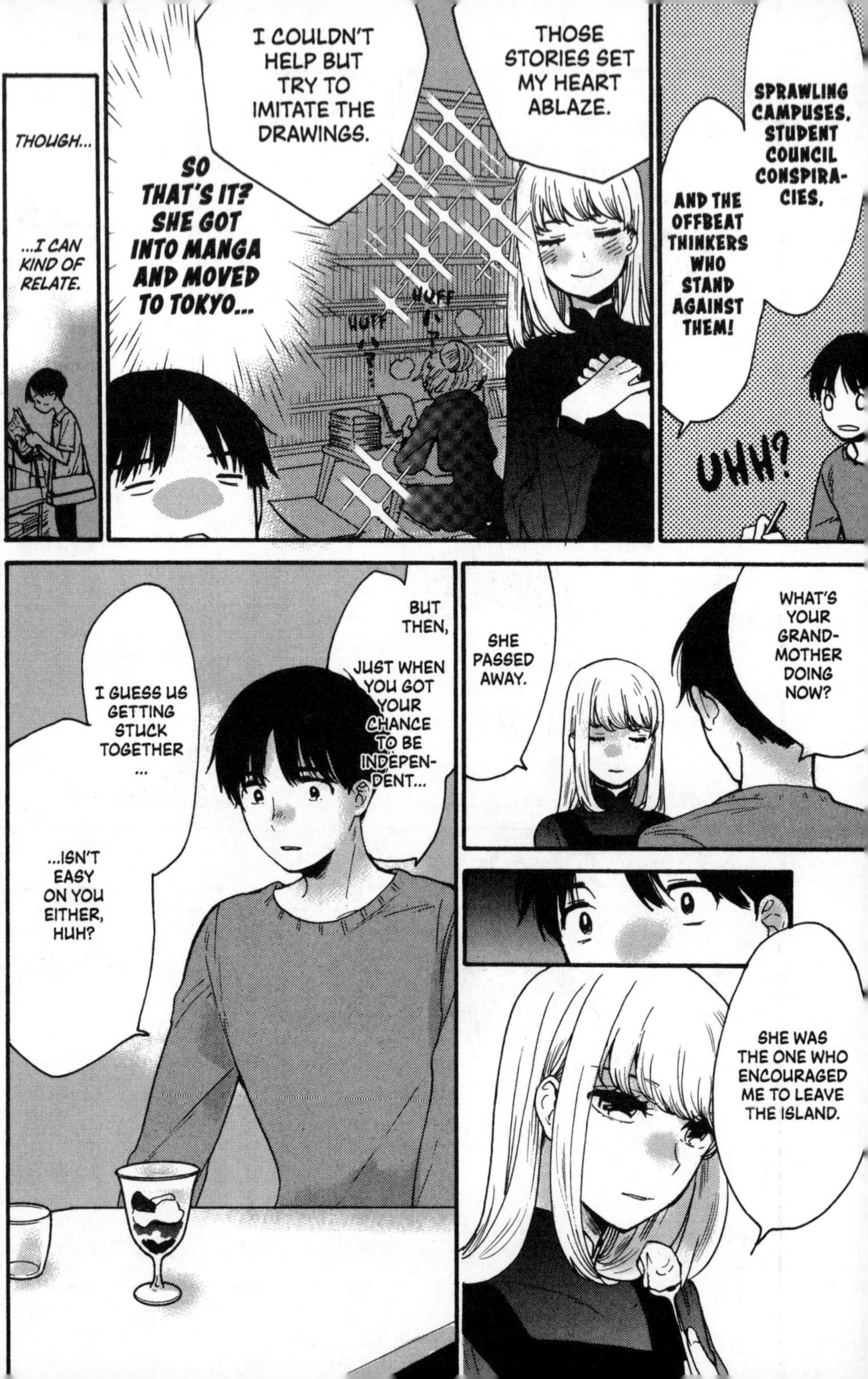
SPRAWLING CAMPUSES, STUDENT COUNCIL CONSPIRACIES,
AND THE OFFBEAT THINKERS WHO STAND AGAINST THEM!
UHH?
THOSE STORIES SET MY HEART ABLAZE.
I COULDN'T HELP BUT TRY TO IMITATE THE DRAWINGS.
HUFF
HUFF
SO THAT'S IT? SHE GOT INTO MANGA AND MOVED TO TOKYO...
THOUGH...
...I CAN KIND OF RELATE.
WHAT'S YOUR GRANDMOTHER DOING NOW?
SHE PASSED AWAY.
SHE WAS THE ONE WHO ENCOURAGED ME TO LEAVE THE ISLAND.
BUT THEN,
JUST WHEN YOU GOT YOUR CHANCE TO BE INDEPENDENT...
I GUESS US GETTING STUCK TOGETHER...
...ISN'T EASY ON YOU EITHER, HUH?

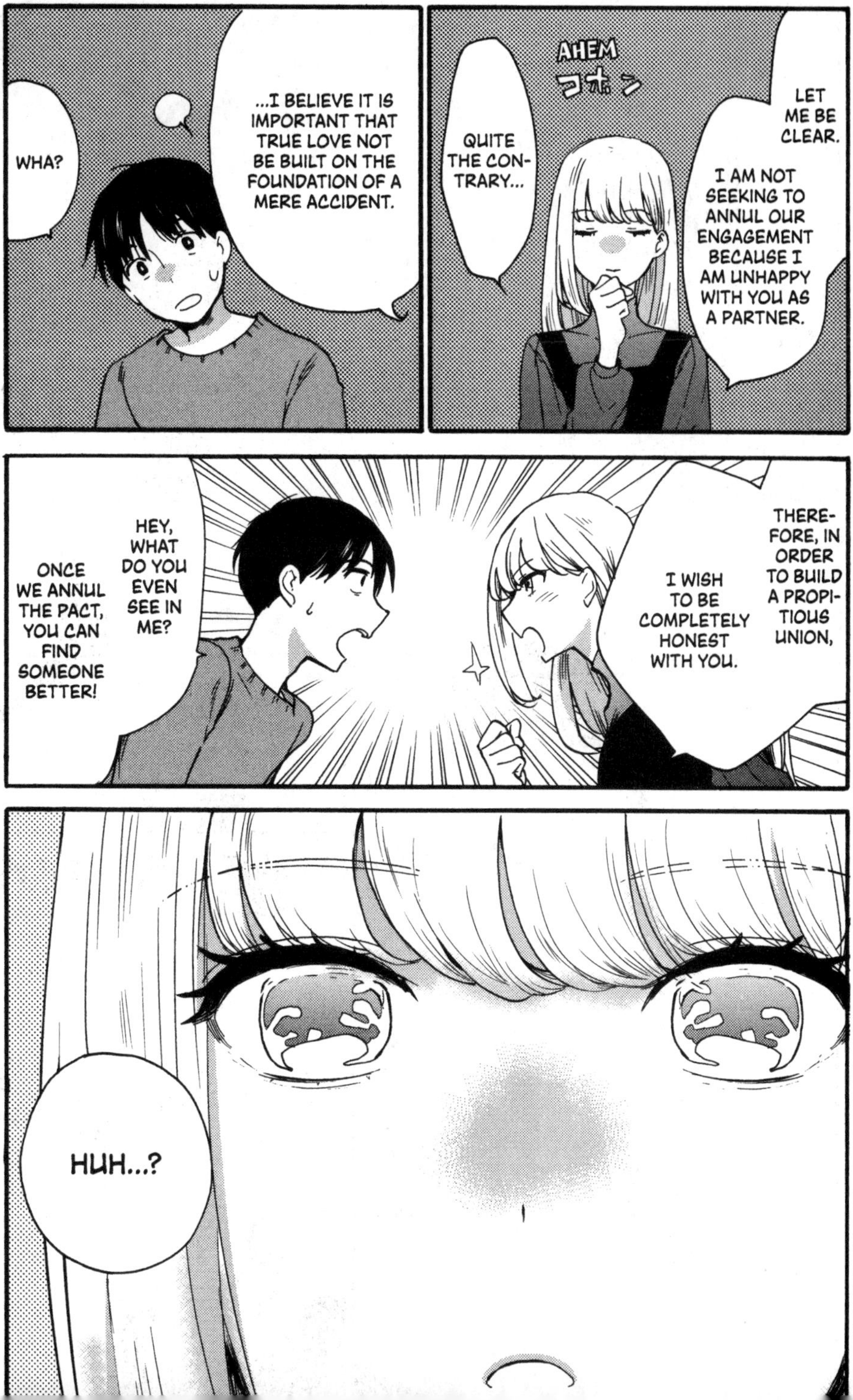
LET ME BE CLEAR.
I AM NOT SEEKING TO ANNUL OUR ENGAGEMENT BECAUSE I AM UNHAPPY WITH YOU AS A PARTNER.
AHEM
コホン
QUITE THE CON-TRARY...
...I BELIEVE IT IS IMPORTANT THAT TRUE LOVE NOT BE BUILT ON THE FOUNDATION OF A MERE ACCIDENT.
WHA?
THERE-FORE, IN ORDER TO BUILD A PROPI-TIOUS UNION,
I WISH TO BE COMPLETELY HONEST WITH YOU.
HEY, WHAT DO YOU EVEN SEE IN ME?
ONCE WE ANNUL THE PACT, YOU CAN FIND SOMEONE BETTER!
HUH...?

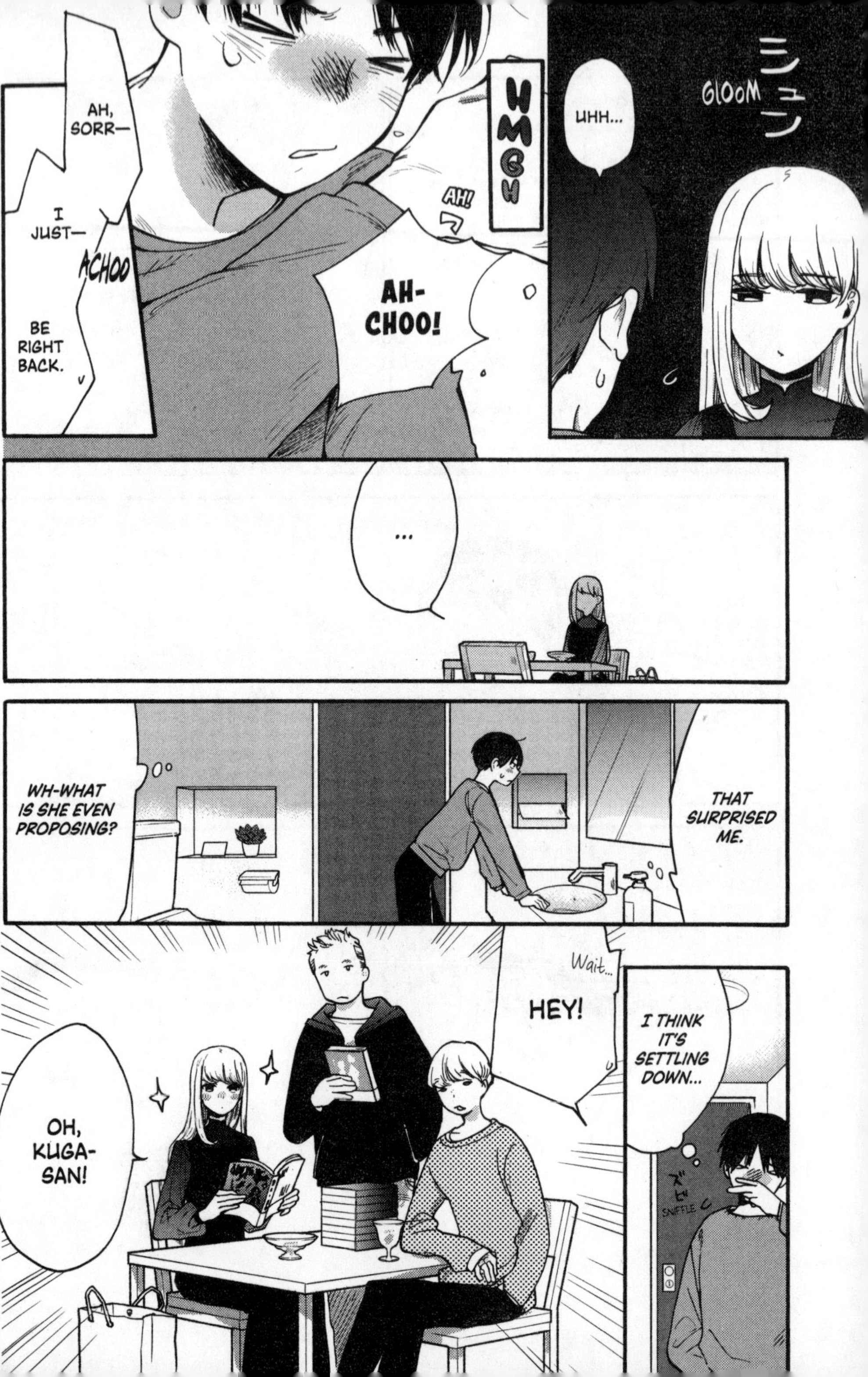
GLOOM
UHH...
HMGH
AH!
AH-CHOO!
AH, SORR—
I JUST—
ACHOO
BE RIGHT BACK.
...
THAT SURPRISED ME.
WH-WHAT IS SHE EVEN PROPOSING?
I THINK IT'S SETTLING DOWN...
SNIFFLE
Wait...
HEY!
OH, KUGA-SAN!

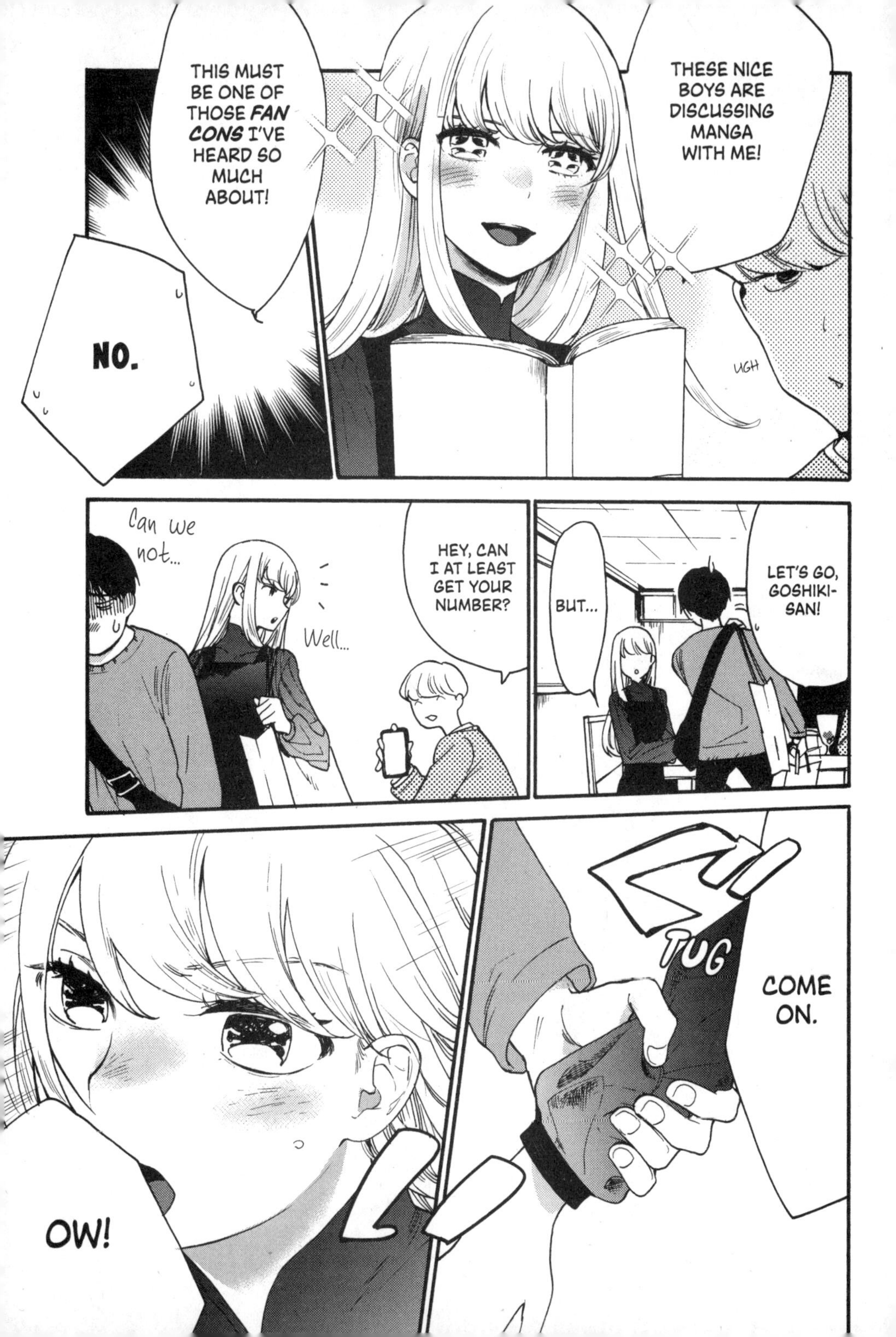

THESE NICE BOYS ARE DISCUSSING MANGA WITH ME!
THIS MUST BE ONE OF THOSE *FAN CONS* I'VE HEARD SO MUCH ABOUT!
UGH
NO.
LET'S GO, GOSHIKI-SAN!
BUT...
HEY, CAN I AT LEAST GET YOUR NUMBER?
Well...
Can we not...
TUG
COME ON.
OW!

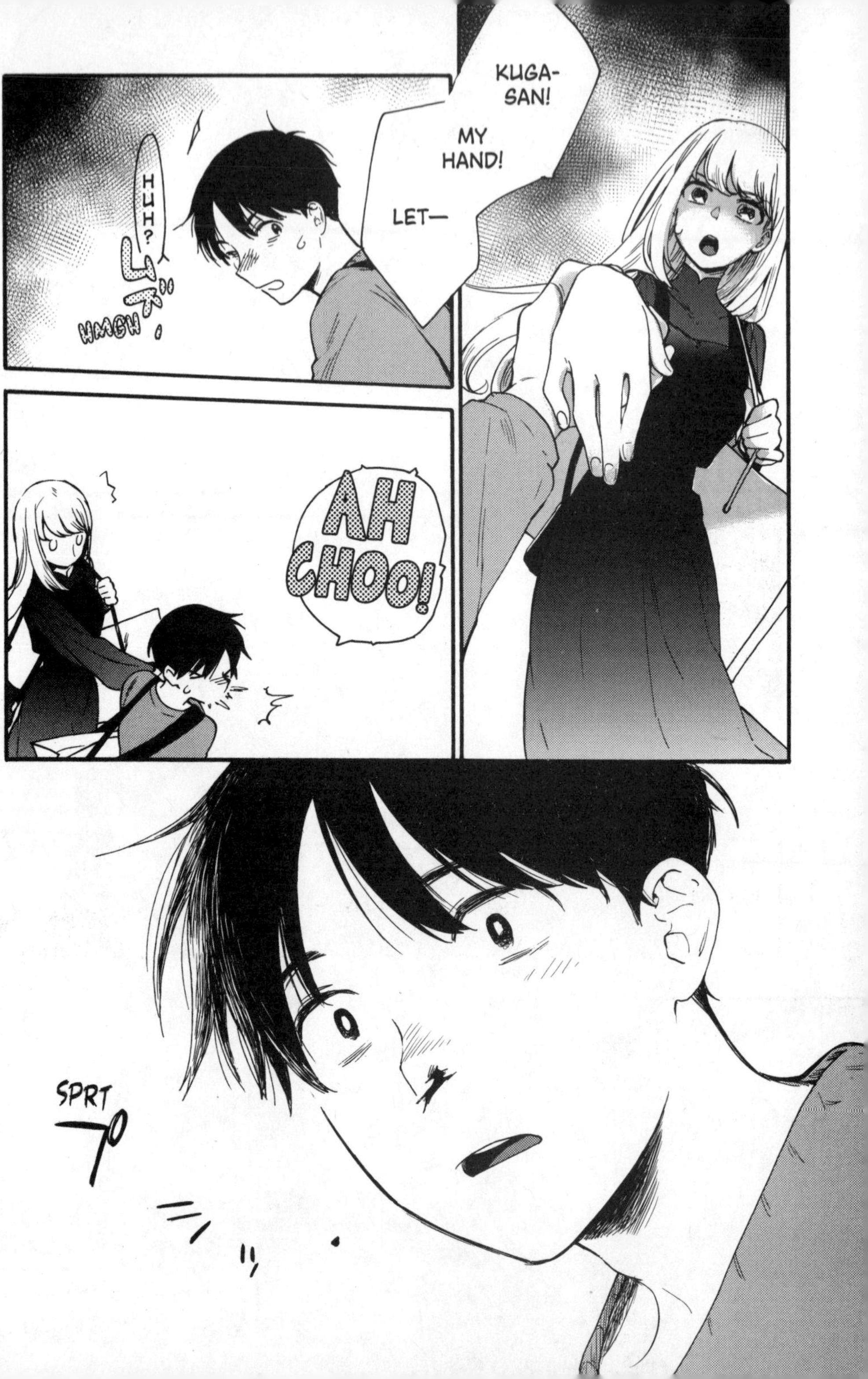
KUGA-SAN!
MY HAND!
LET—
HUH?
ムズ
HMGH
AH CHOO!
SPRT

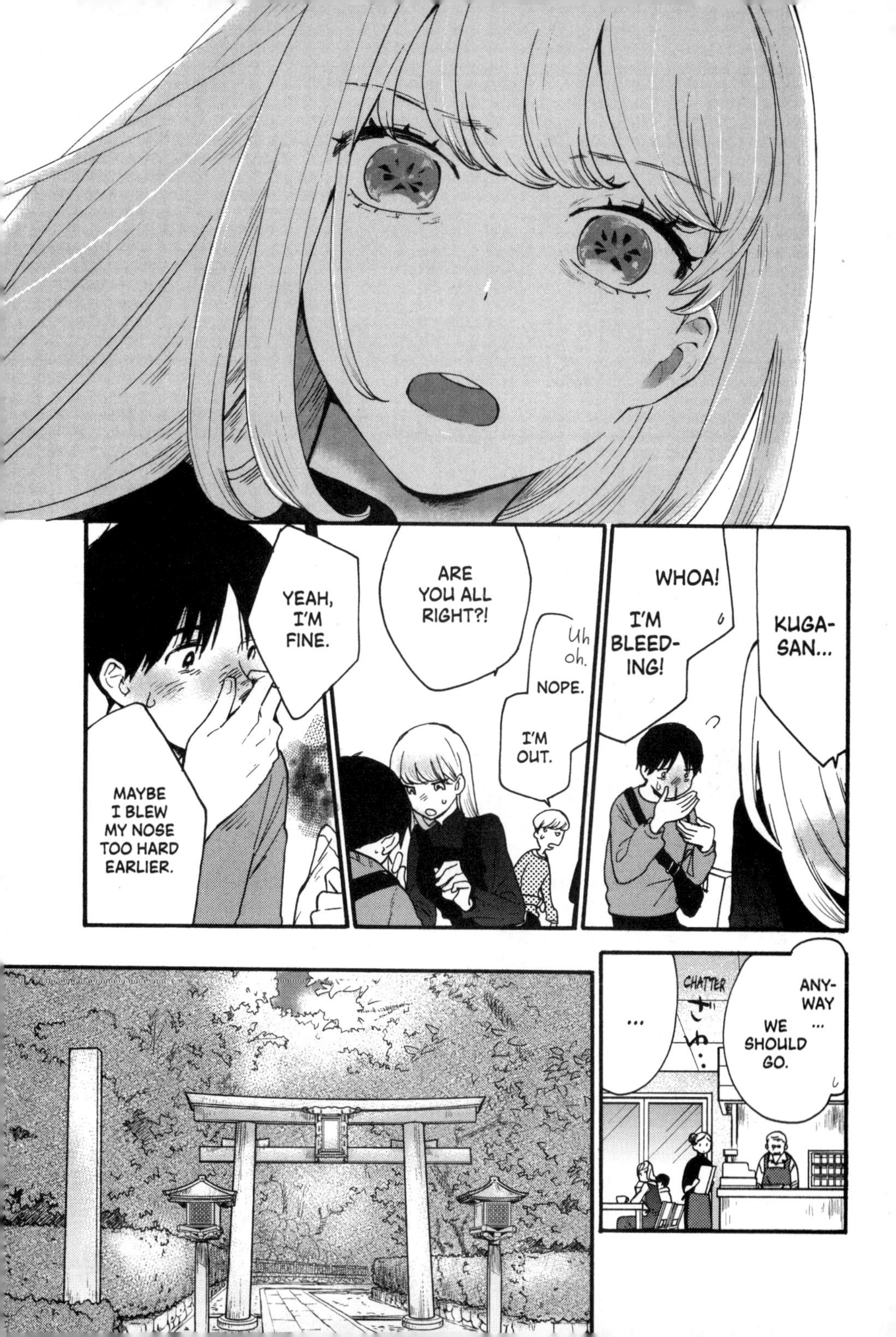
KUGA-SAN...
WHOA!
I'M BLEEDING!
ARE YOU ALL RIGHT?!
Uh oh.
NOPE.
I'M OUT.
YEAH, I'M FINE.
MAYBE I BLEW MY NOSE TOO HARD EARLIER.
ANYWAY... WE SHOULD GO.
...
CHATTER

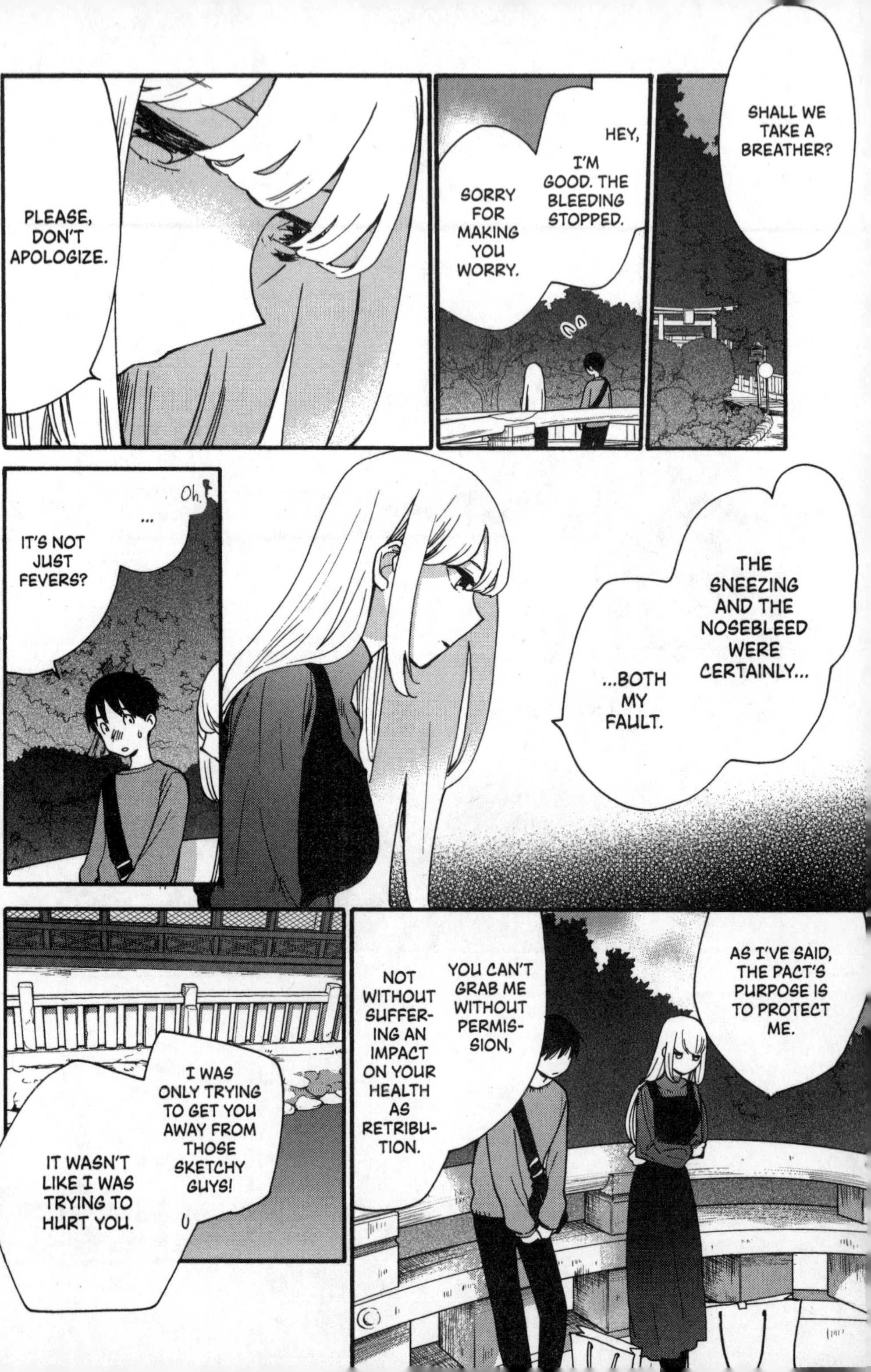
SHALL WE TAKE A BREATHER?
HEY,
I'M GOOD. THE BLEEDING STOPPED.
SORRY FOR MAKING YOU WORRY.
PLEASE, DON'T APOLOGIZE.
THE SNEEZING AND THE NOSEBLEED WERE CERTAINLY...
...BOTH MY FAULT.
Oh.
...
IT'S NOT JUST FEVERS?
AS I'VE SAID, THE PACT'S PURPOSE IS TO PROTECT ME.
YOU CAN'T GRAB ME WITHOUT PERMISSION,
NOT WITHOUT SUFFERING AN IMPACT ON YOUR HEALTH AS RETRIBUTION.
I WAS ONLY TRYING TO GET YOU AWAY FROM THOSE SKETCHY GUYS!
IT WASN'T LIKE I WAS TRYING TO HURT YOU.

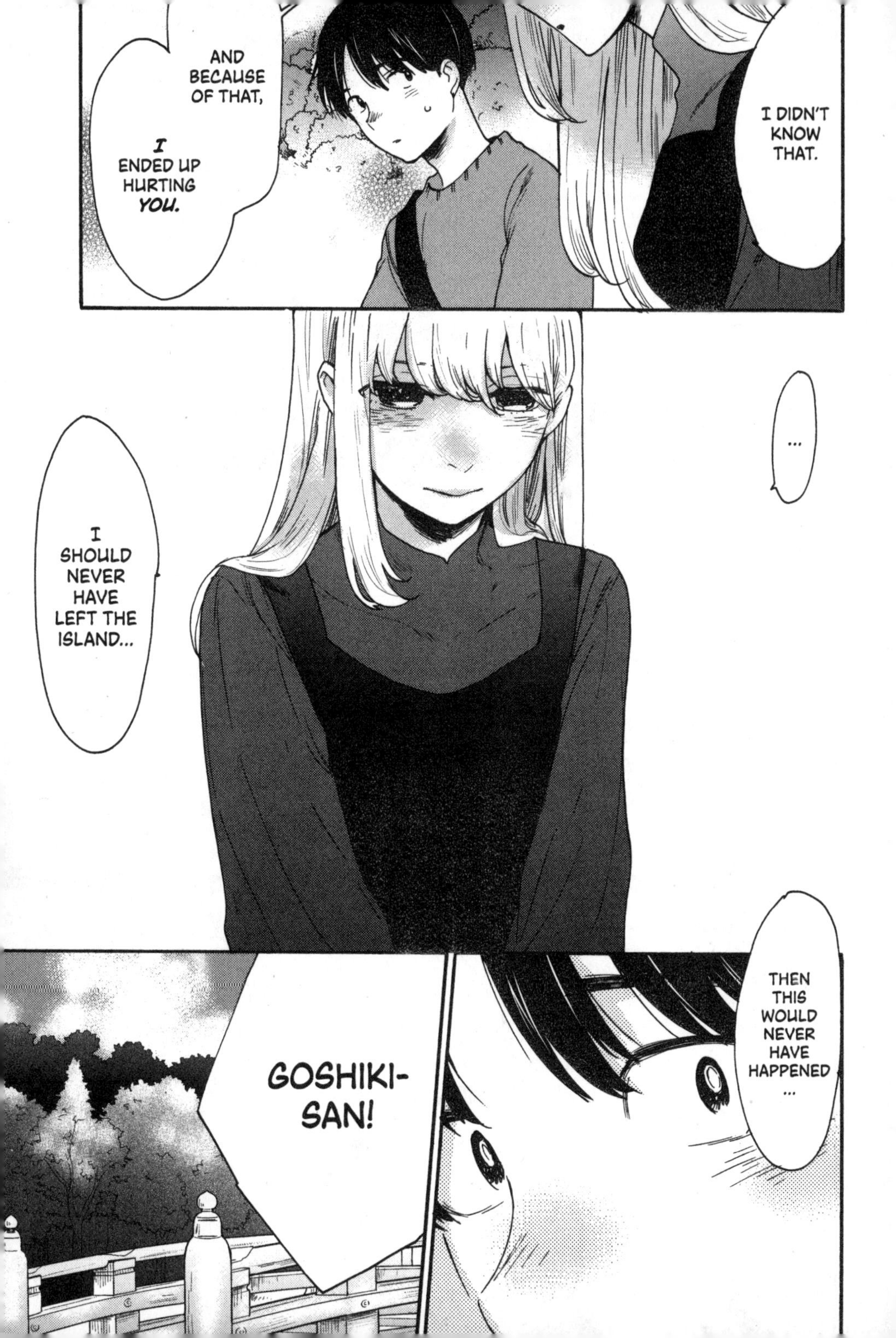
I DIDN'T KNOW THAT.
AND BECAUSE OF THAT, I ENDED UP HURTING YOU.
...
I SHOULD NEVER HAVE LEFT THE ISLAND...
THEN THIS WOULD NEVER HAVE HAPPENED...
GOSHIKI-SAN!

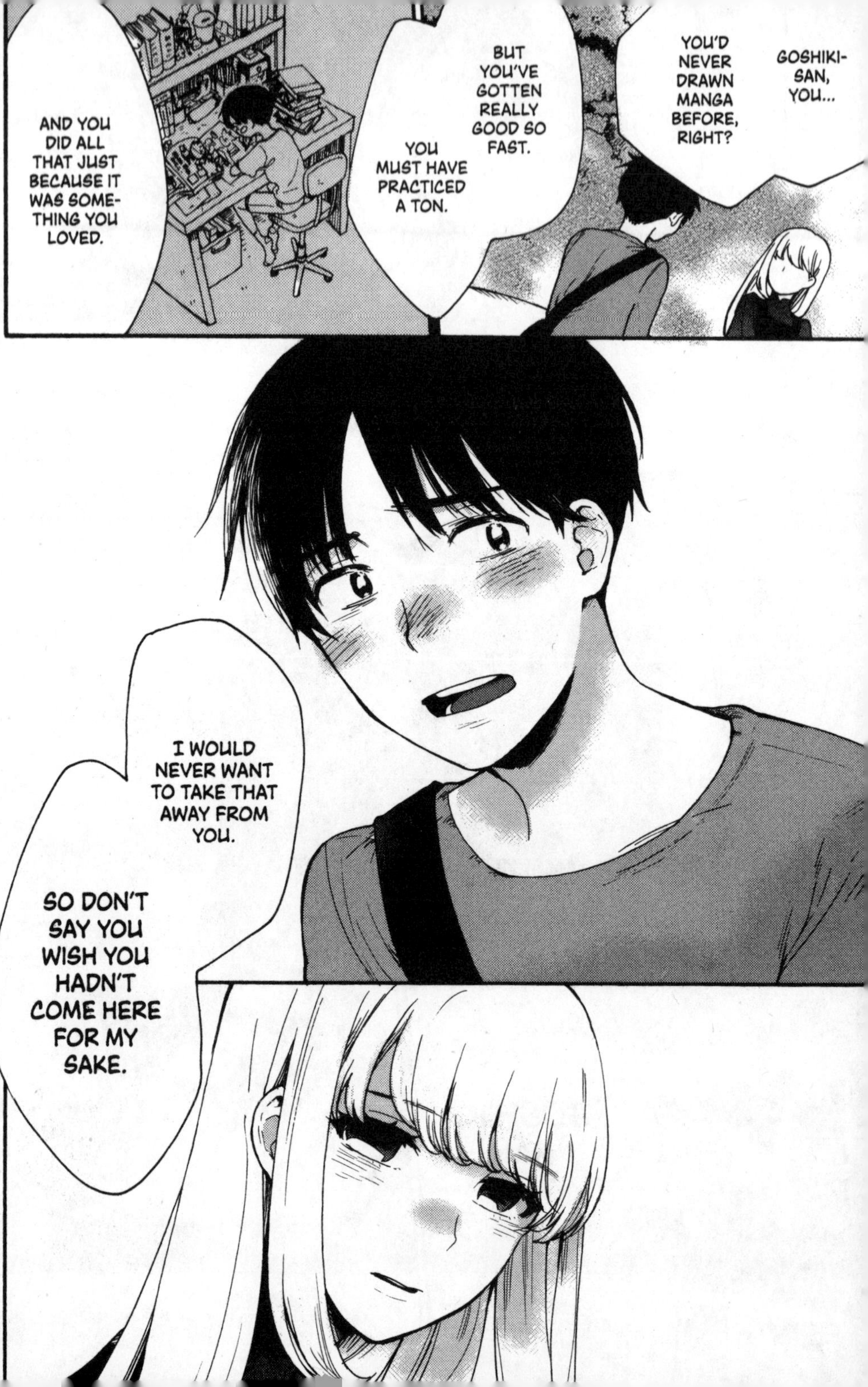
GOSHIKI-SAN, YOU...
YOU'D NEVER DRAWN MANGA BEFORE, RIGHT?
BUT YOU'VE GOTTEN REALLY GOOD SO FAST.
YOU MUST HAVE PRACTICED A TON.
AND YOU DID ALL THAT JUST BECAUSE IT WAS SOMETHING YOU LOVED.
I WOULD NEVER WANT TO TAKE THAT AWAY FROM YOU.
SO DON'T SAY YOU WISH YOU HADN'T COME HERE FOR MY SAKE.

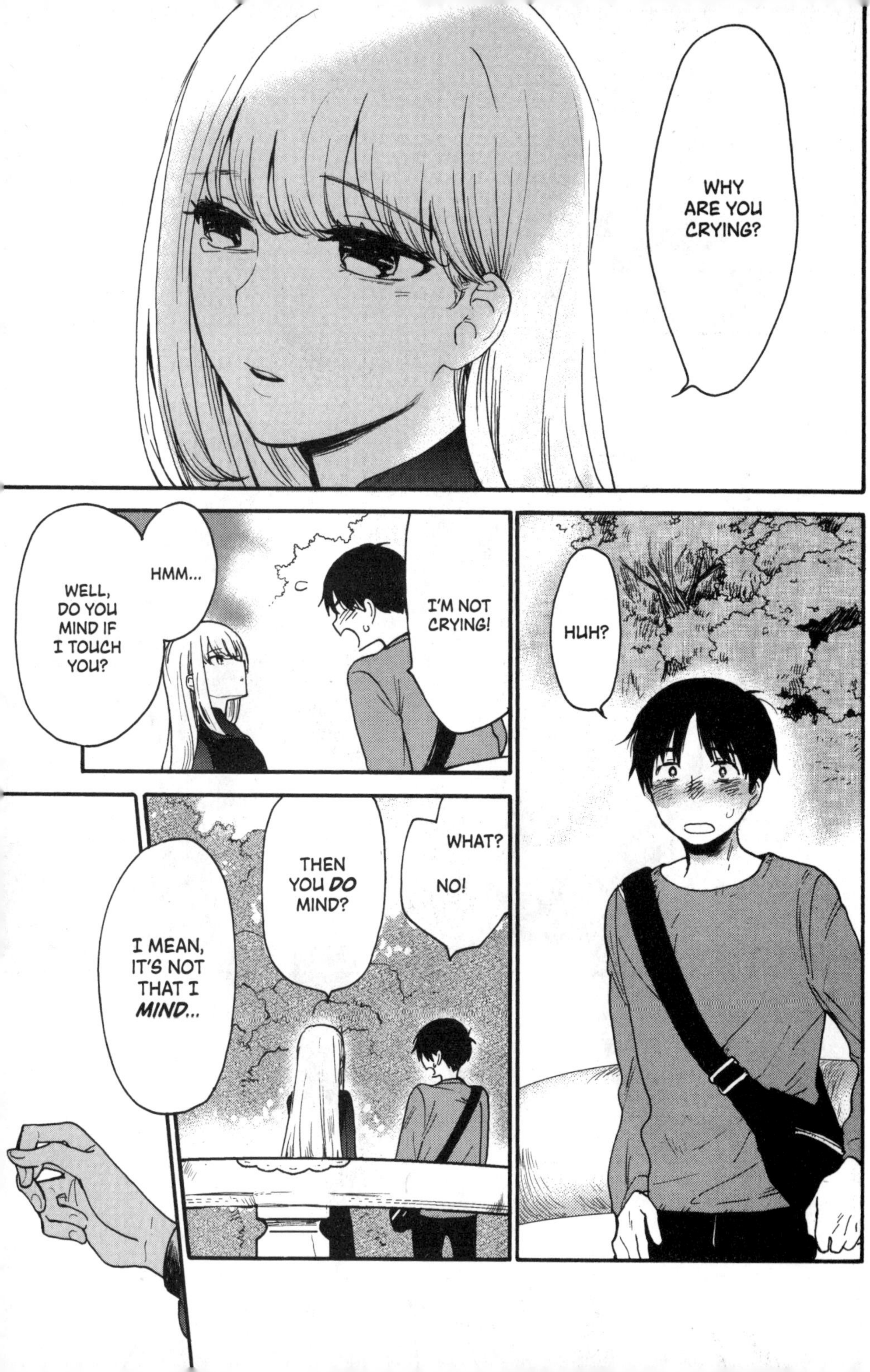

WHY ARE YOU CRYING?
HUH?
I'M NOT CRYING!
HMM...
WELL, DO YOU MIND IF I TOUCH YOU?
WHAT?
NO!
THEN YOU *DO* MIND?
I MEAN, IT'S NOT THAT I ***MIND***...

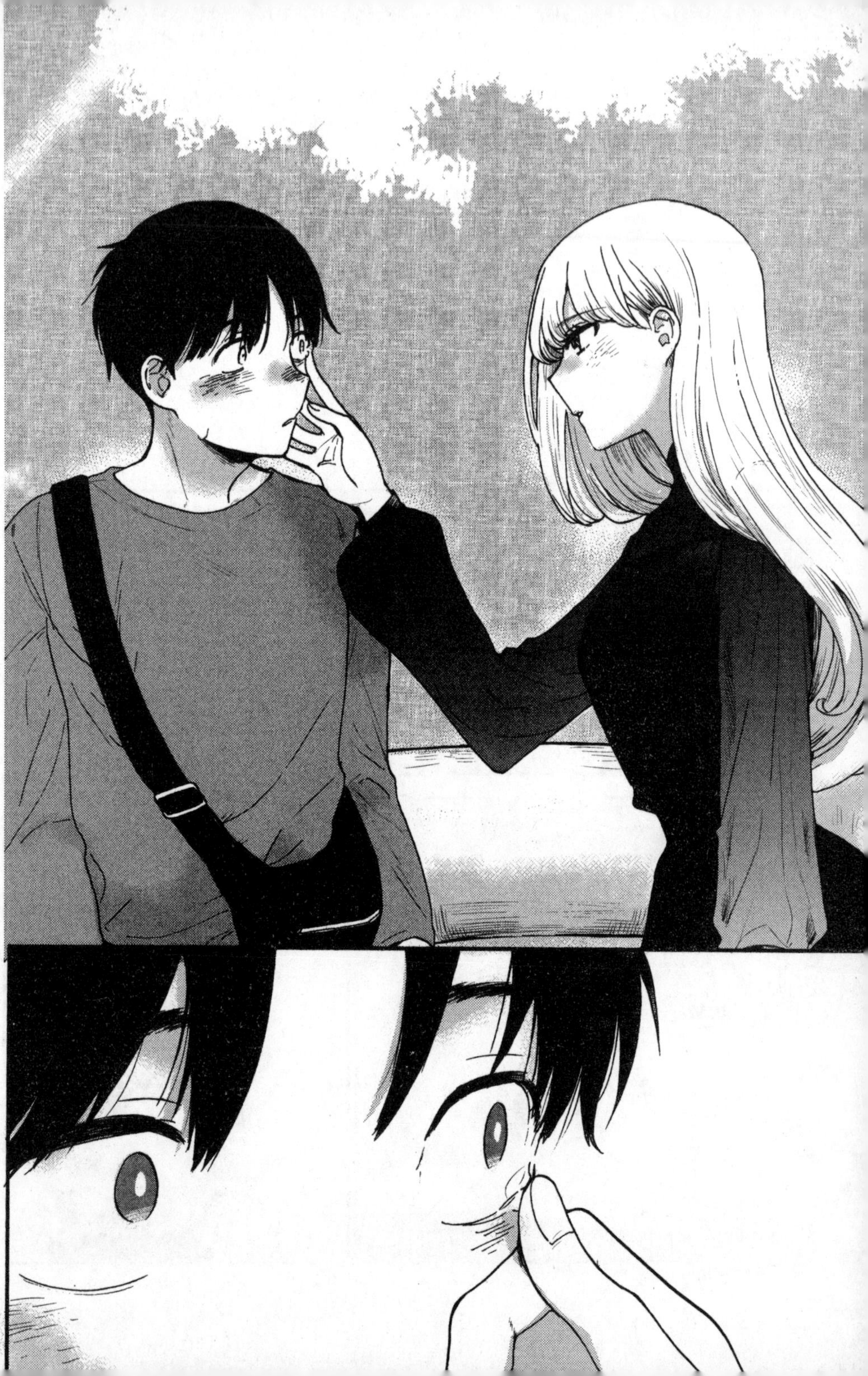

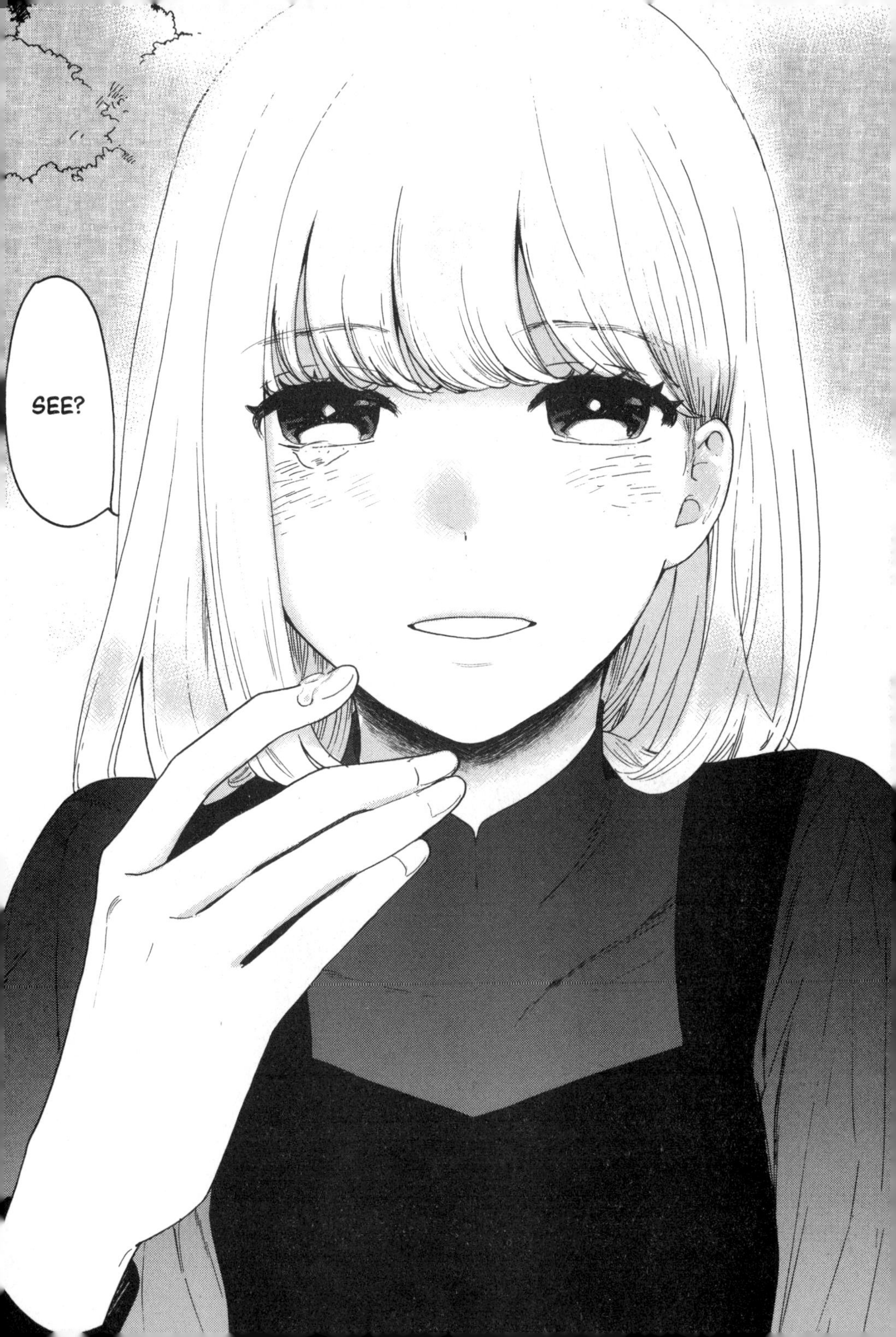
SEE?

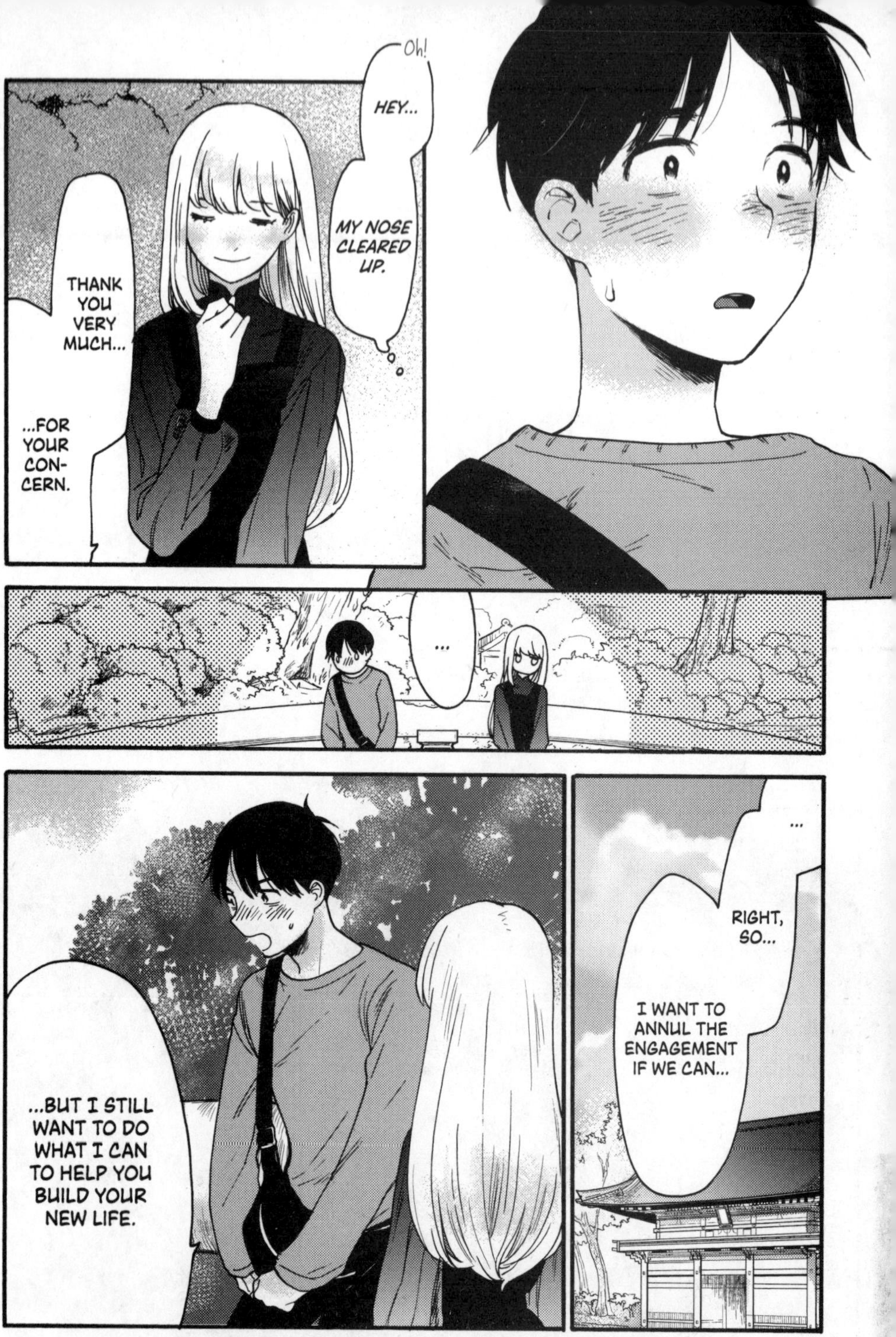
Oh!
HEY...
MY NOSE CLEARED UP.
THANK YOU VERY MUCH...
...FOR YOUR CON-CERN.
...
...
RIGHT, SO...
I WANT TO ANNUL THE ENGAGEMENT IF WE CAN...
...BUT I STILL WANT TO DO WHAT I CAN TO HELP YOU BUILD YOUR NEW LIFE.

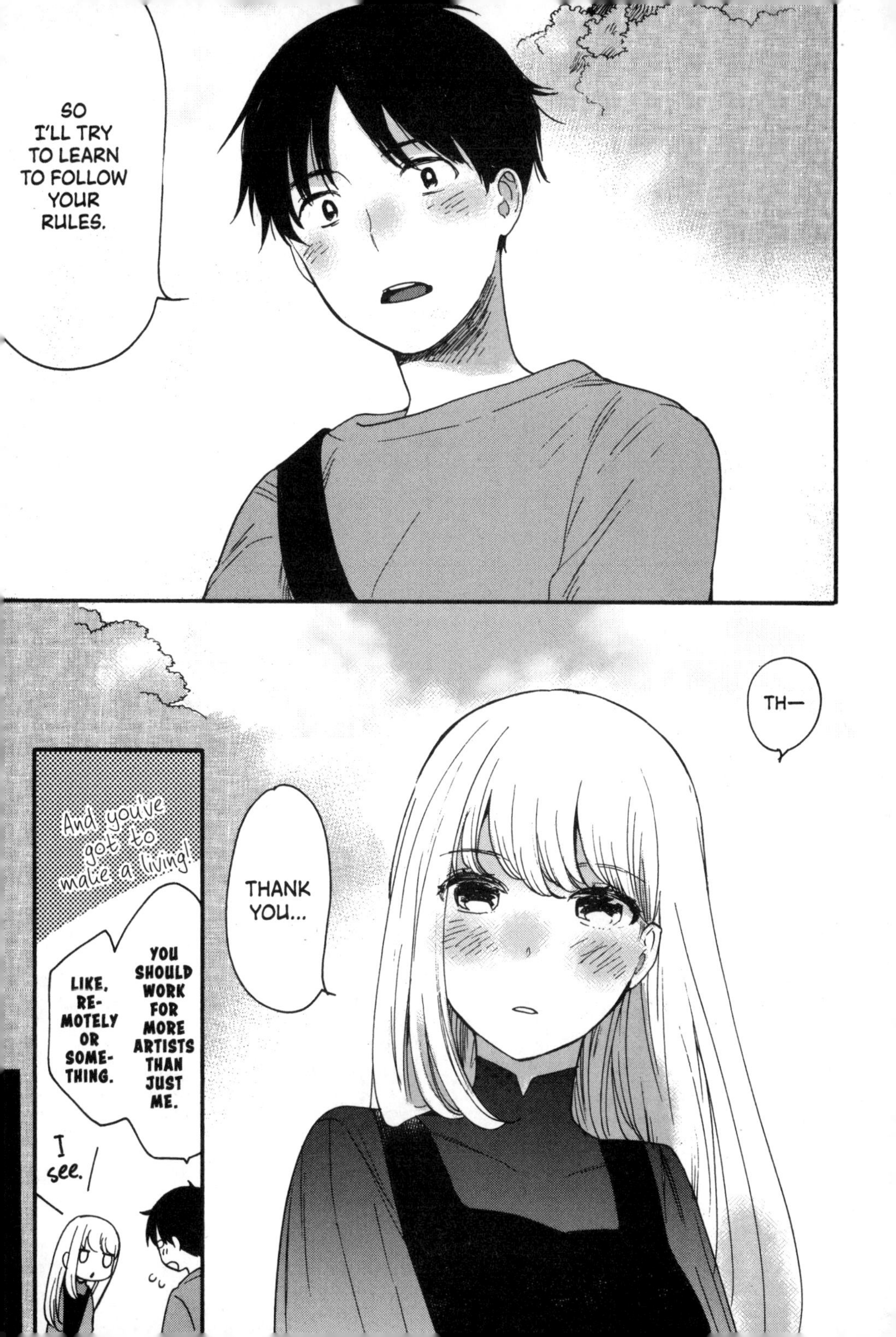
SO I'LL TRY TO LEARN TO FOLLOW YOUR RULES.
TH—
THANK YOU...
And you've got to make a living!
YOU SHOULD WORK FOR MORE ARTISTS THAN JUST ME.
LIKE, RE-MOTELY OR SOME-THING.
I see.

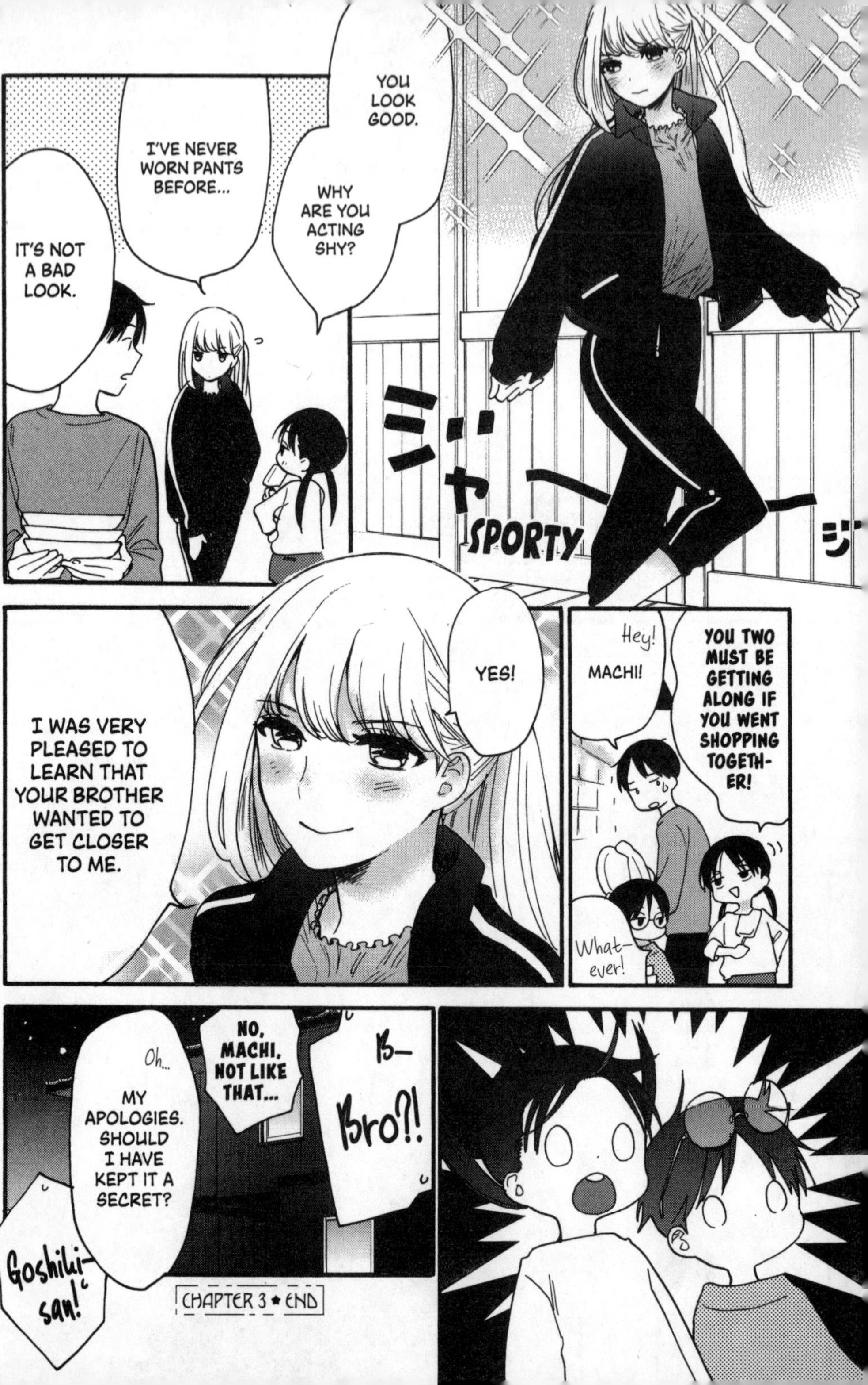
SPORTY
YOU LOOK GOOD.
WHY ARE YOU ACTING SHY?
I'VE NEVER WORN PANTS BEFORE...
IT'S NOT A BAD LOOK.
YOU TWO MUST BE GETTING ALONG IF YOU WENT SHOPPING TOGETH- ER!
Hey! MACHI!
What- ever!
YES!
I WAS VERY PLEASED TO LEARN THAT YOUR BROTHER WANTED TO GET CLOSER TO ME.
B— Bro?!
NO, MACHI, NOT LIKE THAT...
Oh... MY APOLOGIES. SHOULD I HAVE KEPT IT A SECRET?
Goshiki-san!
CHAPTER 3 ★ END

My heart's pounding...

?

A Galaxy
Next Door

Gido
Amagakure

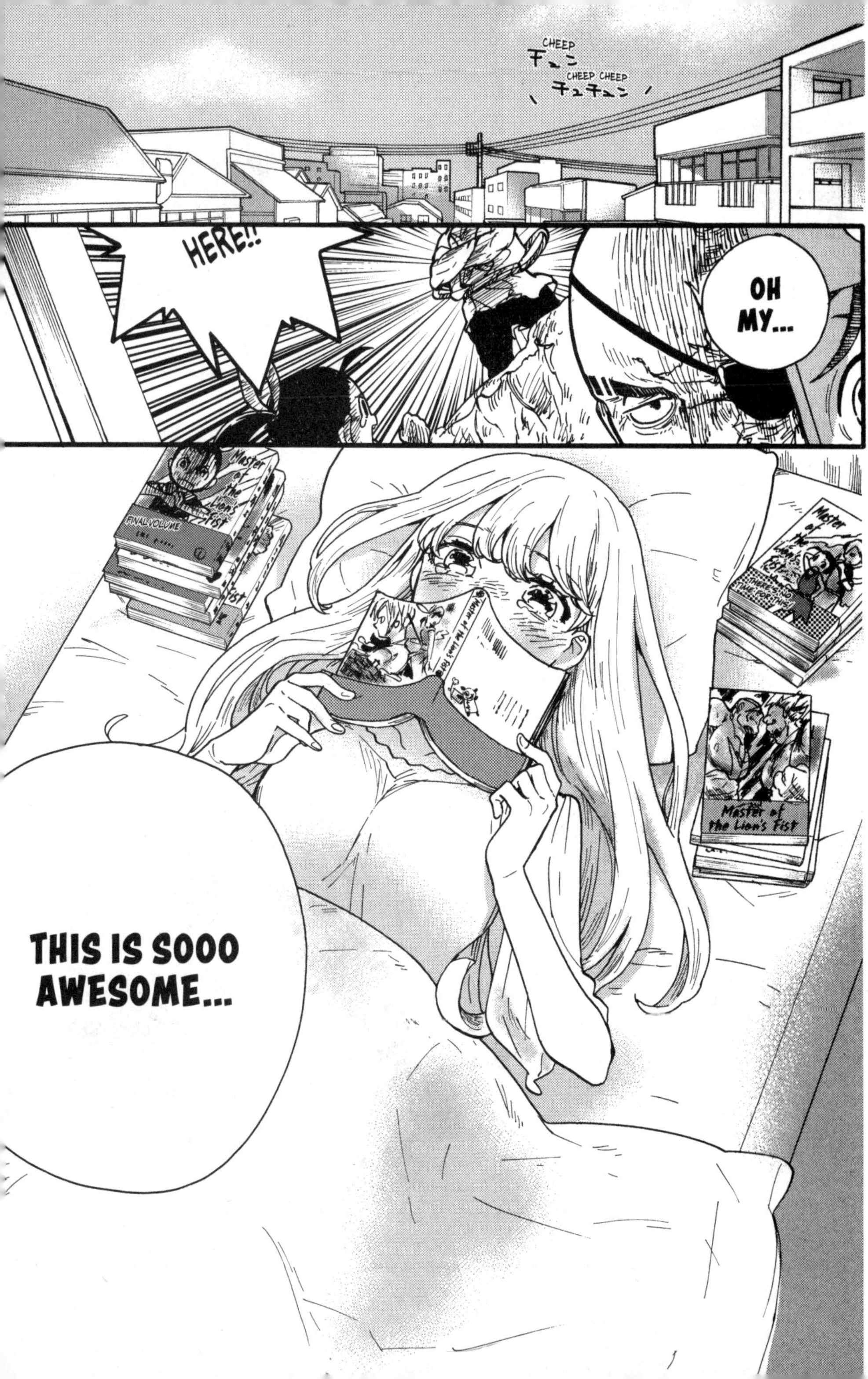
CHEEP
チュン
CHEEP CHEEP
チュチュン
OH MY...
HERE!!
Master of the Lion's Fist
Master of the Lion's Fist
FINAL VOLUME
Master of the Lion's Fist
THIS IS SOOO AWESOME...

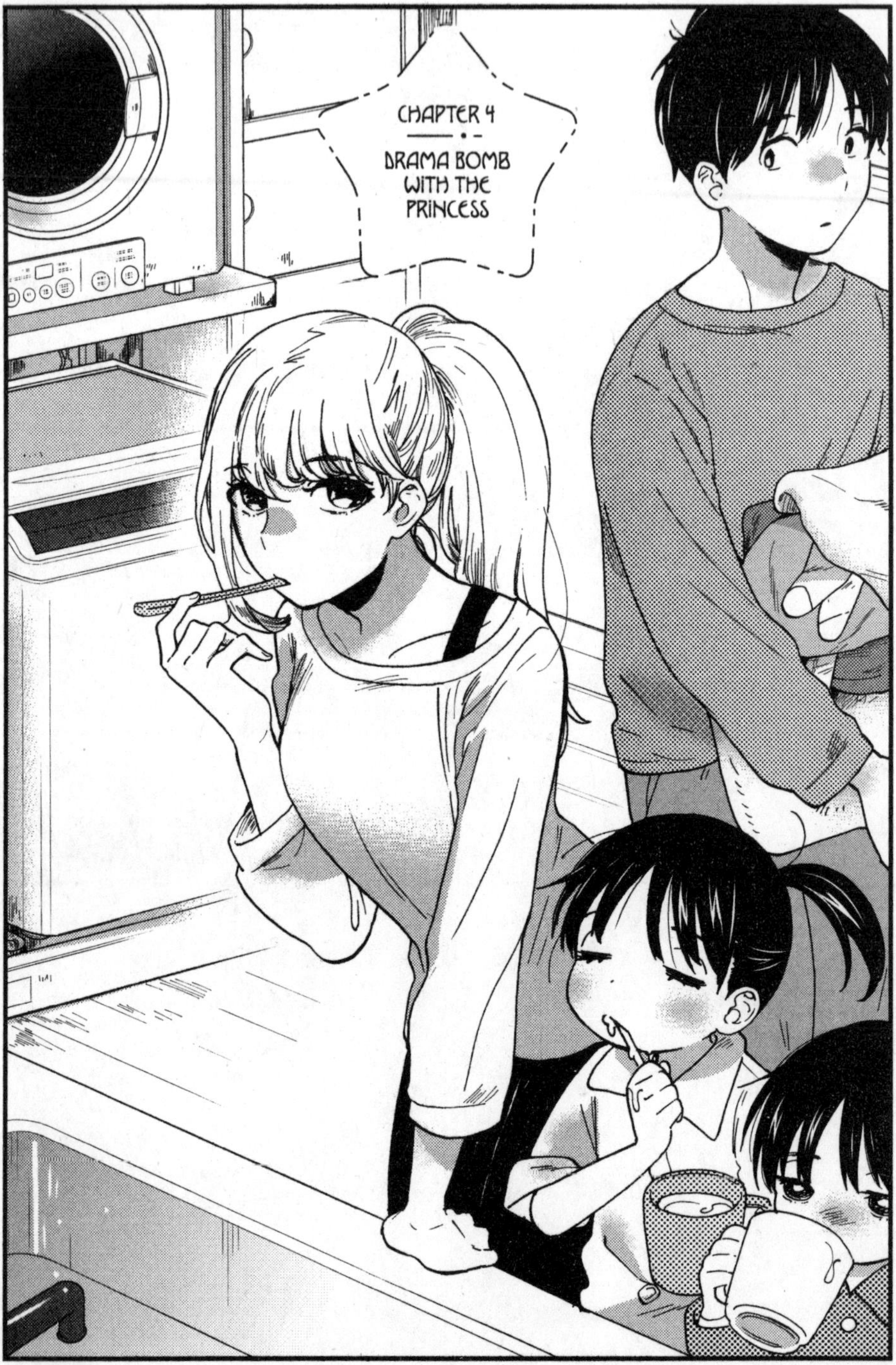
CHAPTER 4
DRAMA BOMB WITH THE PRINCESS

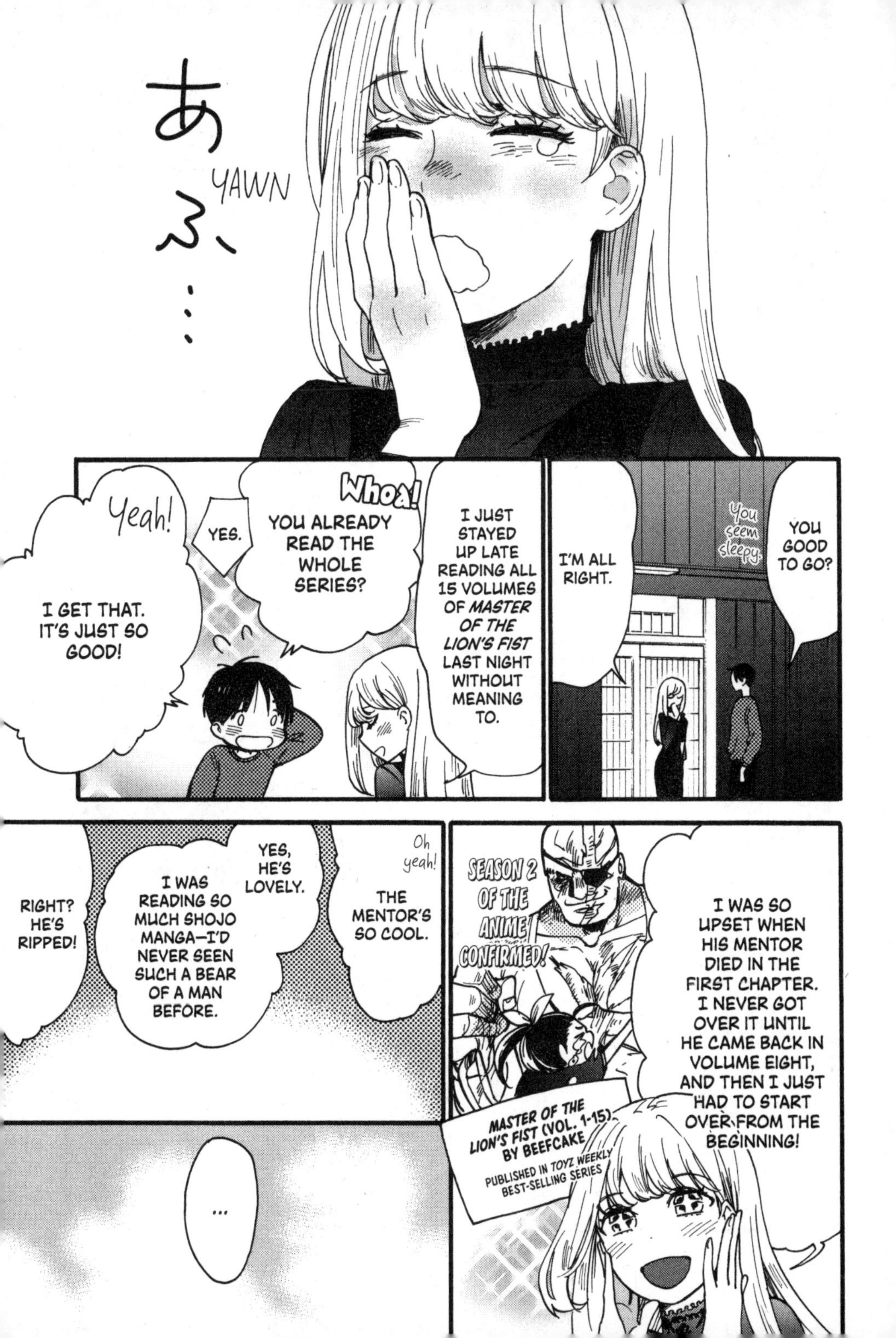
あふ…
YAWN
YOU GOOD TO GO?
You seem sleepy.
I'M ALL RIGHT.
I JUST STAYED UP LATE READING ALL 15 VOLUMES OF *MASTER OF THE LION'S FIST* LAST NIGHT WITHOUT MEANING TO.
Whoa!
YOU ALREADY READ THE WHOLE SERIES?
YES.
Yeah!
I GET THAT. IT'S JUST SO GOOD!
I WAS SO UPSET WHEN HIS MENTOR DIED IN THE FIRST CHAPTER. I NEVER GOT OVER IT UNTIL HE CAME BACK IN VOLUME EIGHT, AND THEN I JUST HAD TO START OVER FROM THE BEGINNING!
SEASON 2 OF THE ANIME CONFIRMED!
MASTER OF THE LION'S FIST (VOL. 1-15) BY BEEFCAKE
PUBLISHED IN *TOYZ WEEKLY* BEST-SELLING SERIES
Oh yeah!
THE MENTOR'S SO COOL.
YES, HE'S LOVELY.
I WAS READING SO MUCH SHOJO MANGA—I'D NEVER SEEN SUCH A BEAR OF A MAN BEFORE.
RIGHT? HE'S RIPPED!
...

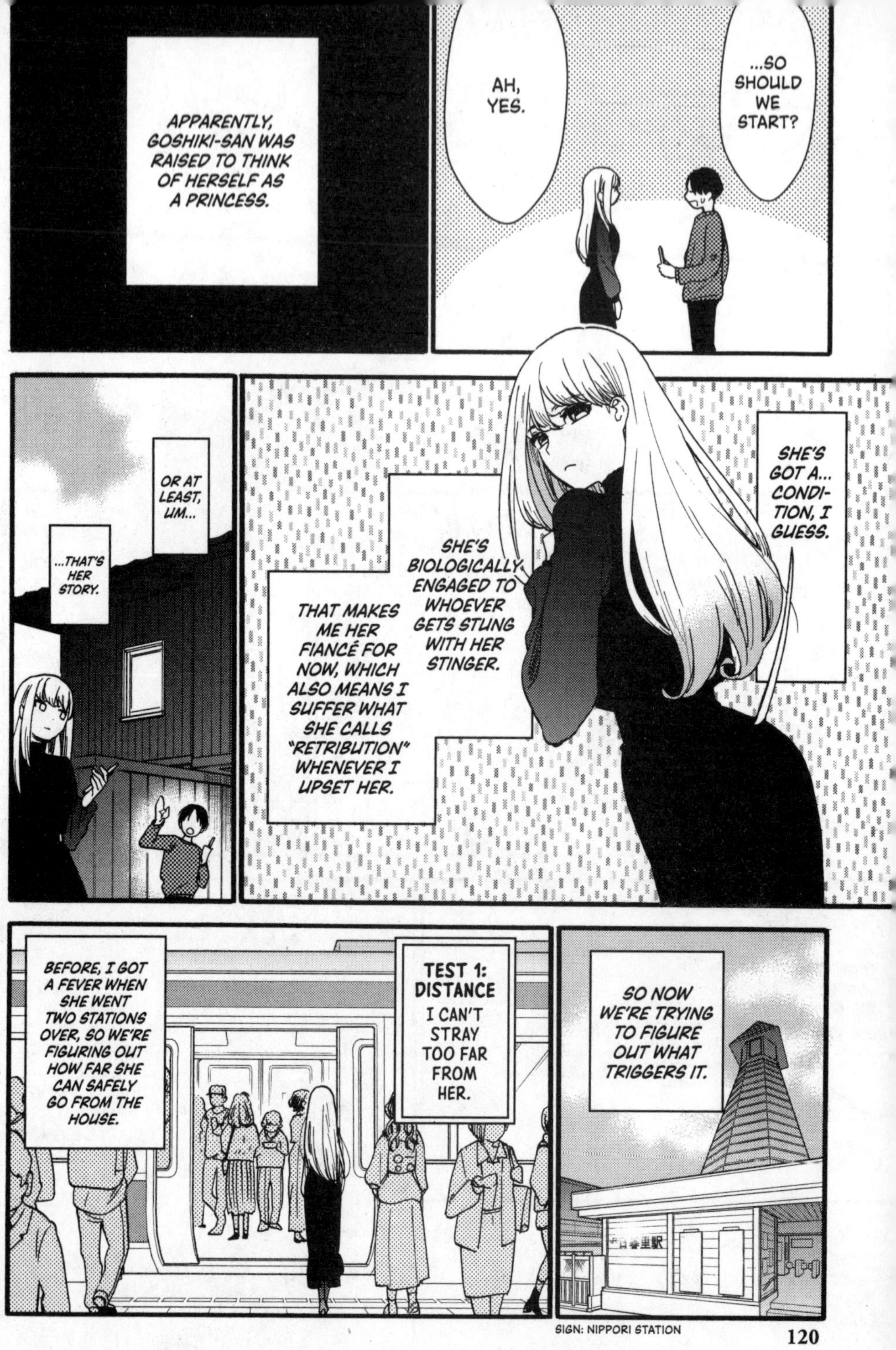
...SO SHOULD WE START?
AH, YES.
APPARENTLY, GOSHIKI-SAN WAS RAISED TO THINK OF HERSELF AS A PRINCESS.
SHE'S GOT A... CONDITION, I GUESS.
SHE'S BIOLOGICALLY ENGAGED TO WHOEVER GETS STUNG WITH HER STINGER.
THAT MAKES ME HER FIANCÉ FOR NOW, WHICH ALSO MEANS I SUFFER WHAT SHE CALLS "RETRIBUTION" WHENEVER I UPSET HER.
OR AT LEAST, UM...
...THAT'S HER STORY.
SO NOW WE'RE TRYING TO FIGURE OUT WHAT TRIGGERS IT.
TEST 1: DISTANCE
I CAN'T STRAY TOO FAR FROM HER.
BEFORE, I GOT A FEVER WHEN SHE WENT TWO STATIONS OVER, SO WE'RE FIGURING OUT HOW FAR SHE CAN SAFELY GO FROM THE HOUSE.

SIGN: NIPPORI STATION

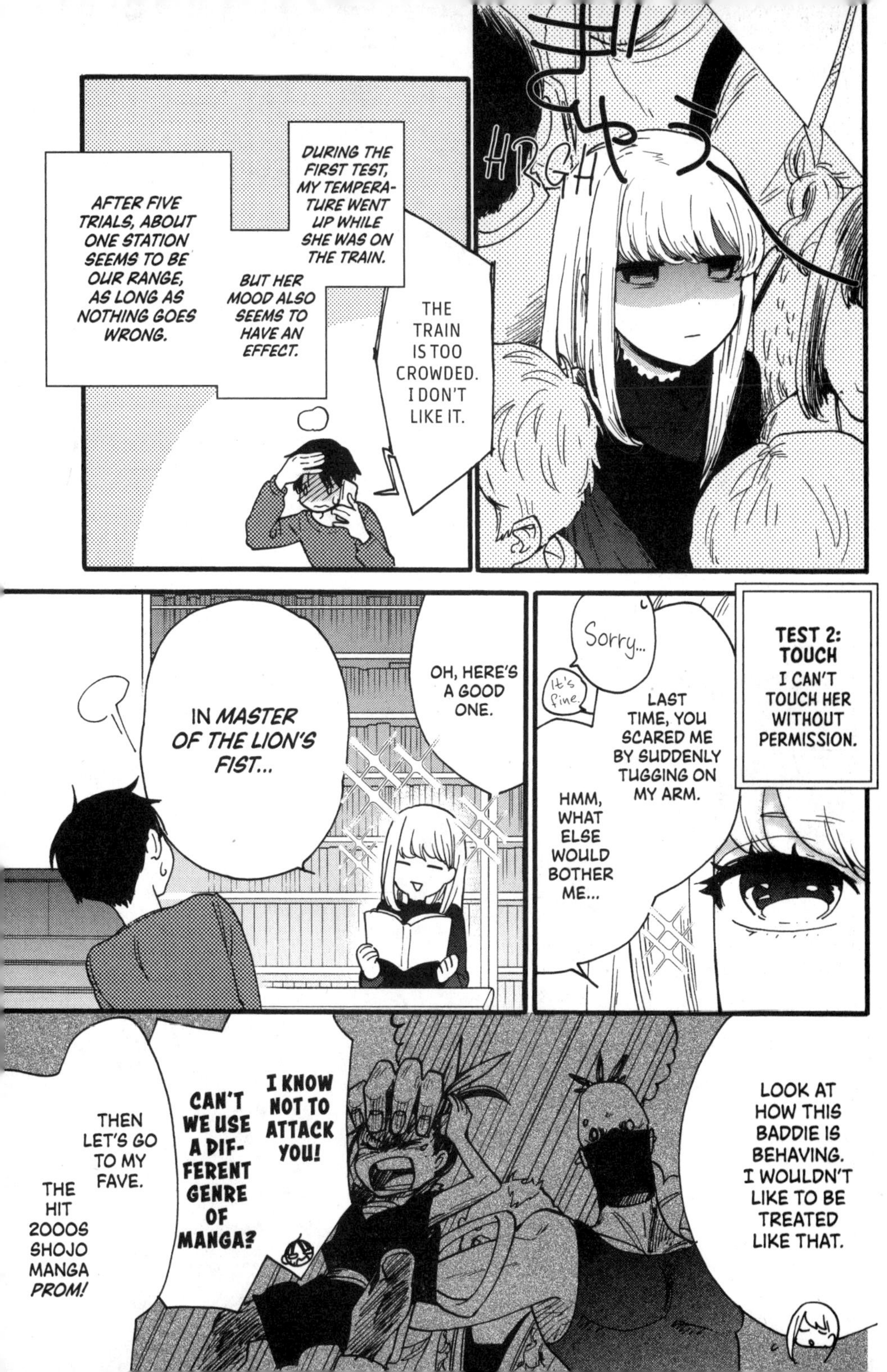
HRGH
THE TRAIN IS TOO CROWDED. I DON'T LIKE IT.
DURING THE FIRST TEST, MY TEMPERATURE WENT UP WHILE SHE WAS ON THE TRAIN.
BUT HER MOOD ALSO SEEMS TO HAVE AN EFFECT.
AFTER FIVE TRIALS, ABOUT ONE STATION SEEMS TO BE OUR RANGE, AS LONG AS NOTHING GOES WRONG.
TEST 2: TOUCH
I CAN'T TOUCH HER WITHOUT PERMISSION.
Sorry...
It's fine.
LAST TIME, YOU SCARED ME BY SUDDENLY TUGGING ON MY ARM.
HMM, WHAT ELSE WOULD BOTHER ME...
OH, HERE'S A GOOD ONE.
IN *MASTER OF THE LION'S FIST*...
LOOK AT HOW THIS BADDIE IS BEHAVING. I WOULDN'T LIKE TO BE TREATED LIKE THAT.
I KNOW NOT TO ATTACK YOU!
CAN'T WE USE A DIFFERENT GENRE OF MANGA?
THEN LET'S GO TO MY FAVE.
THE HIT 2000S SHOJO MANGA *PROM*!

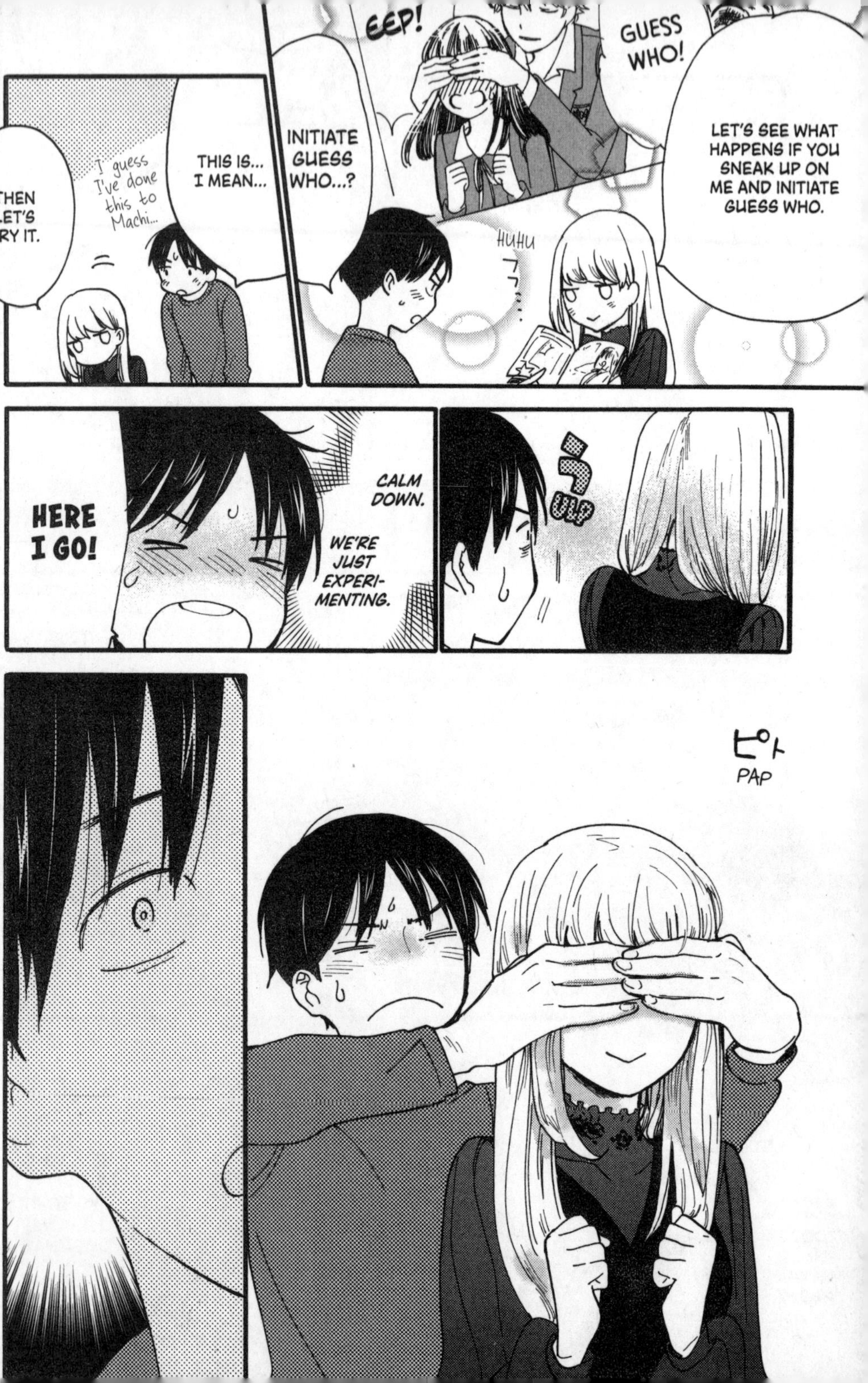
LET'S SEE WHAT HAPPENS IF YOU SNEAK UP ON ME AND INITIATE GUESS WHO.
GUESS WHO!
EEP!
HUHU
フフ
INITIATE GUESS WHO...?
THIS IS... I MEAN...
I guess I've done this to Machi...
THEN LET'S TRY IT.
う
UP!
CALM DOWN.
WE'RE JUST EXPERIMENTING.
HERE I GO!
ピト
PAP

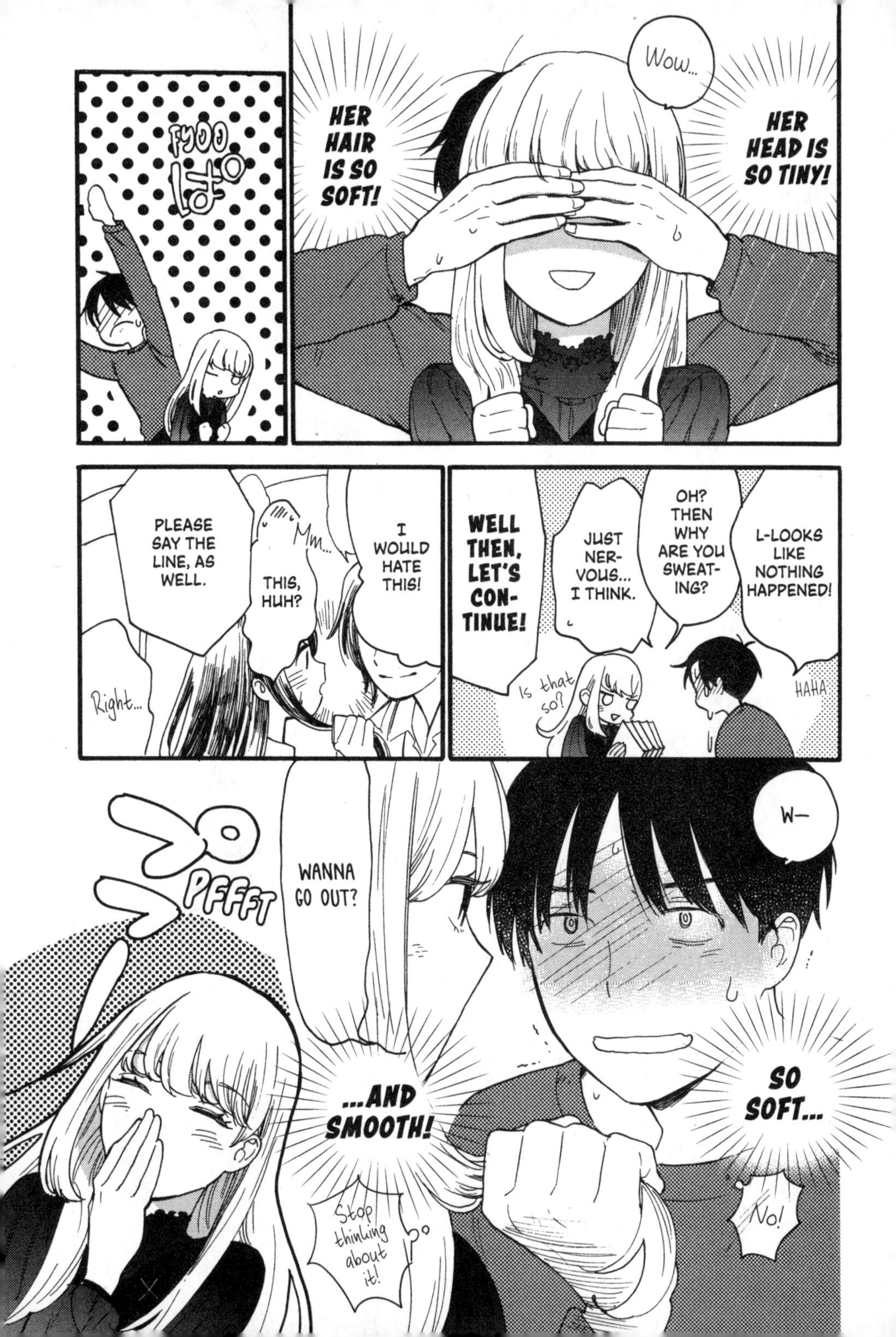
Wow...
HER HEAD IS SO TINY!
HER HAIR IS SO SOFT!
FYOO
L-LOOKS LIKE NOTHING HAPPENED!
HAHA
OH? THEN WHY ARE YOU SWEATING?
JUST NERVOUS... I THINK.
Is that so?
WELL THEN, LET'S CONTINUE!
I WOULD HATE THIS!
Mm...
THIS, HUH?
PLEASE SAY THE LINE, AS WELL.
Right...
W—
WANNA GO OUT?
SO SOFT...
...AND SMOOTH!
No!
Stop thinking about it!
PFFFT

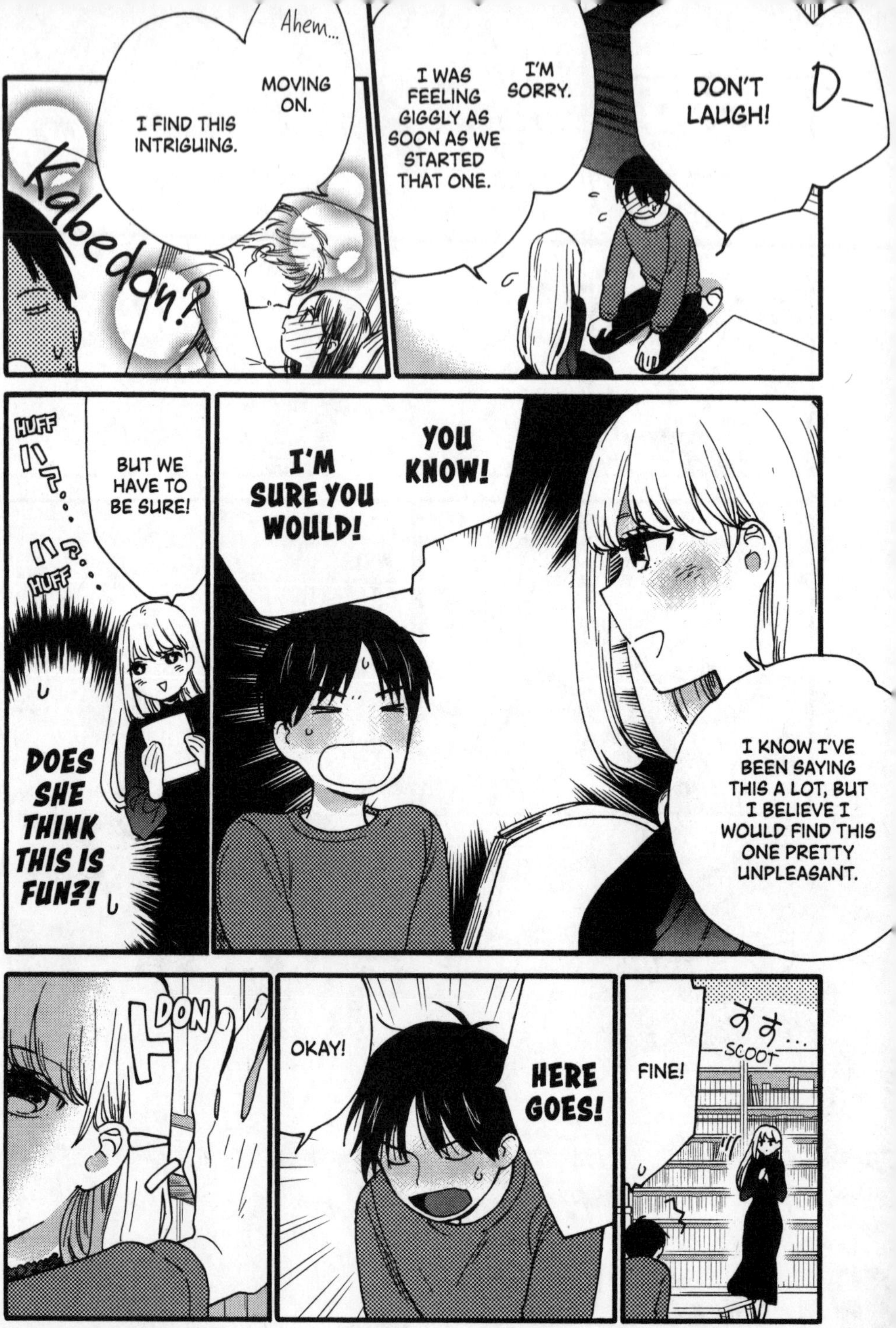
D_
DON'T LAUGH!
I'M SORRY.
I WAS FEELING GIGGLY AS SOON AS WE STARTED THAT ONE.
Ahem...
MOVING ON.
I FIND THIS INTRIGUING.
Kabedon?
I KNOW I'VE BEEN SAYING THIS A LOT, BUT I BELIEVE I WOULD FIND THIS ONE PRETTY UNPLEASANT.
YOU KNOW!
I'M SURE YOU WOULD!
BUT WE HAVE TO BE SURE!
HUFF ハァ...
ハァ... HUFF
DOES SHE THINK THIS IS FUN?!
すす... SCOOT
FINE!
HERE GOES!
OKAY!
ド DON

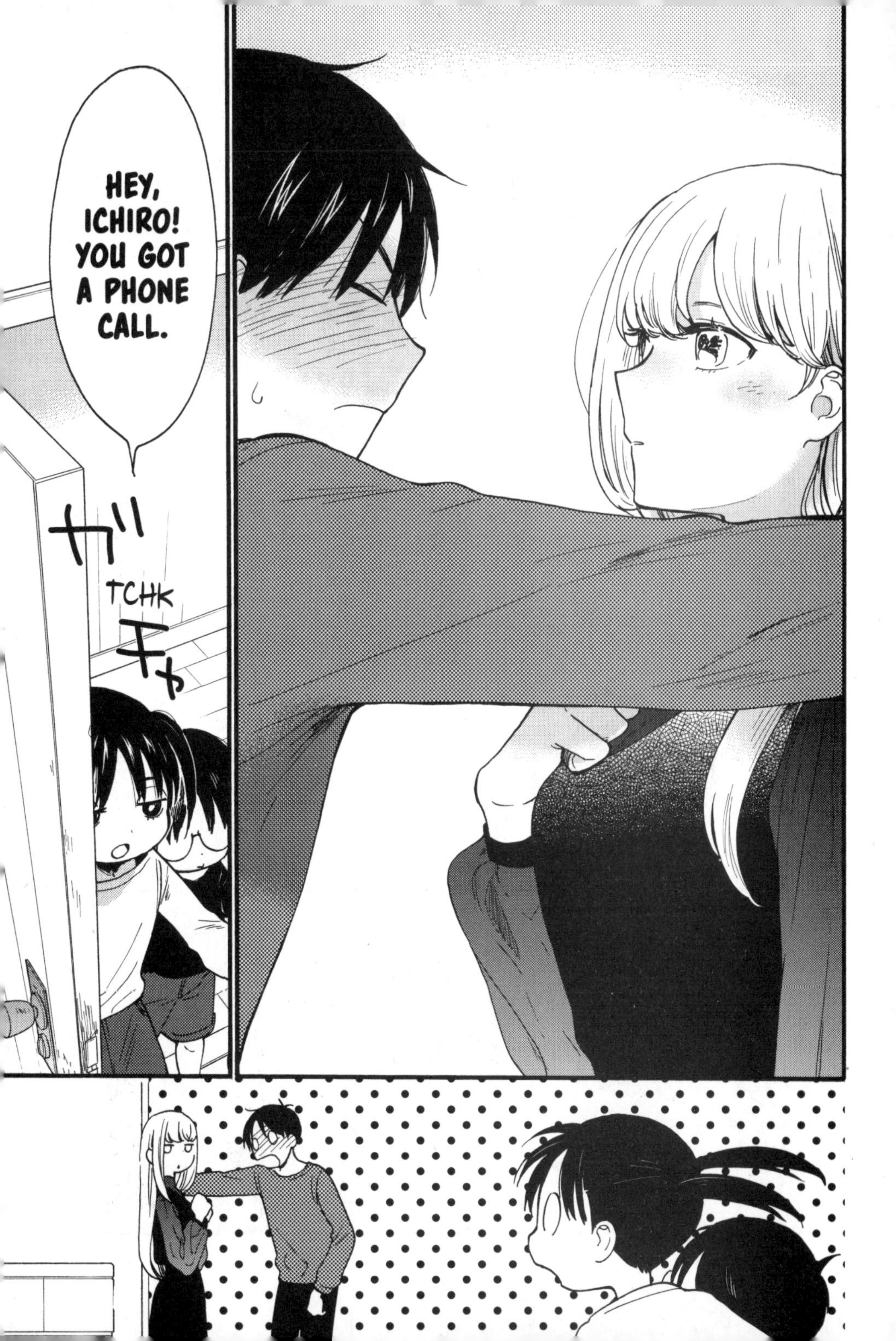
HEY, ICHIRO! YOU GOT A PHONE CALL.
ガチャ
TCHK

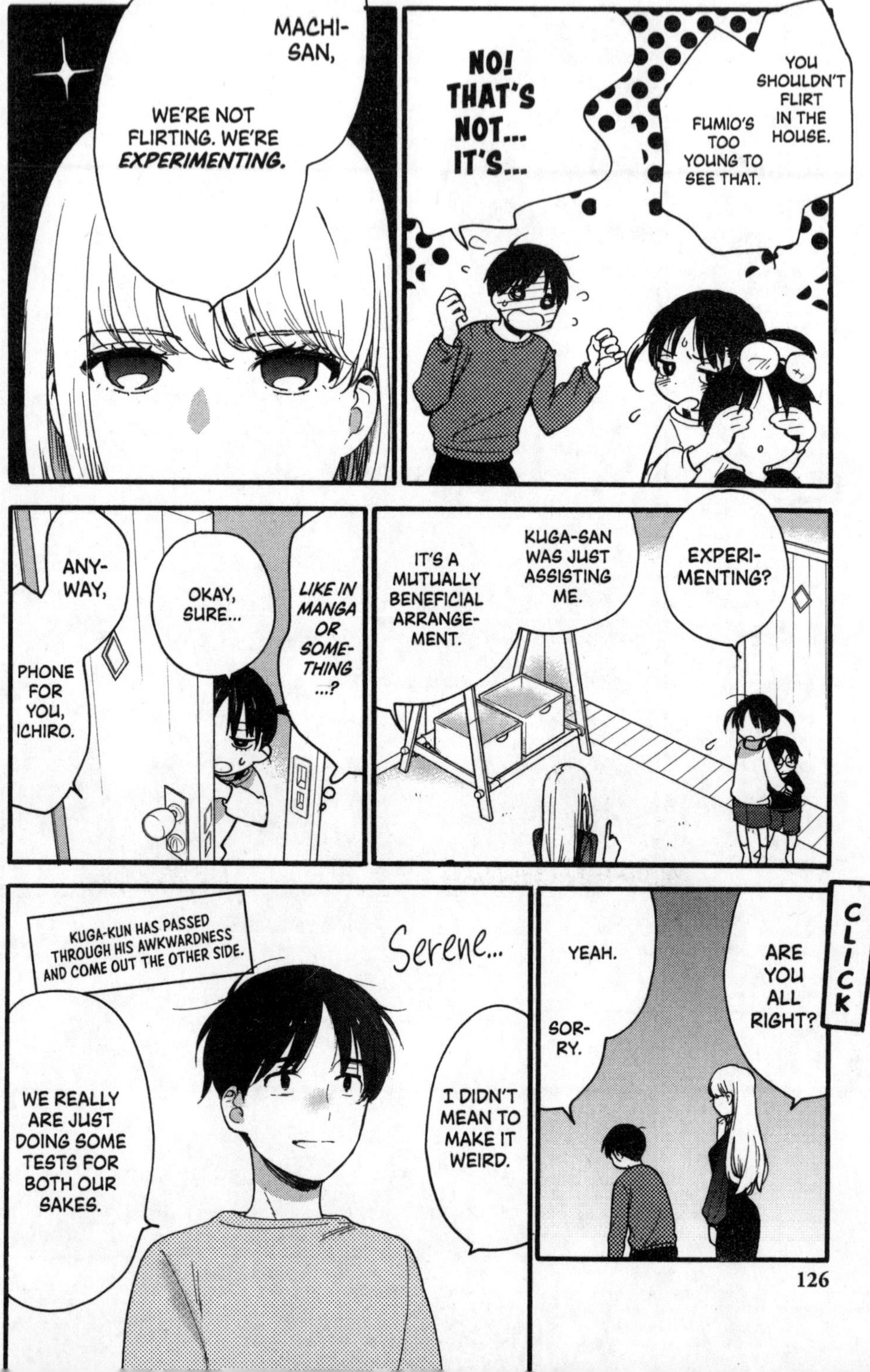
YOU SHOULDN'T FLIRT IN THE HOUSE.
FUMIO'S TOO YOUNG TO SEE THAT.
NO! THAT'S NOT... IT'S...
MACHI-SAN,
WE'RE NOT FLIRTING. WE'RE *EXPERIMENTING.*
EXPERIMENTING?
KUGA-SAN WAS JUST ASSISTING ME.
IT'S A MUTUALLY BENEFICIAL ARRANGEMENT.
LIKE IN MANGA OR SOMETHING ...?
OKAY, SURE...
ANYWAY,
PHONE FOR YOU, ICHIRO.
CLICK
ARE YOU ALL RIGHT?
YEAH.
SORRY.
Serene...
KUGA-KUN HAS PASSED THROUGH HIS AWKWARDNESS AND COME OUT THE OTHER SIDE.
I DIDN'T MEAN TO MAKE IT WEIRD.
WE REALLY ARE JUST DOING SOME TESTS FOR BOTH OUR SAKES.

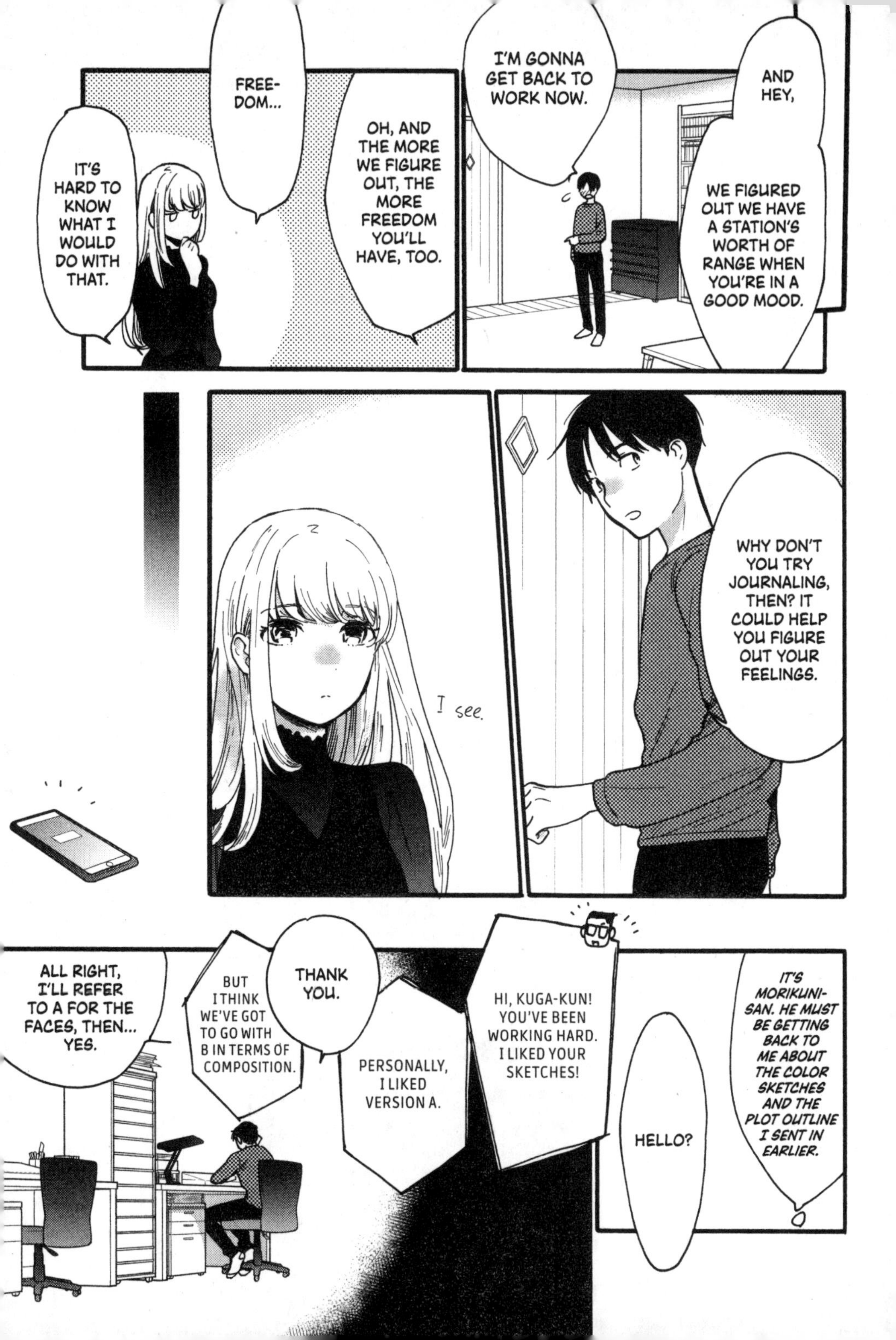
AND HEY,
WE FIGURED OUT WE HAVE A STATION'S WORTH OF RANGE WHEN YOU'RE IN A GOOD MOOD.
I'M GONNA GET BACK TO WORK NOW.
OH, AND THE MORE WE FIGURE OUT, THE MORE FREEDOM YOU'LL HAVE, TOO.
FREE-DOM...
IT'S HARD TO KNOW WHAT I WOULD DO WITH THAT.
WHY DON'T YOU TRY JOURNALING, THEN? IT COULD HELP YOU FIGURE OUT YOUR FEELINGS.
I see.
IT'S MORIKUNI-SAN. HE MUST BE GETTING BACK TO ME ABOUT THE COLOR SKETCHES AND THE PLOT OUTLINE I SENT IN EARLIER.
HELLO?
HI, KUGA-KUN! YOU'VE BEEN WORKING HARD. I LIKED YOUR SKETCHES!
PERSONALLY, I LIKED VERSION A.
THANK YOU.
BUT I THINK WE'VE GOT TO GO WITH B IN TERMS OF COMPOSITION.
ALL RIGHT, I'LL REFER TO A FOR THE FACES, THEN... YES.

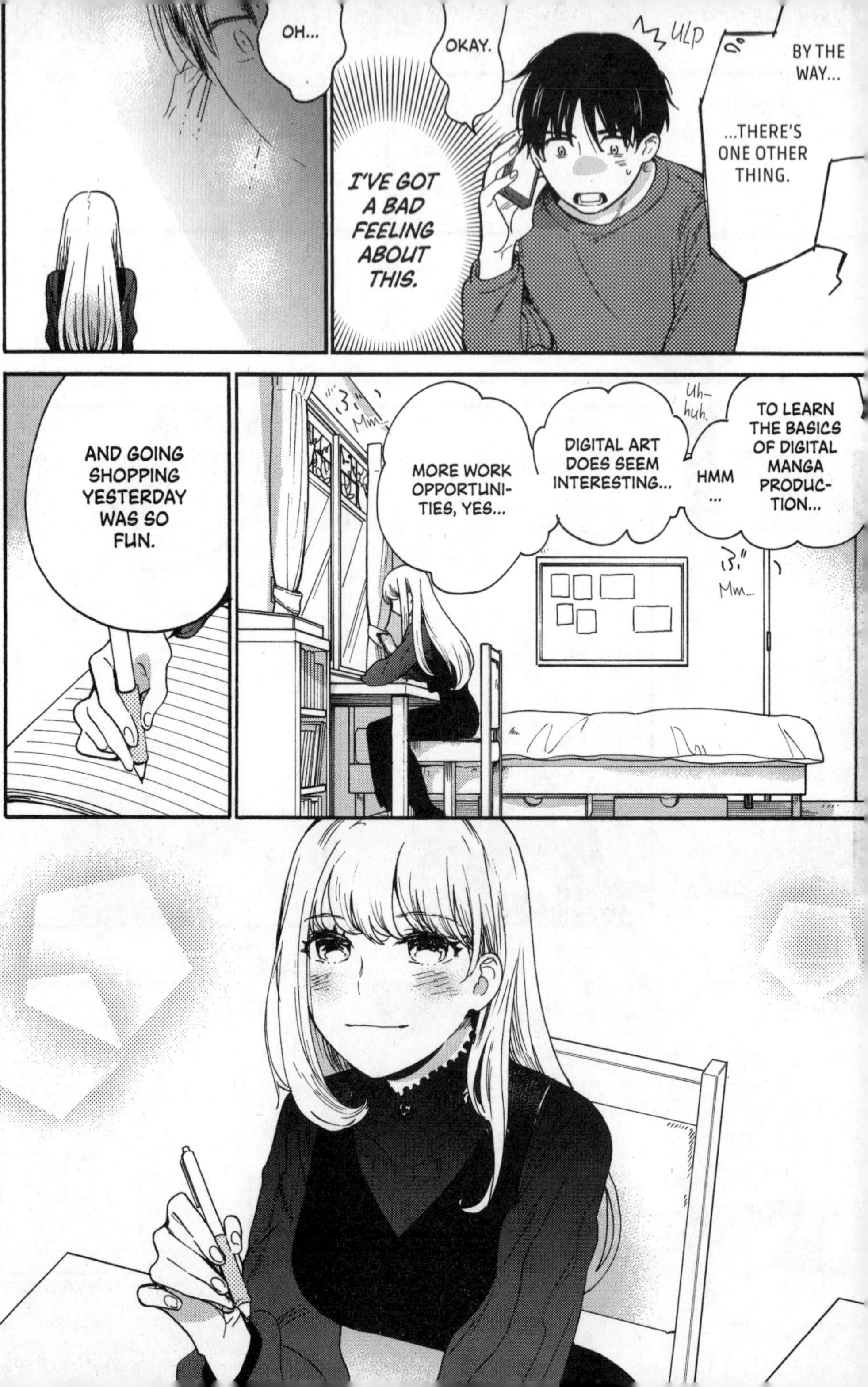
BY THE WAY...
...THERE'S ONE OTHER THING.
ULP
OKAY.
I'VE GOT A BAD FEELING ABOUT THIS.
OH...
TO LEARN THE BASICS OF DIGITAL MANGA PRODUCTION...
Uh-huh.
HMM...
DIGITAL ART DOES SEEM INTERESTING...
Mm...
MORE WORK OPPORTUNITIES, YES...
Mm...
AND GOING SHOPPING YESTERDAY WAS SO FUN.

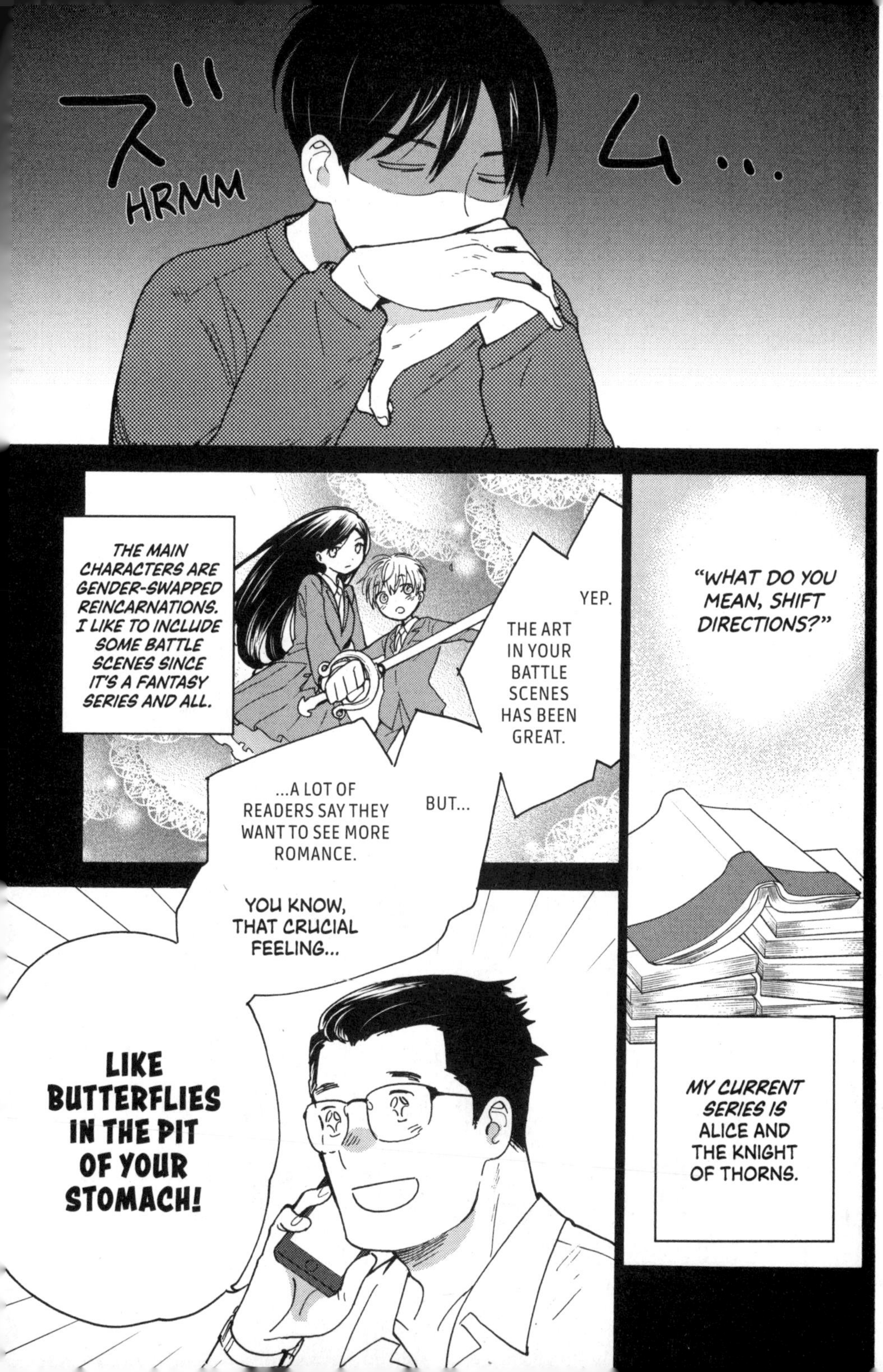
ズム...
HRMM
"WHAT DO YOU MEAN, SHIFT DIRECTIONS?"
MY CURRENT SERIES IS ALICE AND THE KNIGHT OF THORNS.
THE MAIN CHARACTERS ARE GENDER-SWAPPED REINCARNATIONS. I LIKE TO INCLUDE SOME BATTLE SCENES SINCE IT'S A FANTASY SERIES AND ALL.
YEP.
THE ART IN YOUR BATTLE SCENES HAS BEEN GREAT.
BUT...
...A LOT OF READERS SAY THEY WANT TO SEE MORE ROMANCE.
YOU KNOW, THAT CRUCIAL FEELING...
LIKE BUTTERFLIES IN THE PIT OF YOUR STOMACH!

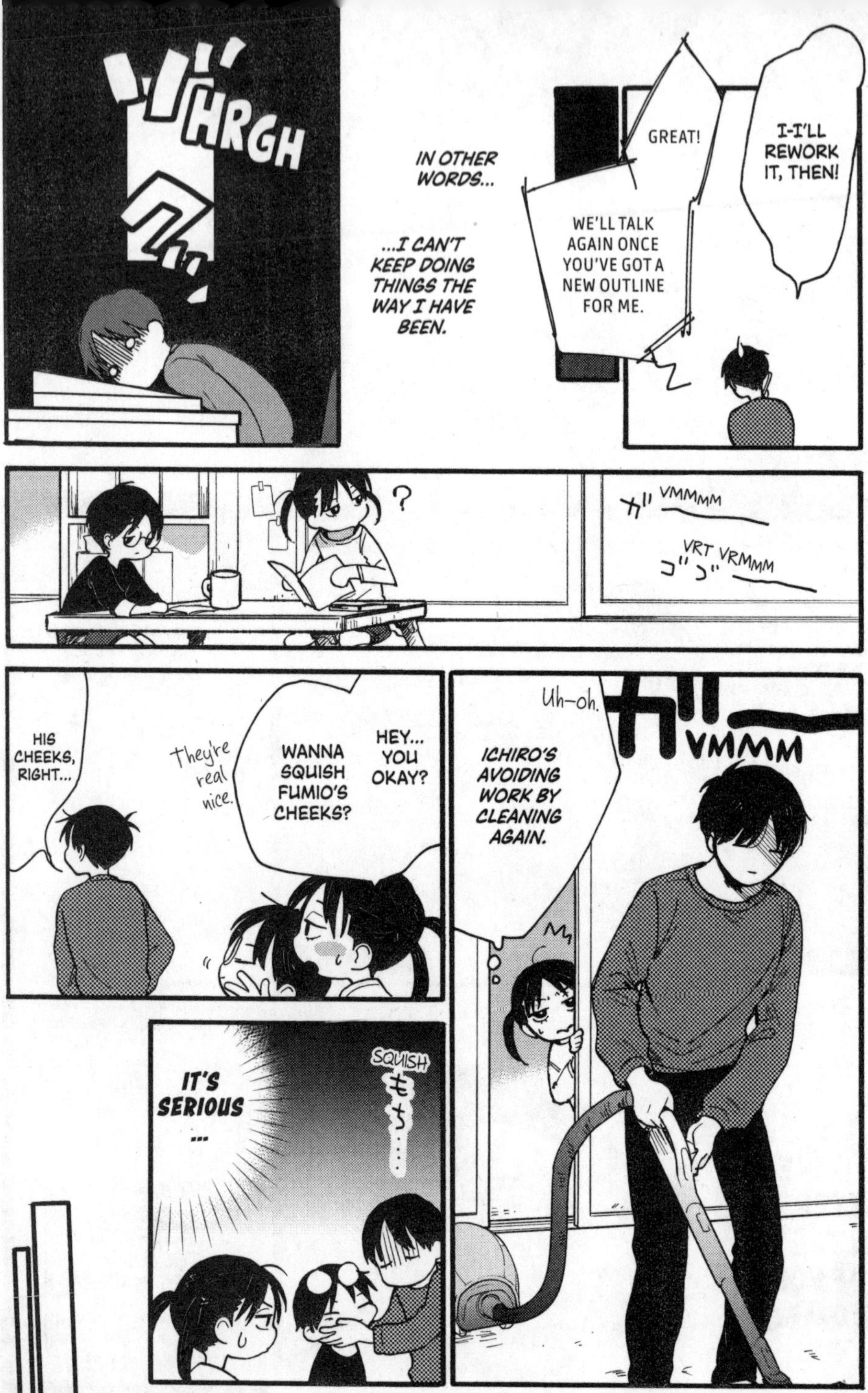
I-I'LL REWORK IT, THEN!
GREAT!
WE'LL TALK AGAIN ONCE YOU'VE GOT A NEW OUTLINE FOR ME.
IN OTHER WORDS...
...I CAN'T KEEP DOING THINGS THE WAY I HAVE BEEN.
HRGH
VMMMM
VRT VRMMM
?
VMMMM
Uh-oh.
ICHIRO'S AVOIDING WORK BY CLEANING AGAIN.
HEY... YOU OKAY?
WANNA SQUISH FUMIO'S CHEEKS?
They're real nice.
HIS CHEEKS, RIGHT...
SQUISH
もち….
IT'S SERIOUS...

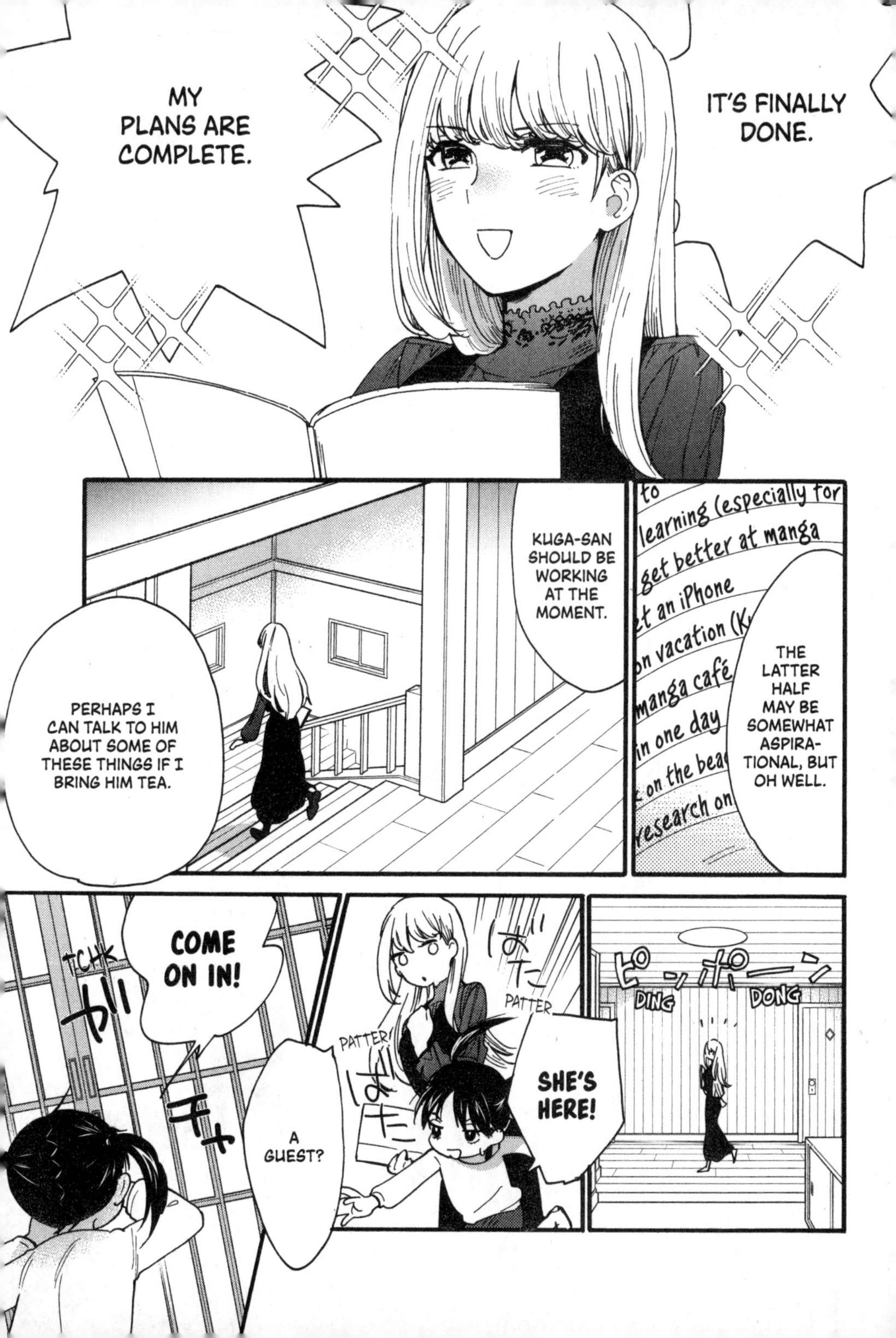
IT'S FINALLY DONE.
MY PLANS ARE COMPLETE.
to
learning (especially for
get better at manga
et an iPhone
on vacation (K
manga café
in one day
on the bea
research on
THE LATTER HALF MAY BE SOMEWHAT ASPIRA-TIONAL, BUT OH WELL.
KUGA-SAN SHOULD BE WORKING AT THE MOMENT.
PERHAPS I CAN TALK TO HIM ABOUT SOME OF THESE THINGS IF I BRING HIM TEA.
DING
DONG
PATTER
SHE'S HERE!
PATTER
A GUEST?
TCHK
COME ON IN!

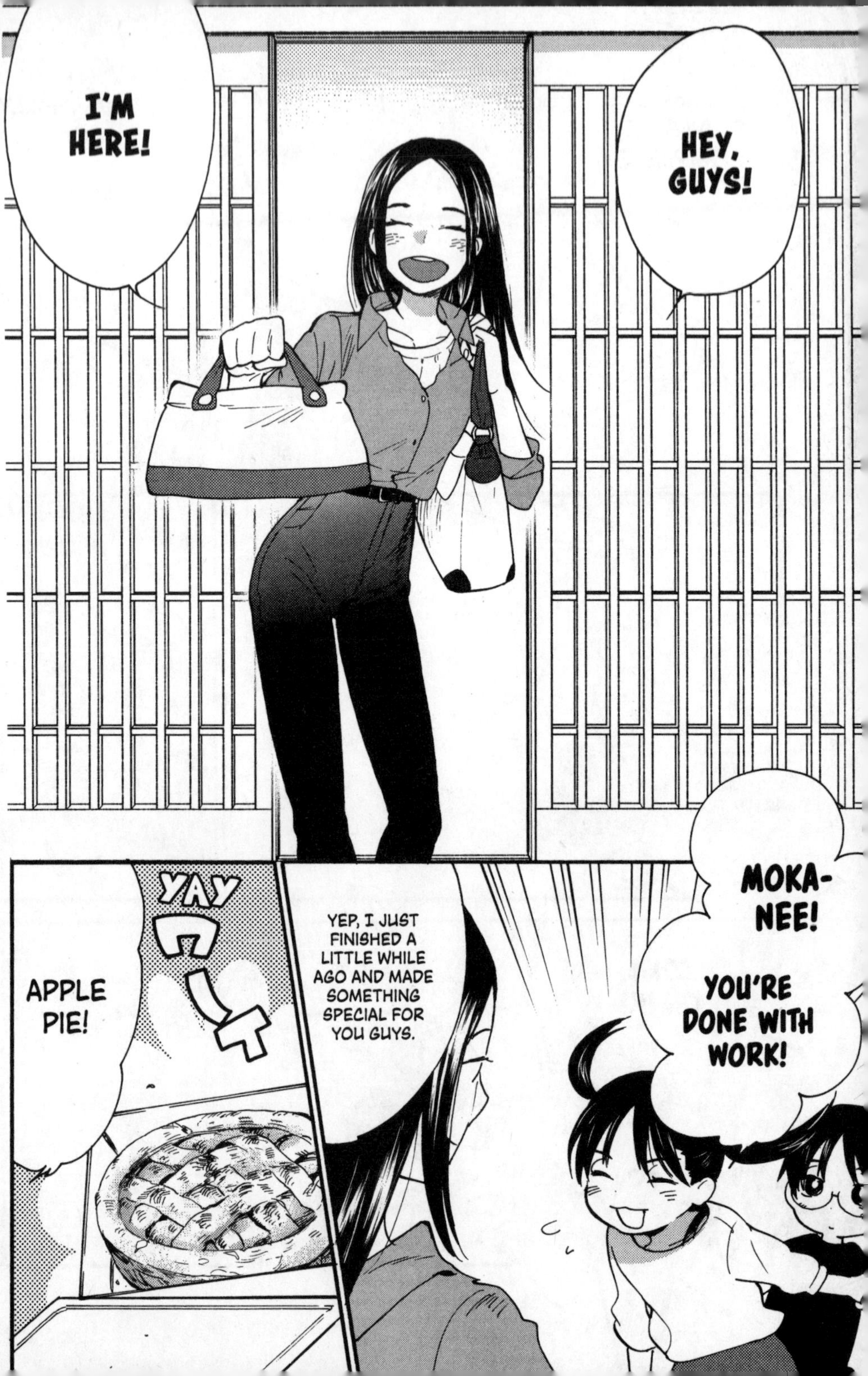
HEY, GUYS!
I'M HERE!
MOKA-NEE!
YOU'RE DONE WITH WORK!
YEP, I JUST FINISHED A LITTLE WHILE AGO AND MADE SOMETHING SPECIAL FOR YOU GUYS.
YAY
APPLE PIE!

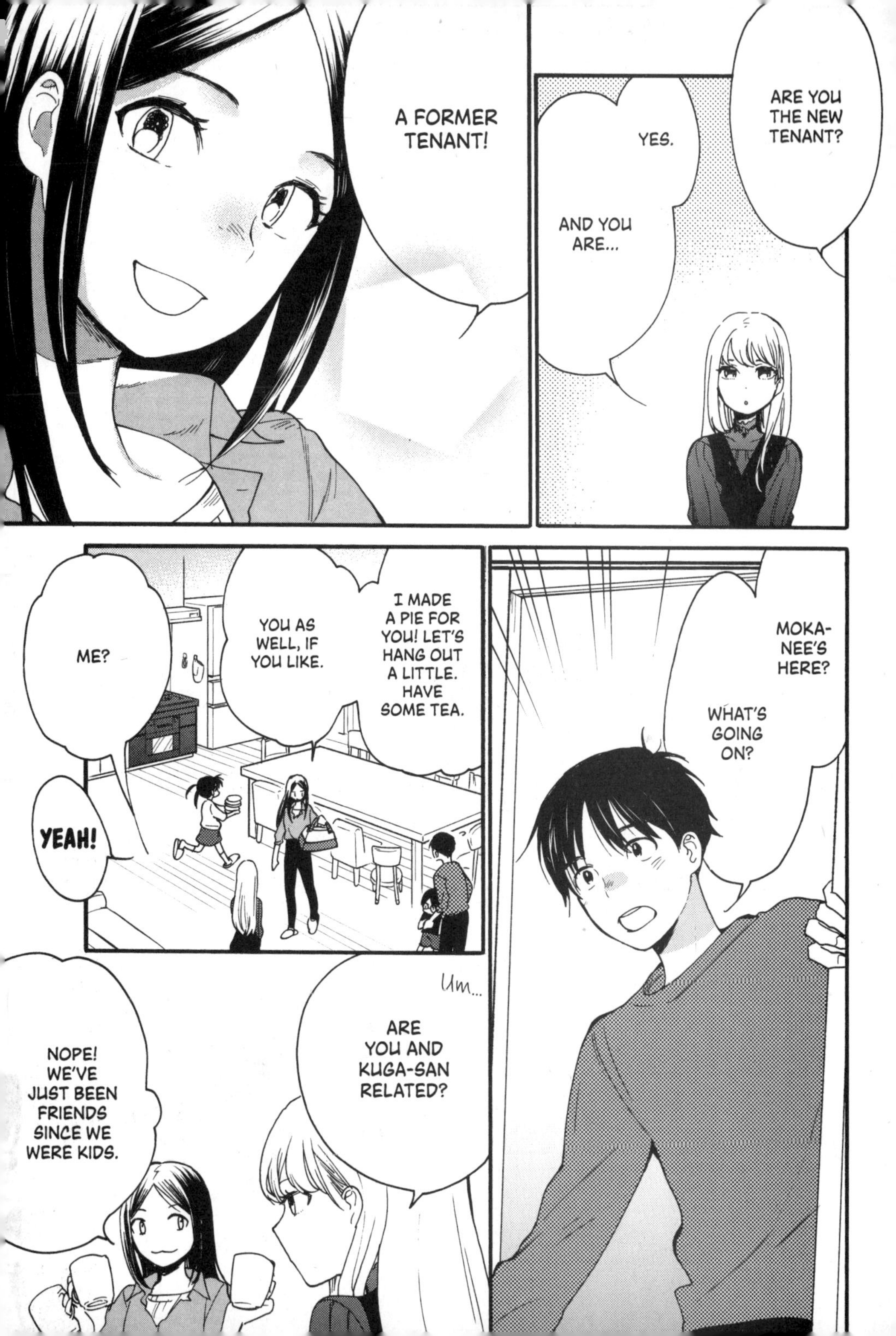
ARE YOU THE NEW TENANT?
YES.
AND YOU ARE...
A FORMER TENANT!
MOKA-NEE'S HERE?
WHAT'S GOING ON?
I MADE A PIE FOR YOU! LET'S HANG OUT A LITTLE. HAVE SOME TEA.
YOU AS WELL, IF YOU LIKE.
ME?
YEAH!
Um...
ARE YOU AND KUGA-SAN RELATED?
NOPE! WE'VE JUST BEEN FRIENDS SINCE WE WERE KIDS.

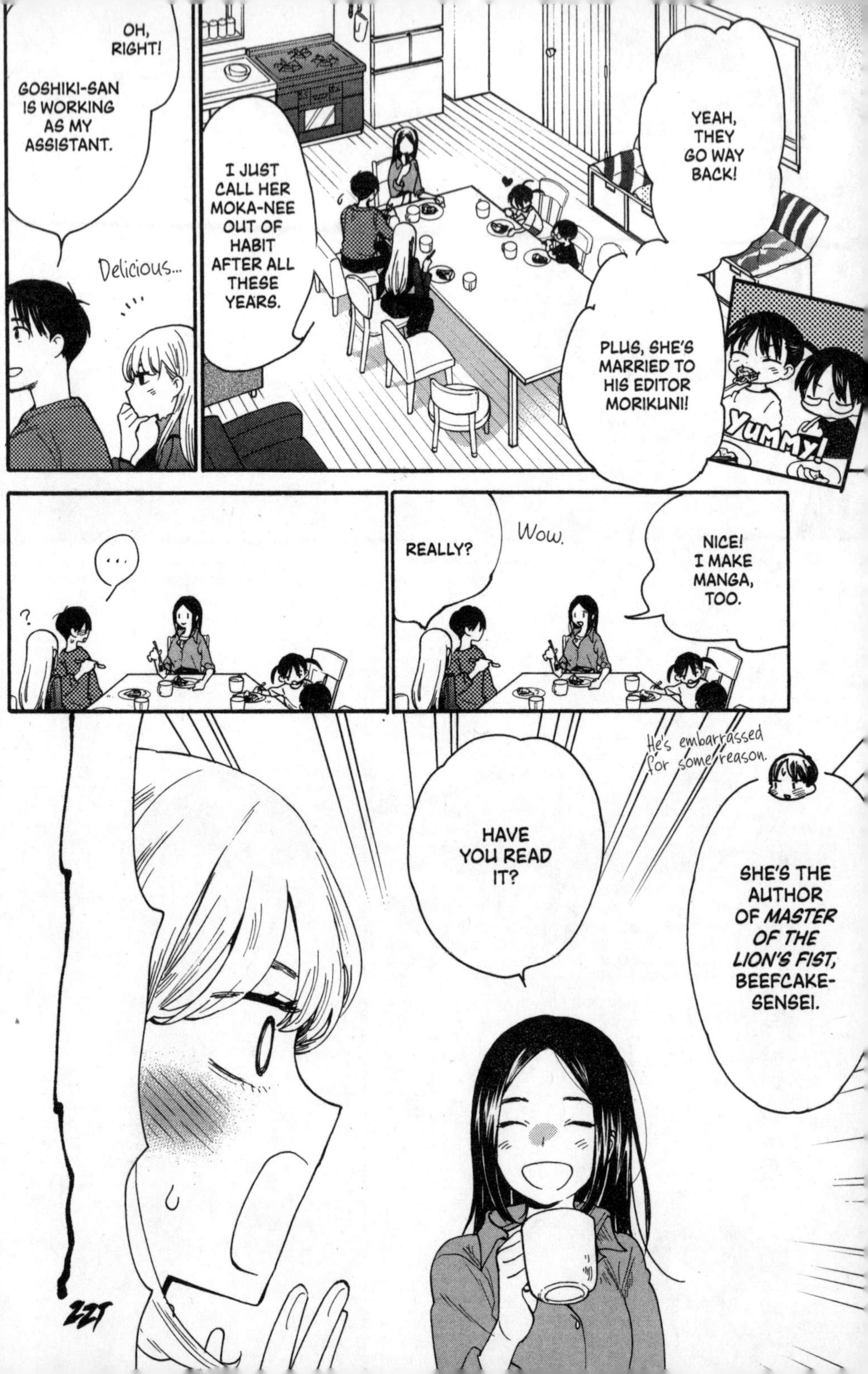
YEAH, THEY GO WAY BACK!
PLUS, SHE'S MARRIED TO HIS EDITOR MORIKUNI!
YUMMY!
I JUST CALL HER MOKA-NEE OUT OF HABIT AFTER ALL THESE YEARS.
OH, RIGHT!
GOSHIKI-SAN IS WORKING AS MY ASSISTANT.
Delicious...
NICE! I MAKE MANGA, TOO.
Wow.
REALLY?
...
?
SHE'S THE AUTHOR OF *MASTER OF THE LION'S FIST*, BEEFCAKE-SENSEI.
He's embarrassed for some reason.
HAVE YOU READ IT?

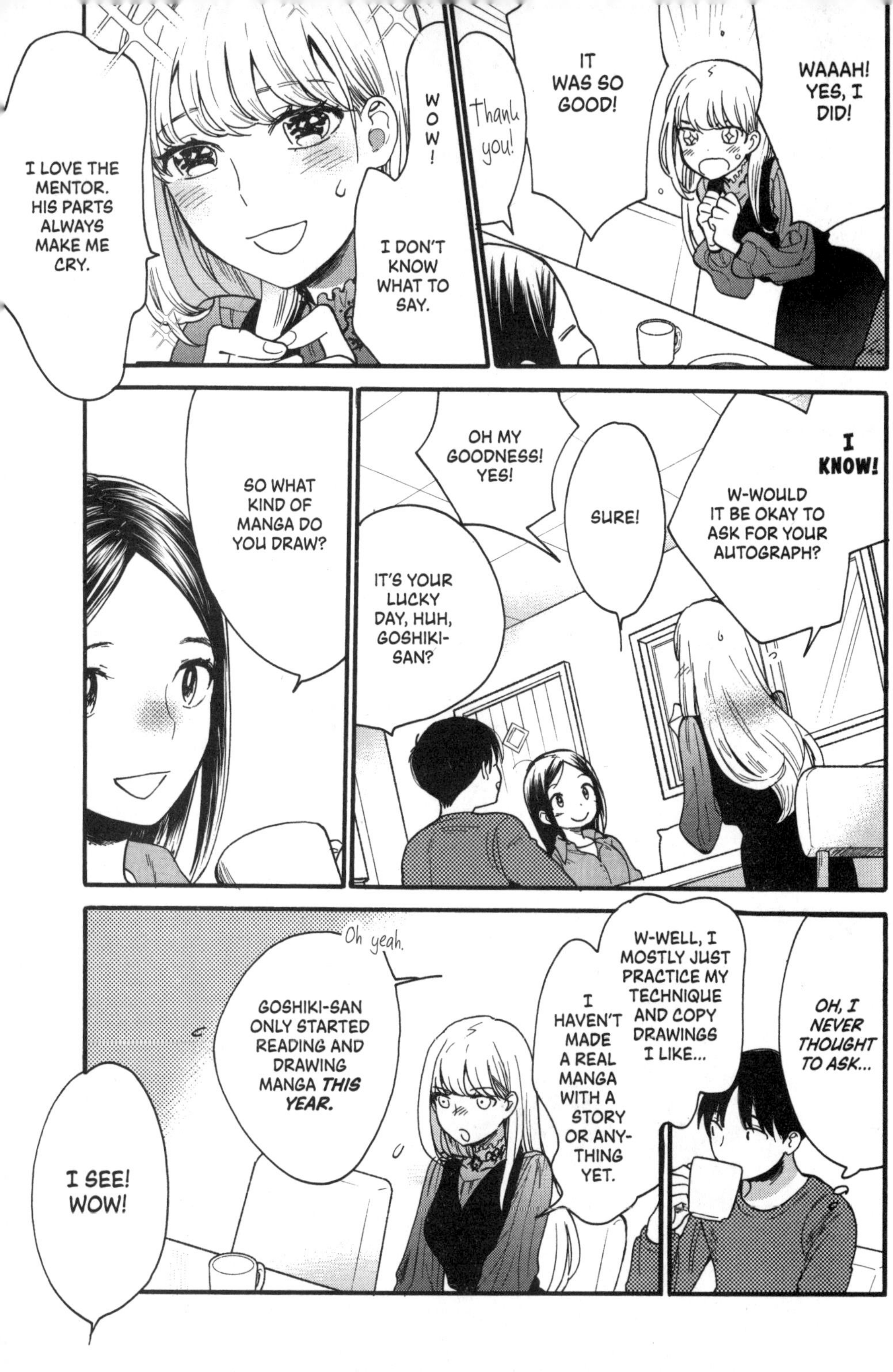
WAAAH! YES, I DID!
IT WAS SO GOOD!
Thank you!
WOW!
I DON'T KNOW WHAT TO SAY.
I LOVE THE MENTOR. HIS PARTS ALWAYS MAKE ME CRY.
I KNOW!
W-WOULD IT BE OKAY TO ASK FOR YOUR AUTOGRAPH?
SURE!
OH MY GOODNESS! YES!
IT'S YOUR LUCKY DAY, HUH, GOSHIKI-SAN?
SO WHAT KIND OF MANGA DO YOU DRAW?
OH, I NEVER THOUGHT TO ASK...
W-WELL, I MOSTLY JUST PRACTICE MY TECHNIQUE AND COPY DRAWINGS I LIKE...
I HAVEN'T MADE A REAL MANGA WITH A STORY OR ANYTHING YET.
Oh yeah.
GOSHIKI-SAN ONLY STARTED READING AND DRAWING MANGA THIS YEAR.
I SEE! WOW!

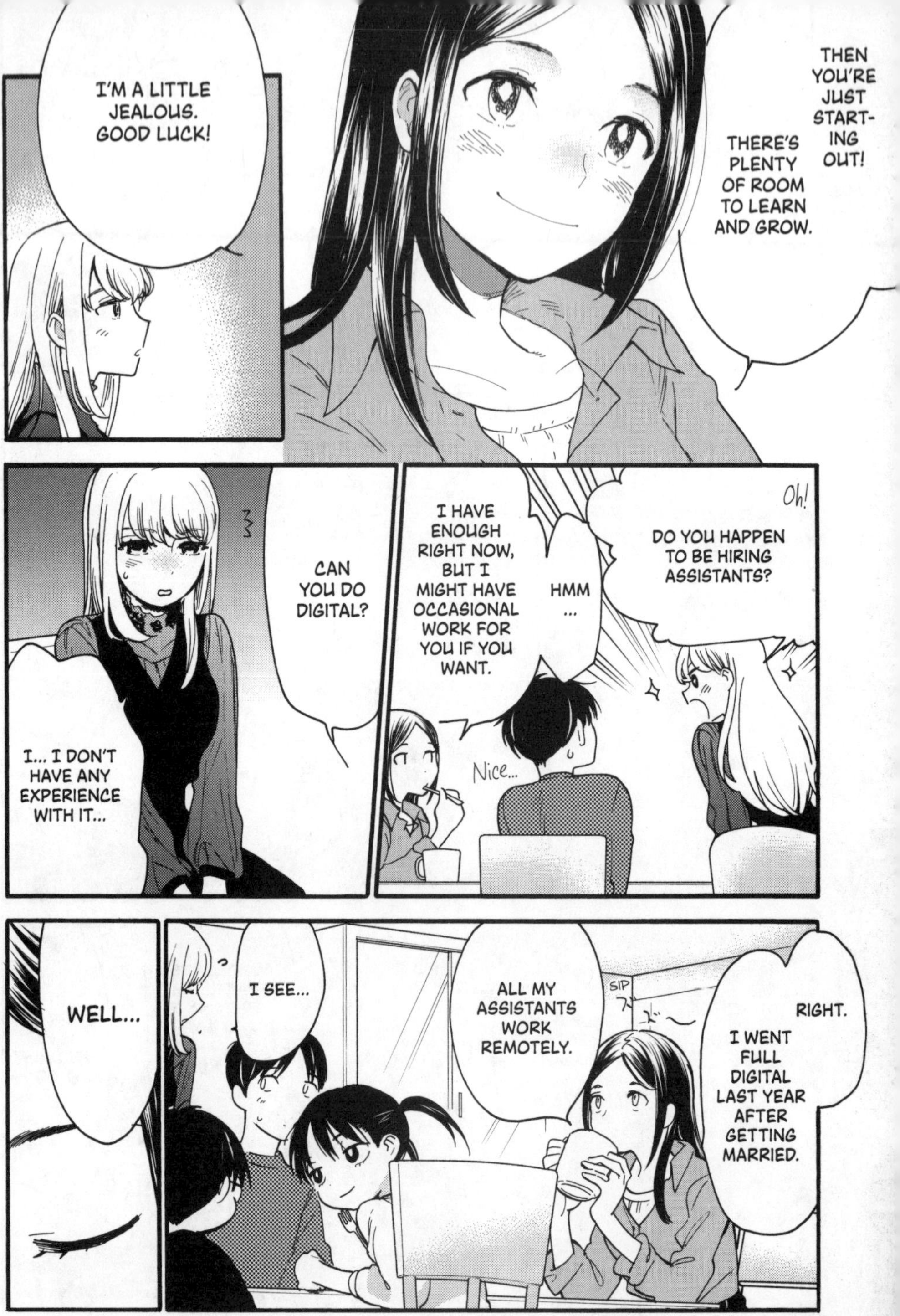
THEN YOU'RE JUST STARTING OUT!
THERE'S PLENTY OF ROOM TO LEARN AND GROW.
I'M A LITTLE JEALOUS. GOOD LUCK!
Oh!
DO YOU HAPPEN TO BE HIRING ASSISTANTS?
HMM ...
I HAVE ENOUGH RIGHT NOW, BUT I MIGHT HAVE OCCASIONAL WORK FOR YOU IF YOU WANT.
Nice...
CAN YOU DO DIGITAL?
I... I DON'T HAVE ANY EXPERIENCE WITH IT...
RIGHT.
I WENT FULL DIGITAL LAST YEAR AFTER GETTING MARRIED.
SIP
ALL MY ASSISTANTS WORK REMOTELY.
I SEE...
WELL...

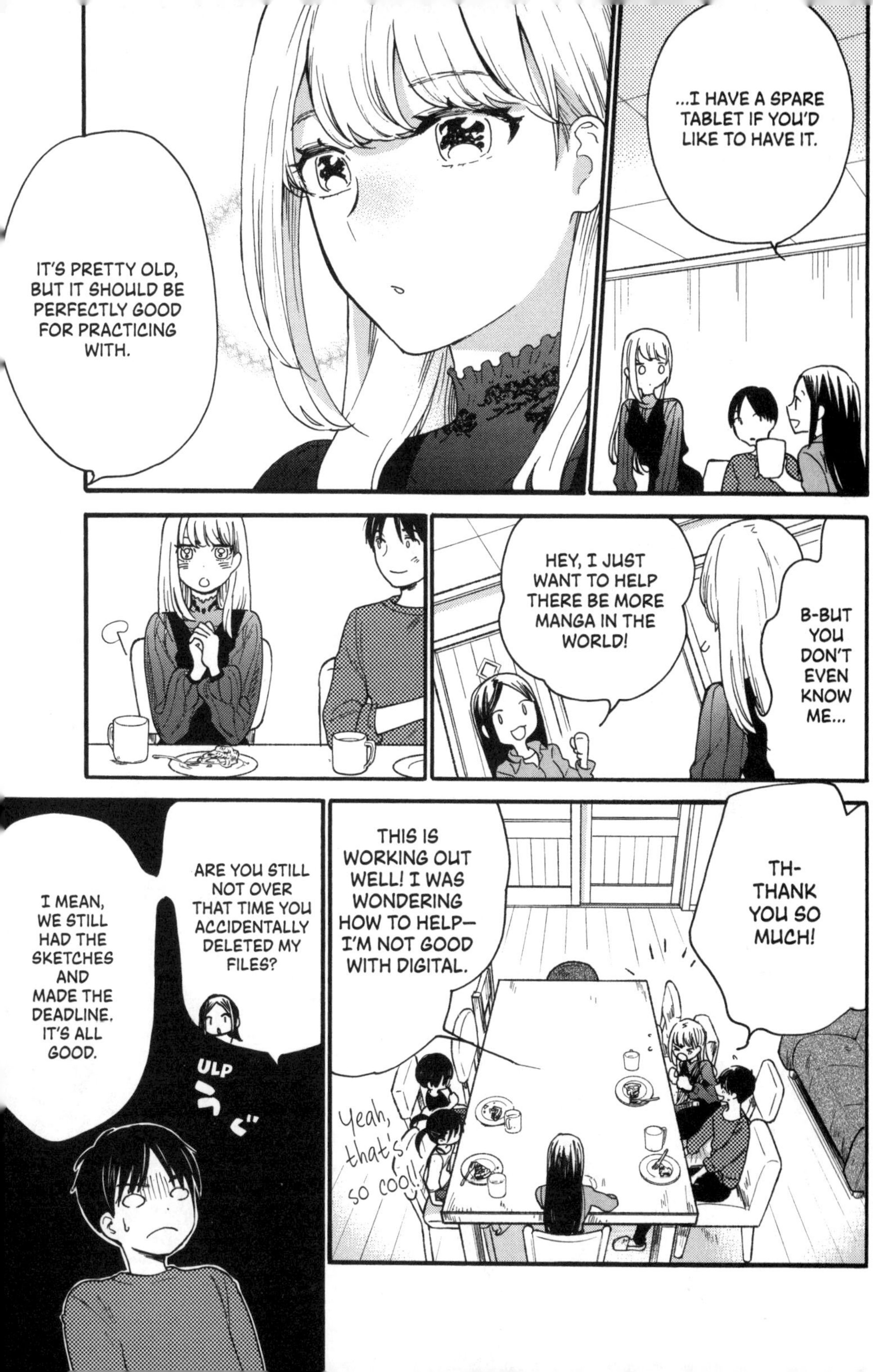
...I HAVE A SPARE TABLET IF YOU'D LIKE TO HAVE IT.
IT'S PRETTY OLD, BUT IT SHOULD BE PERFECTLY GOOD FOR PRACTICING WITH.
B-BUT YOU DON'T EVEN KNOW ME...
HEY, I JUST WANT TO HELP THERE BE MORE MANGA IN THE WORLD!
TH-THANK YOU SO MUCH!
THIS IS WORKING OUT WELL! I WAS WONDERING HOW TO HELP— I'M NOT GOOD WITH DIGITAL.
Yeah, that's so cool!!
ARE YOU STILL NOT OVER THAT TIME YOU ACCIDENTALLY DELETED MY FILES?
I MEAN, WE STILL HAD THE SKETCHES AND MADE THE DEADLINE. IT'S ALL GOOD.
ULP

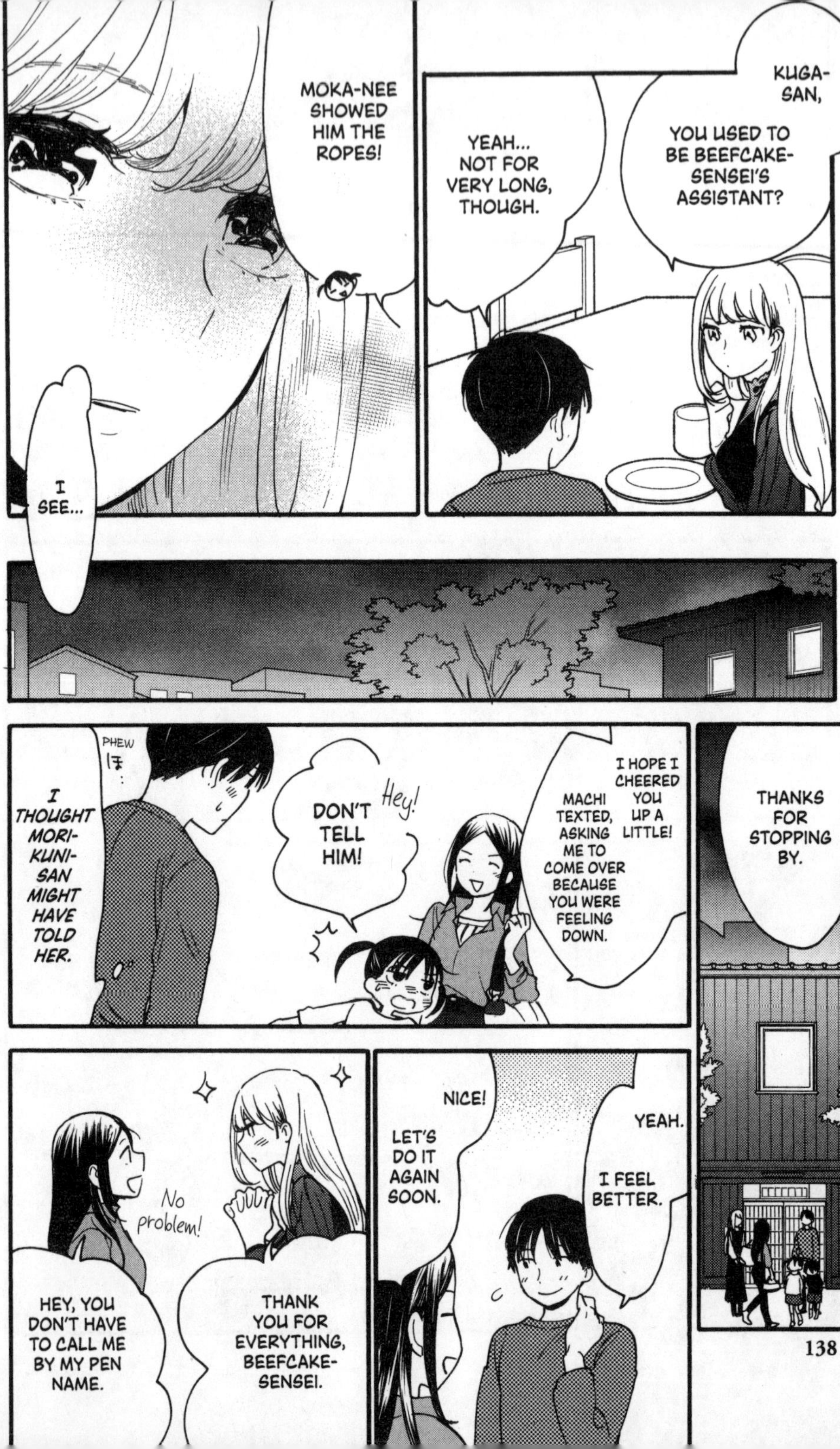
KUGA-SAN,
YOU USED TO BE BEEFCAKE-SENSEI'S ASSISTANT?
YEAH... NOT FOR VERY LONG, THOUGH.
MOKA-NEE SHOWED HIM THE ROPES!
I SEE...
THANKS FOR STOPPING BY.
I HOPE I CHEERED YOU UP A LITTLE!
MACHI TEXTED, ASKING ME TO COME OVER BECAUSE YOU WERE FEELING DOWN.
Hey!
DON'T TELL HIM!
PHEW
I THOUGHT MORI-KUNI-SAN MIGHT HAVE TOLD HER.
YEAH.
I FEEL BETTER.
NICE!
LET'S DO IT AGAIN SOON.
No problem!
THANK YOU FOR EVERYTHING, BEEFCAKE-SENSEI.
HEY, YOU DON'T HAVE TO CALL ME BY MY PEN NAME.

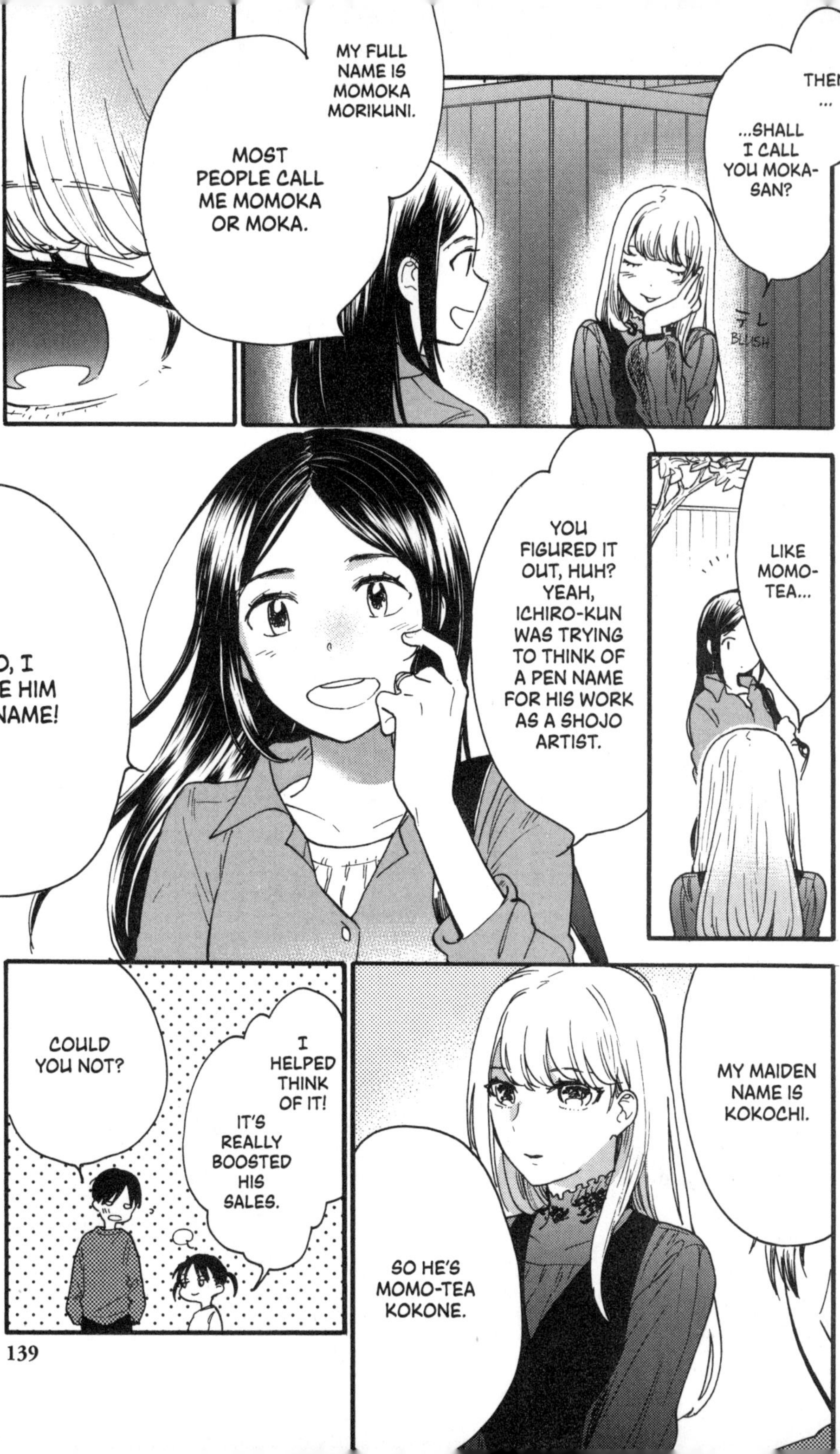
MY FULL NAME IS MOMOKA MORIKUNI.
MOST PEOPLE CALL ME MOMOKA OR MOKA.
THEN ...
...SHALL I CALL YOU MOKA-SAN?
BLUSH
LIKE MOMO-TEA...
YOU FIGURED IT OUT, HUH? YEAH, ICHIRO-KUN WAS TRYING TO THINK OF A PEN NAME FOR HIS WORK AS A SHOJO ARTIST.
SO, I GAVE HIM MY NAME!
MY MAIDEN NAME IS KOKOCHI.
SO HE'S MOMO-TEA KOKONE.
I HELPED THINK OF IT!
IT'S REALLY BOOSTED HIS SALES.
COULD YOU NOT?

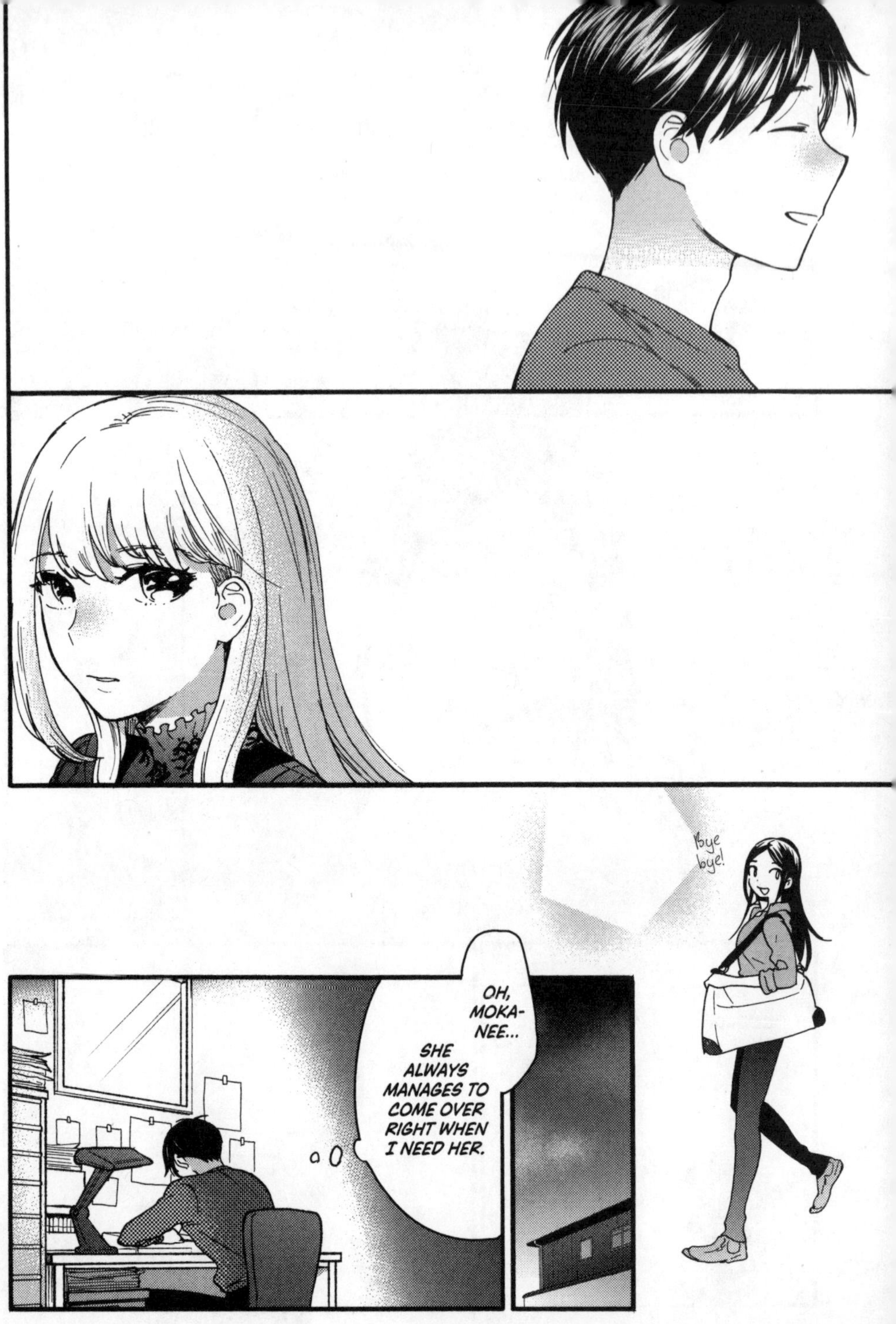
Bye bye!
OH, MOKA-NEE...
SHE ALWAYS MANAGES TO COME OVER RIGHT WHEN I NEED HER.

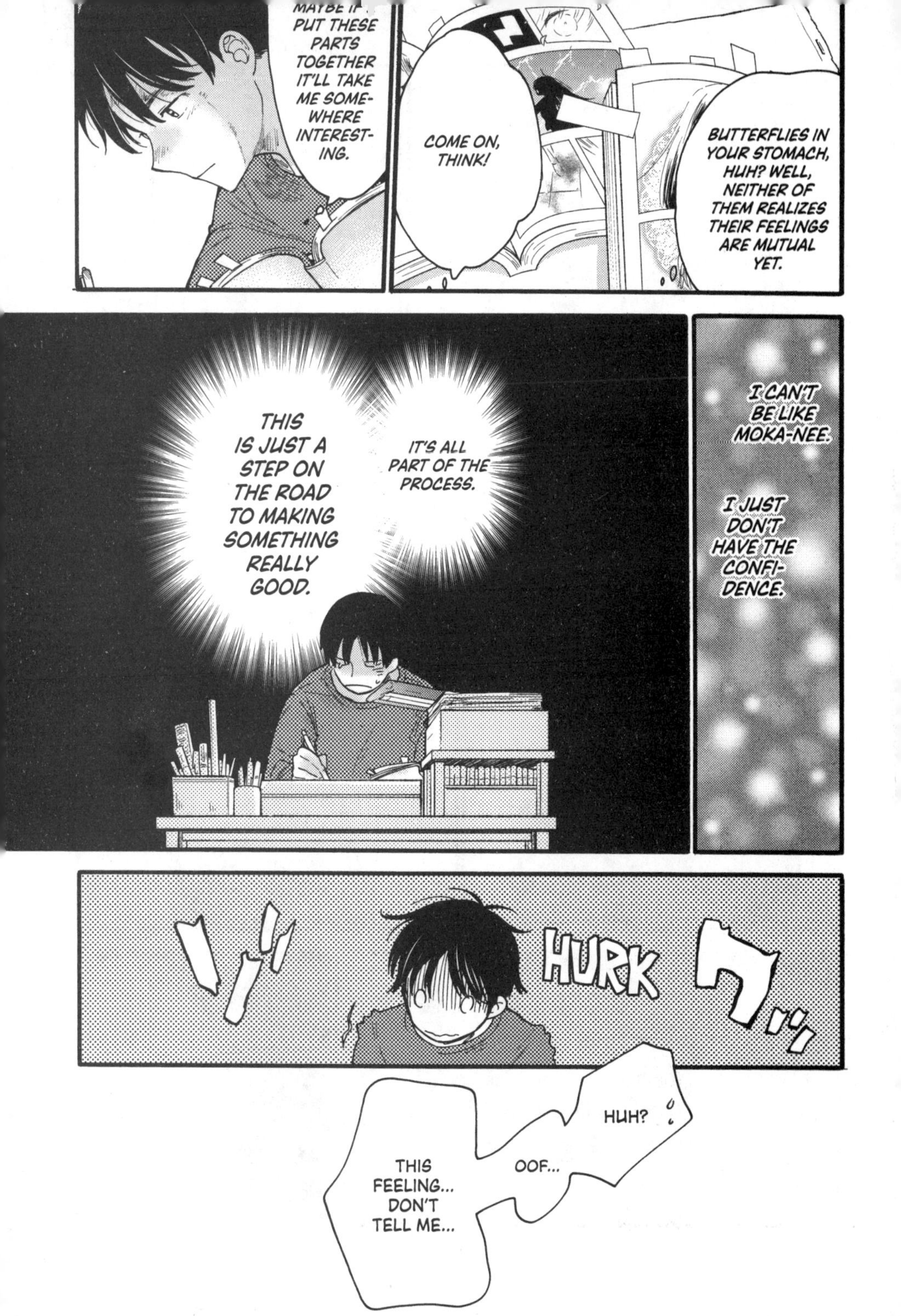
BUTTERFLIES IN YOUR STOMACH, HUH? WELL, NEITHER OF THEM REALIZES THEIR FEELINGS ARE MUTUAL YET.
COME ON, THINK!
MAYBE IF I PUT THESE PARTS TOGETHER IT'LL TAKE ME SOME-WHERE INTEREST-ING.
I CAN'T BE LIKE MOKA-NEE.
I JUST DON'T HAVE THE CONFI-DENCE.
IT'S ALL PART OF THE PROCESS.
THIS IS JUST A STEP ON THE ROAD TO MAKING SOMETHING REALLY GOOD.
HURK
HUH?
OOF...
THIS FEELING... DON'T TELL ME...

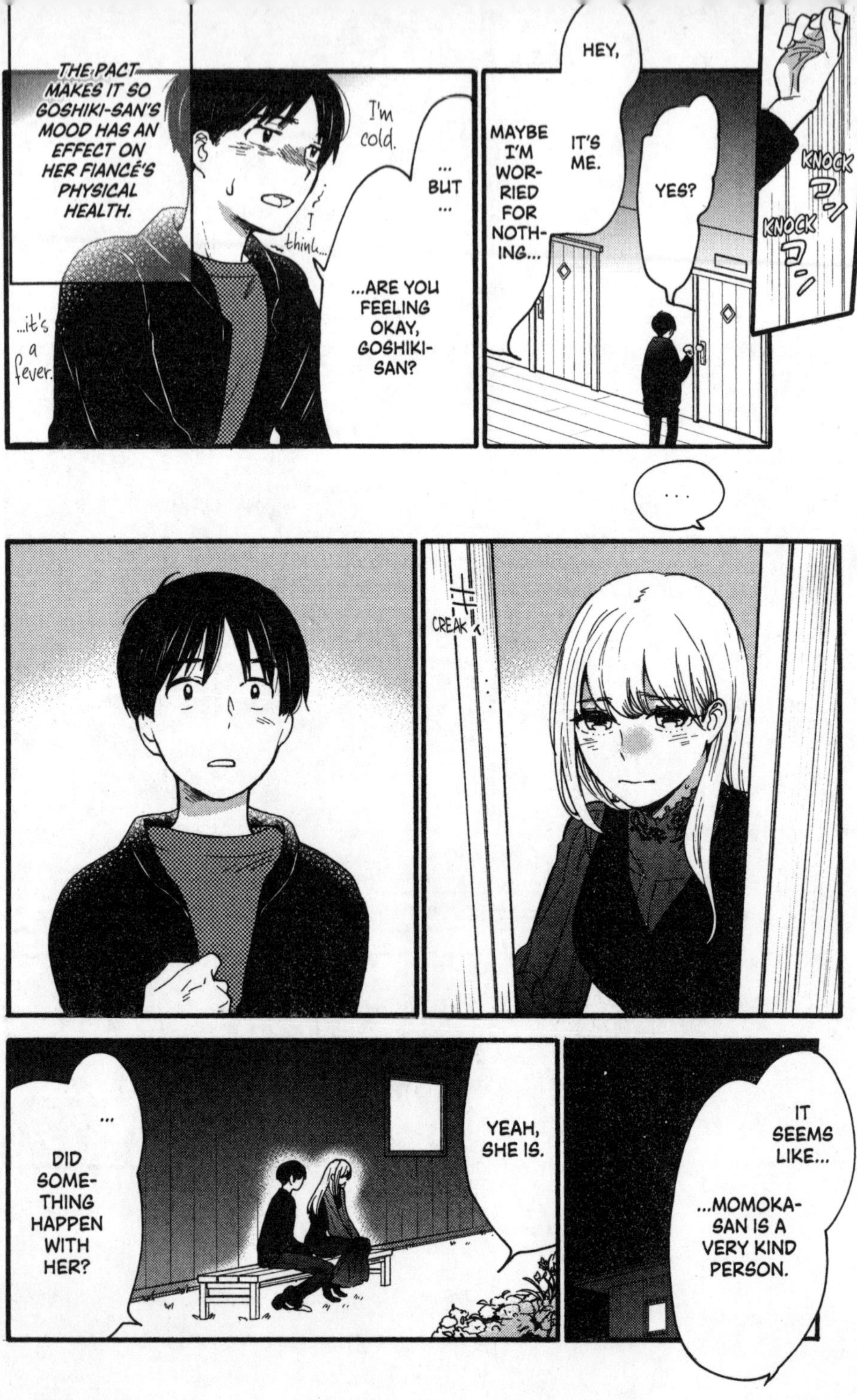

KNOCK
KNOCK
YES?
HEY, IT'S ME.
MAYBE I'M WORRIED FOR NOTHING...
I'm cold.
... BUT ...
...ARE YOU FEELING OKAY, GOSHIKI-SAN?
~I think...
THE PACT MAKES IT SO GOSHIKI-SAN'S MOOD HAS AN EFFECT ON HER FIANCÉ'S PHYSICAL HEALTH.
...it's a fever.
...
CREAK
...
IT SEEMS LIKE...
...MOMOKA-SAN IS A VERY KIND PERSON.
YEAH, SHE IS.
... DID SOMETHING HAPPEN WITH HER?

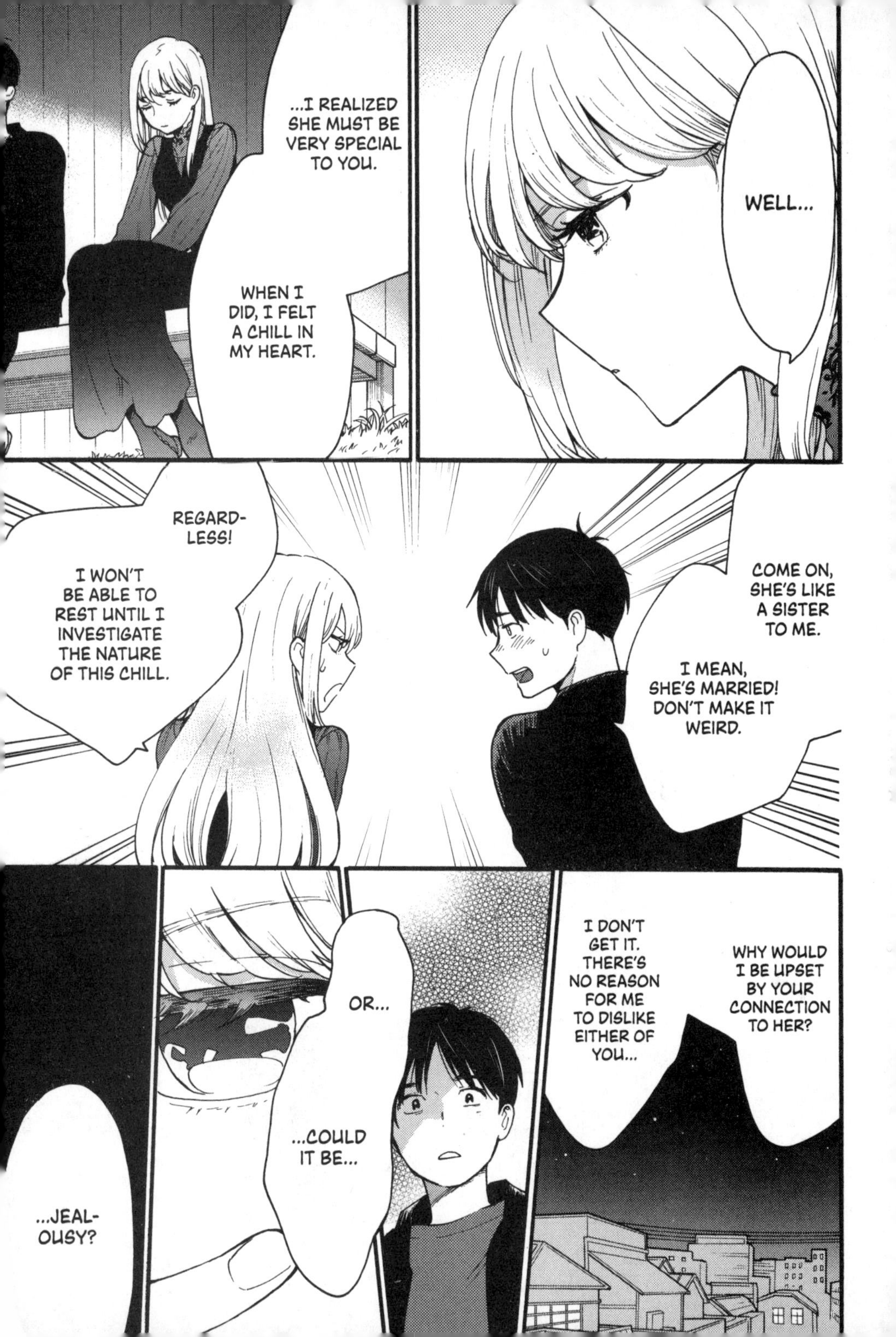
WELL...
...I REALIZED SHE MUST BE VERY SPECIAL TO YOU.
WHEN I DID, I FELT A CHILL IN MY HEART.
COME ON, SHE'S LIKE A SISTER TO ME.
I MEAN, SHE'S MARRIED! DON'T MAKE IT WEIRD.
REGARD-LESS!
I WON'T BE ABLE TO REST UNTIL I INVESTIGATE THE NATURE OF THIS CHILL.
WHY WOULD I BE UPSET BY YOUR CONNECTION TO HER?
I DON'T GET IT. THERE'S NO REASON FOR ME TO DISLIKE EITHER OF YOU...
OR...
...COULD IT BE...
...JEAL-OUSY?

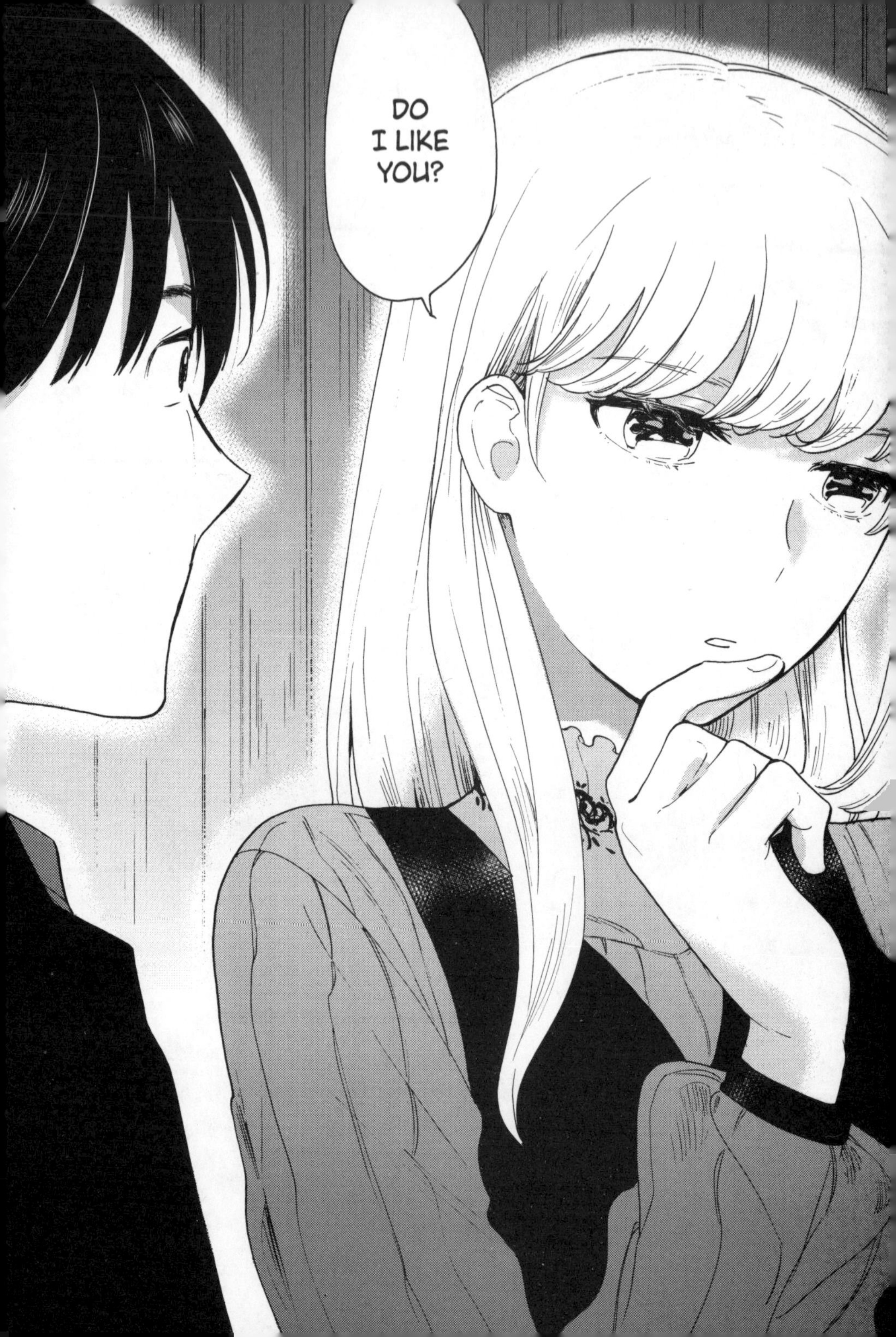
DO I LIKE YOU?

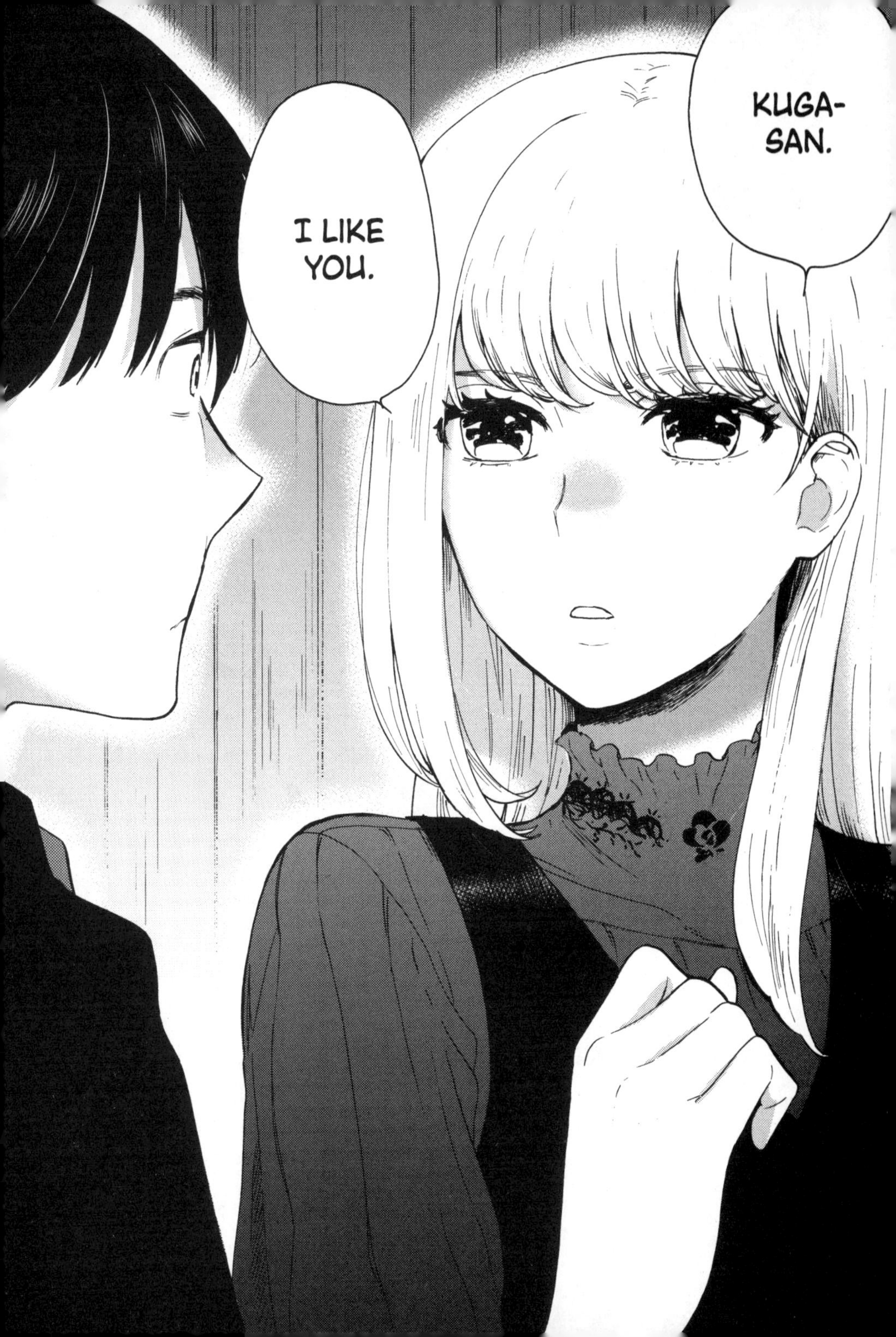
KUGA-SAN.
I LIKE YOU.

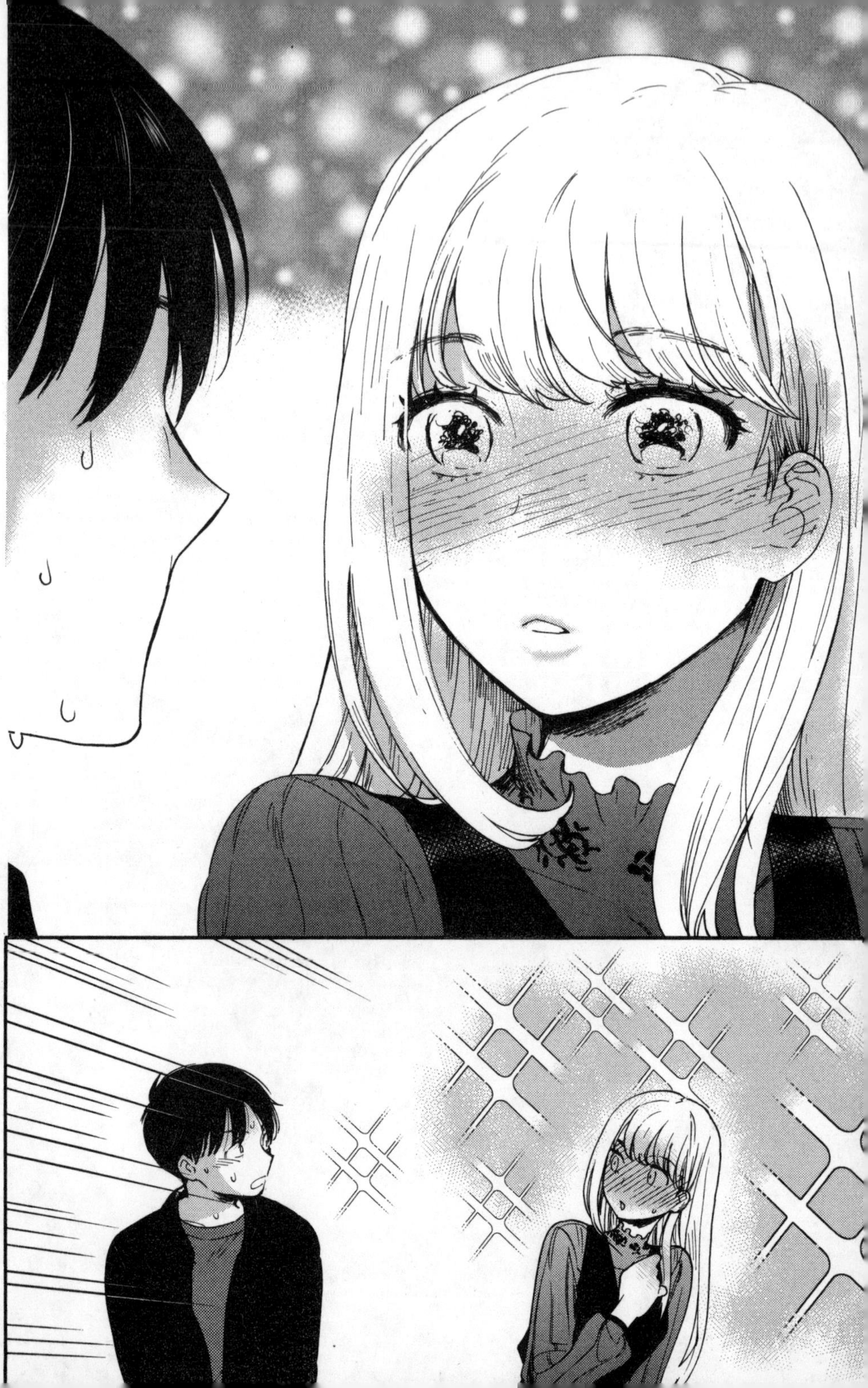

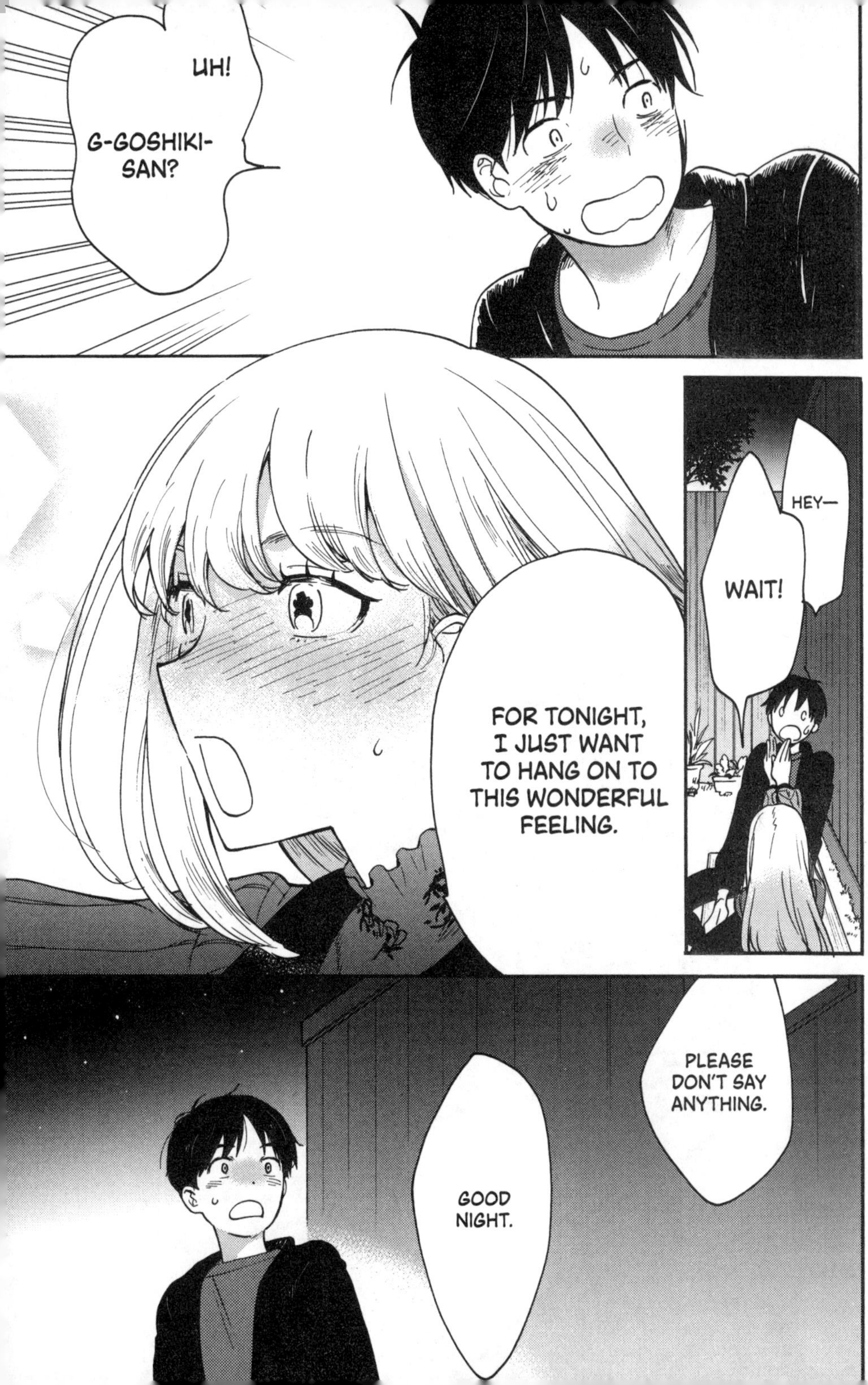
UH!
G-GOSHIKI-SAN?
HEY—
WAIT!
FOR TONIGHT, I JUST WANT TO HANG ON TO THIS WONDERFUL FEELING.
PLEASE DON'T SAY ANYTHING.
GOOD NIGHT.

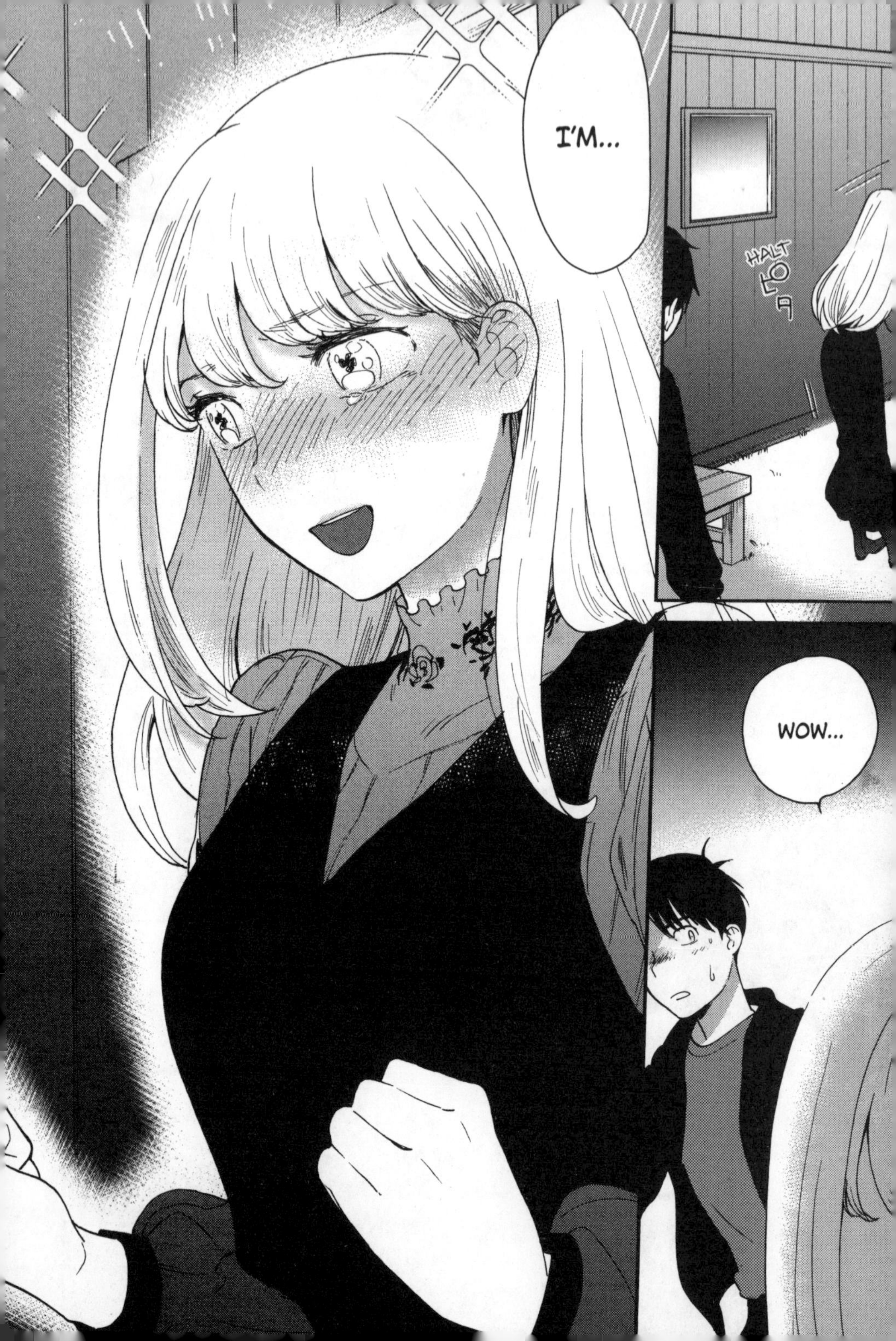
HALT
WOW...
I'M...

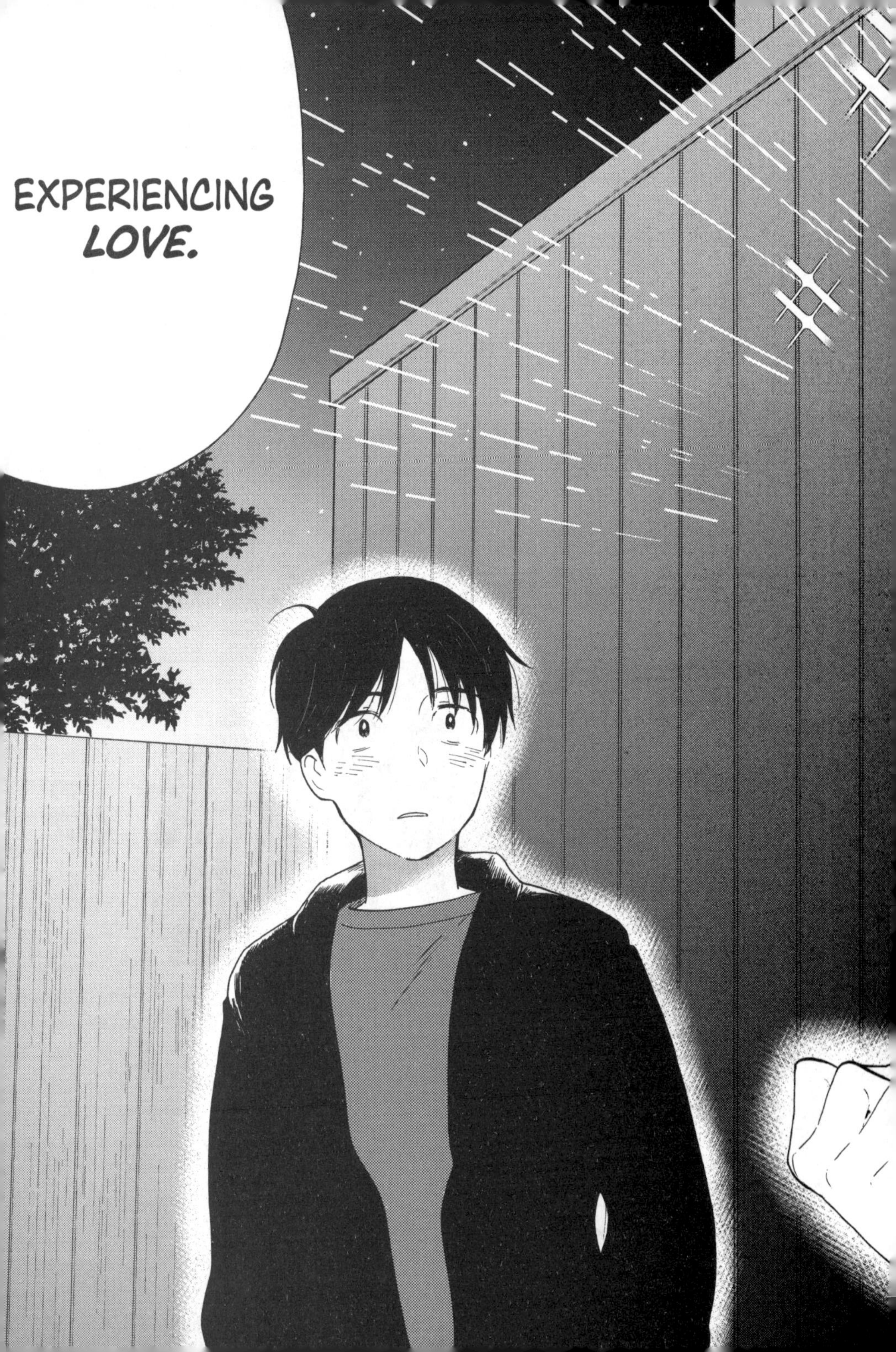
EXPERIENCING LOVE.

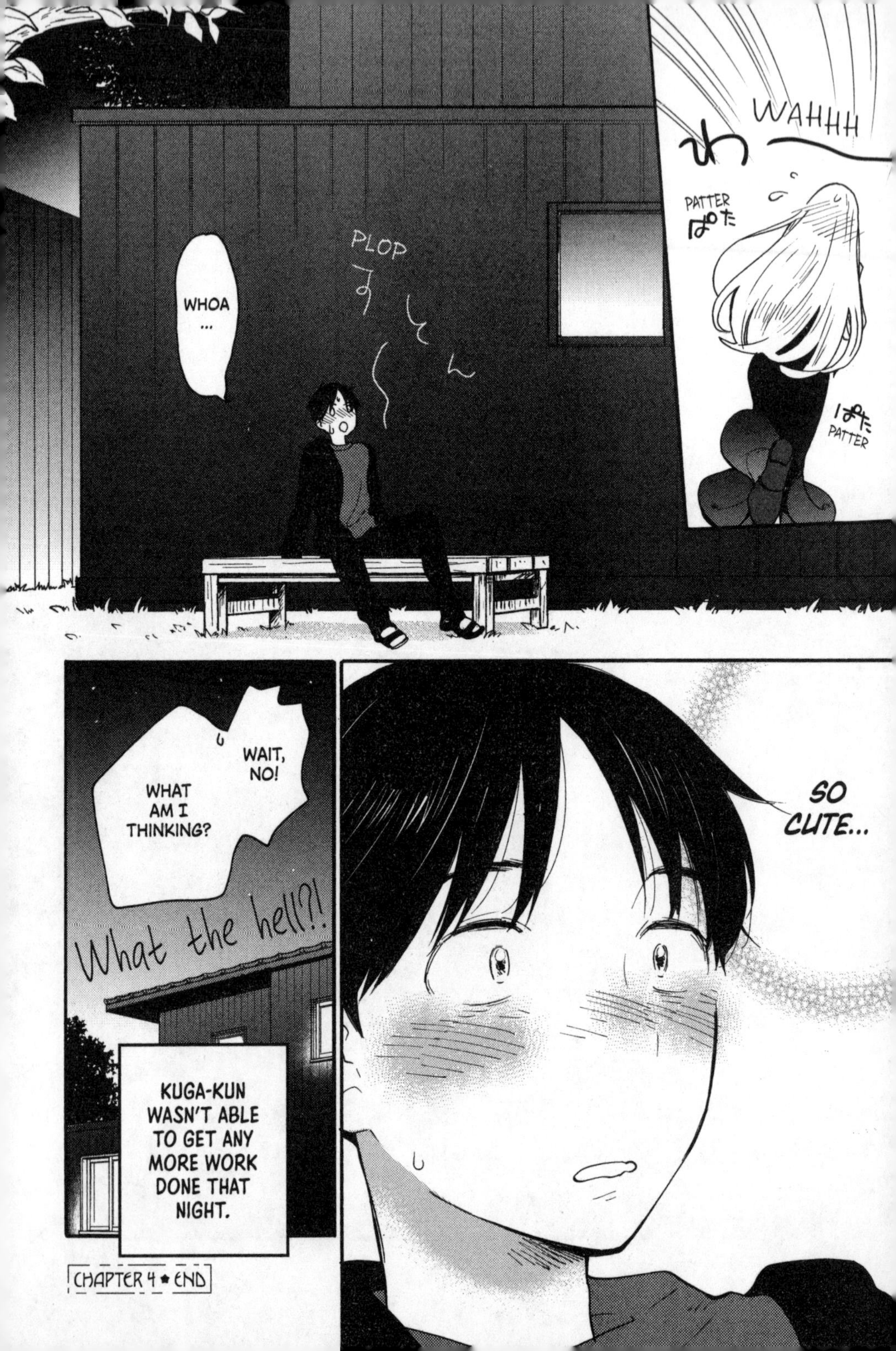
WAHHH
わ―
PATTER
ぱた
ぱた
PATTER
PLOP
すとん
WHOA ...
SO CUTE...
WAIT, NO!
WHAT AM I THINKING?
What the hell?!
KUGA-KUN WASN'T ABLE TO GET ANY MORE WORK DONE THAT NIGHT.
CHAPTER 4 ✿ END

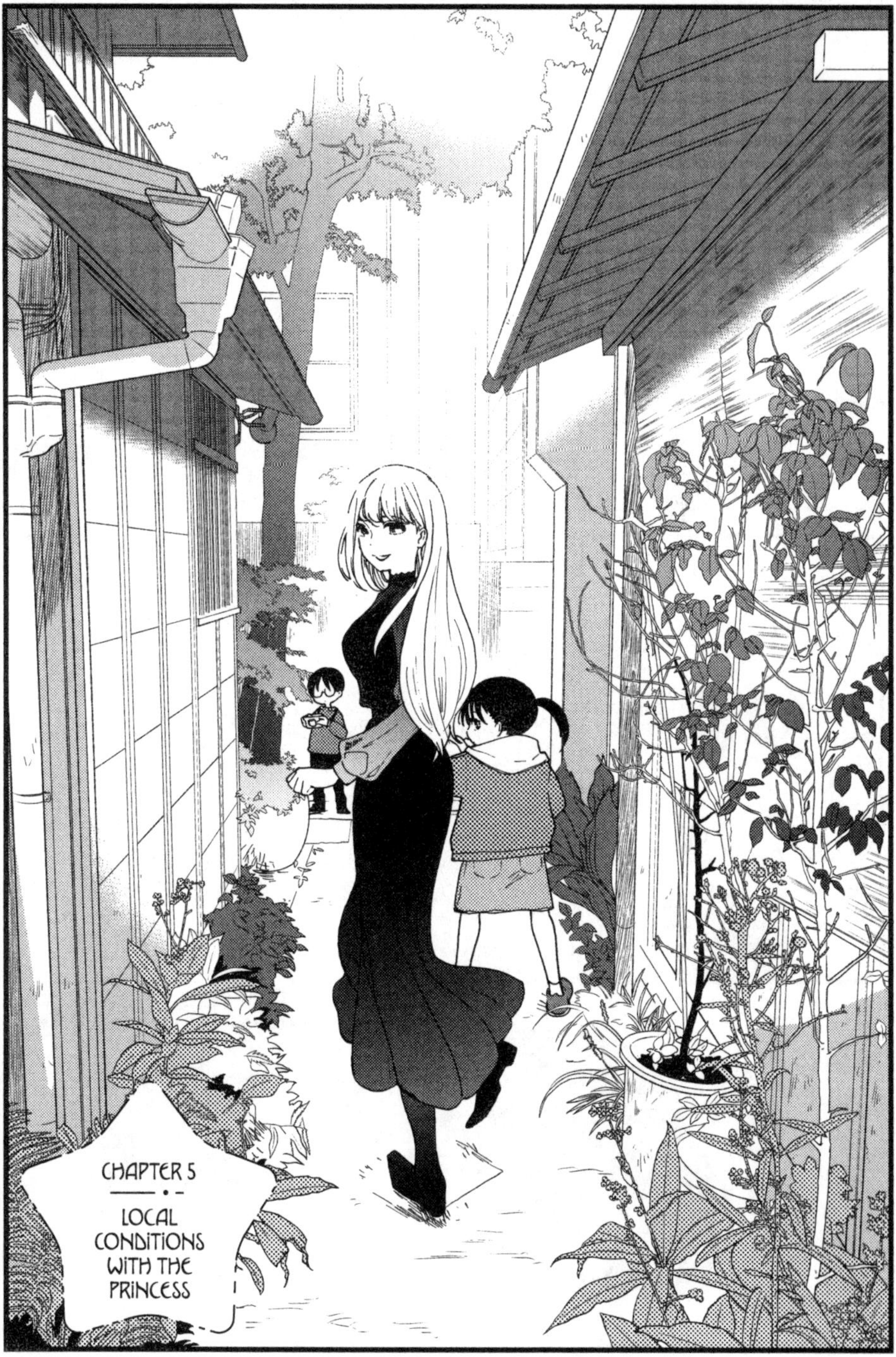
CHAPTER 5
LOCAL CONDITIONS WITH THE PRINCESS

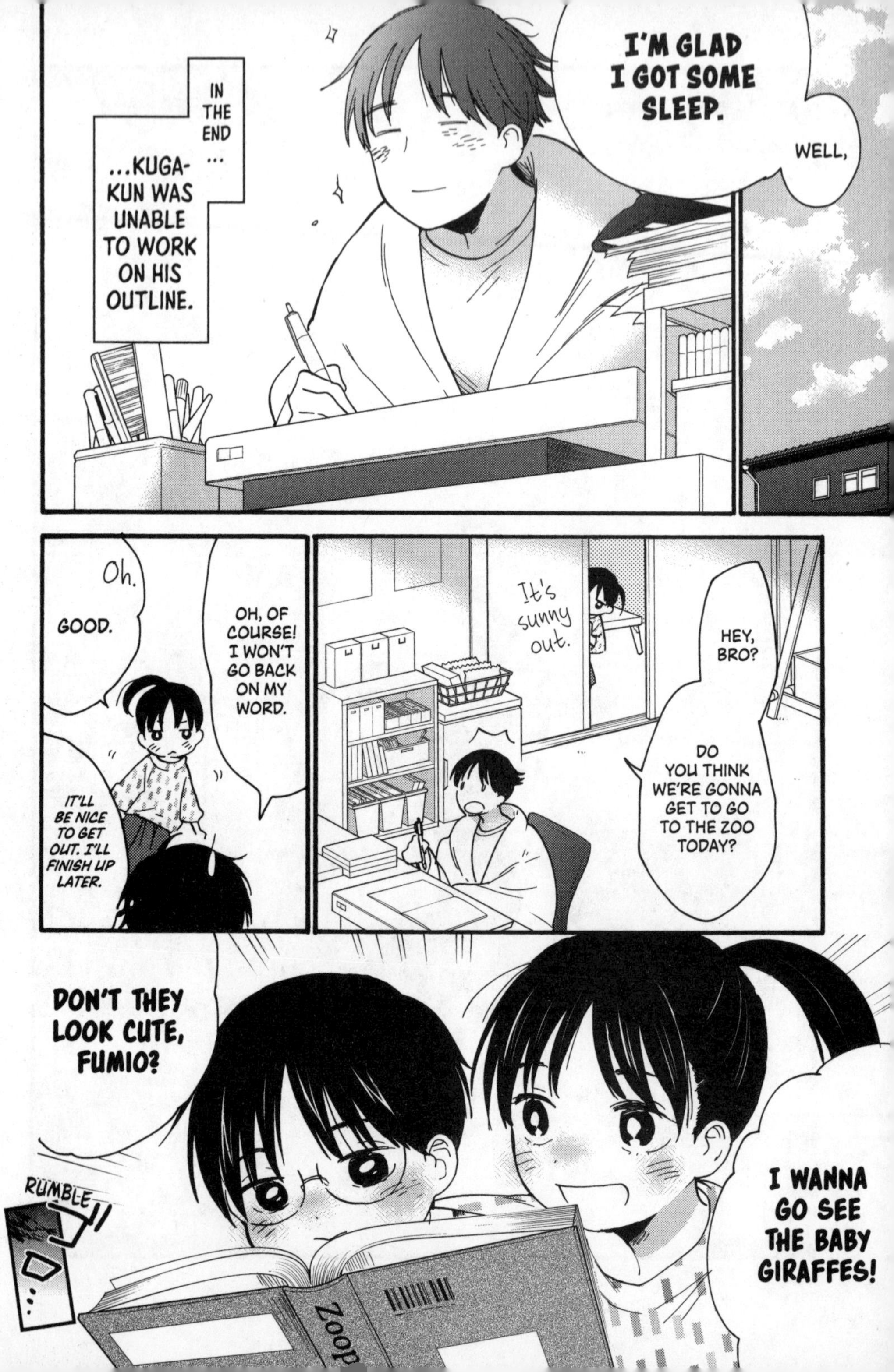
WELL,
I'M GLAD I GOT SOME SLEEP.
IN THE END ...
...KUGA-KUN WAS UNABLE TO WORK ON HIS OUTLINE.
HEY, BRO?
DO YOU THINK WE'RE GONNA GET TO GO TO THE ZOO TODAY?
It's sunny out.
OH, OF COURSE! I WON'T GO BACK ON MY WORD.
Oh.
GOOD.
IT'LL BE NICE TO GET OUT. I'LL FINISH UP LATER.
I WANNA GO SEE THE BABY GIRAFFES!
DON'T THEY LOOK CUTE, FUMIO?
Zoo
RUMBLE
...

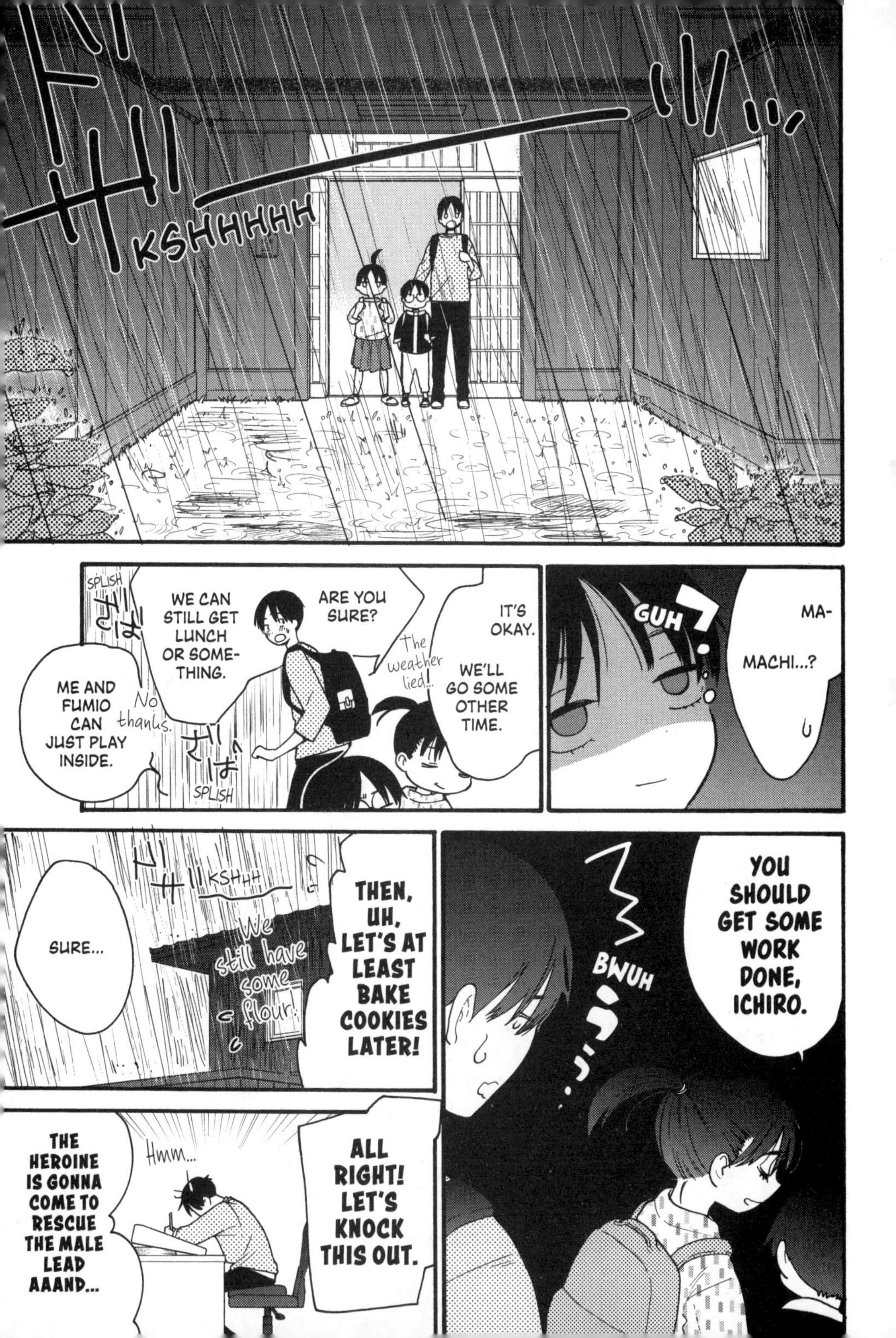
KSHHHHH
GUH
MA-MACHI...?
IT'S OKAY. WE'LL GO SOME OTHER TIME.
The weather lied...
ARE YOU SURE?
WE CAN STILL GET LUNCH OR SOMETHING.
SPLISH
ざば
ME AND FUMIO CAN JUST PLAY INSIDE.
No thanks.
ざば
SPLISH
YOU SHOULD GET SOME WORK DONE, ICHIRO.
BWUH
THEN, UH, LET'S AT LEAST BAKE COOKIES LATER!
We still have some flour!
KSHHH
SURE...
ALL RIGHT! LET'S KNOCK THIS OUT.
Hmm...
THE HEROINE IS GONNA COME TO RESCUE THE MALE LEAD AAAND...

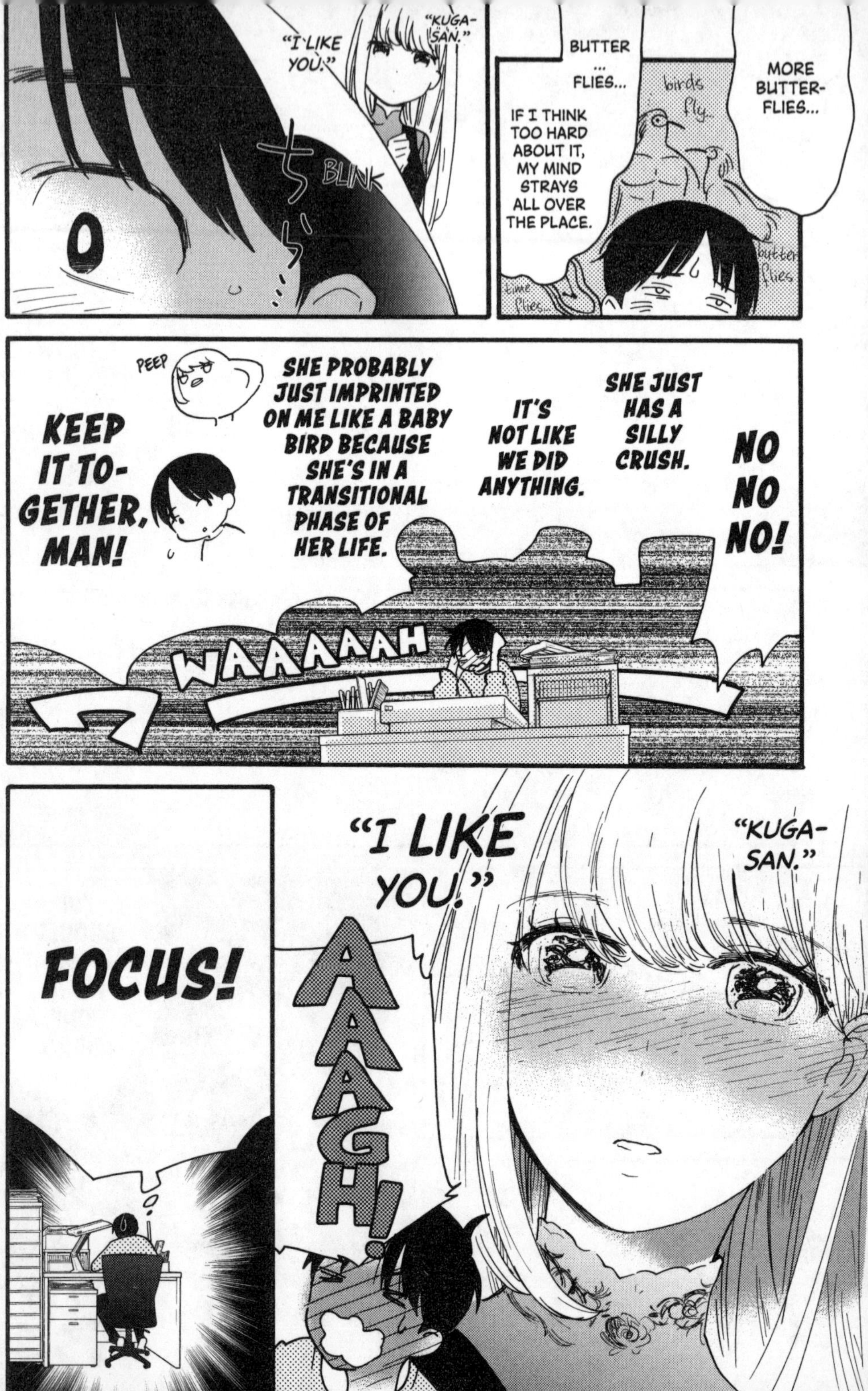
MORE BUTTER-FLIES...
BUTTER ... FLIES...
IF I THINK TOO HARD ABOUT IT, MY MIND STRAYS ALL OVER THE PLACE.
birds fly
butter flies
time flies
"KUGA-SAN."
"I LIKE YOU."
BLINK
NO NO NO!
SHE JUST HAS A SILLY CRUSH.
IT'S NOT LIKE WE DID ANYTHING.
SHE PROBABLY JUST IMPRINTED ON ME LIKE A BABY BIRD BECAUSE SHE'S IN A TRANSITIONAL PHASE OF HER LIFE.
PEEP
KEEP IT TO-GETHER, MAN!
WAAAAAH
"KUGA-SAN."
"I LIKE YOU."
AAAGH!
FOCUS!

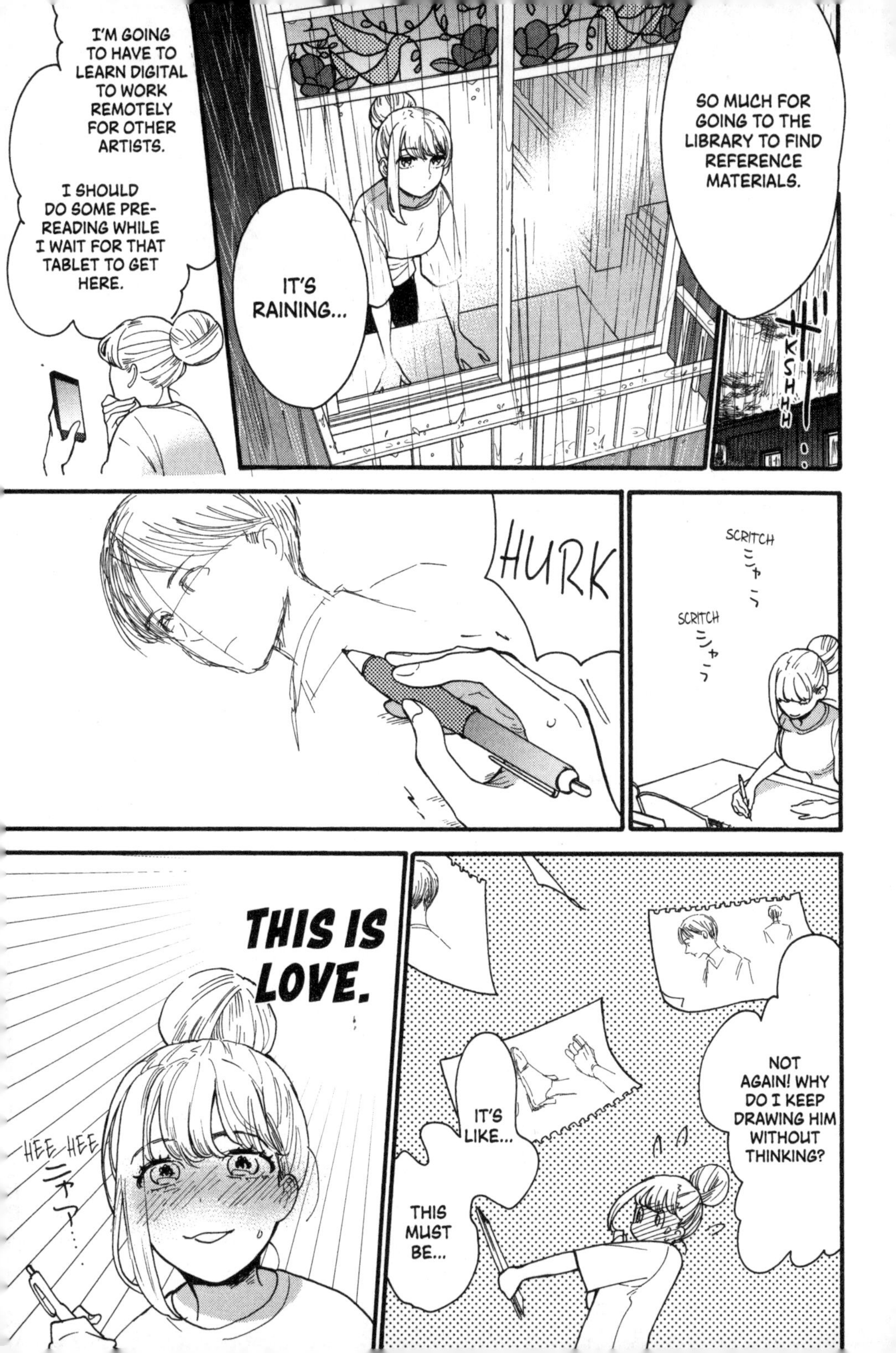

SO MUCH FOR GOING TO THE LIBRARY TO FIND REFERENCE MATERIALS.
KSHHH
IT'S RAINING...
I'M GOING TO HAVE TO LEARN DIGITAL TO WORK REMOTELY FOR OTHER ARTISTS.
I SHOULD DO SOME PRE-READING WHILE I WAIT FOR THAT TABLET TO GET HERE.
SCRITCH
SCRITCH
HURK
NOT AGAIN! WHY DO I KEEP DRAWING HIM WITHOUT THINKING?
IT'S LIKE...
THIS MUST BE...
THIS IS LOVE.
HEE HEE

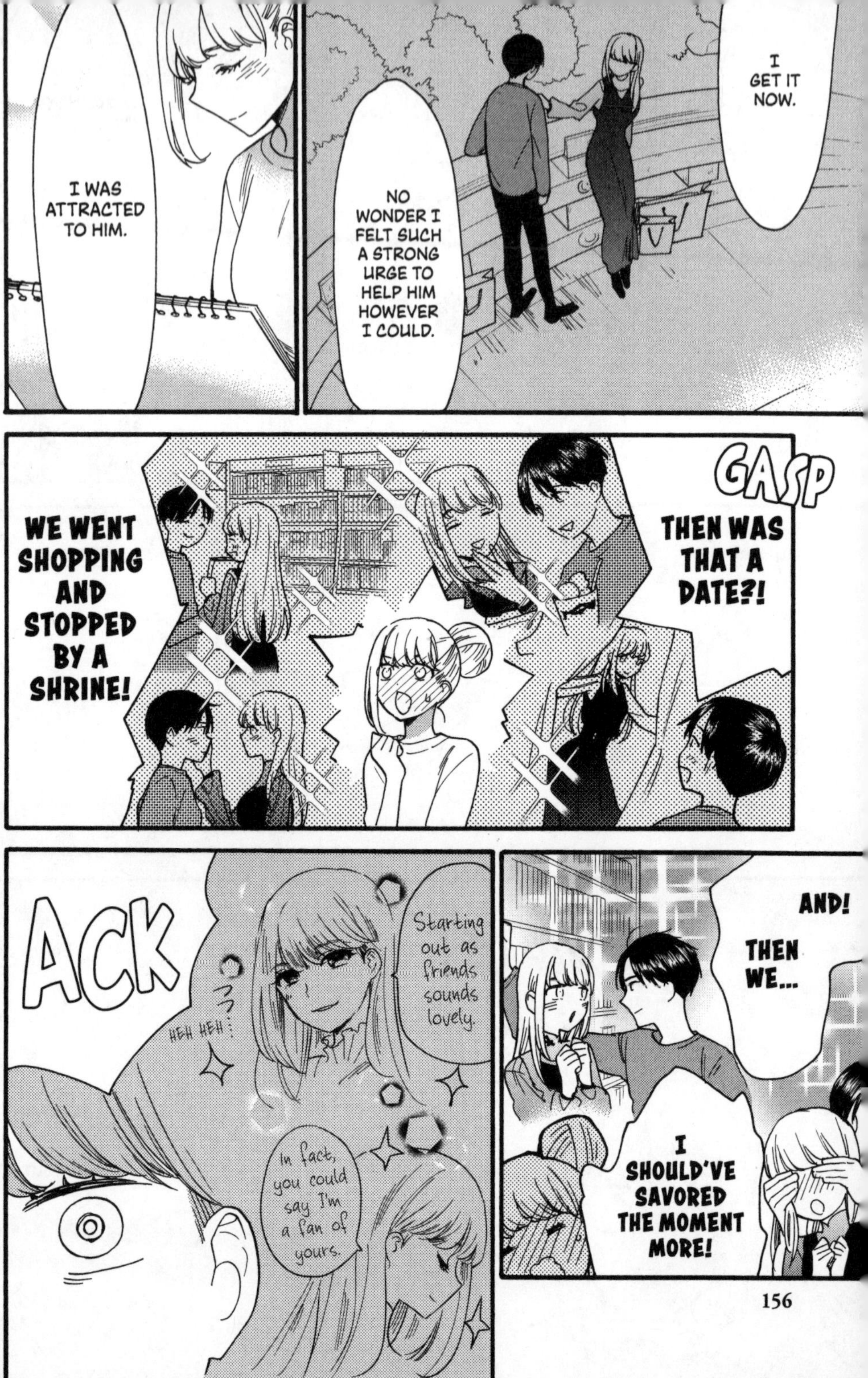
I GET IT NOW.
NO WONDER I FELT SUCH A STRONG URGE TO HELP HIM HOWEVER I COULD.
I WAS ATTRACTED TO HIM.
GASP
THEN WAS THAT A DATE?!
WE WENT SHOPPING AND STOPPED BY A SHRINE!
AND!
THEN WE...
I SHOULD'VE SAVORED THE MOMENT MORE!
Starting out as friends sounds lovely.
ACK
HEH HEH...
In fact, you could say I'm a fan of yours.

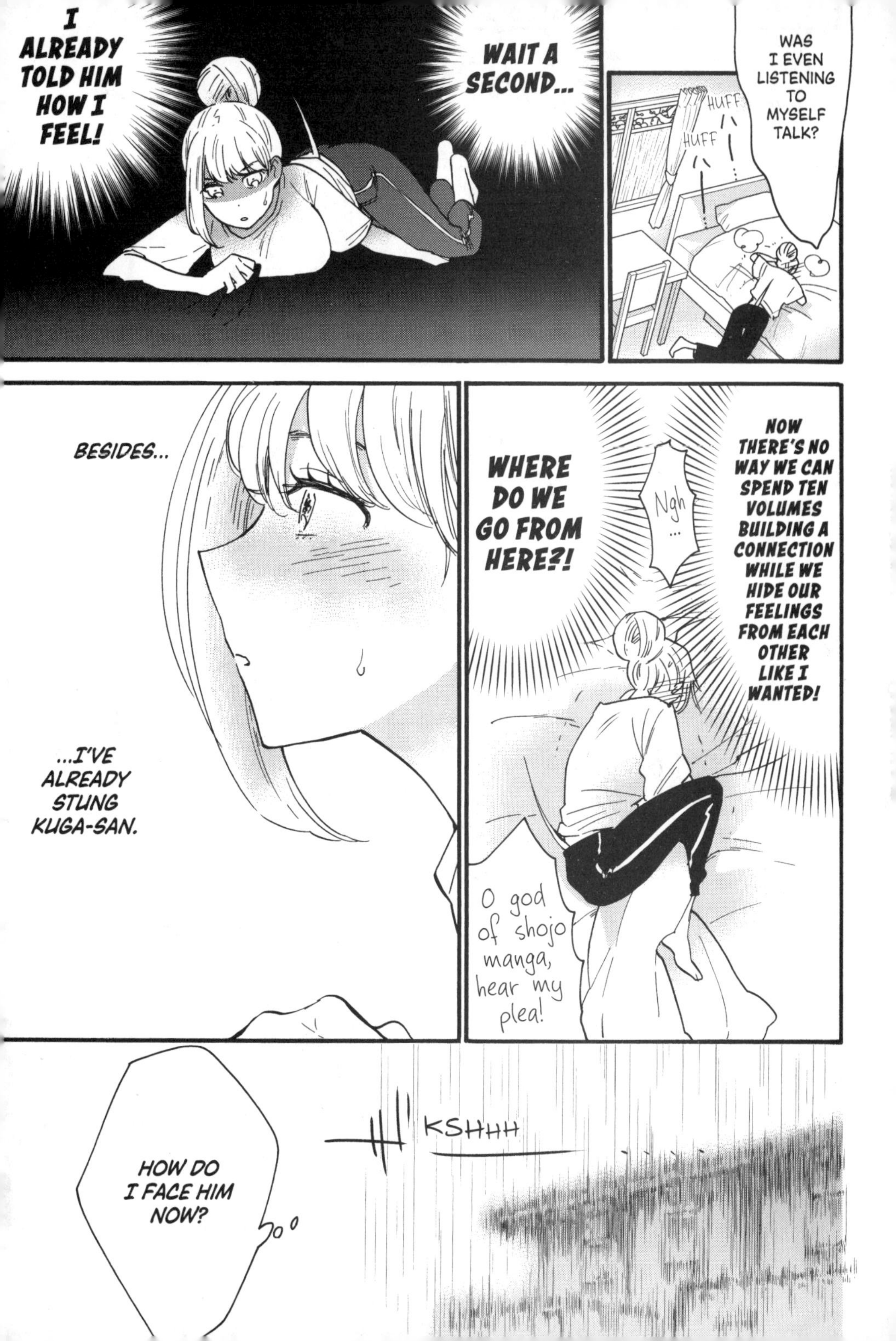

WAS I EVEN LISTENING TO MYSELF TALK?
HUFF
HUFF
WAIT A SECOND...
I ALREADY TOLD HIM HOW I FEEL!
NOW THERE'S NO WAY WE CAN SPEND TEN VOLUMES BUILDING A CONNECTION WHILE WE HIDE OUR FEELINGS FROM EACH OTHER LIKE I WANTED!
Ngh...
WHERE DO WE GO FROM HERE?!
O god of shojo manga, hear my plea!
BESIDES...
...I'VE ALREADY STUNG KUGA-SAN.
KSHHH
HOW DO I FACE HIM NOW?

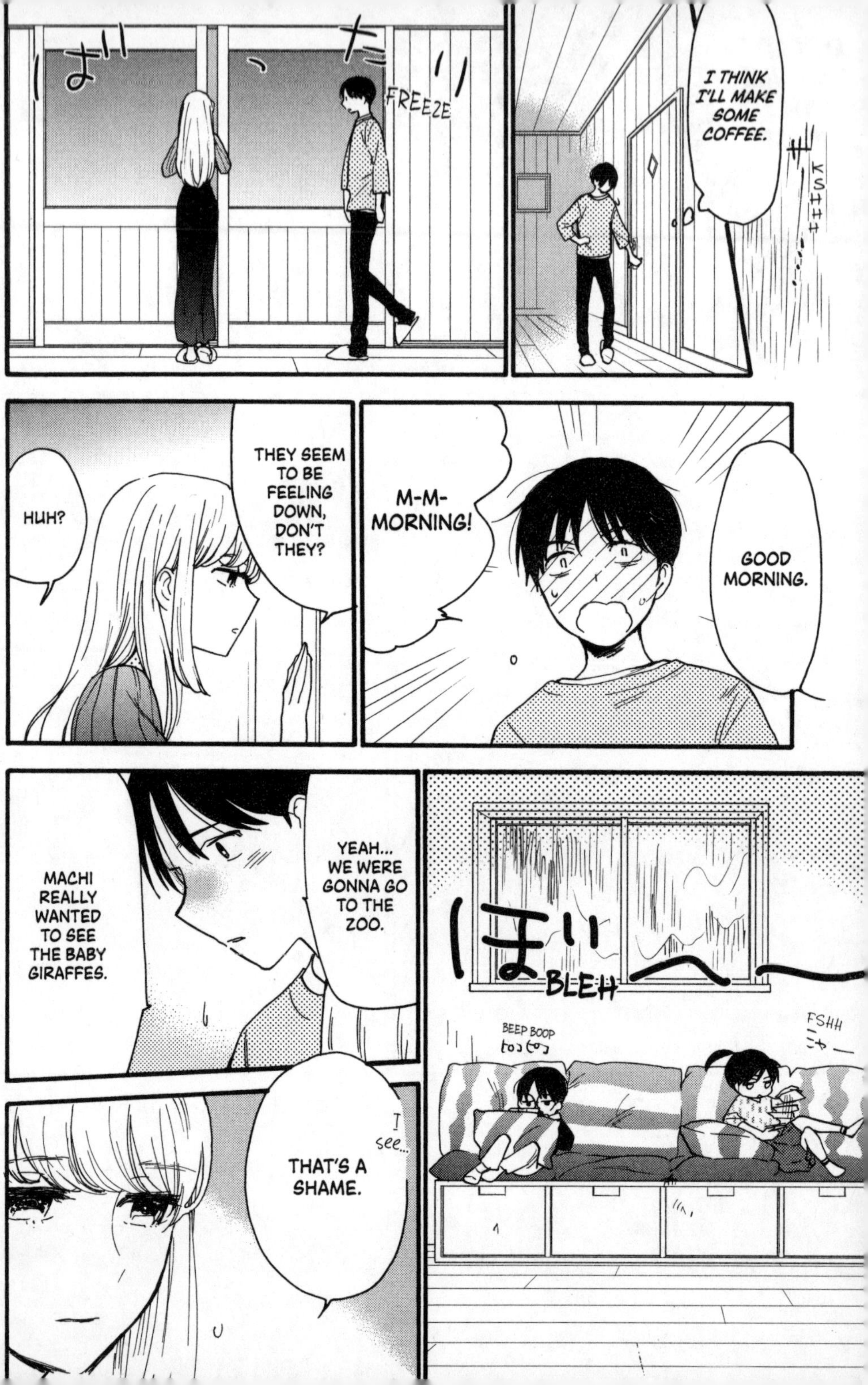
I THINK I'LL MAKE SOME COFFEE.
KSHHH
FREEZE
GOOD MORNING.
M-M-MORNING!
THEY SEEM TO BE FEELING DOWN, DON'T THEY?
HUH?
BLEH
FSHH
BEEP BOOP
YEAH... WE WERE GONNA GO TO THE ZOO.
MACHI REALLY WANTED TO SEE THE BABY GIRAFFES.
THAT'S A SHAME.
I see...

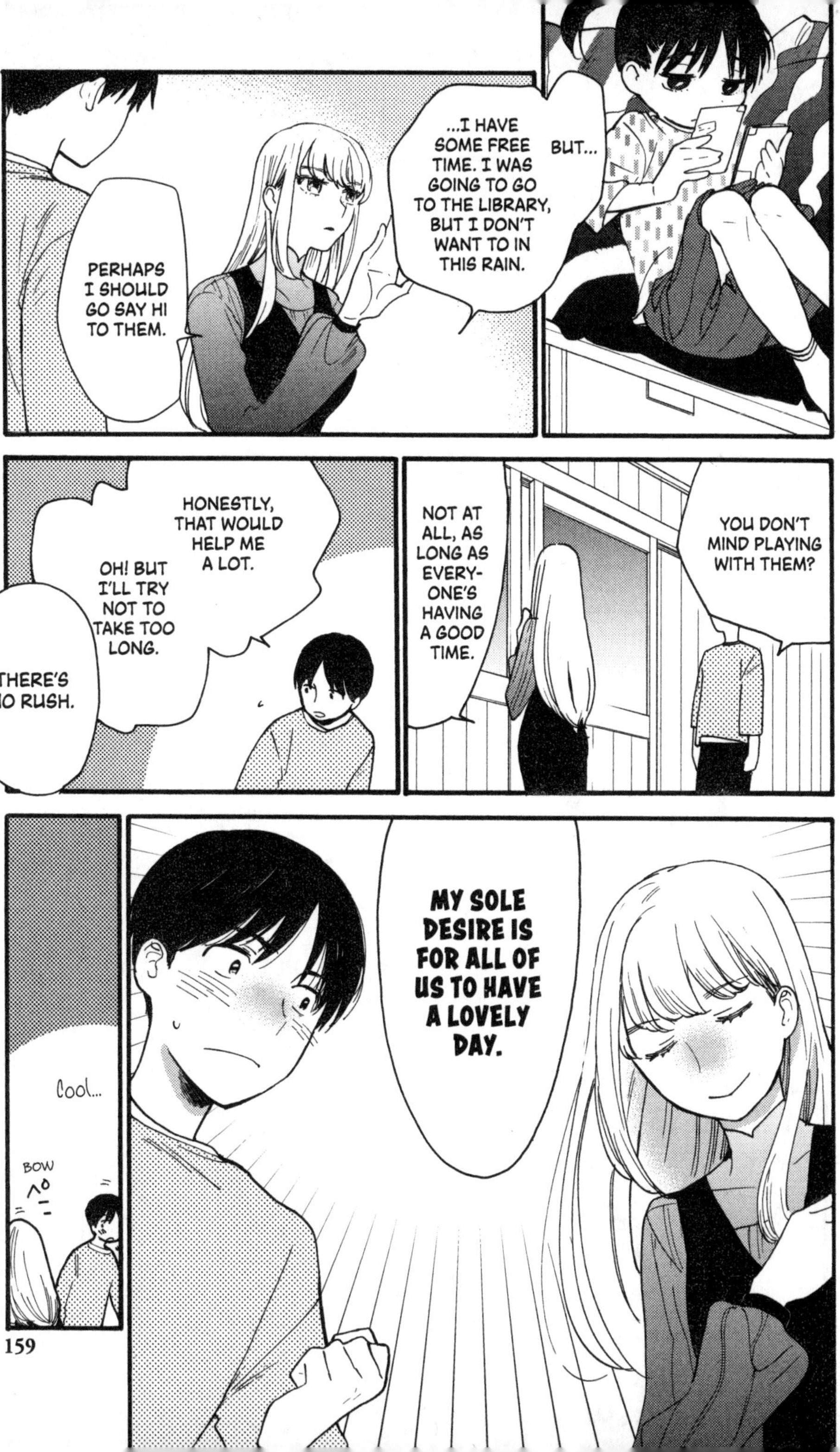
...I HAVE SOME FREE TIME. I WAS GOING TO GO TO THE LIBRARY, BUT I DON'T WANT TO IN THIS RAIN.
BUT...
PERHAPS I SHOULD GO SAY HI TO THEM.
YOU DON'T MIND PLAYING WITH THEM?
NOT AT ALL, AS LONG AS EVERY-ONE'S HAVING A GOOD TIME.
HONESTLY, THAT WOULD HELP ME A LOT.
OH! BUT I'LL TRY NOT TO TAKE TOO LONG.
THERE'S NO RUSH.
MY SOLE DESIRE IS FOR ALL OF US TO HAVE A LOVELY DAY.
Cool...
BOW

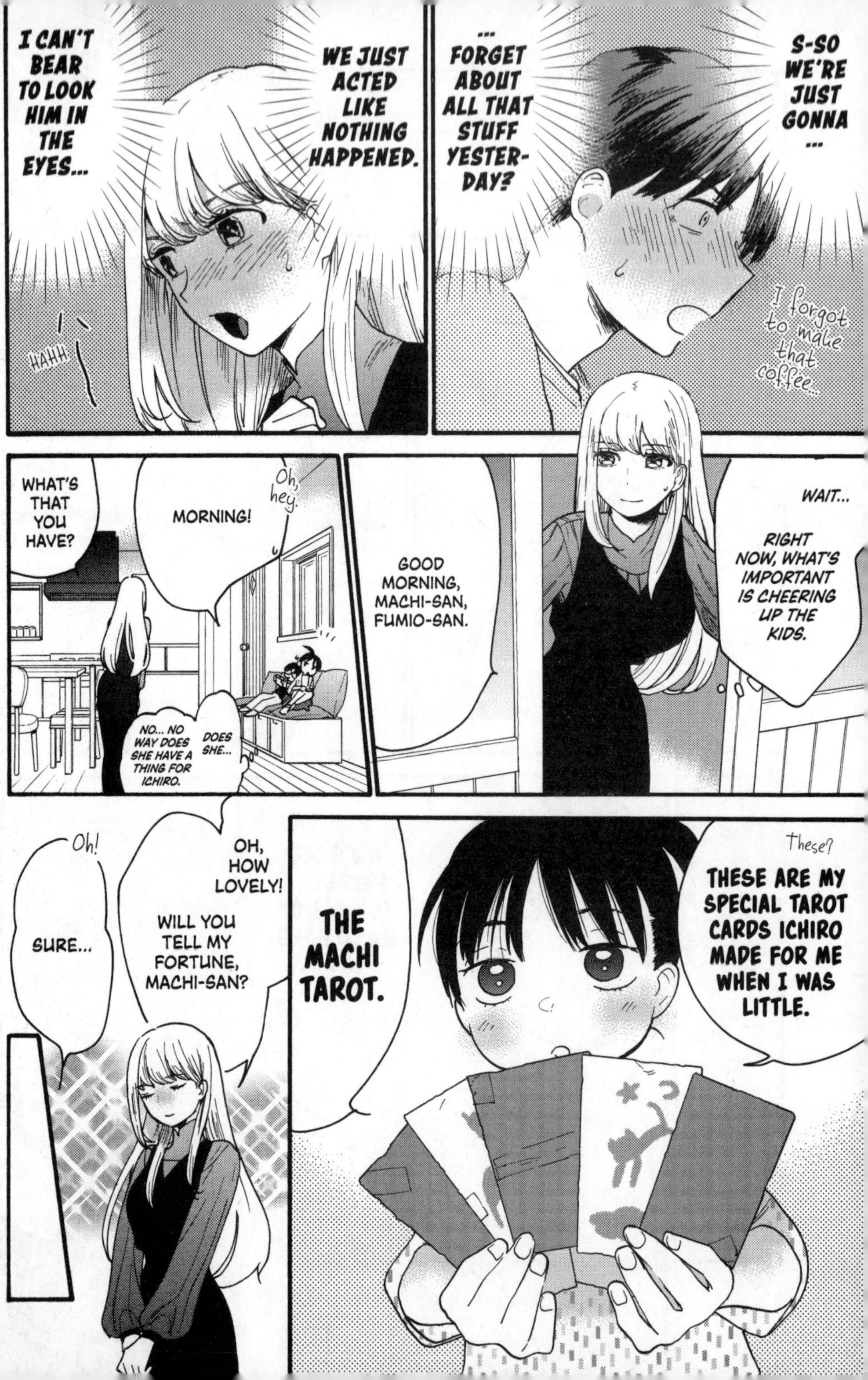
S-SO WE'RE JUST GONNA ...
... FORGET ABOUT ALL THAT STUFF YESTER-DAY?
I forgot to make that coffee...
WE JUST ACTED LIKE NOTHING HAPPENED.
I CAN'T BEAR TO LOOK HIM IN THE EYES...
HAHH
WAIT...
RIGHT NOW, WHAT'S IMPORTANT IS CHEERING UP THE KIDS.
GOOD MORNING, MACHI-SAN, FUMIO-SAN.
Oh, hey.
MORNING!
WHAT'S THAT YOU HAVE?
DOES SHE...
NO... NO WAY DOES SHE HAVE A THING FOR ICHIRO.
These?
THESE ARE MY SPECIAL TAROT CARDS ICHIRO MADE FOR ME WHEN I WAS LITTLE.
THE MACHI TAROT.
OH, HOW LOVELY!
WILL YOU TELL MY FORTUNE, MACHI-SAN?
Oh!
SURE...

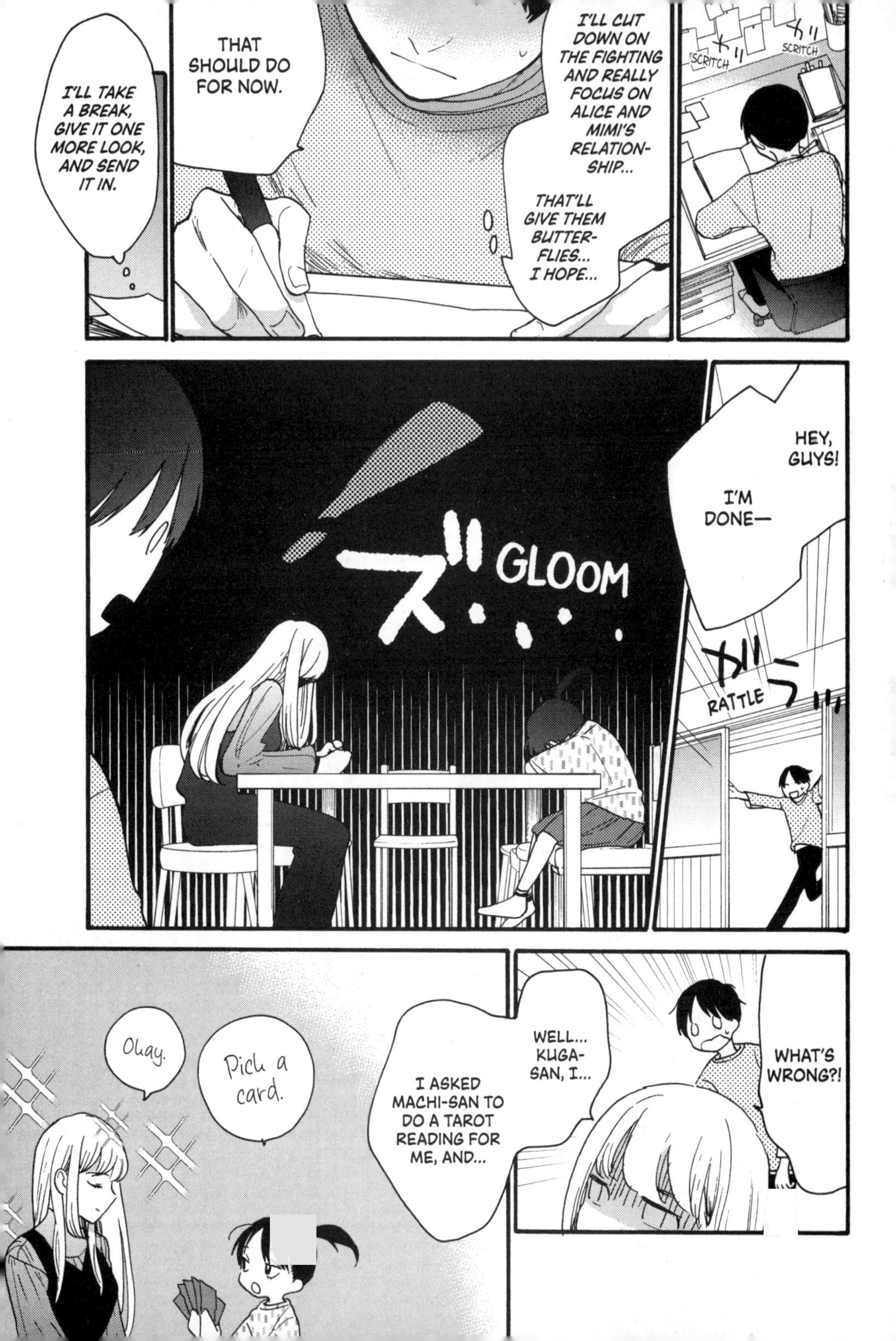
SCRITCH
SCRITCH
THAT SHOULD DO FOR NOW.
I'LL CUT DOWN ON THE FIGHTING AND REALLY FOCUS ON ALICE AND MIMI'S RELATION-SHIP...
THAT'LL GIVE THEM BUTTER-FLIES... I HOPE...
I'LL TAKE A BREAK, GIVE IT ONE MORE LOOK, AND SEND IT IN.
HEY, GUYS!
I'M DONE—
RATTLE
GLOOM
WHAT'S WRONG?!
WELL... KUGA-SAN, I...
I ASKED MACHI-SAN TO DO A TAROT READING FOR ME, AND...
Pick a card.
Okay.

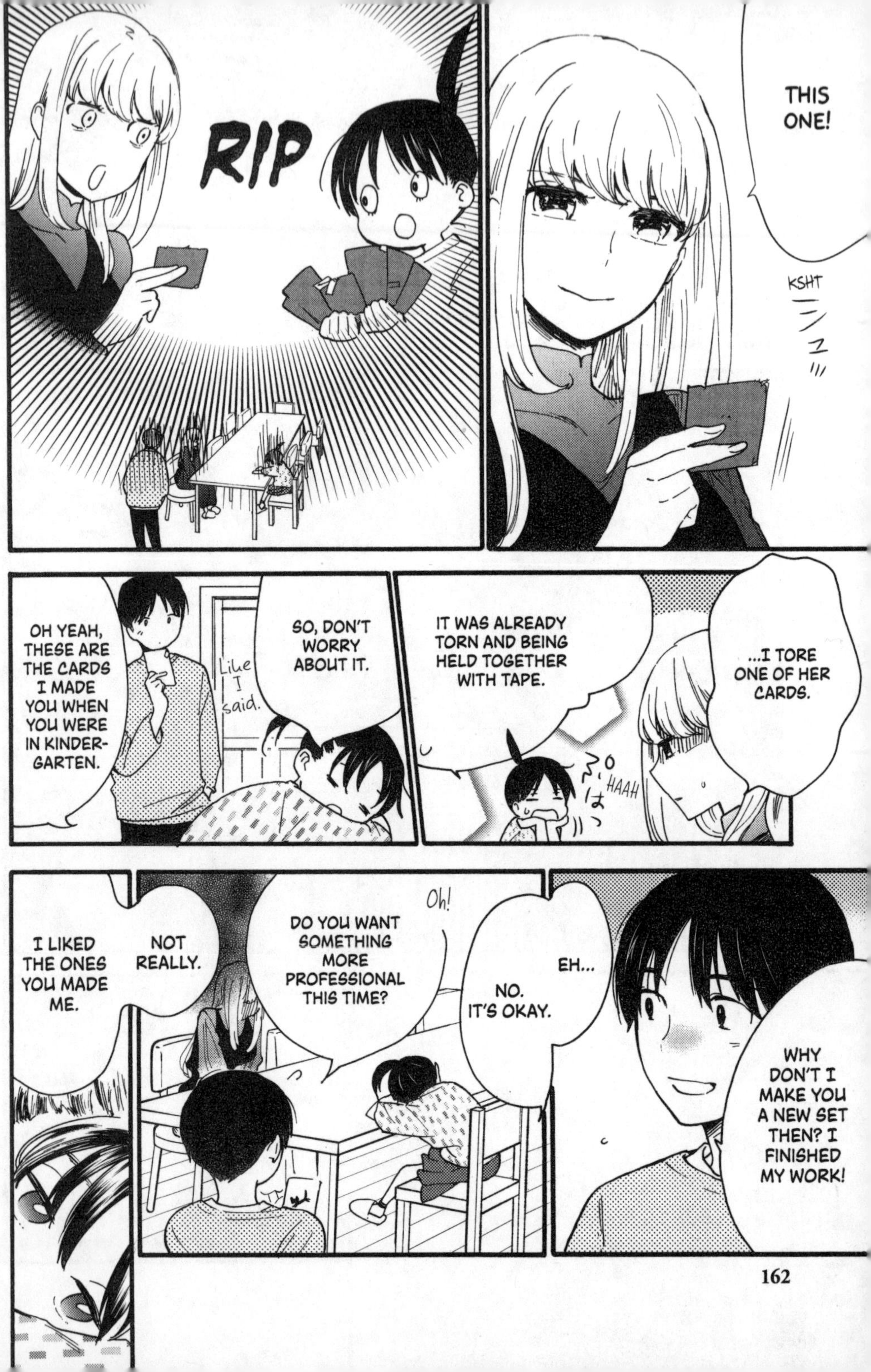
THIS ONE!
KSHT
RIP
...I TORE ONE OF HER CARDS.
IT WAS ALREADY TORN AND BEING HELD TOGETHER WITH TAPE.
HAAH
SO, DON'T WORRY ABOUT IT.
Like I said.
OH YEAH, THESE ARE THE CARDS I MADE YOU WHEN YOU WERE IN KINDER-GARTEN.
WHY DON'T I MAKE YOU A NEW SET THEN? I FINISHED MY WORK!
EH...
NO. IT'S OKAY.
Oh!
DO YOU WANT SOMETHING MORE PROFESSIONAL THIS TIME?
NOT REALLY.
I LIKED THE ONES YOU MADE ME.

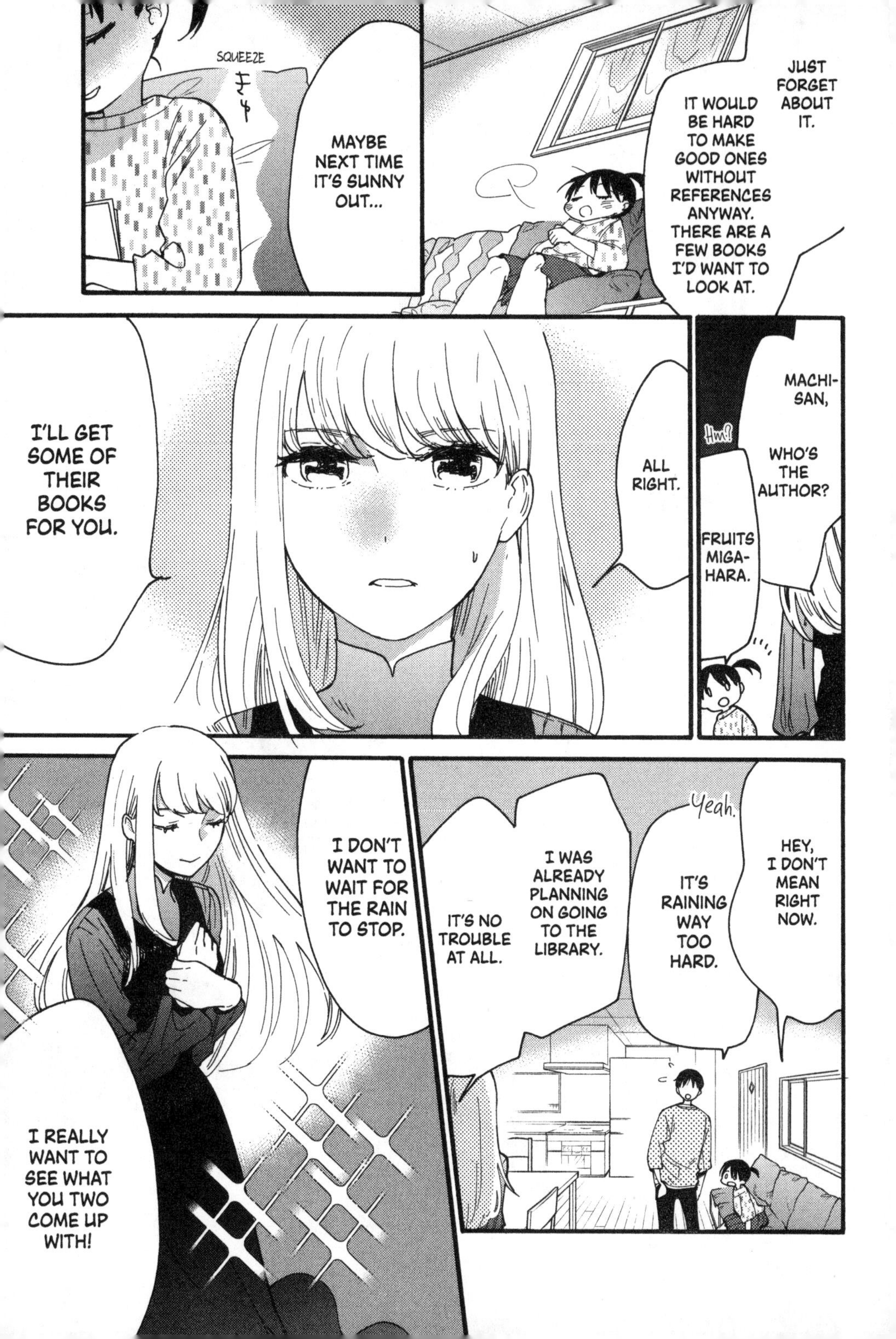
JUST FORGET ABOUT IT.
IT WOULD BE HARD TO MAKE GOOD ONES WITHOUT REFERENCES ANYWAY. THERE ARE A FEW BOOKS I'D WANT TO LOOK AT.
SQUEEZE
MAYBE NEXT TIME IT'S SUNNY OUT...
MACHI-SAN,
WHO'S THE AUTHOR?
Hm?
FRUITS MIGA-HARA.
ALL RIGHT.
I'LL GET SOME OF THEIR BOOKS FOR YOU.
HEY, I DON'T MEAN RIGHT NOW.
Yeah.
IT'S RAINING WAY TOO HARD.
I WAS ALREADY PLANNING ON GOING TO THE LIBRARY.
IT'S NO TROUBLE AT ALL.
I DON'T WANT TO WAIT FOR THE RAIN TO STOP.
I REALLY WANT TO SEE WHAT YOU TWO COME UP WITH!

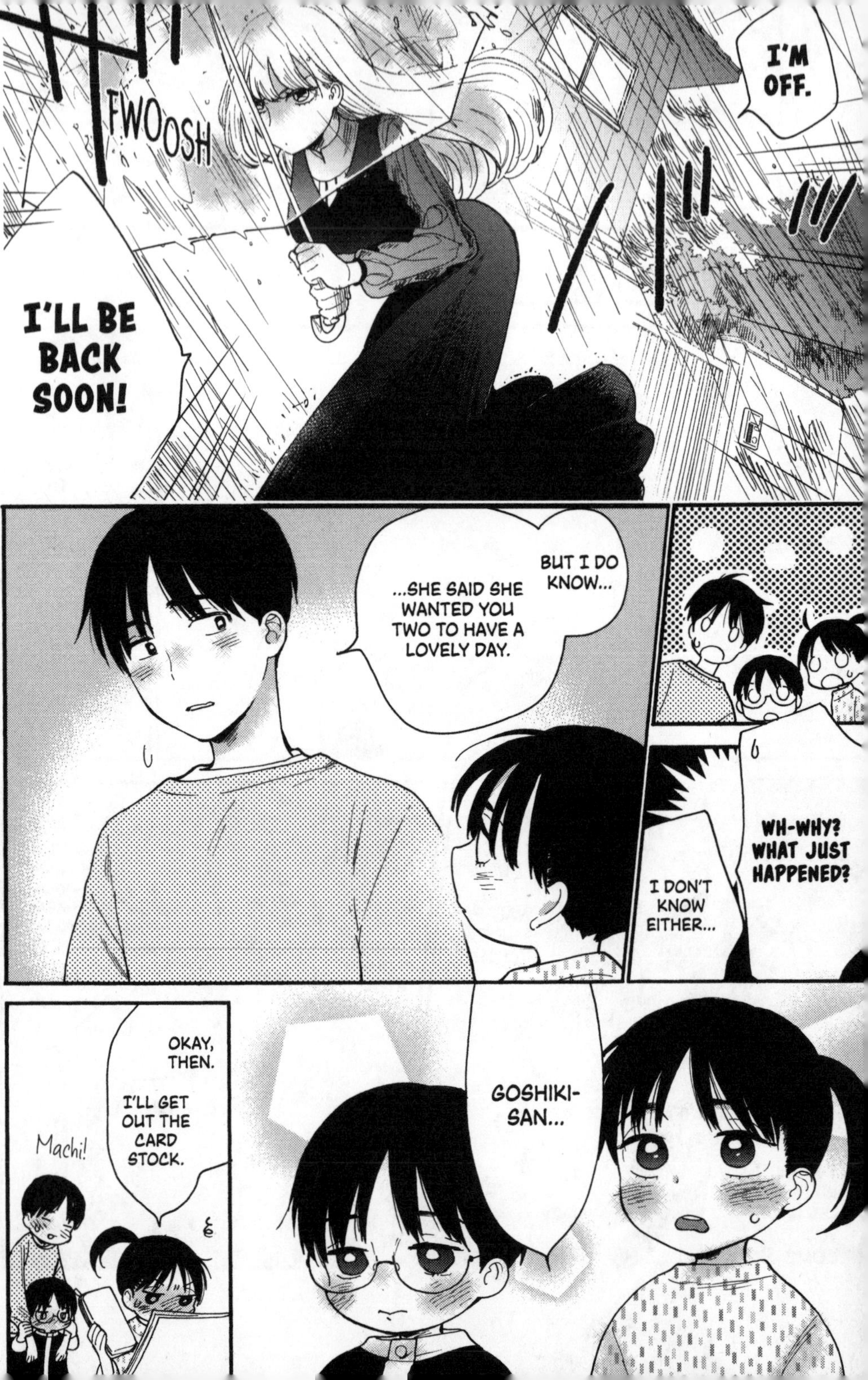
I'M OFF.
FWOOSH
I'LL BE BACK SOON!
WH-WHY? WHAT JUST HAPPENED?
I DON'T KNOW EITHER...
BUT I DO KNOW...
...SHE SAID SHE WANTED YOU TWO TO HAVE A LOVELY DAY.
GOSHIKI-SAN...
OKAY, THEN.
I'LL GET OUT THE CARD STOCK.
Machi!

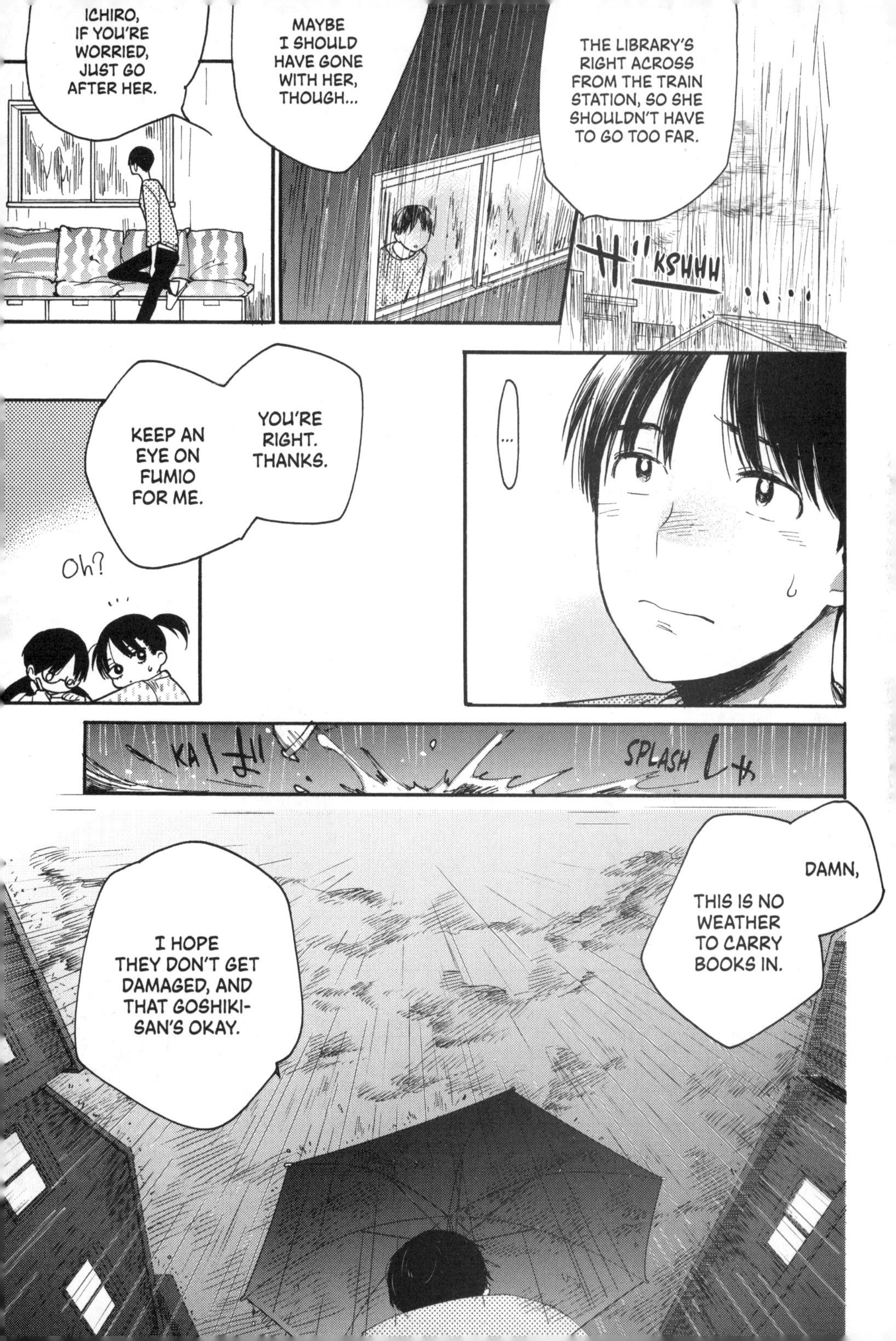
THE LIBRARY'S RIGHT ACROSS FROM THE TRAIN STATION, SO SHE SHOULDN'T HAVE TO GO TOO FAR.
KSHHH
MAYBE I SHOULD HAVE GONE WITH HER, THOUGH...
ICHIRO, IF YOU'RE WORRIED, JUST GO AFTER HER.
...
YOU'RE RIGHT. THANKS.
KEEP AN EYE ON FUMIO FOR ME.
Oh?
SPLASH
DAMN,
THIS IS NO WEATHER TO CARRY BOOKS IN.
I HOPE THEY DON'T GET DAMAGED, AND THAT GOSHIKI-SAN'S OKAY.

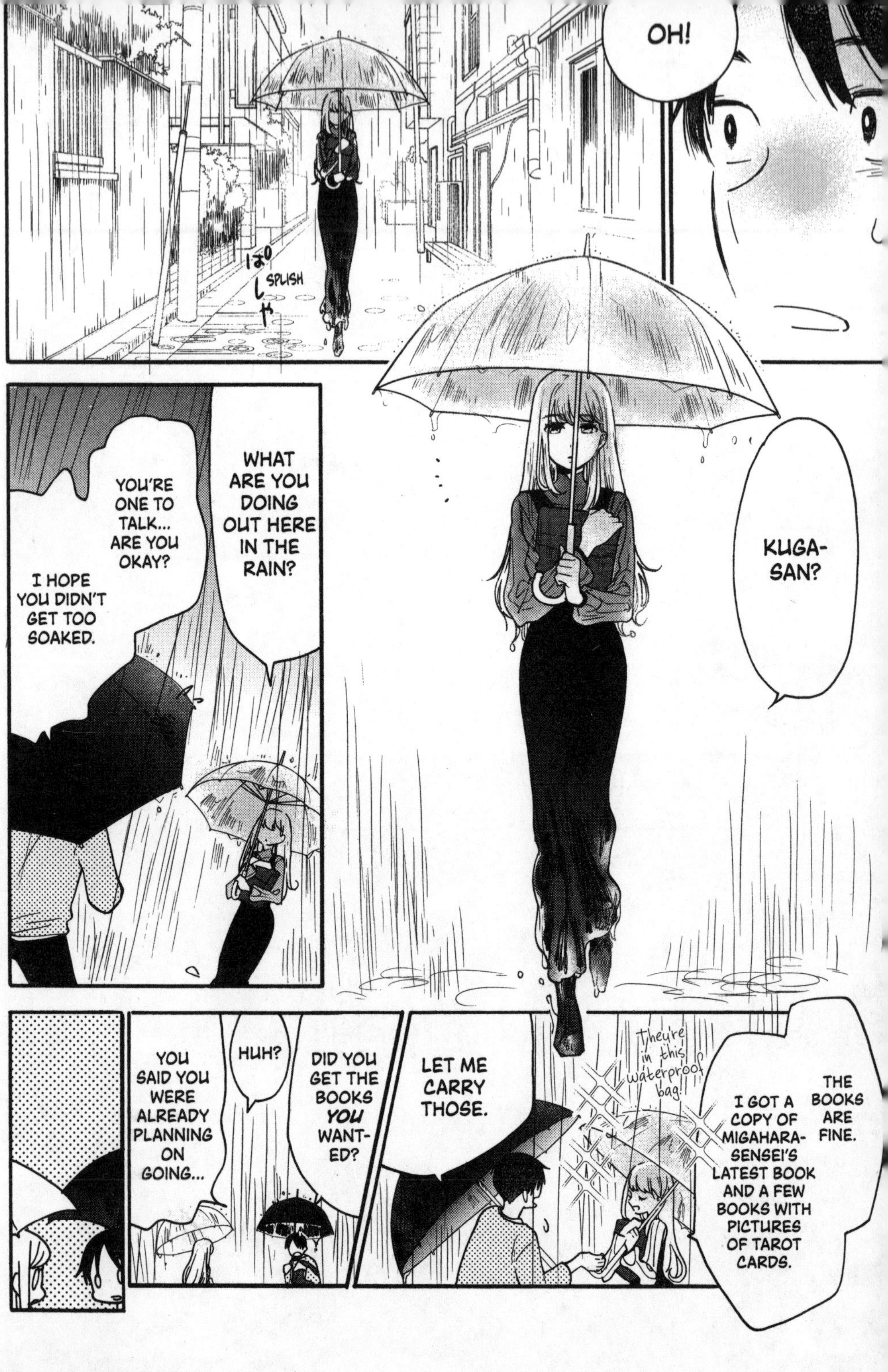
OH!
ぱしゃ
SPLISH
KUGA-SAN?
WHAT ARE YOU DOING OUT HERE IN THE RAIN?
YOU'RE ONE TO TALK... ARE YOU OKAY?
I HOPE YOU DIDN'T GET TOO SOAKED.
THE BOOKS ARE FINE.
I GOT A COPY OF MIGAHARA-SENSEI'S LATEST BOOK AND A FEW BOOKS WITH PICTURES OF TAROT CARDS.
They're in this waterproof bag!
LET ME CARRY THOSE.
DID YOU GET THE BOOKS *YOU* WANTED?
HUH?
YOU SAID YOU WERE ALREADY PLANNING ON GOING...

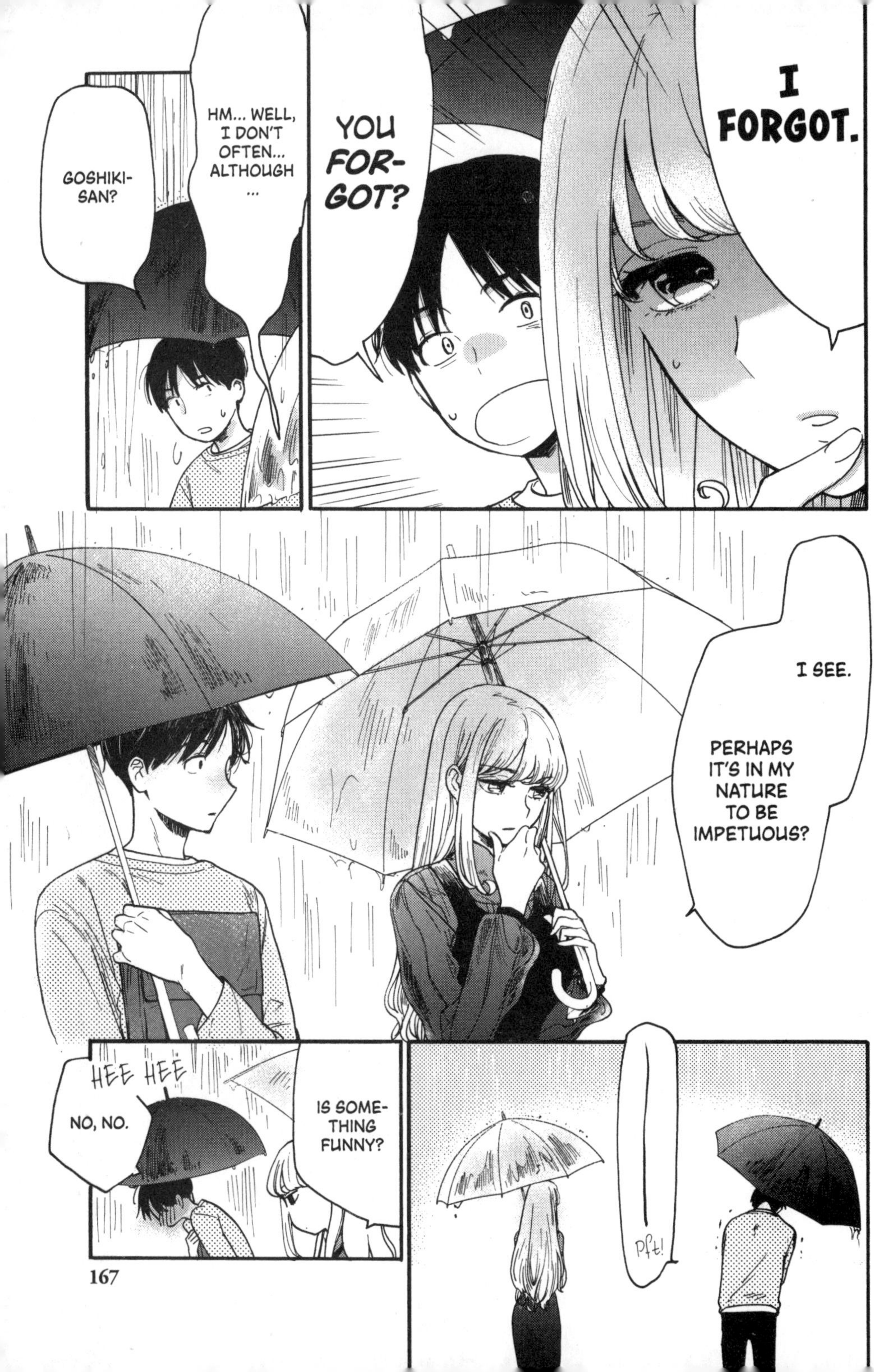
I FORGOT.
YOU FORGOT?
HM... WELL, I DON'T OFTEN... ALTHOUGH ...
GOSHIKI-SAN?
I SEE.
PERHAPS IT'S IN MY NATURE TO BE IMPETUOUS?
Pft!
IS SOMETHING FUNNY?
HEE HEE
NO, NO.

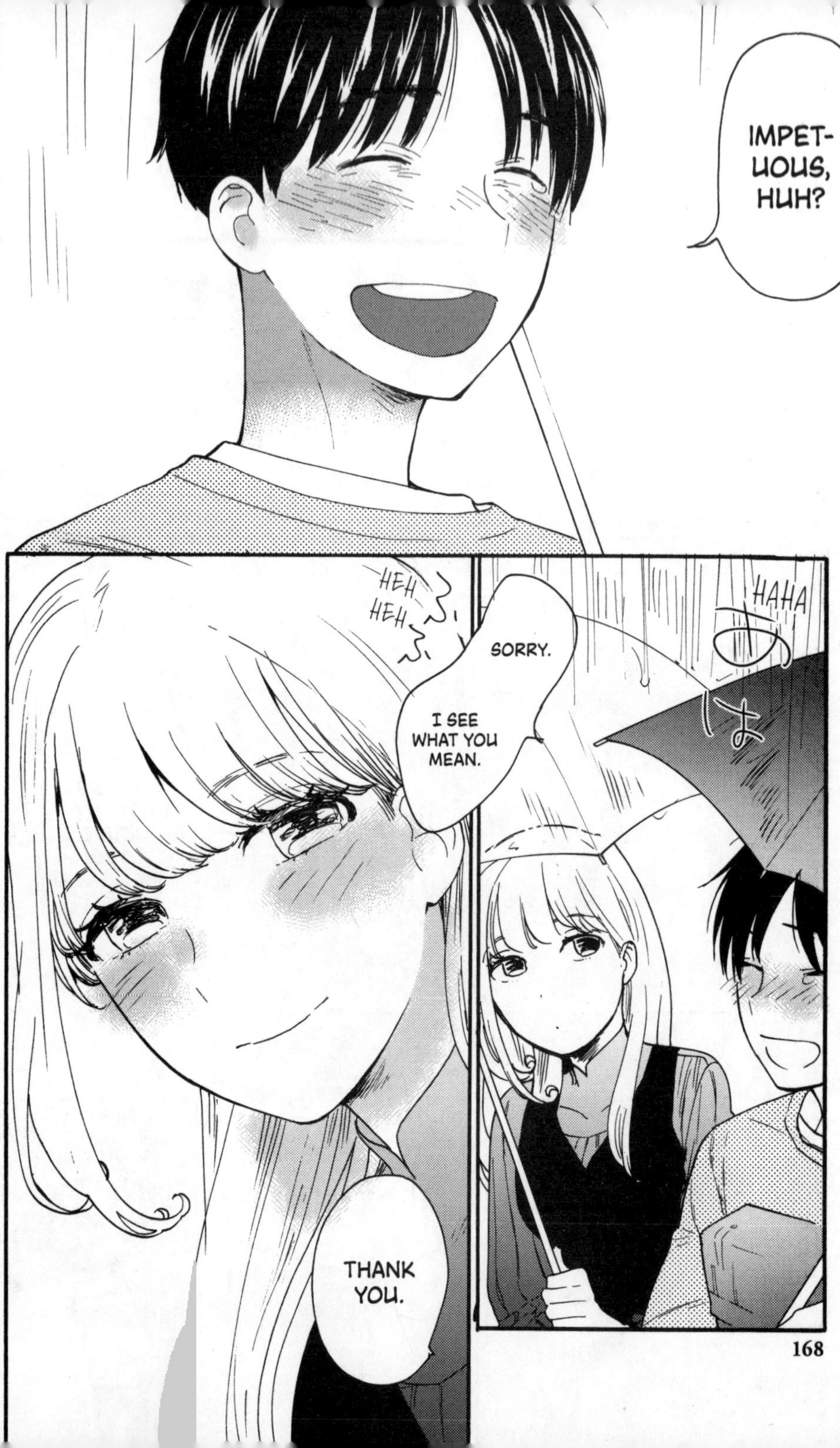
IMPET-UOUS, HUH?
HAHA
あは
SORRY.
I SEE WHAT YOU MEAN.
HEH HEH
ふふ
THANK YOU.

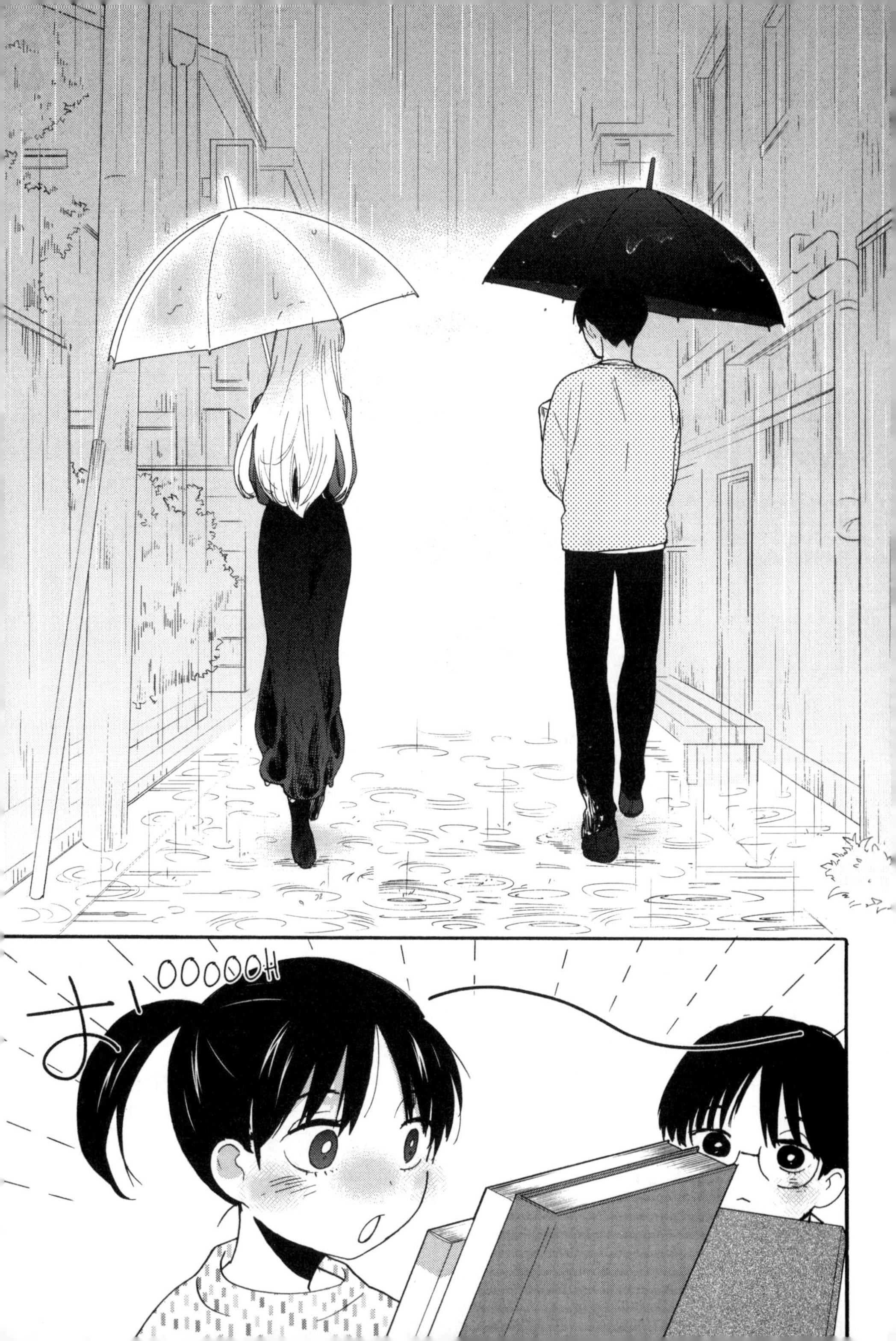
お
OOOOOH

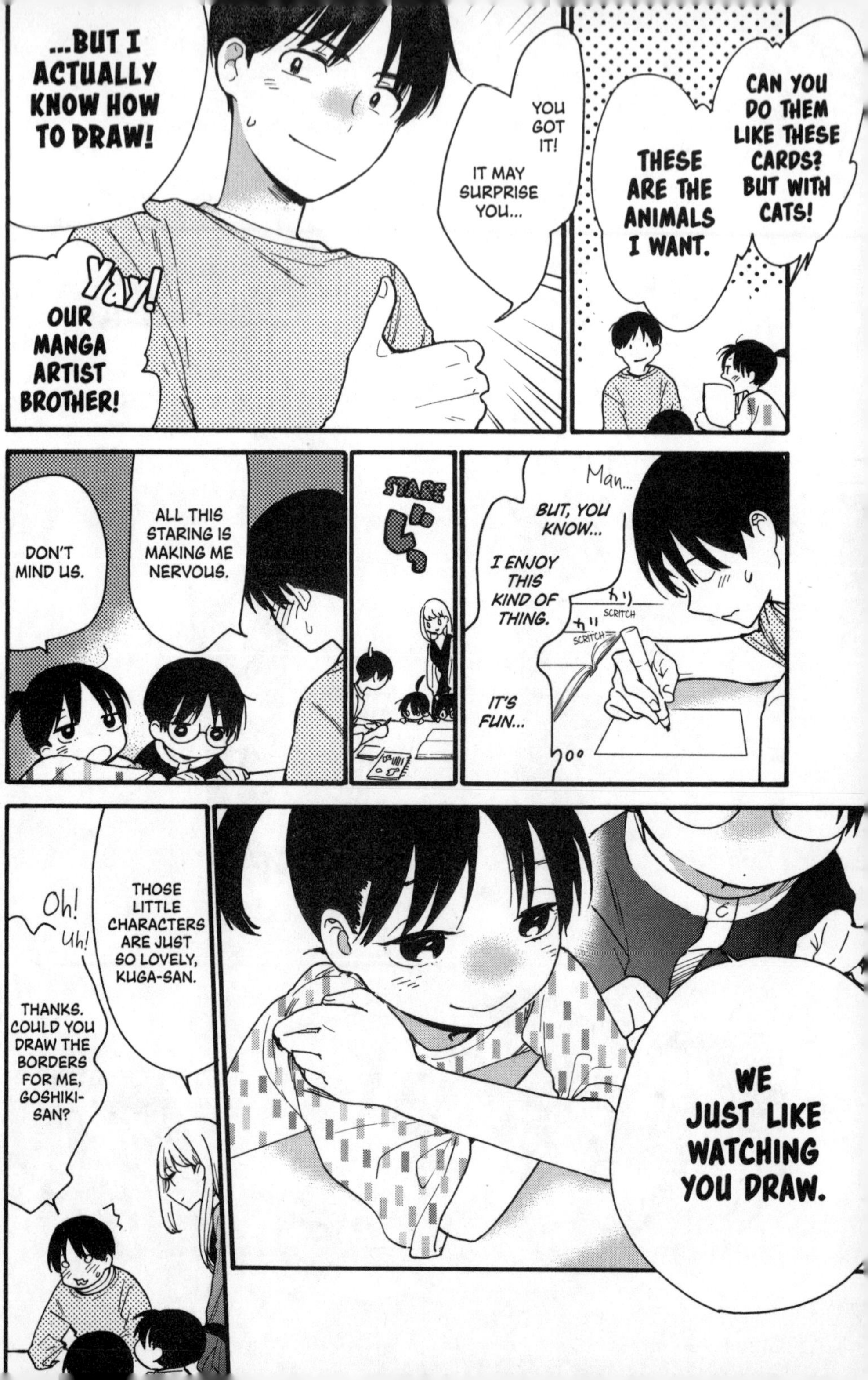
CAN YOU DO THEM LIKE THESE CARDS? BUT WITH CATS!
THESE ARE THE ANIMALS I WANT.
YOU GOT IT!
IT MAY SURPRISE YOU...
...BUT I ACTUALLY KNOW HOW TO DRAW!
Yay!
OUR MANGA ARTIST BROTHER!
Man...
BUT, YOU KNOW...
I ENJOY THIS KIND OF THING.
SCRITCH
SCRITCH
IT'S FUN...
STARE
ALL THIS STARING IS MAKING ME NERVOUS.
DON'T MIND US.
WE JUST LIKE WATCHING YOU DRAW.
THOSE LITTLE CHARACTERS ARE JUST SO LOVELY, KUGA-SAN.
THANKS. COULD YOU DRAW THE BORDERS FOR ME, GOSHIKI-SAN?
Oh!
Uh!

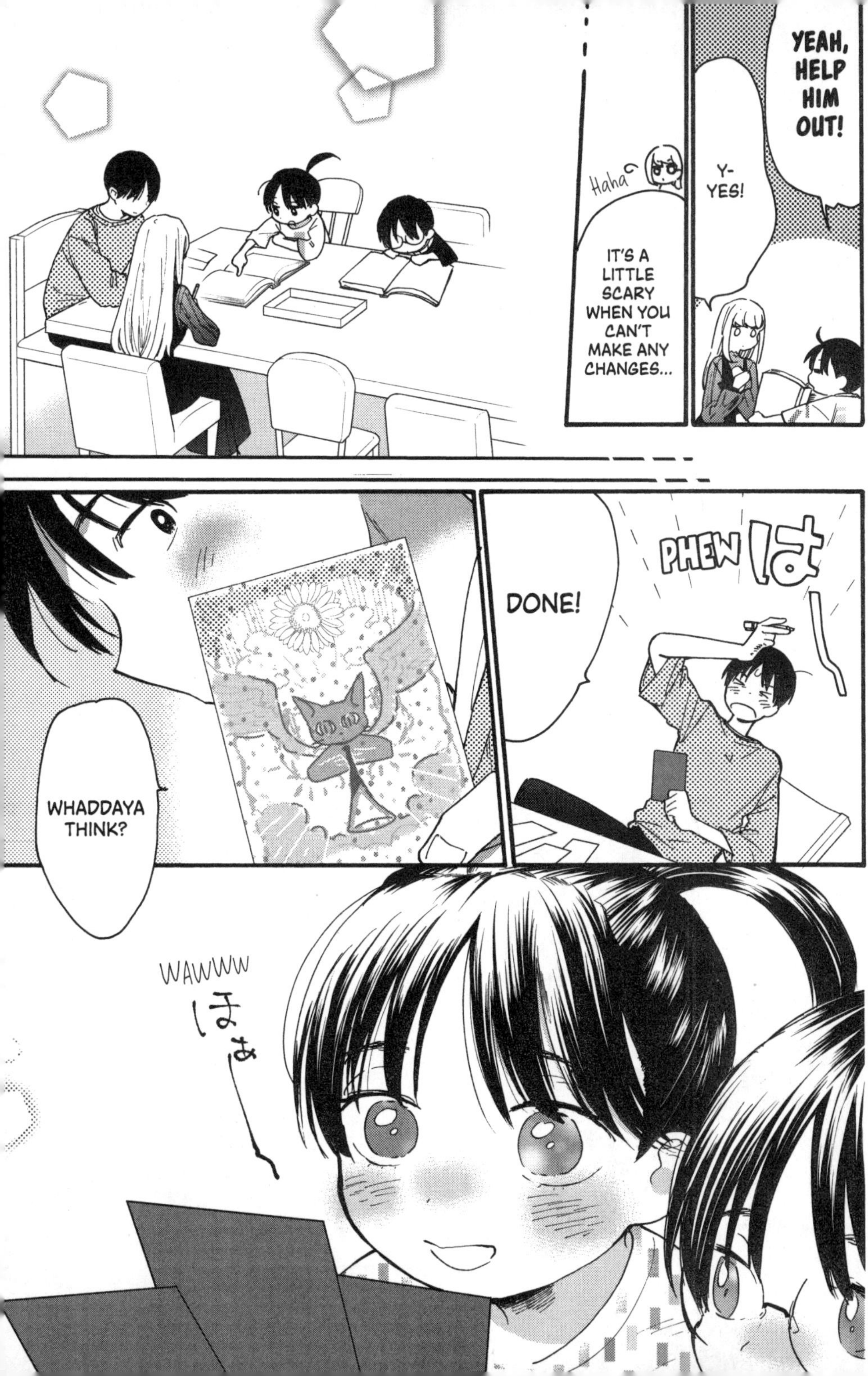

YEAH, HELP HIM OUT!
Y- YES!
Haha
IT'S A LITTLE SCARY WHEN YOU CAN'T MAKE ANY CHANGES...
PHEW
は
DONE!
WHADDAYA THINK?
WAWWW
ほぁ

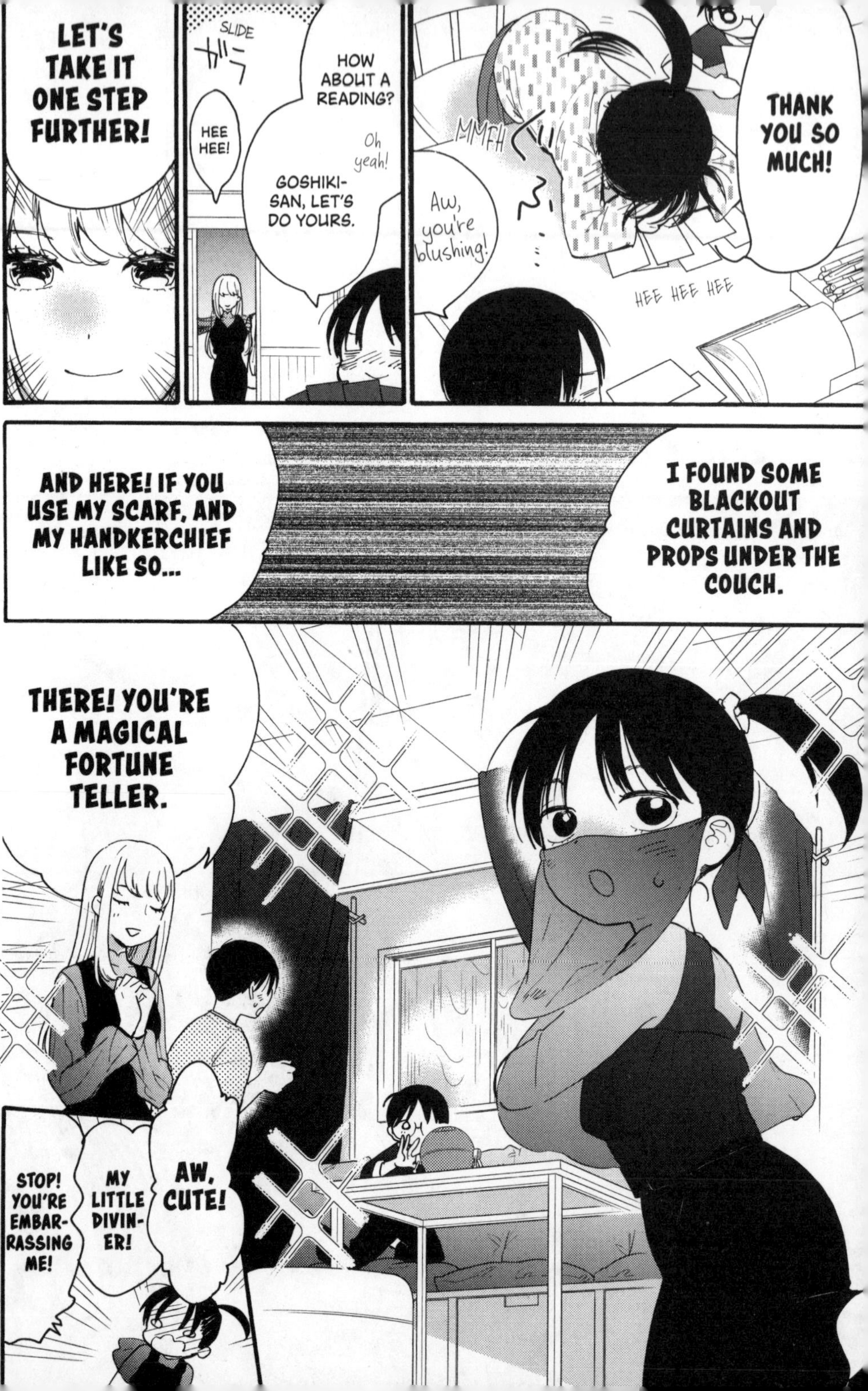
THANK YOU SO MUCH!
MMFH
Aw, you're blushing!
HEE HEE HEE
HOW ABOUT A READING?
Oh yeah!
GOSHIKI-SAN, LET'S DO YOURS.
SLIDE
ガラ
HEE HEE!
LET'S TAKE IT ONE STEP FURTHER!
I FOUND SOME BLACKOUT CURTAINS AND PROPS UNDER THE COUCH.
AND HERE! IF YOU USE MY SCARF, AND MY HANDKERCHIEF LIKE SO...
THERE! YOU'RE A MAGICAL FORTUNE TELLER.
AW, CUTE!
MY LITTLE DIVINER!
STOP! YOU'RE EMBARRASSING ME!

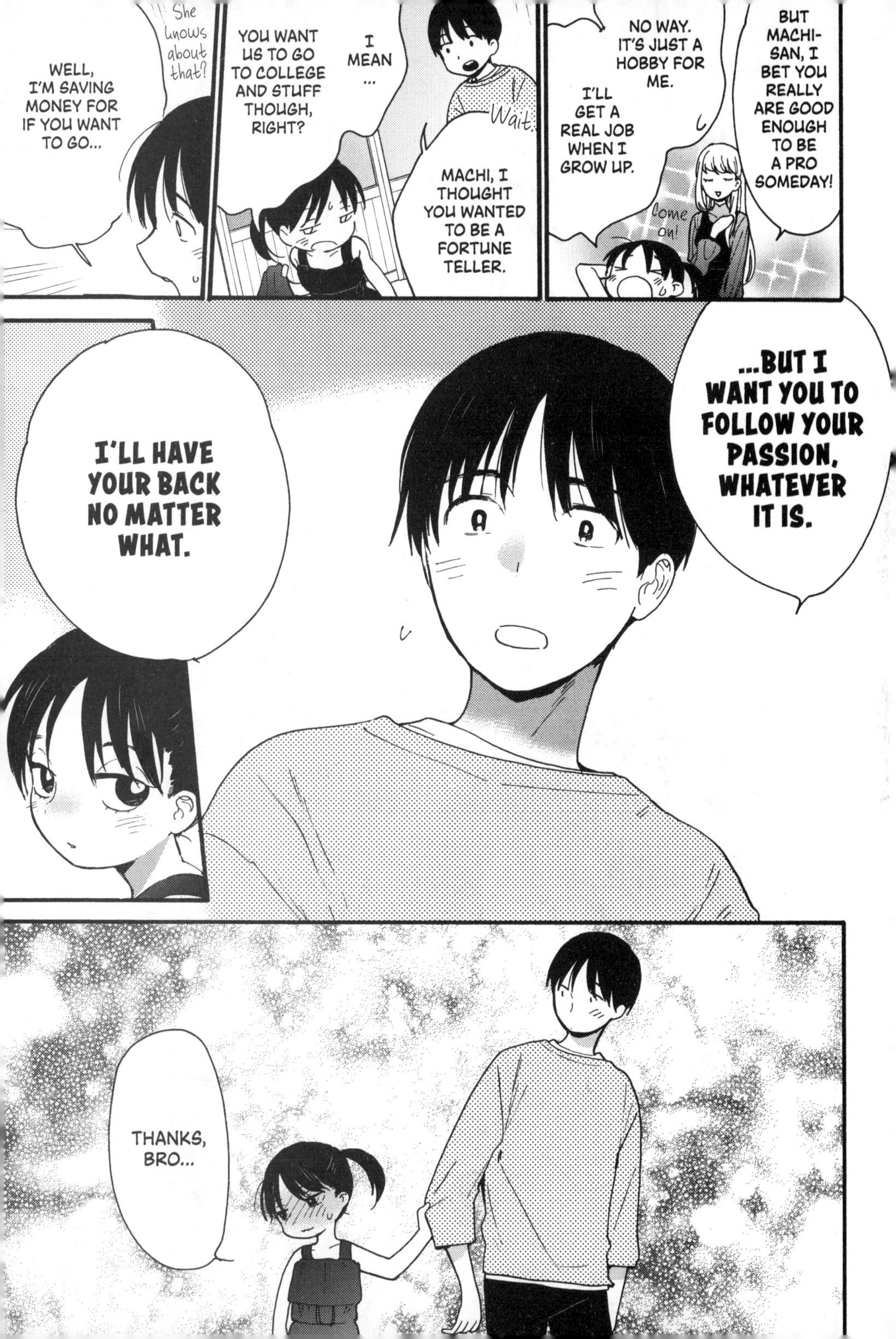
BUT MACHI-SAN, I BET YOU REALLY ARE GOOD ENOUGH TO BE A PRO SOMEDAY!
NO WAY. IT'S JUST A HOBBY FOR ME.
I'LL GET A REAL JOB WHEN I GROW UP.
Come on!
MACHI, I THOUGHT YOU WANTED TO BE A FORTUNE TELLER.
Wait.
I MEAN ...
YOU WANT US TO GO TO COLLEGE AND STUFF THOUGH, RIGHT?
She knows about that?
WELL, I'M SAVING MONEY FOR IF YOU WANT TO GO...
...BUT I WANT YOU TO FOLLOW YOUR PASSION, WHATEVER IT IS.
I'LL HAVE YOUR BACK NO MATTER WHAT.
THANKS, BRO...

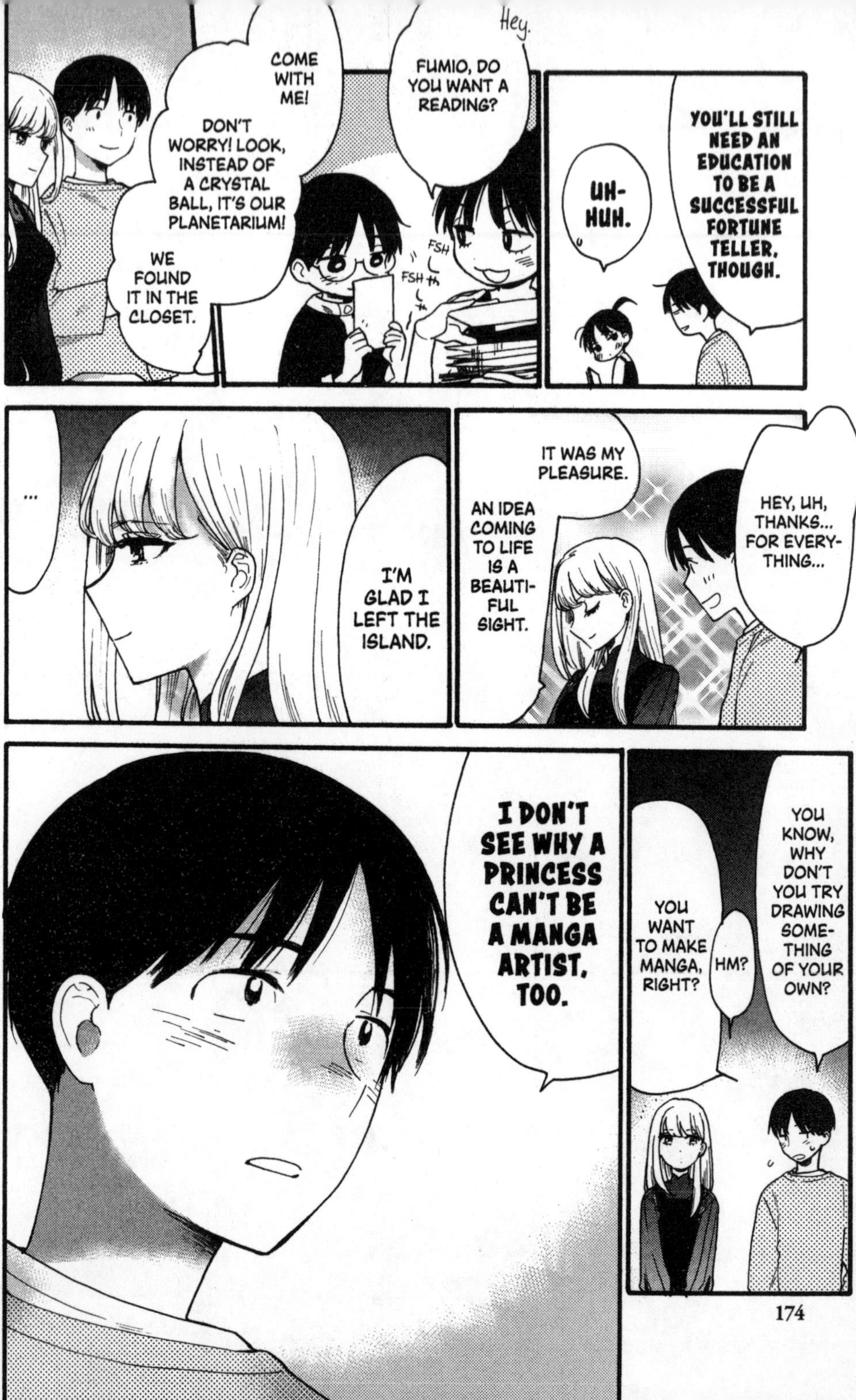

YOU'LL STILL NEED AN EDUCATION TO BE A SUCCESSFUL FORTUNE TELLER, THOUGH.
UH-HUH.
Hey.
FUMIO, DO YOU WANT A READING?
FSH
FSH
COME WITH ME!
DON'T WORRY! LOOK, INSTEAD OF A CRYSTAL BALL, IT'S OUR PLANETARIUM!
WE FOUND IT IN THE CLOSET.
HEY, UH, THANKS... FOR EVERYTHING...
IT WAS MY PLEASURE.
AN IDEA COMING TO LIFE IS A BEAUTIFUL SIGHT.
I'M GLAD I LEFT THE ISLAND.
...
YOU KNOW, WHY DON'T YOU TRY DRAWING SOMETHING OF YOUR OWN?
HM?
YOU WANT TO MAKE MANGA, RIGHT?
I DON'T SEE WHY A PRINCESS CAN'T BE A MANGA ARTIST, TOO.

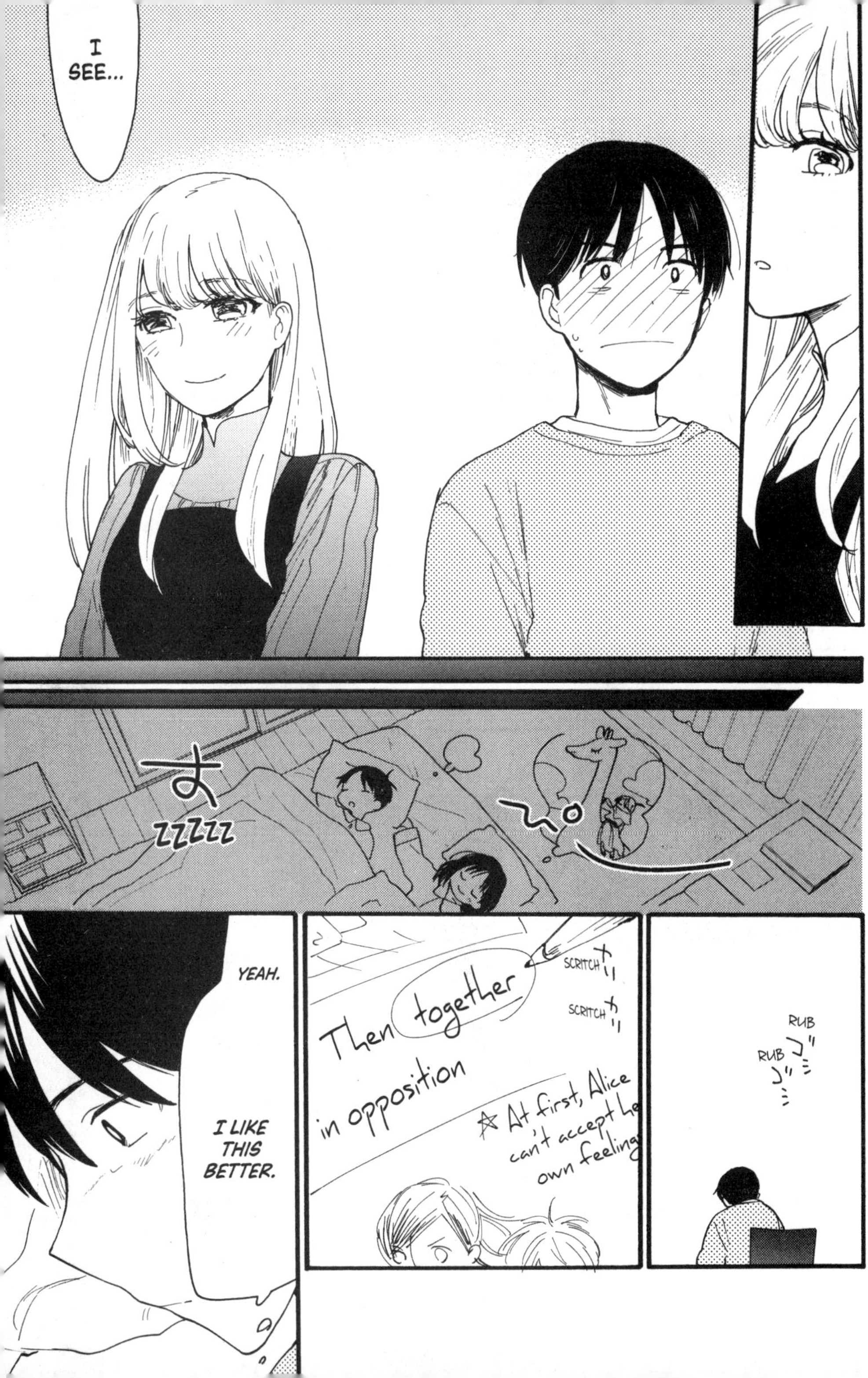
I SEE...
ZZZZZ
RUB
RUB
SCRITCH
SCRITCH
Then together
in opposition
At first, Alice can't accept he
own feeling
YEAH.
I LIKE THIS BETTER.

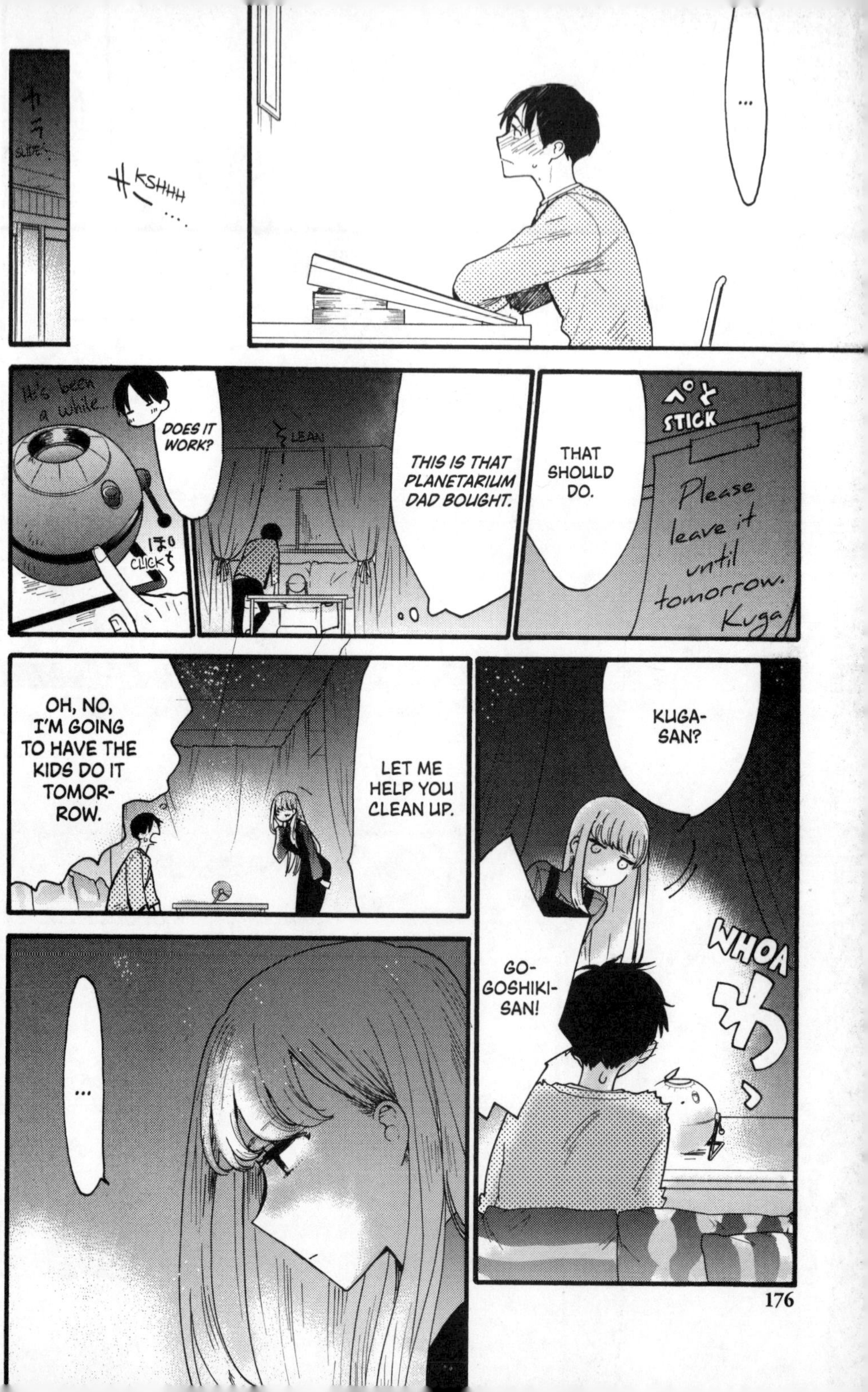
...
SLIDE
KSHHH...
STICK
THAT SHOULD DO.
Please leave it until tomorrow. Kuga
THIS IS THAT PLANETARIUM DAD BOUGHT.
LEAN
It's been a while...
DOES IT WORK?
CLICK
KUGA-SAN?
WHOA
GO-GOSHIKI-SAN!
LET ME HELP YOU CLEAN UP.
OH, NO, I'M GOING TO HAVE THE KIDS DO IT TOMORROW.
...

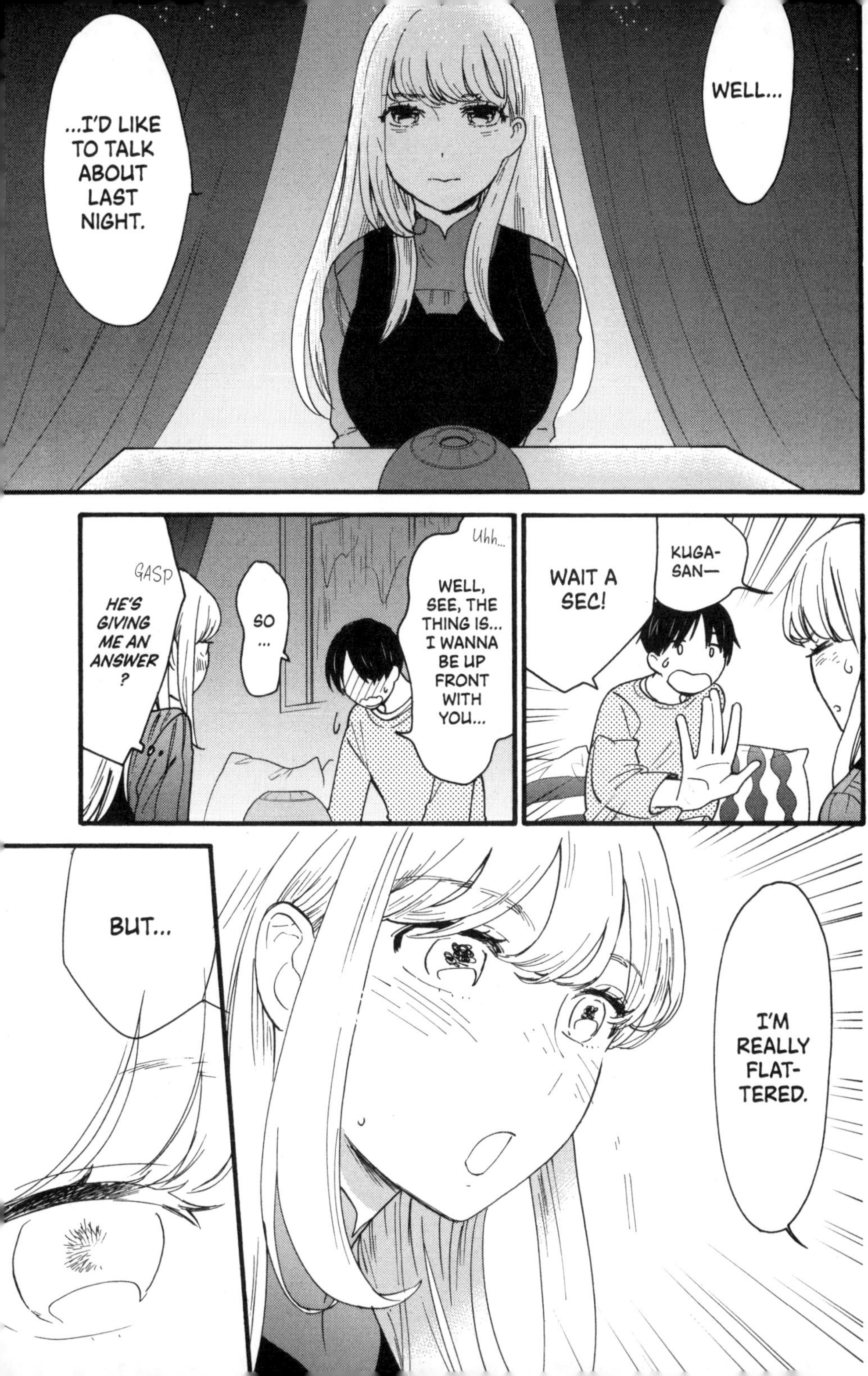
WELL...
...I'D LIKE TO TALK ABOUT LAST NIGHT.
KUGA-SAN—
WAIT A SEC!
Uhh...
WELL, SEE, THE THING IS... I WANNA BE UP FRONT WITH YOU...
SO ...
GASP
HE'S GIVING ME AN ANSWER?
I'M REALLY FLAT-TERED.
BUT...

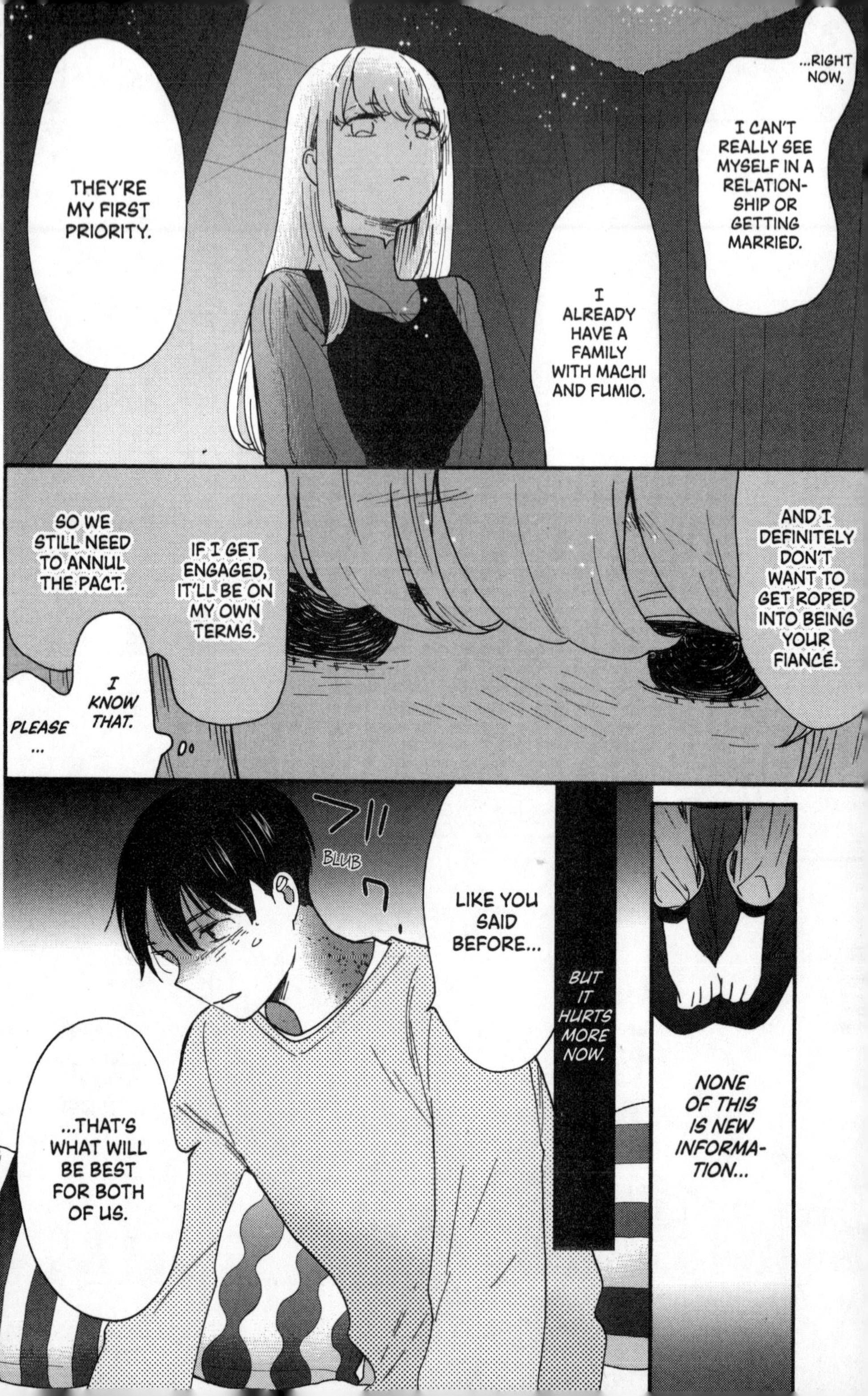
...RIGHT NOW,
I CAN'T REALLY SEE MYSELF IN A RELATIONSHIP OR GETTING MARRIED.
I ALREADY HAVE A FAMILY WITH MACHI AND FUMIO.
THEY'RE MY FIRST PRIORITY.
AND I DEFINITELY DON'T WANT TO GET ROPED INTO BEING YOUR FIANCÉ.
IF I GET ENGAGED, IT'LL BE ON MY OWN TERMS.
SO WE STILL NEED TO ANNUL THE PACT.
I KNOW THAT.
PLEASE...
NONE OF THIS IS NEW INFORMATION...
BUT IT HURTS MORE NOW.
LIKE YOU SAID BEFORE...
BLUB
...THAT'S WHAT WILL BE BEST FOR BOTH OF US.

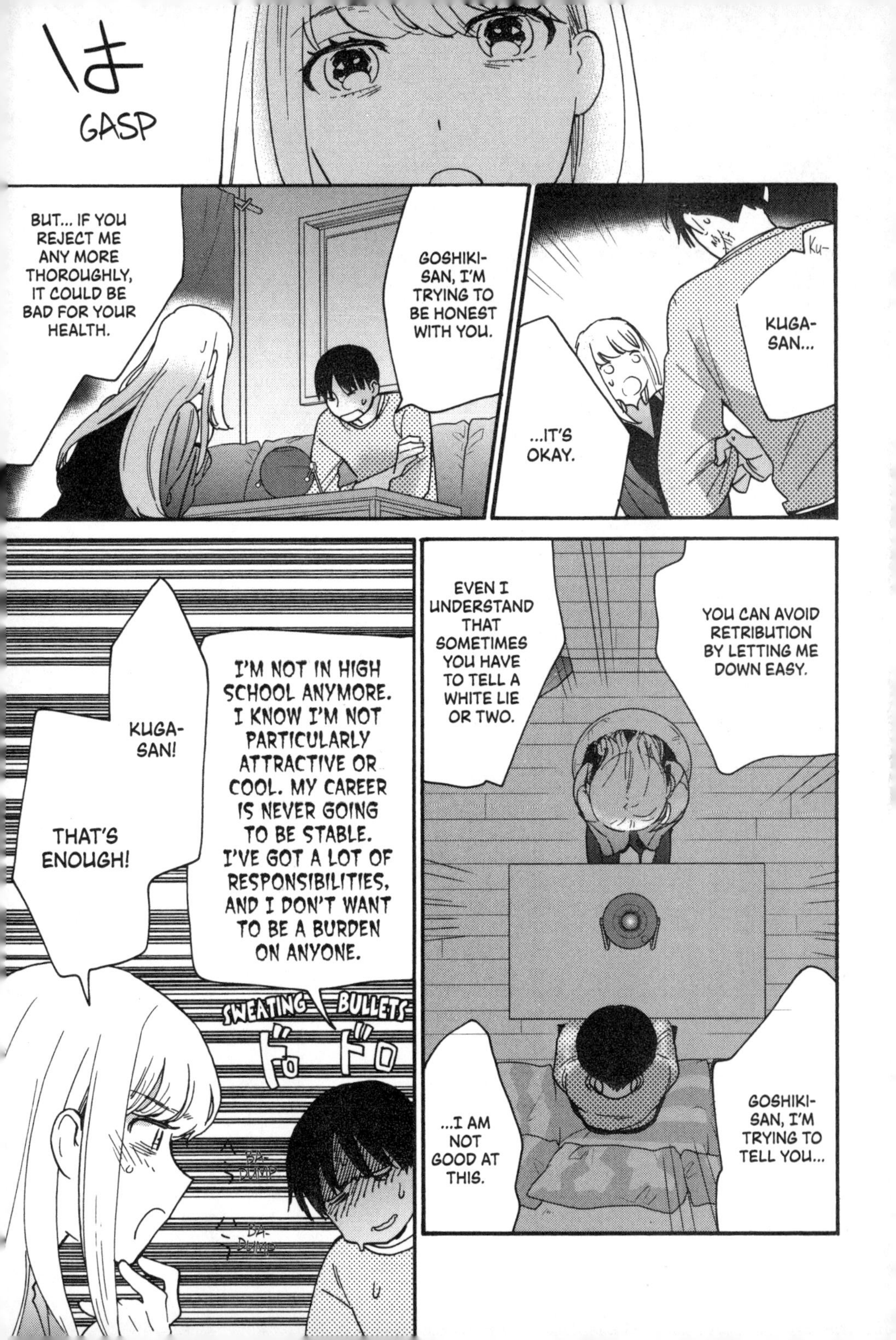
は
GASP
Ku-
KUGA-SAN...
...IT'S OKAY.
GOSHIKI-SAN, I'M TRYING TO BE HONEST WITH YOU.
BUT... IF YOU REJECT ME ANY MORE THOROUGHLY, IT COULD BE BAD FOR YOUR HEALTH.
YOU CAN AVOID RETRIBUTION BY LETTING ME DOWN EASY.
EVEN I UNDERSTAND THAT SOMETIMES YOU HAVE TO TELL A WHITE LIE OR TWO.
GOSHIKI-SAN, I'M TRYING TO TELL YOU...
...I AM NOT GOOD AT THIS.
I'M NOT IN HIGH SCHOOL ANYMORE. I KNOW I'M NOT PARTICULARLY ATTRACTIVE OR COOL. MY CAREER IS NEVER GOING TO BE STABLE. I'VE GOT A LOT OF RESPONSIBILITIES, AND I DON'T WANT TO BE A BURDEN ON ANYONE.
KUGA-SAN!
THAT'S ENOUGH!
SWEATING BULLETS
ドロドロ
BA-DUMP
BA-DUMP

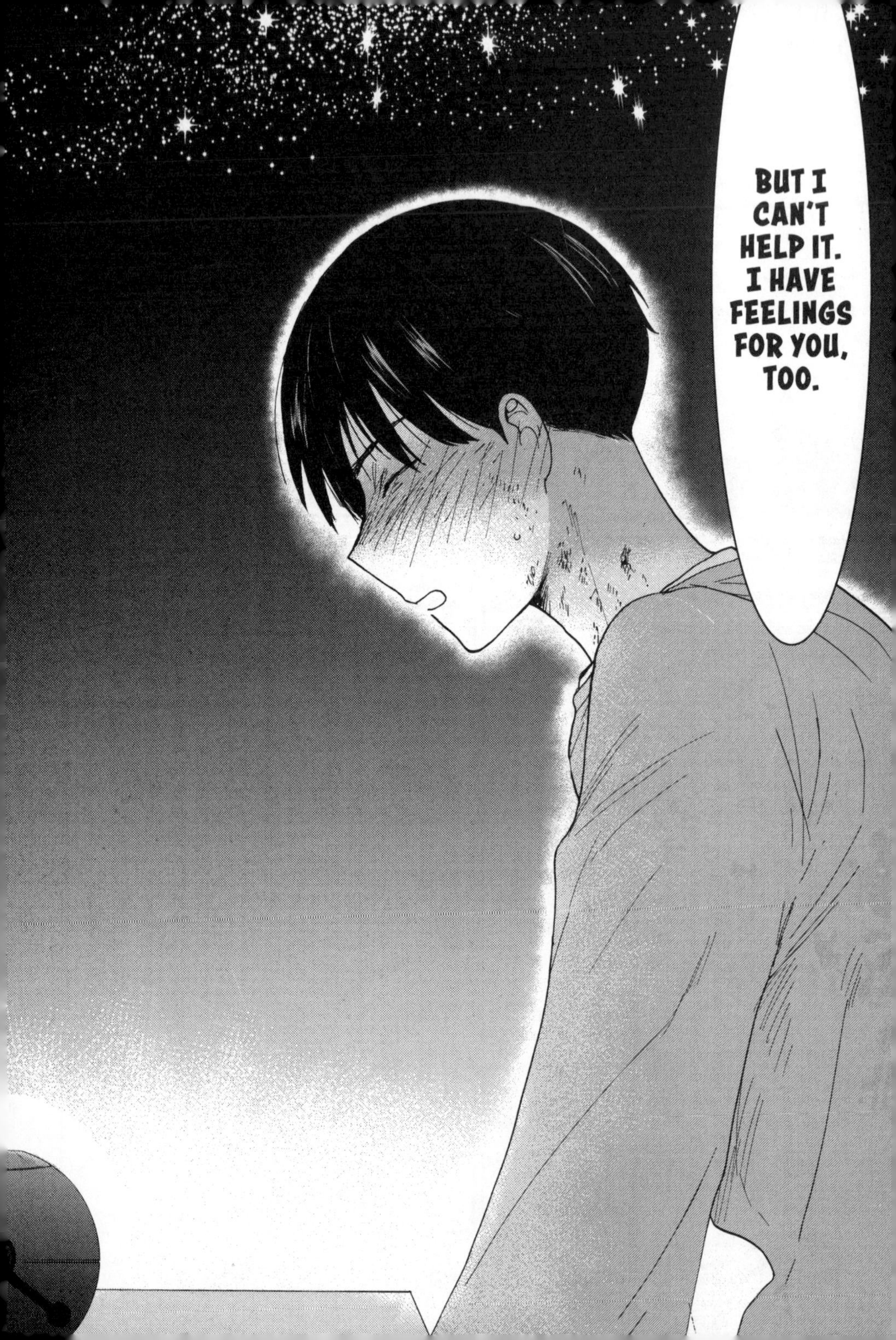
BUT I CAN'T HELP IT. I HAVE FEELINGS FOR YOU, TOO.

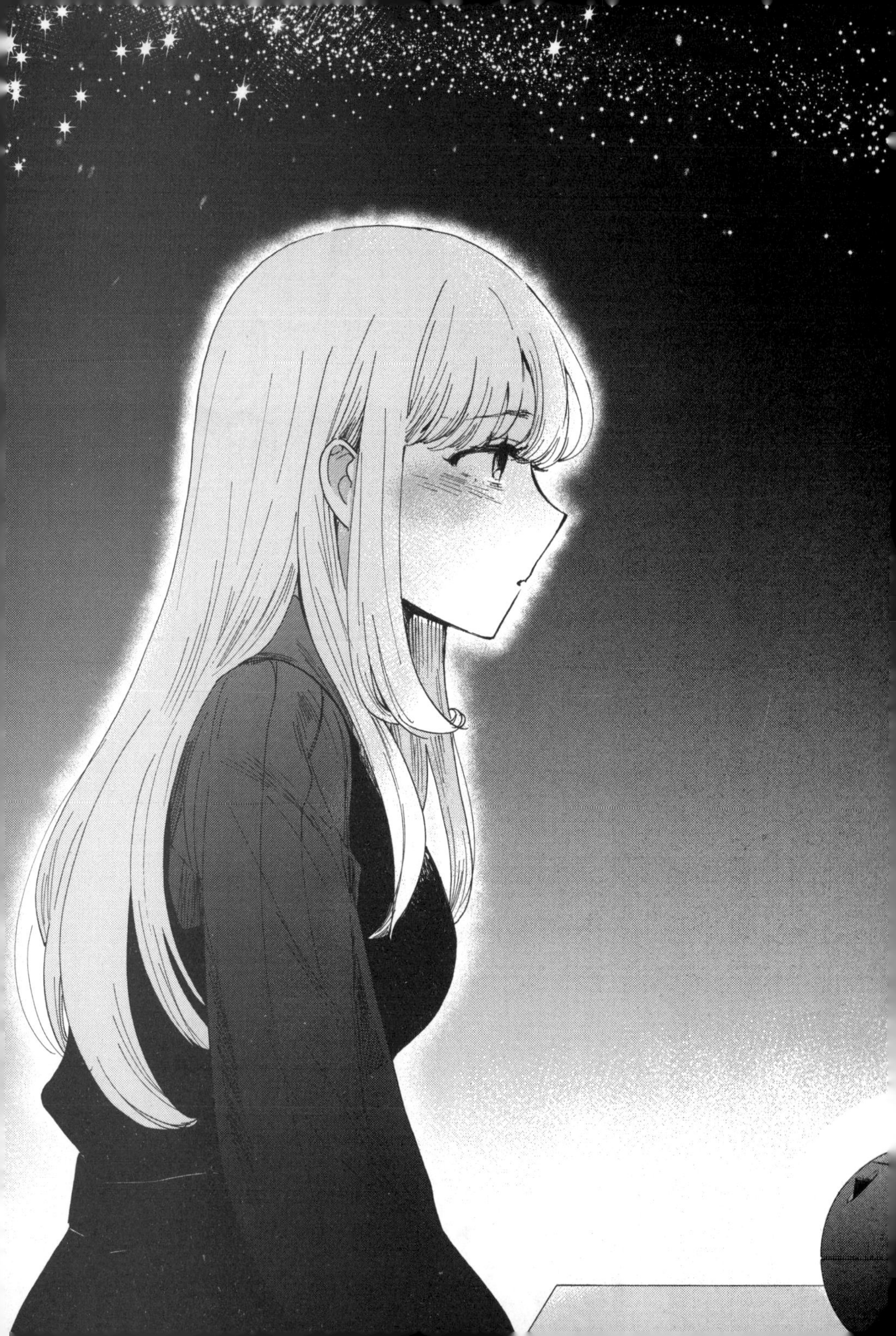

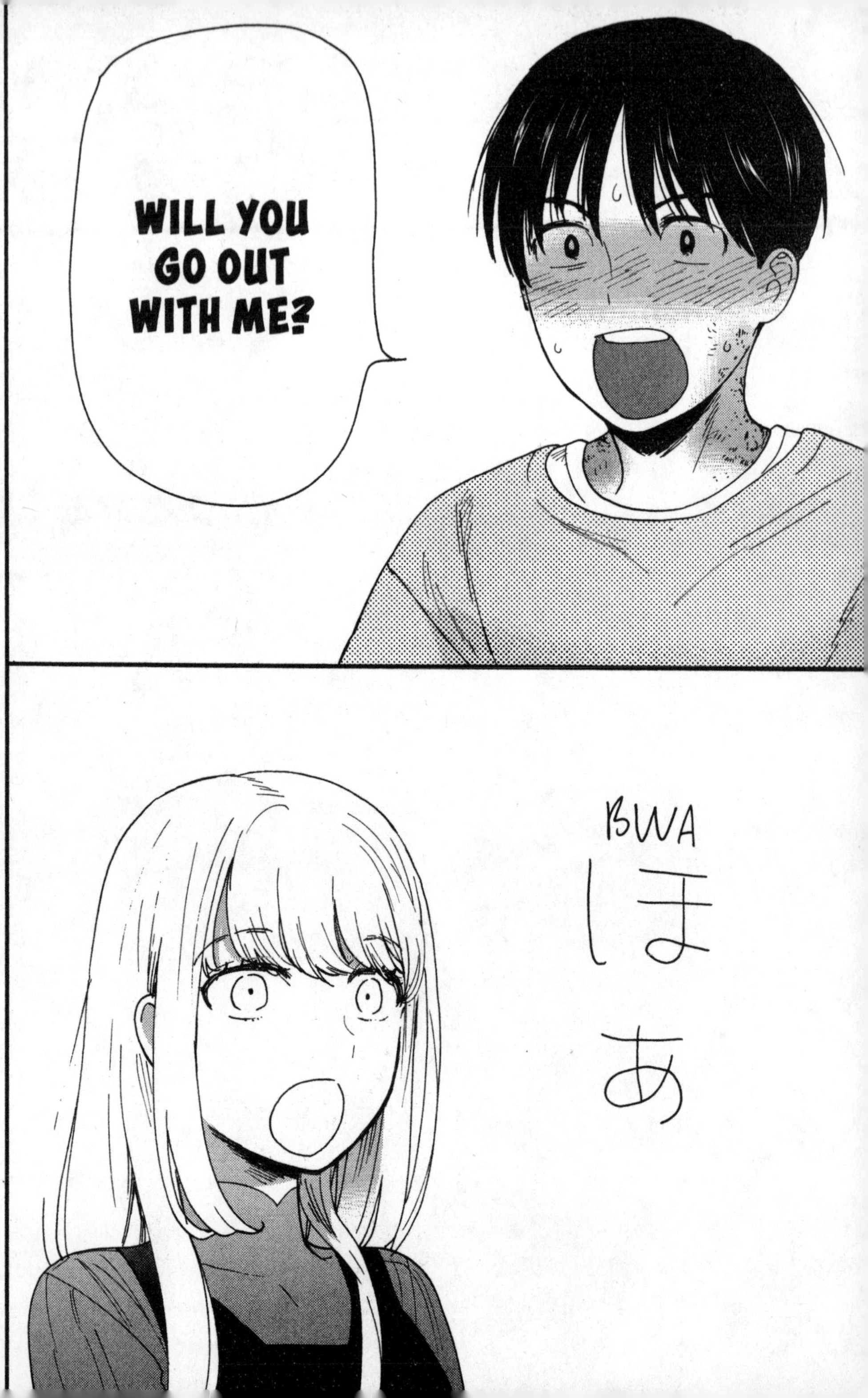
WILL YOU GO OUT WITH ME?
BWA
ほあ

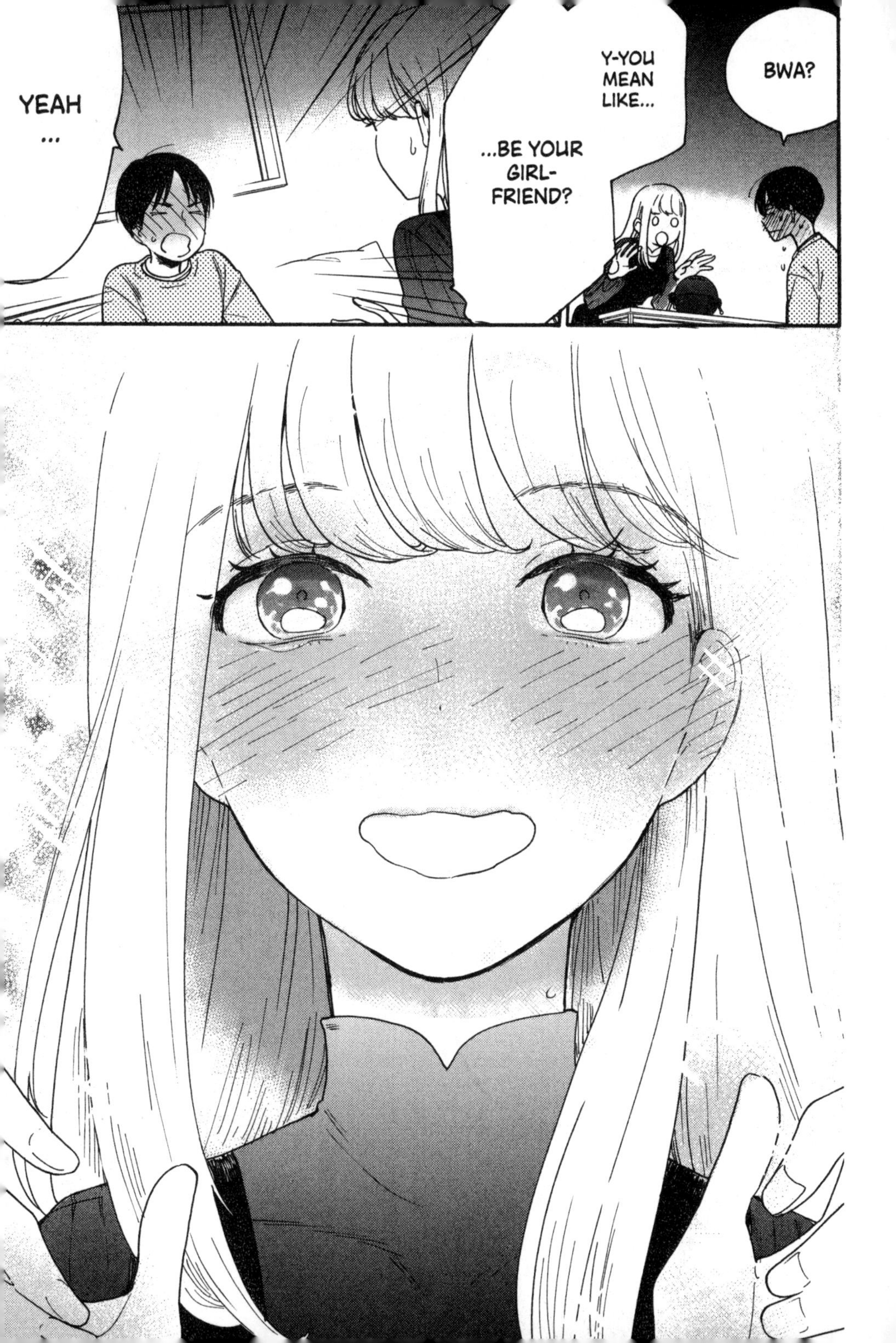
BWA?
Y-YOU MEAN LIKE...
...BE YOUR GIRL-FRIEND?
YEAH ...

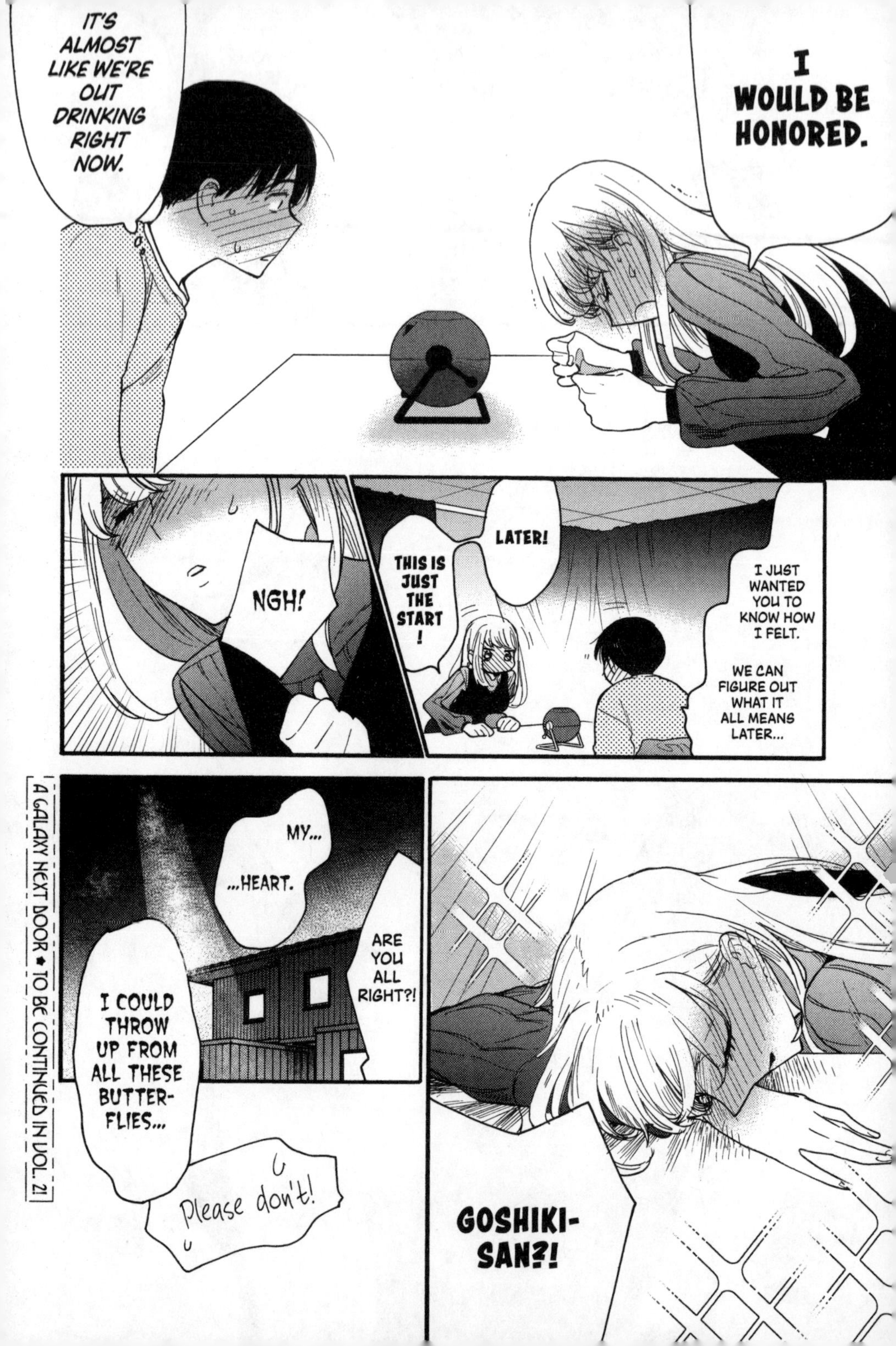
I WOULD BE HONORED.
IT'S ALMOST LIKE WE'RE OUT DRINKING RIGHT NOW.
I JUST WANTED YOU TO KNOW HOW I FELT.
WE CAN FIGURE OUT WHAT IT ALL MEANS LATER...
LATER!
THIS IS JUST THE START!
NGH!
GOSHIKI-SAN?!
MY...
...HEART.
ARE YOU ALL RIGHT?!
I COULD THROW UP FROM ALL THESE BUTTER-FLIES...
Please don't!

A GALAXY NEXT DOOR ♦ TO BE CONTINUED IN VOL. 2!

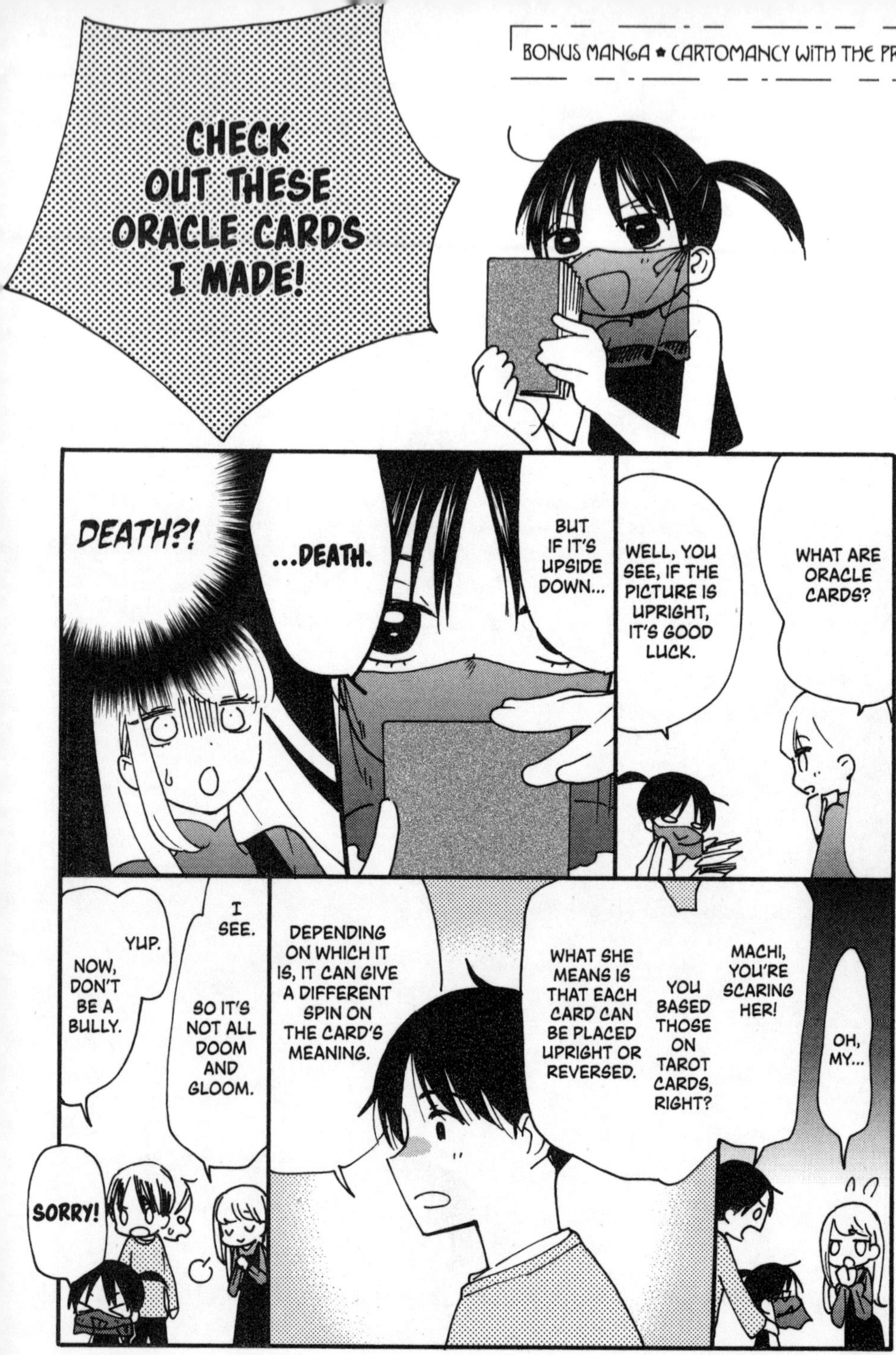
CHECK OUT THESE ORACLE CARDS I MADE!
WHAT ARE ORACLE CARDS?
WELL, YOU SEE, IF THE PICTURE IS UPRIGHT, IT'S GOOD LUCK.
BUT IF IT'S UPSIDE DOWN...
...DEATH.
DEATH?!
OH, MY...
MACHI, YOU'RE SCARING HER!
YOU BASED THOSE ON TAROT CARDS, RIGHT?
WHAT SHE MEANS IS THAT EACH CARD CAN BE PLACED UPRIGHT OR REVERSED.
DEPENDING ON WHICH IT IS, IT CAN GIVE A DIFFERENT SPIN ON THE CARD'S MEANING.
I SEE.
SO IT'S NOT ALL DOOM AND GLOOM.
YUP.
NOW, DON'T BE A BULLY.
SORRY!

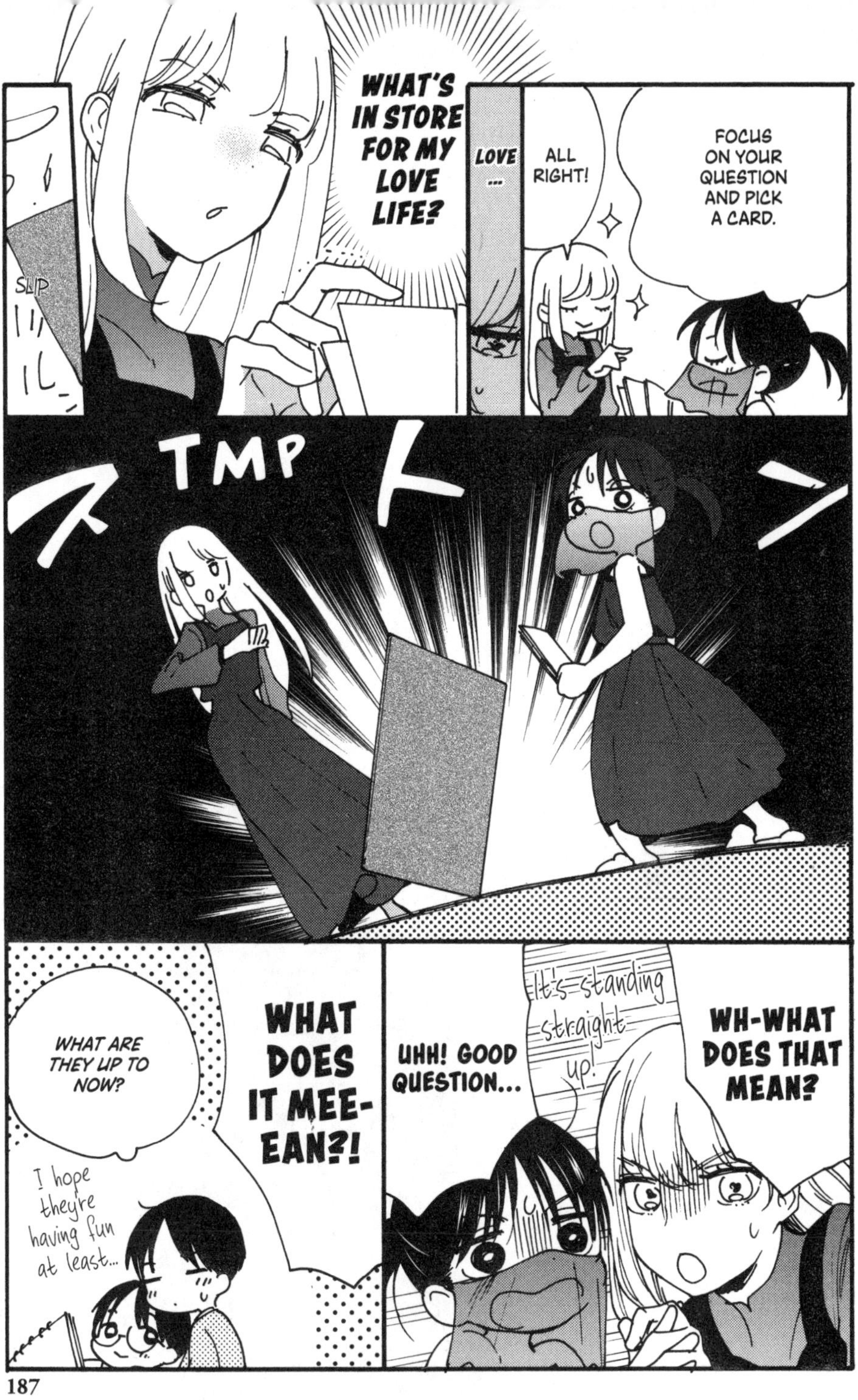
FOCUS ON YOUR QUESTION AND PICK A CARD.
ALL RIGHT!
LOVE ...
WHAT'S IN STORE FOR MY LOVE LIFE?
SLIP
TMP
ストン
WH-WHAT DOES THAT MEAN?
It's standing straight up!
UHH! GOOD QUESTION...
WHAT DOES IT MEE-EAN?!
WHAT ARE THEY UP TO NOW?
I hope they're having fun at least...

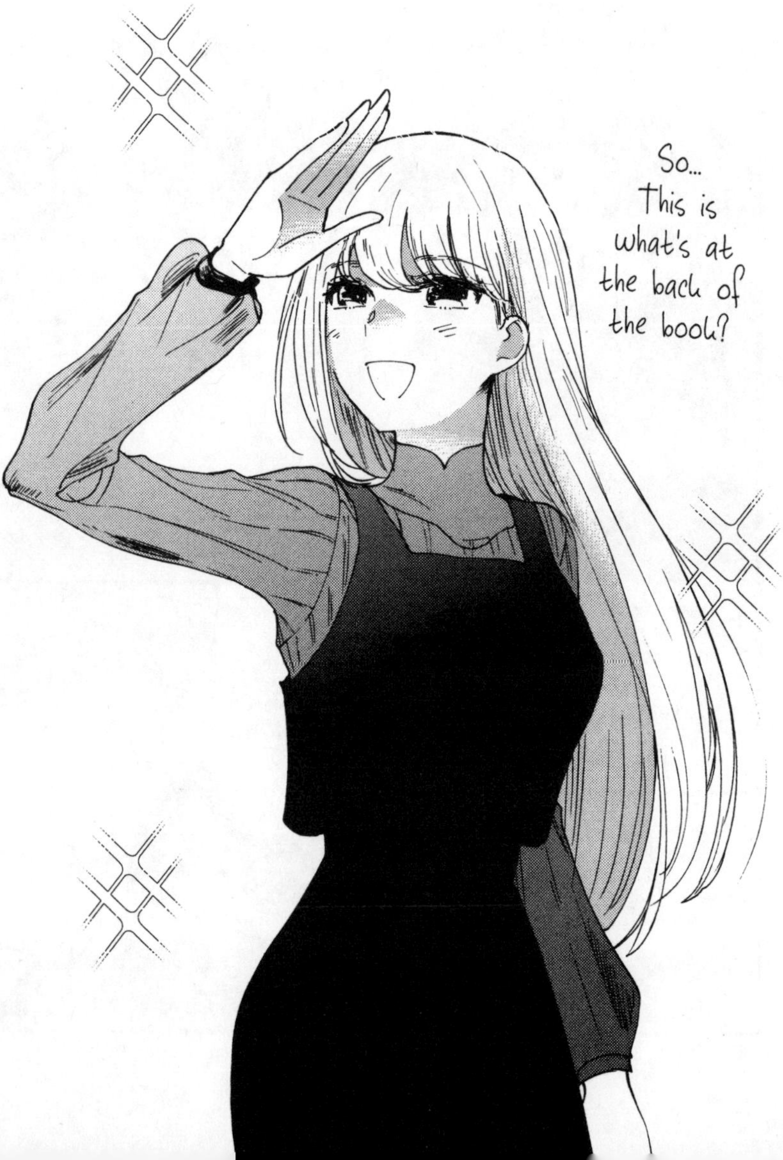
So... This is what's at the back of the book?

Afterword

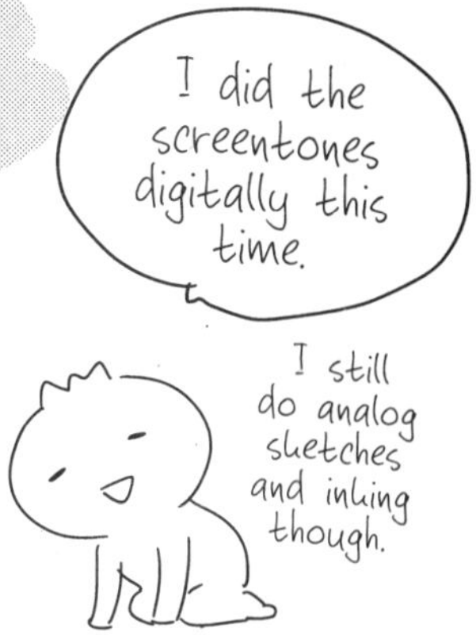

I did the screentones digitally this time.
I still do analog sketches and inking though.

Hi, Gido here.
How is everyone?
I know volume 1 is coming out at a time when everything's kinda crazy, but I'm glad I could do it!
My thanks to everyone who helped make this happen and to all my readers.
I hope to see you in the next volume!

Gido Amagakure, 2020

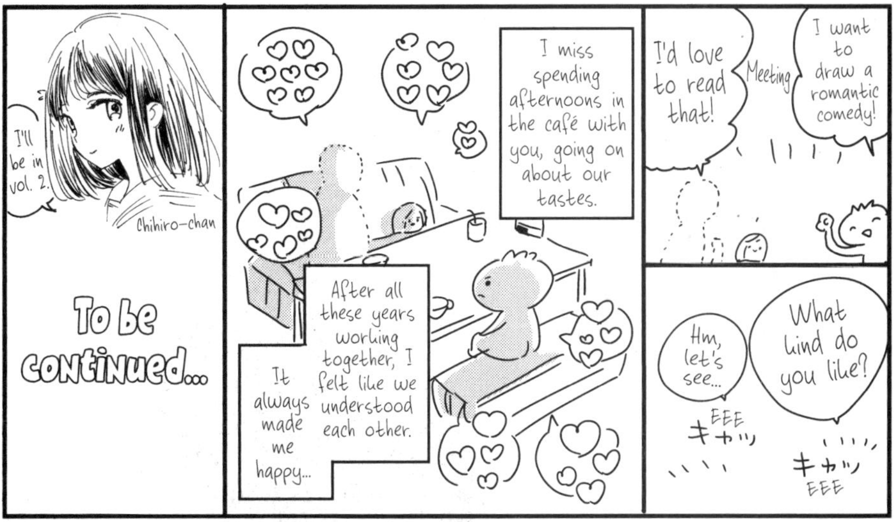

I want to draw a romantic comedy!
Meeting
I'd love to read that!
What kind do you like?
Hm, let's see...
キャッ EEE
キャッ EEE
I miss spending afternoons in the café with you, going on about our tastes.
After all these years working together, I felt like we understood each other.
It always made me happy...
I'll be in vol. 2.
Chihiro-chan
To be continued...

Thank you! to...

W-yama-san, Chii-chan, Teba-san, Gon-chan, Tsuru-san, M-chan.
My editor

Graphic Design: Kohei Nawata Design Office

Next Issue

KUGA-KUN &
GOSHIKI-SAN
THEY LIKE EACH OTHER...
...BUT NEITHER HAS BEEN IN A RELATIONSHIP BEFORE.
WHAT ARE WE SUPPOSED TO DO NEXT?
OH YEAH!
THERE IS ONE THING.
THEY CALL IT...
DATING
SO...
LET'S START THERE!

A Galaxy Next Door 2

COMING SOON!

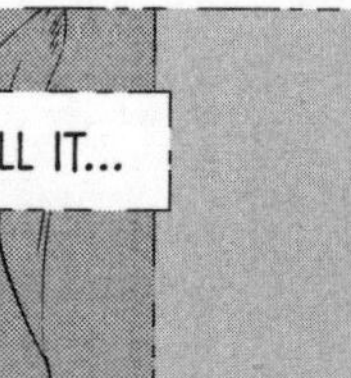

GOOD LUCK, BRO!

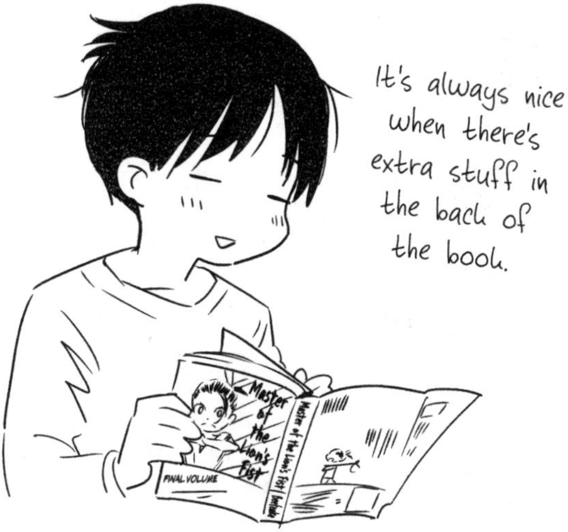
It's always nice when there's extra stuff in the back of the book.
Master of the Lion's Fist
FINAL VOLUME

Translation Notes

Honorifics:
While most readers are likely familiar with many of the honorifics used in Japanese (typically attached after the addressee's name), here's a refresher:
***-kun*, pg 8:**
Typically used to address boys, or close male friends, but can also be used to refer to younger colleagues of any gender.
***-sensei*, pg 13:**
Sensei, meaning "teacher," is commonly used as a term of respect not just for actual teachers, but also for doctors and those considered masters of their craft, such as authors and manga makers!
***-san*, pg 18:**
The polite default honorific, used for strangers, acquaintances, colleagues, and other non-specific relationships.
***-chan*, pg 19:**
Typically used by young children, female friends, family members, couples, and parents and adults to children (usually to young girls). Denotes a closeness with the addressee.
***-nee*, pg 132:**
A variation on older sister, denoting closeness, familiarity, and seniority. In this case, Momoka is being greeted like she is part of the family, even though they aren't blood related, as other honorifics like -*san* would be too formal and distant for their relationship.

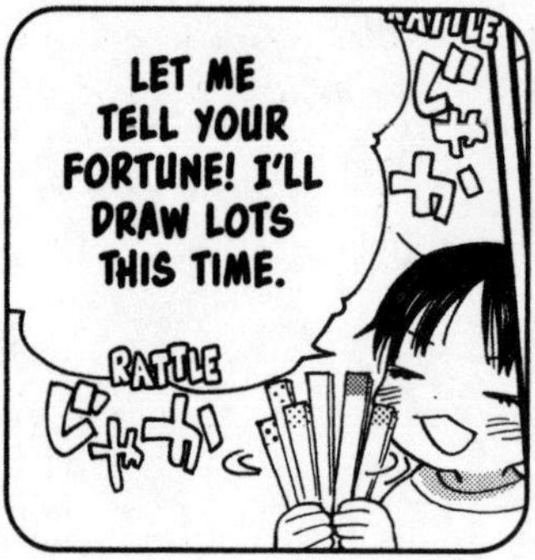
LET ME TELL YOUR FORTUNE! I'LL DRAW LOTS THIS TIME.
RATTLE

Fortune, pg 9:
Different methods of fortune telling, or *uranai*, are fairly common in Japan, including methods of using fortune sticks, or *o-mikuji*. Usually such sticks have numbers on them that correlate to a preset fortune, but in this case, Machi has colored her sticks and assigned a meaning to each of the colors.

Momo-Tea Kokone, pg 13: Momo-Tea is a kind of peach-flavored tea drink that's fairly popular in Japan. Kuga's pen name here is meant to evoke that kind of sweet image, particularly because he is drawing shojo manga. In the original Japanese, his name is: *Kokone Momoti*. Such peculiar pen names are quite common in Japan, to give the authors a measure of privacy. In fact, many Japanese manga authors choose to never reveal their faces or even their genders to the public.

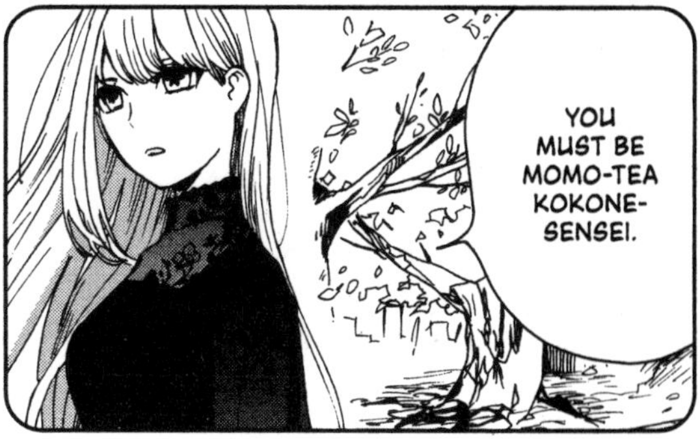
YOU MUST BE MOMO-TEA KOKONE-SENSEI.

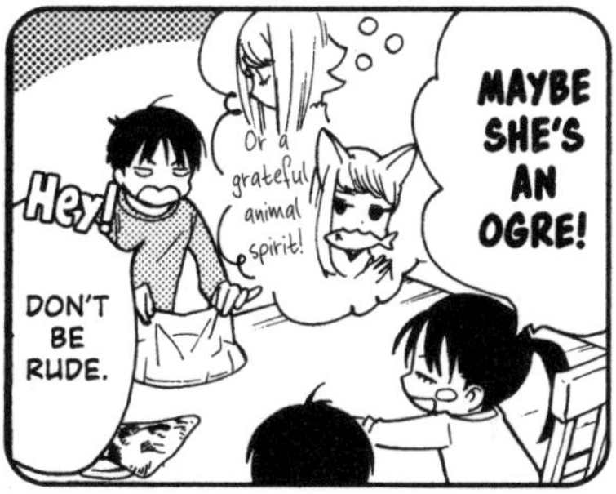
MAYBE SHE'S AN OGRE!
Or a grateful animal spirit!
Hey!
DON'T BE RUDE.

Ogre & Grateful Animal Spirit, pg 21: The joke here is that Machi is thinking of different folklore explanations for Goshiki's actions. She jokes that the reason Goshiki is taking her meal alone is because she might be a type of supernatural entity, often collectively translated as "ogre," called *futakuchi-onna*, who eats from a mouth in the back of her head (and thus must take all her meals in private, lest she be discovered). Kuga scolds Machi for being rude to suggest such a thing, so then she instead imagines Goshiki as a benevolent animal spirit, such as a *kitsune*, or shapeshifting fox spirit, who are sometimes said to bestow a favor in return for an offering. They often take the form of a beautiful woman, just like Goshiki.

Beefcake, pg 119:
Once again, we have an unusual pen name for a manga author: "Beefcake." The original Japanese is *katamari niku*, which more literally translates to "lump of meat." Again, this pen name was likely chosen to represent the spirit of the manga the author is drawing, but also to hide their true identity.

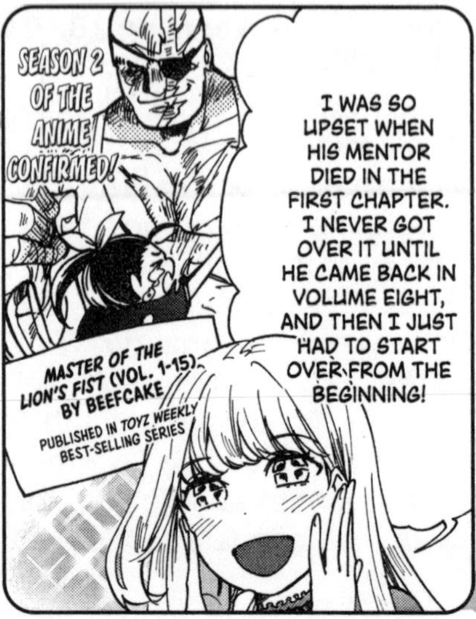
I WAS SO UPSET WHEN HIS MENTOR DIED IN THE FIRST CHAPTER. I NEVER GOT OVER IT UNTIL HE CAME BACK IN VOLUME EIGHT, AND THEN I JUST HAD TO START OVER FROM THE BEGINNING!
SEASON 2 OF THE ANIME CONFIRMED!
MASTER OF THE LION'S FIST (VOL. 1-15) BY BEEFCAKE
PUBLISHED IN TOYZ WEEKLY BEST-SELLING SERIES

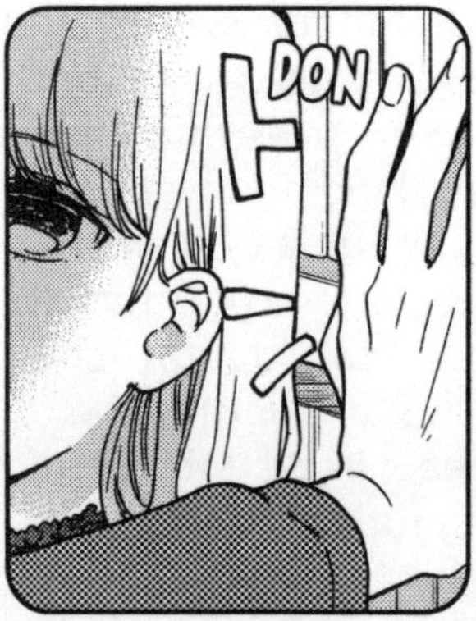
DON

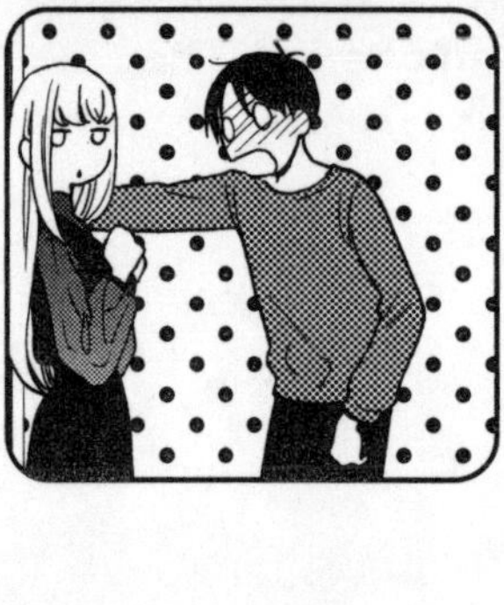

***Kabedon*, pg 124:**
Kabedon is a romantic trope that appears frequently in shojo manga and has now become a well-known cliché. Loosely translated as "wall slam," it has taken on a romantic context wherein a suitor, usually a man, will trap their love interest (usually a girl) against a wall by slapping it hard enough to make a *don!* sound. While many shojo readers have expressed that they enjoy this trope, others eschew it as too aggressive, which is why Goshiki claims it is something she won't like and wants to add it to her experiments.

Having lost his wife, high school teacher Kōhei Inuzuka is doing his best to raise his young daughter Tsumugi as a single father. He's pretty bad at cooking and doesn't have a huge appetite to begin with, but chance brings his little family together with one of his students, the lonely Kotori. The three of them are anything but comfortable in the kitchen, but the healing power of home cooking might just work on their grieving hearts.

"This season's number-one feel-good anime!" —Anime News Network

"A beautifully-drawn story about comfort food and family and grief. Recommended." —Otaku USA Magazine

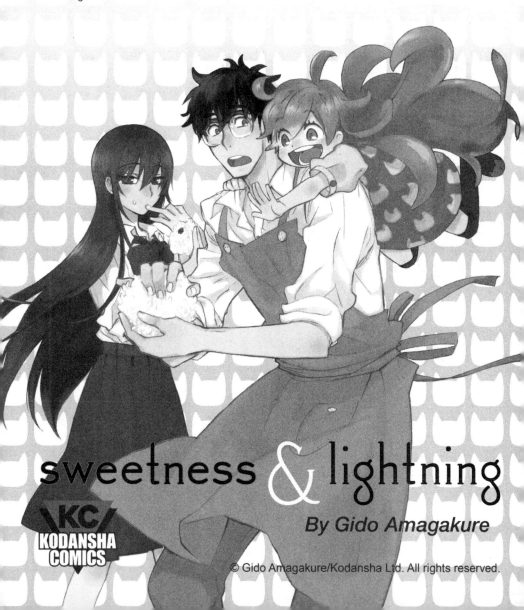

sweetness & lightning

By Gido Amagakure

KC
KODANSHA
COMICS

In love, there are
no save points.

ヲ
タ
ク
に
恋
は
難
し
い

NOW AN
ANIME!

KC
KODANSHA
COMICS

WOTAKOI:
LOVE IS HARD FOR OTAKU

by FUJITA

Narumi has had it rough: Every boyfriend she's had dumped her
once they found out she was an otaku, so she's gone to great
lengths to hide it. At her new job, she bumps into Hirotaka, her
childhood friend and fellow otaku. When Hirotaka almost gets
her secret outed at work, she comes up with a plan to keep him
quiet. But he comes up with a counter-proposal:
Why doesn't she just date him instead?

A SMART, NEW ROMANTIC COMEDY FOR FANS OF *SHORTCAKE CAKE* AND *TERRACE HOUSE!*

A romance manga starring high school girl Meeko, who learns to live on her own in a boarding house whose living room is home to the odd (but handsome) Matsunaga-san. She begins to adjust to her new life away from her parents, but Meeko soon learns that no matter how far away from home she is, she's still a young girl at heart — especially when she finds herself falling for Matsunaga-san.

A Kodansha Trade Paperback Original

A *Galaxy Next Door* 1 copyright © 2020 Gido Amagakure
English translation copyright © 2022 Gido Amagakure

Published in the United States by
Kodansha USA Publishing, LLC, New York.

Publication rights for this English edition arranged through
Kodansha Ltd., Tokyo.

First published in Japan in 2020 by Kodansha Ltd., Tokyo
as *Otonari ni ginga*, volume 1.

ISBN 978-1-64651-463-2

Printed in the United States of America.

1st Printing

Translation: Rose Padgett
Lettering: Lys Blakeslee
Editing: Cayley Last
Kodansha USA Publishing edition cover design by Matthew Akuginow

Publisher: Kiichiro Sugawara

Director of Publishing Services: Ben Applegate
Associate Director of Operations: Stephen Pakula
Publishing Services Managing Editors: Alanna Ruse, Madison Salters
Production Managers: Emi Lotto, Angela Zurlo

KODANSHA.US

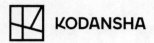